TROPICANA

NIGHTS

TROPICANA

NIGHTS

*The Life and Times of
the Legendary Cuban Nightclub*

Rosa Lowinger AND Ofelia Fox

IN SITU PRESS

New York   Miami   Los Angeles

IN SITU PRESS

Requests for permission to make copies of any part of the work should be submitted to: info@rosalowinger.com

www.rosalowinger.com

Photo on page 249 is courtesy of the Vicki Gold Levi Collection.
All photos in the insert, unless noted, are courtesy of Ofelia Fox.

The Library of Congress has cataloged the hardcover edition as follows:
Lowinger, Rosa.
Tropicana nights: the life and times of the legendary Cuban nightclub/
Rosa Lowinger and Ofelia Fox.
p.   cm.
Includes bibliographical references and index.
1. Tropicana (Nightclub: Havana, Cuba)—History. *2*. Music-halls
(Variety-theaters, cabarets, etc.)—Cuba—Havana—History—*20*th century.
I. Fox, Ofelia. II. Title.
PN1968.C9L*68 2005*
792.7'097291'23—dc22   2005002398
ISBN-13: 978-0-9898085-2-1 ISBN-10: 0-9898085-2-1

Text set in Fournier MT

Cover art by Alexandre Arrechea
Cover design by Little Gables Group
Printed in the United States of America

First IN SITU PRESS edition 2016

The 10th Anniversary Edition

Rosa Lowinger

The idea for this book originated on a windy afternoon in the first days of the 21st century, during a conversation with the great Cuban film director Humberto Solás. We were in an outdoor Havana café built in the ruins of a collapsed building, drinking coffee and reflecting on Cuba's cultural attainments during the previous century. It was an upbeat way to begin the new millennium, because Cuban cultural history easily inspires pride, as opposed to our political history, which is fraught, to say the least. Our greatest achievement, we readily agreed, is Cuban music and its related dance forms. But there were also painting and sculpture, literature, ballet, and architecture. On and on we went, our self-congratulatory banter underscored with yearning as we drank cafecito after cafecito on that chilly January Sunday.

At some point the conversation turned to Tropicana. Tropicana, mused Humberto, might just be the confluence of everything we had been discussing. Right then and there I began to think about the fictional possibilities of the place. For Tropicana was not only Cuba's most famous nightspot, it was a place of legendary musical innovation and prizewinning modernist architecture. It had been fictionalized before, most notably in Guillermo Cabrera Infante's 1967 tour de force novel *Tres Tristes Tigres*, but mostly as a backdrop. Tropicana as a protagonist, as a venue where Cuban history unfolded among mobsters, showgirls, and revolutionaries, remained relatively unexplored. The dramatic prospects made my head spin.

Then something happened, something bordering on the magical, which I describe a few pages from now. A world was set in motion for me, and within a few months I was on the doorstep of Ofelia Fox, the vivacious octogenarian widow of Tropicana's owner Martin Fox. It took one conversation with Ofelia for me to abandon the idea of a novel. Her stories were far more fascinating than anything I could make up.

I am a materials conservator by training. When I am not writing my days are spent restoring sculpture and architectural elements. Embarking on this book appeared to be a different sort of task. Yet, as I researched the history of Cuba's premier cabaret, I realized that this also constituted an act of preservation. In materials conservation, we're concerned with the retention of original fabric—the stone and bronze of an artwork or historic building. Tropicana's original fabric is largely ephemeral. It's composed of memories, shared with me by the people I interviewed for this book—dancers, musicians, bandleaders, wives, waiters, roulette dealers, makeup artists, hustlers, stars, mobsters, showgirls, chefs, chauffeurs, ballerinas, architects, and my own family members.

Many of these people are no longer alive. But this is their story. It is our story: a Cuban tale of love, loss, and history, featuring the showgirl, the mobster, the revolutionary, and all that other sexy stuff. And best of all, it really happened.

CONTENTS

For
Martin Fox,
Leonardo and Hilda Lowinger
and Todd Kessler

Life is an old casino in a park.

<small>WALLACE STEVENS, "ACADEMIC DISCOURSE AT HAVANA"</small>

PROLOGUE

The Flight

Volar por Cubana de Aviación. ¡Qué emoción!
from *Rumbo al Waldorf*

On January 1, 1959, sometime after one in the morning, an airplane rose over the swanky seaside high-rises in the Havana neighborhood known as Vedado. All over Vedado people stopped their New Year's revelry and stepped out onto their balconies to watch it. Airplanes did not normally take off in the middle of the night. And this one, flying dangerously low, looked like it was going to graze a rooftop, maybe crash onto one of the city's leafy avenues. The plane made several slow circles overhead, its engines drowning out the dance music that poured out of almost every apartment. *"Está borracho,"* people shouted to each other across balconies, thinking that the pilot might be drunk. Some rushed back inside, worried about an accident. Then, just as suddenly as it had appeared beneath the crescent moon, the plane banked sharply to the east over the ocean and disappeared. With it went Cuba's leader, General Fulgencio Batista.

After the plane was gone, my parents were among those who went back indoors to continue partying. They were at their neighbors' apartment, in the building where we all lived on Fifth Street, near the Avenida de los Presidentes and five blocks inland from the seaside boulevard known as the Malecón. My paternal grandfather, a Jewish immigrant from Hungary, had financed the building in 1952. It had sixteen units, six with wide square balconies that faced south to the city. The balcony—or *terraza*, as it was called—was the focus of middle-class domestic life in Cuba; yet that night, from their neighbor's *terraza*, my parents watched the departure of the plane that signaled the end of Cuban middle-class life. At the time they did not know that. They were caught up in celebrating a raucous New Year's Eve, the favorite holiday in a country that celebrates every holiday with gusto. In their neighbors' two-bedroom apartment, my parents and their friends danced the night away, my father in a white handkerchief-linen *guayabera* and matching cuffed trousers with razor-sharp creases, my mother in a pale grey satin cocktail dress that was tight in all the right places and slit high enough to allow for easy movement on the dance floor. On her feet were slingback heels; in her earlobes, pearl drop clusters. In his pocket was a pressed perfumed handkerchief to blot away perspiration from the sultry night.

On the radio was station CMQ's special all-night New Year's program, featuring music by Machito, Pérez Prado, Orquesta Aragón, Orquesta Riverside, Ñico Saquito, Celeste Mendoza, Celia Cruz, and the unquestionable favorite of all habaneros, Benny Moré, the Barbarian of Rhythm, as he was called. The guests knew every number and the dances that accompanied them: the mambo, cha-cha-cha, and what was called "rhumba" by the Americans who came down to Havana in droves each winter. They sang along, drinking rum-and-Cokes and whiskey, feasting on a traditional meal laid out on the bottle-green glass dining table: black beans, white rice, fried plantains, salad, and sliced pork that had marinated all day and then roasted in the spacious oven of a nearby bakery. At midnight, the hostess laid out bowls of purple grapes.

The guests ate twelve apiece for *buena suerte,* good luck, and toasted each other with champagne. Then, for more good luck, they hurled buckets of water off the balcony.

Normally my parents and their friends would have gone out to a cabaret for New Year's Eve. They would have reserved a table at one of their favorites—the Ali Bar, where Benny Moré was a regular performer; the Panchín or the Rumba Palace at the beach in Marianao; or possibly at the Hotel Capri, where the host of the casino was the American tough-guy actor George Raft. There were dozens of cabarets to choose from in Havana. They could be found in Vedado basements, on the crowded boulevards of Central Havana, or lined up in a row along the coast in the nearby suburb of Marianao. There were posh ones, like the Copa Room in Meyer Lansky's recently opened Riviera Hotel, where men wore tuxes and the women dripped with jewels; or rustic places that served drinks and *un sala'ito*—something salty to keep you drinking well into the night—for a few pennies. Most clubs stayed open until three or four A.M.; some barely got going until that hour. But they all featured live music and some sort of show consisting of anything from a four-piece conjunto and a pair of dancers, to full-blown extravaganzas replete with showgirls and star headliners like Eartha Kitt, Nat "King" Cole, and Ginger Rogers.

The year before, my parents had celebrated New Year's Eve at the most celebrated of all the Havana cabarets, Tropicana. They had been guests of radio host Mario Lavín, another of my grandfather's tenants, who broadcasted his show directly from the nightclub. From Lavín's ringside table you could see every curve on Tropicana's hourglass-shaped showgirls, you could hear the scrape of the dancers' feet on the stage, and almost touch the hems of costumes thick with lace, embroidery, and rhinestones. My parents adored Tropicana. They stayed out that New Year's Eve until well after the sun came up, ending the revelry with a breakfast of thick hot chocolate and buttered toast at a Vedado café.

Mario Lavín had extended the invitation again this New Year's Eve—1958—but my parents had decided not to go. Civil war was heating up across the island. Attacks by anti-Batista rebels and government reprisals had soared to frightening levels. There had been sabotage, kidnappings, and killings by the guerrillas. Thousands had been summarily arrested and tortured by Batista's police and army, and then had disappeared. The country was in a constant state of emergency. Constitutional rights had been suspended half a dozen times over the previous two years. The police were edgy and trigger-happy. There was less violence in Havana, but it still seemed as if every day the front pages of newspapers carried pictures of dead young men. And there were bombings—package bombs exploding in movie theaters, and paper bags with dynamite found in trash cans, stairwells, alleys. The police were picking people up for anything even remotely suspicious. My father had been stopped repeatedly during the year; in April he had been detained simply because his car matched a description of one the police were looking for. The word on the street was that the rebels were planning to sabotage the cabarets on New Year's Eve. No one knew if it was true or a ruse to scare away the tourists. But for my parents it was reason enough to stay away from Tropicana that night.

My parents' worries notwithstanding, Tropicana was enjoying brisk business on that New Year's Eve. Since eight in the evening, a long line of cars had been backed up on Truffin Avenue, inching their way toward the cabaret entrance. The club's four valet parking attendants worked at double speed, helping ladies in evening gowns and men in tuxedos out of Oldsmobiles and Cadillacs. The entire staff of four hundred was on that night—dancers, models, singers, waiters, croupiers, cooks, musicians, busboys, bartenders, cigarette girls, seamstresses, makeup artists.

Inside the club's plush, carpeted casino, no one felt more optimistic about the coming year than Tropicana's owner, Martín Fox. Holding his customary highball glass of Dewar's Ancestor whiskey, Martín strolled through his domain, greeting locals and tourists with holiday cheer. A quartet was playing at the casino bar, but the only sound Martín was interested in was the ringing of slot machines and the clacking of roulette balls. Despite the turmoil of the last few years, which had included a terrible bombing exactly two years before at Tropicana itself, things were beginning to look up. Nineteen fifty-eight had not been quite as good a year for tourism as 1957, but if tonight's crowd was any indication, 1959 was going to turn out fine. Of course, Martín had heard the same rumors as everyone else—that the revolutionaries were advancing, that Batista and his family had been issued U.S. visas—but he knew that what the country longed for more than anything was an end to the violence. No matter who eventually resided in the presidential palace, Batista or the bearded rebel leader, Fidel Castro, the real business of doing business would carry on. Still, it was always smart to be on amicable terms with the powers that both are and might be, and for this reason Martín had hedged his bets over the last year, laying money in the hands of both sides. In addition to the usual monthly payoffs to Batista's people, he had also made a sizeable donation to Fidel Castro's 26th of July Movement, just in case. The expense mattered little to him. For Martín, money was for sharing with his partners, friends, and family, and mostly for investing back into his beloved Tropicana, so that it retained its place as Cuba's, maybe the world's, most beautiful nightclub.

And beautiful it truly was. Stepping out through the casino's glass doors, Martín threaded his way through the tightly packed tables of the Bajo las Estrellas (Under the Stars) cabaret, slapping backs and shaking hands. Though the outdoor show would not start for another two hours, the place already glittered like a showgirl. Lights were strung between the outdoor catwalks and the palms; the tables glowed with candles set into glass holders to protect them from the warm but sometimes gusting December breezes. The orchestra was deep into a sizzling mambo, and everyone was dancing or eating a four-course dinner served on china bearing the Tropicana emblem, a semi-abstract figure of a ballerina by sculptor Rita Longa. Martín breathed in the scents—the balmy lushness of the gardens, men's cigars, the perfume of elegant women. Tropicana was like his mistress. Recently he had used that very analogy with the press. Luckily, his wife, Ofelia, shared his passion for the special magic of the place known as a Paradise Under the Stars.

If not for that passion, Ofelia would have been in bed nursing a terrible cold this New Year's Eve, not to mention a back ailment that sent shooting pains down her leg every time she coughed. Instead, she was seated at her and Martín's usual table, one tier up from ringside in the Arcos de Cristal (Arches of Glass) salon, where Armando Romeu's orchestra was playing the last few dance numbers before the floor show got underway. Despite the back pain that made her feel twice her age, Ofelia tried to maintain her role as the First Lady of Tropicana. Wearing an embroidered white satin Pierre Balmain original that Martín had bought for her, she presided over a table around which sat her sisters and sisters-in-law. By this point in the evening all the men in the family were hard at work. Ofelia's brother, Osvaldo Suarez, was at the baccarat table; her brother-in-law Atilano Taladrid was the casino's comptroller; Martín's brother Pedro Fox, his closest associate, was busy supervising the cabaret's food and beverage services.

The two other profit-sharing partners, Oscar Echemendia and Alberto Ardura, were also hard at work that New Year's Eve. Oscar was the casino's manager and Ardura, as he was known to nearly everyone, kept a watchful eye on the progress of the entertainment. These men were closer to Martín than anyone except his family. As the partner who had hired Rodney, the club's celebrated choreographer, and handled star contracts and payments to musicians, dancers, and acrobats, Ardura was largely responsible for turning Tropicana into one of Cuba's key tourist destinations. Tonight's show, *Rumbo al Waldorf*, was a testament to his and Pedro's marketing acumen. Only weeks before, the Tropicana dance corps had performed it at the American Society of Travel Agents (ASTA) conference at New York's Waldorf-Astoria Hotel (the next ASTA conference was scheduled to take place in Havana in late 1959). The idea was not only to lure more tourists down to Cuba, but to guide them all directly to Tropicana. If tonight's crowds were any indication, this was exactly what was happening.

At eleven thirty, around the time that General Batista and his family were heading to the airport, Tropicana's dance floor was slowly elevated and transformed into a stage. Martín slipped into his seat beside Ofelia. The lights dimmed and a spotlight came up on master of ceremonies Miguel Angel Blanco. "Ladies and gentlemen," boomed the Latin-lover-handsome Blanco. "The Tropicana cabaret is proud to present . . . *Rumbo al Waldorf*!"

The show began with a film of a landing airplane projected onto the curtain. At the precise moment the plane appeared to touch down on the tarmac, bandleader Romeu lifted his baton and the orchestra struck the first chords of the overture. The curtain opened to a stage set of an airplane, and out danced Tropicana's male chorus, dressed as baggage handlers and attendants. They rolled a tall staircase up to the airplane door, from which emerged ballet stars Henry Boyer and Leonela González. Leonela was on pointe, wearing a stylish-looking travel suit with a fur slung over her shoulder and carrying a live white poodle. Henry, in an English-style tweed suit and brown derby, escorted her down the stairs. The chorus sang, "Volar por Cubana de Aviación. ¡Qué emoción!" (What a thrill to fly Cubana Airways!).

At midnight, Romeu began the countdown to 1959: cinco, cuatro, tres, dos, uno! Felicidades! The cast released twelve doves for good luck in the coming year. There was champagne, hugs, kisses, confetti, noisemakers. Martín gingerly embraced the suffering Ofelia then slipped off to extend New Year's greetings to his partners. The show ended with the entire cast onstage again, dancing a cha-cha-cha to the theme music from the film *The Bridge on the River Kwai* while waving Cuban and American flags.

General Batista, meanwhile, had gathered his top generals and ministers. A line of airplanes sat on the tarmac of Cuban army headquarters, their engines warming.

At one A.M., Martín took Ofelia home to bed. As with my parents, their New Year's Eves usually ended long after sunup, but Ofelia, who would be diagnosed the following day with two herniated discs, was in such agony that she barely managed to hobble to their Cadillac using a cane.

Batista's plane swooped low over Vedado, crossed into international waters, and headed toward the Dominican Republic. Two other airplanes followed it. No one at Tropicana noticed. Then slowly, like the first fat raindrops of a tropical thundershower, the rumors started.

The first phone call came in for a man who was slumped, dead drunk, at the roulette table. An ophthalmologist, he had plans to run for office in the upcoming elections as a member of Batista's party. Seeing that the man was passed out, croupier Valentín Jodra handed the phone to the man's wife. The woman listened for a second, then grew pale. *"No me digas, no me digas!"* she gasped over and over, like a broken record. When she hung up she was trembling. She turned to Valentín.

"Help me get my husband out of here."

While someone helped the woman with her husband, Ardura began pacing nervously in and out of his office. He, too, had received a phone call. Ardura and his wife were close friends of Batista's brother-in-law Roberto Fernandez Miranda, and there was talk that the rebels were going to arrest anyone who had had anything to do with Batista. Ardura left without saying good-bye to anyone. Two uniformed policemen from the nearby Marianao precinct rushed in looking for their chief, who happened to be on the dance floor. The news spread quickly. There were sporadic cheers and clapping. "Abajo Batista!" Some raised champagne glasses. Others hurried to their cars. At four A.M., the last car drove out past the towering acacia trees that flanked the entrance to the cabaret.

At five thirty the phone rang in Martín and Ofelia's bedroom. Martín bolted out of bed. It was Ardura.

"Martín," he whispered frantically. "I need money. My plane is ready. I'm leaving for Florida and I'm taking Carmelina with me." Through the sluggishness caused by her head cold and her back pain, Ofelia could make out her husband's words.

"Have others been arrested? Are Fidel's men are in the city? Go to the safe, compadre, take what you need."

Martín hung up and began dressing. Ofelia struggled to sit up. "Martín, *qué pasó?* Where are you going at this hour?"

Martín considered what to say. He never told Ofelia unpleasant things. "Don't worry, *china*. The war is over. Batista's gone."

"But Ardura's leaving, isn't he? Is he in danger? Are we in danger?"

Martín hesitated before replying. "No, no, china. It's just that he's such good friends with Fernandez Miranda." Martín paused again, then added, "It's only temporary, until things get worked out with the new government. That's what always happens, right? One group comes in, another goes out, and things settle down. Go back to sleep."

But Ofelia could not sleep now. Martín sat by her side and stroked her hair until she finally surrendered to exhaustion. Then, as the sun rose over the Straits of Florida, he got into his car and sped back to Tropicana, where he would soon learn that nothing would ever again be the way it was.

PART I

CHAPTER 1

Introductions

A little more than four decades after that momentous New Year's Eve in Havana, I was driving up the Glendale Freeway near Los Angeles, on my way to meet Ofelia Fox. It was a hot summer afternoon, and the foothills of the San Gabriel Mountains loomed above the city, shrouded in yellow smog. Glendale is the third-largest city in Los Angeles County and home to the region's largest Cuban population. Though roughly fifteen miles east of where I had lived for over ten years, until a month earlier I had had no idea I lived so close to the widow of Tropicana's last owner. Until a few years before that, I had never given much thought to Tropicana, or any cabaret for that matter, Cuban or otherwise. I was in diapers when Batista's DC-6 flew over my grandparents' apartment building. Two years later, my parents and I were living in Miami. Tropicana belonged to the world that had been left behind, though my parents and their friends often spoke of it. "The most beautiful cabaret that ever existed," said my mother with characteristic Cuban bravado. "They called it 'A Paradise Under the Stars' because it was just that—a paradise," echoed my father, his voice thick with nostalgia.

If you grow up among Cuban exiles in Miami, you quickly become used to such hyperbole, to memories clouded by grief and loss. Everything in Cuba had once been more beautiful, more elegant, more glamorous. To many, Tropicana was the ultimate symbol of those days. But it belonged to my parents' world, not mine.

Then I saw it. The first time was in 1998. I had been going back to Cuba for a number of years. All four of my grandparents were Jewish immigrants, so our Cuban-based family was small and everyone left soon after the 1959 revolution. Yet I am an art conservator by training, and for years I had been eager to see the country's architecture, and particularly that of Havana, where I was born. Havana is an architectural historian's dream. Walk from one end of the city to the other and you will pass stunning examples of almost every major architectural style that has existed since the mid-fifteen hundreds. Many of the buildings are in terrible disrepair. But look behind the peeling paint and rusting grillwork and you will find astonishing details: murals, stained glass, black terrazzo, iridescent tiles, glazed terracotta, and granite facades inlaid with bronze. The list goes on and on. I began returning to Havana to participate in restoration workshops with my Cuban colleagues and to teach aspiring conservators there techniques to repair bronze and marble monuments and modern art. By the late 1990s, when tourism was flourishing in Cuba, I was often sought out to lead groups of Americans who were prohibited by U.S. law from visiting Cuba other than for the purpose of cultural research, or a type of travel termed "People-to-People Exchange," intended to foster socio-cultural understanding between the two nations. Between 1998 and 2003, Havana was jam-packed with tour groups from practically every museum, alumni group, film society, and religious and cultural institution in America. Tropicana was a common evening destination for these tour groups,

touted as offering the archetypal Cuban song-and-dance experience. It was mainly for tourists now; the minimum entry price was
three times the average Cuban monthly salary.

In 1998 I went to Tropicana with a group from the National
Trust for Historic Preservation's study tour to Cuba. After a day
of sightseeing, we sat at a long table in Tropicana's Bajo las Estrellas, the club's outdoor performance space, drinking rum-and-
Cokes and watching the spectacle of silky-skinned, scantily clad
dancers and muscled acrobats. Singers belted out Afro-Cuban
songs. The show was astounding—an hour and a half of satin,
feathers, fishnets, G-strings, towering headdresses that looked like
chandeliers, and blaring horns and hammering congas. Some in
my group covered their ears. "This is too loud!" they complained.
Others got up and danced. Still others were struck dumb by the
six-foot-tall women parading down the catwalks and inviting
members of the audience to dance with them.

I, too, was struck dumb, but for entirely different reasons. Before that night, Tropicana had only been a name, a place as removed from my life as the archeological sites in the Middle East I
had worked at during my art conservation training. Now it was as
if I were walking into someone else's dream and realizing it was
also mine. Tucked among clusters of fruit trees, flowering shrubs,
and vine-choked royal palms, was some of the finest modernist architecture I had ever seen. It was like discovering an ancient temple
in a jungle, though here the structures were made of glass and concrete, and the forms were 1950s-era shell vaults, parabolic arches,
geometric sculptures, and Charles Eames furniture. The architectural centerpiece of Tropicana is a building known as Arcos de
Cristal, a cavernous performance space formed by slender concrete
arches and soaring walls of glass. Giant fruit trees, left in situ during construction, punctuate the interior. Arcos de Cristal, I later
learned, won numerous international prizes when it was built and
was one of only six Cuban buildings included in the landmark

1954 Museum of Modern Art exhibit entitled "Latin American Architecture since 1945."

Tropicana was designed to be experienced at night, but I returned the following morning. Stripped of the colored stage lights, the structures seemed even more audacious; Arcos de Cristal's arches, which support the entire building, were barely three inches thick. Whoever built it had been making a deliberate statement about modernism, about how functionalism could harmonize with the lyrical garden setting and the sound, which at that moment was being made only by gardeners' and custodians' voices and the soft swish of the wind in the trees. I stayed there for a long time. For some reason, I started to remember the tear-jerking boleros that my parents liked, music that, as a child, would send me running from the room. That morning I began to listen.

OFELIA FOX lives on a steep street I had passed many times. Her block, located technically a few doors down from Glendale's city limits, dead-ends at the back entrance to the Forest Lawn Memorial Park, the most "Hollywood" of cemeteries. Errol Flynn, Nat "King" Cole, and Sammy Davis Jr. are buried there, and every half hour there is a sound-and-light show in front of a large stained glass mural depicting Leonardo Da Vinci's *Last Supper*. Years ago, when I first moved to Los Angeles, I restored some marble sculpture for Forest Lawn. When the project was finished, I never thought I'd be back in the area again. Yet there I was, parking my car in front of a neat red-tile-roofed Spanish house. A long flight of steps led to the front door. They were lined with planters in the shape of dogs, cats, elephants, deer, and, of course, foxes. When I reached the top, I stopped to catch my breath on a porch crowded with orchids, palms, and gnomes. Colored flags and wind chimes hung mutely in the August stillness. Next to the doorbell was an engraved bronze plaque. "On this site, in 1897, nothing happened." Another smaller plaque read, "Happiness lives here. We do too."

I'm in pretty decent shape, but I was winded. I wondered whether it was from nervousness, though I couldn't imagine why. I had learned of Ofelia Fox's existence by accident, several years after my first visit to Tropicana. I had been playing hooky from one of my tour groups and sitting in an Old Havana café with a noted Cuban filmmaker, who introduced me to a relative of hers. When the relative learned I was from Los Angeles, he sidled over to me and began crowing about his family's connection to the Tropicana. His great aunt had been married to Tropicana's owner. "I want to write a screenplay," he said. "It would make a great movie. I can see it. We just need to add a love interest, a showgirl, and a revolutionary. Two lovers separated by political circumstance. Something like that." He and his great aunt were not on good terms, he admitted, but he still carried her phone number. I took down the number, surprised to see that the area code was the same as mine.

Three weeks later, I was standing on Ofelia Fox's porch. My finger had barely grazed the buzzer when she opened the door. She had been watching from the window. She herded me in quickly— "so the cats don't escape"—then shook my hand in an entryway in which the carpeting was so thick I felt as if I was sinking. Like the porch, the interior was resolutely cheerful. There were ornaments and candles, bubbling fountains, dried flower and feather arrangements, and a Noah's ark's worth of ceramic animals. An oil painting of a young woman wearing pearls and a white mink stole hung over the fireplace. It did not seem to be Ofelia, but there were similarities that I could detect even after a short acquaintance— something about the combination of serenity and liveliness. By my calculations, Ofelia had to be around eighty years old, yet she was amazingly youthful looking. Her round face was barely lined. Her silky white, shoulder-length hair was tied back in a ponytail. Her brown eyes twinkled behind black, square-rimmed glasses. She wore perfume that was both smoky and floral. She said little at first, but when she spoke—in English at first—her voice was deep and warm, but also carried a tone of quiet bemusement. This, I thought, is someone who has lived a long and interesting life.

She led me into a bright old-fashioned-looking kitchen. On a small, round Formica table were letters, a stack of manuscript pages, and several thick red leather photo albums. I read the first words of her manuscript, which was entitled *Tropicana y Yo* (Tropicana and Me): "*Envuelta en años y recuerdos he vivido de esperanzas y añoranzas y no sé cuál de ellas pesa más o si en números una alcanza o sobrepasa a la otra.*" "Wrapped in years and memory," I translated silently as Ofelia walked to the refrigerator, "I've lived on hope and longing, and I don't know which of them weighs more, or if in number one matches or exceeds the other." I continued reading, silently translating: "I believe that all of us Cubans have lived this way, whether we've been in exile for ten or for forty years. But I also believe that I have more memories than other Cubans because so many of them have shared their memories of Tropicana with me."

"What are you drinking?" asked Ofelia, as she opened the freezer. A big snowy cat with gray markings brushed my leg. I hesitated, waiting for the grandmotherly offer of iced tea or soft drinks. Instead, she pulled out a silver cocktail shaker and two frosted glasses. "How about a martini?"

THE PICTURES in Ofelia's photo albums brim with cocktail glasses and ice buckets set on tables covered with pristine white tablecloths and already crowded with bottles of whiskey, rum, vermouth, and Canada Dry. There are tall white pillar candles in white holders, bouquets of roses and chrysanthemums. The men sport white suits or black tuxedos, the women are in satin and wear diamonds and mink. Ofelia showed me pictures of herself with Joan Crawford, Steve Allen, Jayne Meadows, Nat "King" Cole, Liberace, and Carmen Miranda.

"There were so many famous guests," she said, sighing and reaching for her manuscript. She looked up, adjusting her glasses. "I've started making a list. These were visitors to Tropicana, not performers." In addition to those in the photos, she read off more names:

Errol Flynn, Cesar Romero, Tyrone Power, Ava Gardner, Ernest Hemingway, Marlon Brando, Elizabeth Taylor, Eddie Fisher, Pier Angeli, Vic Damone, Debbie Reynolds, Anne Miller, Dorothy Dandridge, Eva Marie Saint, Frankie Lane, Johnny Matthis, Jimmy Durante, Rocky Marciano, Tony Bennett, Jack Paar, Diane Carroll, Sammy Davis Jr., George Raft, Jennifer Jones, David O. Selznick, Maurice Chevalier, Augustín Lara, Arturo de Cordoba, and Edith Piaf.

Other names were not as familiar to me. They were Latin American musicians, comedians, and actors—icons of their era, such as Mexican actresses María Félix and Evangelina Elizondo, Spanish actress Sarita Montiel, Italian starlet Silvana Pampanini, rumba dancer Tongolele, Mexican singers Pedro Vargas and Tito Guizar, Spanish crooner Juan Legido, and exiled Argentinian singer, Libertad Lamarque. Ofelia pulled out two more pages and began to read off the Tropicana headliners. Again, there were names most Americans know—Nat "King" Cole, Josephine Baker, Billy Daniels, Carmen Miranda, Xavier Cugat, Celia Cruz, Christine Jorgensen, Paul Robeson, and Yma Sumac—and others that may be less well-known now to American audiences but were nonetheless huge stars in their day, such as Miguelito Valdés, Johnny Puleo, Olga Guillot, Elena Burke, Omara Portuondo, Celeste Mendoza, Erlinda Cortés, and Benny Moré.

"There were many, many others," said Ofelia. "But I forget. The photographs help me remember, but so many got left behind."

The subject of missing photographs, I soon learned, remained one of the touchiest issues involving her relatives in Cuba. "All I want is access to my memories," she said, bristling as she refilled my martini glass. "Does that seem like so much to ask?"

It did not seem like much at all. But Ofelia's memories are now a central part of Cuban history, and as with most things Cuban, claim to them is hotly disputed on both sides of the Straits of Florida. While we talked, it also became clear that Ofelia herself was at the heart of the Tropicana story. In the photographs, she is always sitting next to the movie star or guest of honor. A poised, dark-haired beauty, she looks elegant but approachable. Her smile seems genuine.

"*Mira,* this was one of those nights you never forget." She pointed to a photograph of a group sitting around a table that has been painted black and white. In it, Ofelia sits beside a strikingly handsome young man in a white tuxedo with a printed cummer-bund and matching bow tie. She is deep in conversation with him, hands folded neatly on the table, wearing a white lace halter dress.

"Is that Liberace?" I asked.

Ofelia nodded, pleased and slightly surprised that I recognized the baby-faced pianist. "It was his birthday. We made him a huge table shaped like a piano." This was in 1954, when the flamboyant performer was the most popular star on television, receiving more fan mail even than Lucille Ball and earning $50,000 a week at the Riviera Hotel in Las Vegas. Everyone in America recognized the trademark white tuxedo and candelabras. Apparently, Liberace was just as popular in Cuba.

"After a concert in Havana, he chose Tropicana to host a party in honor of Cuba's press," said Ofelia, as she turned to a photo in which the Kandelabra Kid (as Liberace was known in Cuba) stood by his black piano-table, hands held aloft, pretending to play. The table has all eighty-eight keys, a huge white wooden music stand, and is adorned with three-tined silver candelabras. All thirty or so people at the table seem to be having a rollicking good time. Even those sitting a tier up from the stage are clearly enjoying the party. Liberace was not scheduled on the Tropicana program that night, but the public got to watch him perform, anyway. There he is, posing with an impersonator named Armando Roblán, who that evening had performed a Liberace bit in honor of the cabaret's guest of honor. In another picture, Liberace is onstage, beaming, his hands around the waist of a young star of mambo dance named Ana Gloria Varona.

The old black-and-white photographs were alive with laughter, conversation, congas, horns and clinking glasses. I asked Ofelia about the show the night the Liberace photographs were taken. She explained that they were called *En Broma* and *En Serio* (Joking, Seriously), a pair of revues staged by Tropicana's choreographer, known simply as Rodney, in tribute to the Alhambra Theater in Havana's Chinatown. The show blended Chinese dance and costumes with Cuba's popular mambo and rumba dance styles.

While Ofelia described it, I could see it coming to life: the models strutting down catwalks set among the trees, wearing billowing satin pantaloons slit at the sides and gold slippers with upturned toes. Everything is opulent. Everything sparkles. One of Cuba's most celebrated showgirls of the 1950s, the statuesque Alicia Figueroa, is dressed as a peacock, trailing a ten-foot train of white feathers. There is modern dancer Emilia "La China" Villamíl, wearing a pagoda headdress festooned with crystal pendants. Prima ballerina Leonela González pirouettes around Emilia in her Chinese silks, her partner Henry Boyer close behind her. Then it's mambo time and Ana Gloria Varona spins out with her lithe partner, Rolando—dipping, turning, knotting their arms into combinations that could foil a contortionist. Varona (the Princess of Mambo) finishes her set by hopping down from the stage and returning with the grinning Liberace.

"You should have heard that audience," said Ofelia, pouring us a third round of martinis. "A hurricane couldn't drown out the roar when Ana Gloria got up with Lee."

Ofelia talked about Tropicana like a proud parent. Yet her photos revealed more than the glamour of 1950s Cuban cabaret life. There she is, in one instance, draped in silver mink and sitting next to mobster Santo Trafficante, who ran several of the big-name casinos in Havana. "The mink stole was a gift from Santo," admitted Ofelia.

In the photo, the bespectacled Trafficante (whose name in Spanish translates as "saintly trafficker") looks demure and unassuming, more like a college physics professor than a man with a three-page FBI rap sheet linking him to the numbers racket in Tampa; narcotics trafficking in Cuba; the infamous Mafia conference that took place in Apalachin, New York on November 14, 1957; and, most bone-chilling of all, the murder of Albert Anastasia in the barbershop of New York's Park Sheraton Hotel on October 25, 1957. In another photo, Martín poses in front of Tropicana's Fountain of the Muses alongside Lefty Clark, the casino's onetime credit manager. Clark, who was also known as William Buschoff and Frank Bischoff, was a two-bit hood linked by the FBI to narcotics trafficking in Cuba and to Meyer Lansky's illegal South Florida casino, Greenacres. Advertisements of the time refer to Tropicana's casino as "Lefty Clark's Casino."

According to Ofelia, Trafficante was her husband's friend, and Clark was merely someone his casino had hired to lure gamblers from the United States. In any case, the appearance of these men raised unsettling questions: Was Tropicana's cabaret just a front? What really lay behind the glorious architecture and gorgeous showgirls, the costumes, the music, and the dancing? The popular view of 1950s Cuba is that it was riddled with mobsters who owned all the casinos. I wondered whether that was also the story of Tropicana. Was it a haven for criminals, or for artists?

I had many, many questions, but it was getting dark in Glendale, and while I'd been looking at Ofelia's pictures, she had been continuously refilling my martini glass. The questions faded in the California twilight as I spooled back in time with her. We were at Tropicana and the music was playing. I was wearing lavender organza and a diamond bracelet, tapping my black satin stilettos. I wanted to dance. I had to dance! There were dozens of willing men. My attention was caught by one in particular: a large, dark-haired man who sat at a ringside table, wearing a white suit and a thin dark tie. He wasn't handsome, but there was something in his gaze that told you that he had power. He also seemed to have a sense of humor—crinkles at the edges of his eyes, a sly smile drawing the corners of his mouth. He looked like someone who could tell a good off-color joke yet wear an elegant suit with authority.

Ofelia saw me looking at him. "You want to know the story of Tropicana?" She pointed to the man in the photograph. "Start with him. My husband, Martín Fox."

CHAPTER 2

A Nickel on
the Butterfly

Some say the island of Cuba is shaped like a crocodile, an analogy that may be based on the fact that the reptile inhabits most of the island's swamps and rivers. A better comparison would be to a woman. Facing the Atlantic Ocean, lithe yet curvaceous, she is kneeling and arched backward, her hair flowing from the middle of the island to the westernmost province of Pinar del Rio, her thighs and legs comprising the eastern area once known simply as Oriente.

The city of Ciego de Avila sits at the center of the woman's slender waist, where the Atlantic and Caribbean coasts are less than eighty miles apart. Between 1871 and 1873, while the Spanish rulers were battling an independence movement born on October 10, 1868, in the rural town of Bayamo and led by freedom fighters known as Mambises, they took advantage of this geographic feature to keep the revolution from moving westward to Havana. Clearing away isolated strands of palm and mahogany forests, the colonial army built a string of thirty-six small fortresses, each big enough to accommodate only a single sentry and stretching all the way from the city of Morón in the north to the port of Júcaro on the Caribbean. Known as La Trocha (string of fortresses) Júcaro a Morón, the constructions were a charming addition to the landscape, but also ineffective. Less than a year after it was built, the Mambí general Manuel Suarez broke through the Spanish line of defense with his machete-wielding rebels and swept westward, with the Spaniards in hot pursuit. Over time, the fortresses began to crumble. Their ruins still stand, poignant reminders that nothing is permanent—neither structures built of brick and stone nor the ideologies they are meant to defend.

The landscape in this part of Cuba (and indeed, much of the center of the island) is notable for its total lack of drama. Flat, scruffy, occasionally marshy, and ferociously hot most of the year, it has no alluring tropical features—no palm forests, no wooded mountains, and no sinuous rivers. What it does have is the richest soil in the entire country. The area around Ciego de Avila is the breadbasket of Cuba, and the city itself is the island's Kansas City.

Founded in 1847 as a rural outpost that saw minor growth when soldiers from the Trocha settled in the area, Ciego de Avila is a relatively new city for Cuba. The region only began to flourish in the early twentieth century, after Cuba had won independence from Spain. The main reason was *caña de azucar*, "sugarcane," the mainstay of the island's economy since the late eighteenth century and the primary source of the wealth that had built the colonial cities of the eighteenth and nineteenth centuries, such as Matanzas, Trinidad, Camagüey, and Cienfuegos, as well as the imposing baroque and neoclassical buildings that made Havana one of the most European-looking cities in the entire Western Hemisphere. Ciego de Avila's flat, rich terrain was perfect for growing sugarcane. The fact that the area's refineries, or *centrales*, were built after the industrial revolution meant that, unlike the *centrales* in the old colonial towns, they started out as fully mechanized facilities, able to compete on the world market despite the lack of slave labor. By 1914, Cuba was producing 12 percent of the world's sugar. This was actually a decline from the 1850s, when it produced a quarter of the world's sugar. Yet now the island benefited from a reciprocal trade agreement with the United States, enacted by Teddy Roosevelt following a four-year period of American occupation of Cuba that came after the end of the Spanish-Cuban-American war. The treaty gave Cuba a 20 percent tariff preference over other countries (American shippers also received a rate reduction ranging from 25 to 40 percent) that effectively obliterated Cuba's competition in the American market. By the end of the first decade of the twentieth century, Ciego de Avila's flat alluvial plain (*ciego* means "savannah") was home to seven fully mechanized sugar refineries. One of these, the Central Stewart, which was owned by the American firm Atlantic Sugar Company of the Gulf, was the largest in all Cuba. Between them these refineries churned out a third of the sugar produced on the island, an amount greater than that refined in the entire state of Florida. The region also produced oranges, bananas, cotton, tomatoes and pineapples so sweet and juicy that they are still highly prized today; and its rice paddies supplied half of Cuba's population. But sugar was the main reason that Ciego's fortunes boomed. Sugar turned the area into a magnet for a vast internal migration by rural folk from the surrounding provinces. These *guajiros,* as Cuban country people are known, flocked to the great centrales to eke out livings as field hands, laborers, mechanics, machinists, drivers—anything that was required to keep the *caña* going from the fields to the mills, to line the pockets of the sugarmill owners and, ultimately, the Cuban and American bankers who financed them.

One such guajiro was a young man named Martín Fox Zamora. Born in 1896, the year after the outbreak of Cuba's War of Independence from Spain, Martín was brought up in Amarillas, a tiny town just north of the Zapatas swamp in the province of

Matanzas. His parents, Martín Fox Pita and Domitila Zamora Alvarez, had come to Amarillas from the colonial town of Cárdenas. Little is known about Martín's early years, except that he was probably around twenty when he decided to join the eastward migration to Ciego de Avila. It was the time of World War I, when the decimation of the European beet fields had caused the price of cane sugar to skyrocket—first from 1.9 to 3.6 cents a pound between July and August of 1914, eventually reaching an astronomical 29.2 cents by mid-1920. These were heady times in Cuba. The fortunes of landowners, sugarmill owners, bankers, railroad magnates, and American companies like the United Fruit Company, American Sugar Refining Company, John Deere, and International Harvester grew at such dizzying rates that the epoch came to be known as *la danza de los millones,* or "dance of the millions." The term, which came from the title of a 1916 musical by Cubans Jorge Anckermann and Federico Villoch, was used in Havana more than in the provinces. Yet its effects were felt around the country. In towns like Ciego de Avila, the danza de los millones created jobs for thousands of guajiros. It also spawned a solid middle class made up of engineers, agronomists, doctors, barbers, lawyers, nurses, shopkeepers, and other professionals who moved to the region to support the burgeoning sugar industry. This middle class flourished in the friendly and open-minded atmosphere of Ciego de Avila. Unlike the great Cuban cities of the eighteenth century, here a man's worth was measured by his accomplishments, not his long string of last names.

Upon arriving in Ciego de Avila, Martín Fox found work at the Central Jagüeyal, a smaller mill also owned by the Atlantic Sugar Company of the Gulf, which was located north of the city. A large-boned guajiro with broad shoulders and thick hands, Martín seemed one of those men fated by his size for manual labor. At Jagüeyal he worked as a *tornero,* lathe machinist, fabricating metal parts to maintain the mill's vast grinding machines and caramelization apparatus. It was not the backbreaking labor of cutting sugarcane, but it was hot, dirty, hands-on work. During the period of the *zafra,* the winter months when caña was harvested, Martín and his coworkers would practically become part of the milling apparatus themselves. On duty eighteen hours a day, seven days a week, the machinists wouldn't catch a full night's sleep or get a hot bath for months at a time.

It was probably during one of those sleepless workshifts that the middle finger of Martín's left hand got caught in a lathe. The accident left him unfit for the dexterous work of a *tornero.* Unable to continue working at the refinery, he suddenly found himself looking for a way to earn a living. No one alive can recall how Martín chose gambling, and specifically the venerated Cuban occupation of bookmaking, as his second profession; but the accident at the central set his destiny in motion. He took to gambling; he excelled at it. And it could not have happened at a better time.

By Christmas of 1920, it had become clear that the dance of the millions was a prelude to economic disaster. The price of sugar, which had teetered at an artificial, war-fueled 22.5 cents a pound in May of 1920, plunged to 3.5 cents by December. Cuba's banks went into crisis, and within a few years half of Ciego de Avila was out of work. Martín, meanwhile, was making a steady living *apuntando terminales,* a term which means "the taking down of bets," for an off-the-record numbers lottery known as *la bolita.* An illegal practice that was played parallel to the official national lottery, la bolita was—and still is—a national passion, as distinctly Cuban as royal palms, cigars, sugarcane fields, and the Matanzas-born guajiro who eventually became one of its kingpins in the heartland.

It was a postcard-perfect evening in Glendale. The mountains and the spindly California palms were crisply silhouetted against the dusky blue twilight. It was my second visit with Ofelia and I was in the den, the center of her domain in exile. With us was Rosa Sanchez, a lively, olive-skinned woman who introduced herself as Ofelia's *comadre* and housemate.

"When Martín began with la bolita, I had not even been born yet," said Ofelia as she folded an eight by ten-inch sheet of paper lengthwise to show me how the *listeros*, the listkeepers who kept track of the bolita bets, used to record the numbers. "He was twenty-eight years older than me. Twenty-nine, if you go by my birth certificate."

Her comment begged for a question. Rosa Sanchez gave me the answer before I had a chance to ask it. "What Ofelia means is that she was born on November 6, 1923, but because her father was away with the army at the time, and there was a law in Cuba that said you had to register your children within three months of their birth or pay a fine, they changed the birthdate on the certificate to February 5, 1924."

As Rosa Sanchez talked, I began to recognize her as the subject of the portrait hanging over the fireplace in the living room. She seemed a spirited individual—a sharp contrast to Ofelia's droll serenity. The two women had moved to California together in 1964, after Martín Fox suffered a debilitating stroke and Ofelia had fought a bitter custody battle with his family. At the time, Ofelia was forty-one years old, and Rosa was twenty-nine. Ofelia had left Cuba three years before. Yet, sitting in Ofelia's house, it was becoming evident to me how much of the Tropicana lifestyle she still maintained. The cabaret's legacy was like a comet's tail, extending far behind the original source of the brightness. Tropicana was not merely a subject of nostalgia, but an ongoing and seemingly inextinguishable source of celebration.

Ofelia and Rosa's den seemed to symbolize this seize-the-day philosophy. In addition to the cozy sofa and entertainment center, there was a red Formica bar, and here was where we sat as Ofelia prepared the sample bolita list. Behind her was a gigantic mirror that read OFELIA'S BAR AND GRILL. To her left was a pair of mirrors advertising Miller and Corona beer. The bar itself was stocked with dozens of bottles of spirits and wine, and twelve-packs of soda. A nearby refrigerator contained olives, cocktail onions, maraschino cherries, seltzer, tonic, cranberry juice, several kinds of dips, jalapeños, sliced cheese, sausages, and a full array of condiments to complement a pantry full of chips and crackers. There were goblets full of matchbooks, collections of shot glasses, and playing cards. There were cigarettes (this is one of the few houses in Southern California where people smoke indoors), gambling (I sat with my computer at a felt-covered poker table), and music. Ofelia's favorites are torrid boleros, especially those sung by Olga Guillot, a star of Tropicana who had remained one of her close friends over the years.

"I recently learned that the bolita is still played all over Cuba," I said, watching Ofelia tear the paper into columns roughly an inch wide. "I'm not surprised," she replied, laughing. "It was always the poor man's lottery. It was played on the last three numbers of the Cuban national lottery, but it was cheaper, so you could play for less and win more money. The listeros would keep the bets on thin strips of paper. They would write the numbers next to the bet amount. For example, let's say you wanted to put five centavos on the number two, the butterfly. You'd say, *'Un nickel a la mariposa,'* and the guy knew what you meant."

"It was a secret code, though of course everyone knew it," added Rosa Sanchez. "The long strips of paper made it easy when the police came around. The listeros just swallowed the evidence."

"The numbers all have names," Ofelia continued. "Number one is *el caballo* [horse]; number two, *la mariposa;* three, *el marinero* [sailor]; four, *el gato* [cat]; and up to a hundred in the same way."

"What's number forty-three?" I asked.

"The scorpion," replied Rosa and Ofelia together, without missing a beat or looking at each other.

BY THE mid-1920s, Ciego de Avila was teeming again. The price of sugar had gone back up a bit and, like their fellow countrymen, the residents of Ciego were regaining confidence. People began building houses, shops, and theaters. The streets, which for nearly a century had been exposed to the relentless sun and driving rain, were covered by a series of connected porticos that made it possible to walk from one end of the town to the other in any weather.

For years Martín Fox walked these streets as a listero, but he had quickly risen through the bolitero's hierarchy, saving enough money on the way to become his own *banquero,* or the one who financed the bets. This was lucrative but risky work. A particularly "charged" number—one that had been heavily bet on by many people, like eight on September 8, the date of the feast of the Virgin of Charity, Cuba's patron saint; or seventeen on December 17, the feast of San Lazaro, patron saint of the sick—could bring a banquero to ruin. But Martín had an innate feel for the finances of gambling. Almost as soon as he began as a banquero, he was careful to spread the risk of "charged" numbers, even if it meant giving up some of his profits.

Martín's next accomplishment was to consolidate most of the bolita operations in Ciego de Avila and become the region's biggest banquero. His "bank" was in a storefront shop on Calle Independencia, one of Ciego de Avila's prime commercial streets. Under one of the town's porticos, within sight of the Parque Martí, the town square named for José Martí, the poet and essayist who was the spiritual father of Cuban independence, Martín set up a kiosk, or *vidriera,* that he called La Batallita, "the little battle," which sold cigarettes, cigars, candy, and official lottery tickets, and where one could place bolita bets on the sly. Though tucked at the end of a

long corridor between the town pharmacy and a men's haberdash-
ery called La Elegante, the kiosk soon became a popular gathering
place. Men would hang around to smoke, buy lottery tickets, and
place their daily bolita bets. Among them were the town's elite—
doctors, lawyers, local politicians, and sugar planters—men who
belonged to the exclusive Club Atlético, where a thousand-peso
membership and twenty-peso monthly fee gave you the privilege
of playing billiards and poker with others of your social class, getting a shave and haircut in the private upstairs barbershop, or
spending the night in a mahogany-appointed bedroom after you'd
had a fight with your wife. Martín, a mere guajiro, went up a notch
in social standing simply by associating with these men. When the
Depression hit, Martín became privy to their concerns about the
economy and their fledgling nation's political stability. He learned
the names of their wives, children, mistresses, and remembered
their favorite places to hunt and fish. Most importantly, he understood how deeply vital gambling was to Cuban society.

During the 1930s Martín did nothing with this knowledge.
Then, like all ambitious men who make a mark in a nation's rural
backwaters, he decided to try his luck in the big city.

CHAPTER 3

The Boulevard of the New World

Havana never was what one might call a rendezvous of prohibitionists.

—Basil Woon, *When It's Cocktail Time in Cuba*

T he defining feature of a Cuban," pronounced Ofelia, "is a person who will do just about anything to get a minute of pleasure."

Ofelia offered me this laconic bit of wisdom on her cellphone one morning while she and Rosa Sanchez headed south on the I-15 to the Harrah's casino located on an Indian reservation near San Diego. Today was the last of her seven lucky days that month, according to the Chinese horoscope, and she was not about to let it slip away without a roll of the dice. Ofelia's favorite place is the casino, and she prefers craps to all other forms of gambling. "Craps is where the action is, and she loves the excitement," explained Rosa. "It's where you hear the shouting, the egging on of dice. You see the people leaning over the felt, feeling the challenge."

Ofelia's love of gambling is nothing less than a national characteristic. "The Cuban is nothing if not a sport. But he doesn't consider a game worth playing unless he can bet on it," wrote travel writer Basil Woon in *When It's Cocktail Time in Cuba*, a

1928 guide to the city where America's top social set, including the Astors, Vanderbilts, Irenée DuPont, Will Rogers, and New York Mayor Jimmy Walker wintered every year. Written when the Eighteenth Amendment to the Constitution and the Volstead Act prohibited the legal manufacture, sale, or transportation of alcoholic beverages in the United States, Woon's book extolls the virtues of a country that, as he describes it, "has 'personal liberty' carried to the nth degree," and where "everyone is drinking and not a soul is drunk." He highlights Cuba's licentiousness and sensuality: "Every restaurant and nearly every grocery in Havana is a barroom." And, "You can stare at the pretty señoritas because such staring in Cuba is a compliment—not a crime." Pages and pages of the book are devoted to cocktails like the daiquiri, "the most popular and healthful drink," as well as to the bars of the period, many of which were owned by Americans driven south by Prohibition. But Woon's greatest admiration is reserved for the unquenchable optimism of the Cuban gambler. "He always believes that his luck will change—that tonight he will pick the winners at *jai-alai*—a ball game of Basque origin that consists of hurling balls against forty foot high concrete walls from baskets, called *cestas,* which are attached to the players' wrists—that Sunday his cock will vanquish the opponent, and that within ten days he will win the Grand Prize of the lottery."

Woon could just have easily been describing Ofelia Fox. At the casino she is always certain that she's just a roll of the dice away from recouping the day's losses. At home, where she and Rosa frequently entertain, every guest knows that at some point in the evening she will break out the dice or cards or dominoes. Bets are even placed on pick-up sticks and on Jenga, that Milton Bradley game that involves pulling blocks of wood from a tall stack until it topples over.

"It's more fun when there's something at stake—pennies or a Cuban sandwich at the local bakery," insisted Ofelia one evening in Glendale, while uncovering the green felt poker table. It was time for Rosa and Ofelia's weekly game with a trio of Cuban co-madres who had just driven an hour from Orange County. The atmosphere was rowdy even before cocktails were served. Alina, the jokester of the group, prowled the room in search of ciga-rettes. Maria and Virginia, cousins from Mission Viejo, unloaded a twenty-four-pack of Corona beer and the largest bag of tortilla chips I'd ever seen. "Maria's father was that wine importer who used to sell Martín his whiskey," said Rosa as she laid out the decks of cards and chips. "He only used to drink Ancestor."

Ofelia and Rosa pay a great deal of attention to the details of their entertaining. Their costume theme parties are the talk of their social group. "We've had so many different types of parties—British, Moroccan, African, Polynesian, French—it's hard to re-member them all," said Rosa. During their African dinner, the Glendale dining room was cleared of furniture and covered in grass cloth; recipes for the food were obtained from the Kenyan consulate in Los Angeles. The Gypsy party featured a palm reader who insisted on staying after her work was finished to sample the authentic Romanian dishes Rosa had prepared. Even the weekly poker parties are studies in enthusiastic entertaining. The tequila is Jimador and the chips used for the game are made of clay like the kind one finds in Las Vegas casinos. "I had those made and in-scribed with Ofelia's initials for her sixtieth birthday," Rosa told me as she distributed them among the five women players. "Our stakes may be low, but we take our games seriously."

Since 1518, when the Spanish crown moved the settlement named San Cristobal de la Habana from a swampy, malarial cove on Cuba's southern Gulf of Batabanó, to a broad, narrow-mouthed harbor on the island's north coast, Havana has always been a haven for gamblers. The reason is strategic. Being posi-tioned at the entrance to the old Bahamian Channel made the city the perfect stopping-off point for the Spanish fleet as it sailed home to Cádiz and Seville laden with the New World's precious metals. The tall, two-masted galleons would begin arriving from Central and South American ports every spring. The ships would harbor in Havana until the full fleet was assembled for the long homeward journey. While hulls and sails were mended and maintained in local shipyards and the galleon's larders stocked with cured meats, vegetables, grains, and potable water for the three-month voyage across the Atlantic, the port filled up with as many as four thousand sailors for three to six weeks every year. Havana catered to them like a courtesan. The cobbled streets were lined with taverns, houses of prostitution, and gambling parlors where a sailor's meager salary could quickly be squandered or spun into gold, spices, tobacco, and other products that could be clandestinely traded. By the eighteenth century, Havana was the teeming gateway to the Americas—"the boulevard of the New World," as the philosopher-historian Guillaume Raynal put it in 1776. By 1810, a census put the city's population at 96,114, only 259 fewer souls than lived in New York. There was a national lottery by 1812, and several good hotels, bars, and restaurants, which were enjoyed by visitors like British novelist Anthony Trollope. The Prussian historian and naturalist Baron Alexander von Humboldt made a three-month visit in 1800. The entrance to Havana harbor, he wrote in his "Political Essay on the Island of Cuba," "is one of the gayest, most picturesque and enchanting on the shore of equinoctorial America." Enrico Caruso, who headlined Havana's 1920 opera season, put it somewhat differently in a letter to his wife from the Hotel Sevilla: "Here is so noise and I cannot have a moment of quite rest," he wrote, in his inimitable English. "Autos, tramways, trollys and talking machines makes terrible noise, that my mind go over terribly. Imagine that is a continual play of auto horn, one have not stop than another beginning, at that all day and night! You can imagine my nervs."

———

WHEN MARTÍN FOX, the bolita kingpin of Ciego de Avila, arrived in Havana in 1939, he found a city vastly different than any other in Cuba. Indeed, Havana didn't look like any other city in the Western Hemisphere. The old part of the city near the port still retained the rough-and-tumble character of the colonial backwater. Yet Havana had now been the capital of the largest republic in the Caribbean for nearly forty years, and its closest neighbor and trading partner was the world's most powerful nation. The city flaunted its importance. The streets grew even more crowded with trolleys and automobiles than in Caruso's day; the populace bustled like that in New York or Chicago, not the relatively sleepy and swampy town ninety miles away known as Miami. Visually, the city resembled a major European capital. In place of the narrow, cobbled, eighteenth-century streets, with their tightly packed buildings embroidered with elaborate ferrous grillwork, twentieth-century Havana boasted leafy, spacious boulevards where houses, factories, office buildings, and hotels all stood side by side, representing every architectural style of the burgeoning century. Within a five-block radius of the city's Parque Central, the city's epicenter, were the Moorish art nouveau Sevilla Biltmore, headquarters of the American social set described in Woon's book; the birthday-cake neobaroque presidential palace whose interior was decorated by Tiffany & Co.; a pair of massive, ornate social centers representing the Spanish Asturian and Galician communities; the terra-cotta-clad art deco headquarters of Bacardi; block upon block of eclectic mansions that blended elements from a variety of styles; and a neoclassical capitol building based on the design of the Washington Capitol Building, its interior bedecked with marble pillars, gold-knobbed bathroom fixtures, and the renowned Capitolio Diamond, a 24-carat stone set into the floor of its main reception hall. By the time Martín began to run bolita numbers from its streets, Havana looked and felt like the fulcrum of the Americas, the crossroads between Europe, South America, and the United States.

Unfortunately, the city's newfound status as the commercial capital of the Americas did not translate into political stability. Though Cuba had gained independence from Spain in 1898, it had been occupied for four years by the United States military, which had arrived to fight what Americans refer to as the Spanish-American War. ("What Spanish-American War?" remarked Rosa Sanchez with vehemence. "For us that's called the War of Independence!") At the time, there were rumblings that the United States would try to annex the island, as it had recently done with Hawaii. When Cuba finally gained its proper independence, it did so only by accepting an amendment, formulated in 1901 by Senator Orville Platt of Connecticut, which barred Cuba from entering into any treaty with any foreign power without the consent of the United States; allowed the United States to intervene in Cuban affairs "for the preservation of Cuban independence"; and, further, required Cuba to both effect sanitation measures in its cities to protect the southern ports of the United States, and to "sell or lease to the United States lands necessary for coaling or naval stations, at certain specified points, to be agreed upon with the President of the United States." The Platt Amendment effectively made Cuba, once again, into a colony. However the restrictions it posed were only part of the new nation's problems. Cuba's governments were plagued by corruption. Thievery was rampant among elected officials (one of the most efficient methods of illegal enrichment was skimming profits off the national lottery), and Cuba's politics, though nominally democratic, were often decided at gunpoint. The darkest years were 1925–1933, when President Gerardo Machado parlayed what had been a relatively clean election into a brutal free-for-all and seized a second term in office. In her book *Cuba, Island of Paradox,* Ruby Hart Phillips, the wife of then-*New York Times* Cuba correspondent James Doyle Phillips (whose post was filled by his wife after his death in 1937), describes the time as so chaotic—the government armed a group of civilian vigilantes called the *porristas,* who openly murdered students, labor unionists, journalists, and anyone else who challenged the regime—that people began to telephone her Havana home to ask when the U.S. Marines planned to land.

The Marines did not have to land—Machado resigned—but his middle-of-the-night departure was followed by a bloodbath, as warring factions within the army, student groups, and organized vigilantes sought vengeance for the viciousness of the regime. Thousands were killed. One of the worst encounters took place at the Hotel Nacional, a luxurious Vedado hotel designed by McKim, Mead, and White, the prestigious American architectural firm responsible for New York's Pennsylvania Station, the Morgan Library, the Boston Public Library, and Columbia University Library. The Nacional was a popular residence for American businessmen, journalists, and diplomats, including U.S. Ambassador Sumner Welles. A group of Machado's former army officers, wary of reprisals, holed up in the hotel for weeks. The new army besieged them, cutting off their water supply and electricity. Welles and the Americans evacuated in September. Two weeks later, the officers surrendered to a group of sergeants (the battle became known as the Sergeant's Revolt); but as the officers were leaving the hotel, the army opened fire. The ensuing battle lasted days and left eighty soldiers dead and two hundred wounded.

Similar clashes took place in the following months. The army shelled the Castillo de Atarés, a military fortress built by Spain in 1763 in response to the only British occupation of Havana. The fort's two-foot-thick stone walls were destroyed and two hundred soldiers were killed. Among the wounded was Lieutenant Victor Ceferino Suarez Hernandez, Ofelia's father. She was ten years old at the time, but even a child could see how dangerous it was to be a member of the military.

As soon as he was hurt, my father stripped off his uniform.
He tossed it aside so no one would know what side he was on.
He lay there in his underwear until he got into an ambulance

headed for the hospital. When my sisters found out where he was, they snuck him out and hid him. Weeks later, they took me to see him. It was in Old Havana, I think. The building had many rooms. We walked from one room into another, then another, until I finally got to him. And then I didn't recognize him because he had grown a mustache and he was in civilian clothes. He was a career army officer and before then I'd never seen him out of uniform.

THE STREETS of Old Havana, where Ofelia's father was hidden in 1933, seem to groan under the weight of centuries of secrets. The buildings, which are crammed together, discourage access. Sneaking through these stone and stucco canyons undetected is a futile exercise; everyone is watched from the wood and iron balconies. Inside the colonial buildings, it is easier to mask clandestine activity, for most contain labyrinths of rooms fanning out from central courtyards. The interiors of the nineteenth-century buildings of *Centro Habana*, an area bordered by the Parque Central on one side and by the Vedado district on the other, keep even better secrets. These stacked, multi-story concrete structures are pressed together more tightly. Many are mansions that were later subdivided into apartments, and they house scores of tiny rooms, closets, dead-end hallways, and attics whose narrow entryways can easily be concealed behind furniture, portraits, and statues of saints.

For Martín Fox and the other denizens of Havana's gambling underground, these warrens provided ideal cover for their operations. Martín's first venture in Havana was running bolita numbers in Central Havana. His *banco*, which he called La Buena, was run out of varying locales, mostly the apartments of friends. Details about these days are hard to come by, but it seems clear that Martín brought loyal cohorts with him to Havana, including his brother Pedro, who intermittently lived in New York, and Oscar Echemendia, a portly, broad-faced, easygoing man who had run bolita numbers with Martín in Ciego de Avila. Another was a woman named Antonia Valles, nicknamed Niquita. She may or may not have been Martín's lover at one time, but she was certainly a close friend, and someone he relied upon to lend her home for card games. Martín had married in December 1939. His wife, Rosita García, a quiet, well-educated woman who happened to be his first cousin, showed little interest in the gambling life. Her father, Leonardo García Fox, was a wealthy landowner with large holdings on the Icacos Peninsula, where the powdery white-sand beaches of Varadero are located. Rosita urged Martín to let her father bankroll him in a different sort of business, something more respectable and with more regular hours. It was a marriage doomed from the start. In 1940 Martín and Rosita went on a cruise, probably courtesy of her father, and Martín spent the entire trip in a private card game. One rumor had it that Martín's winnings were so huge that he used the money to buy his share of Tropicana, but this is untrue. Nonetheless, the story illustrates the depth of Martín's obsession: neither the law nor his wife was going to keep him from the gambling world.

His marriage notwithstanding, Martín set Niquita up in a house on Concordia Street in Central Havana that he used as a base of operations. Oscar Echemendia's place was also available to keep La Buena as ephemeral as smoke to the police. Martín then began to make inroads into Havana's gambling underground, which was broad based, highly competitive, and worked largely out of those back rooms and hidden corners within its aging neighborhoods. This world was as stratified as the rest of Cuban society. Rich men gambled in the smoky, wood-paneled rooms of private social clubs. On the Malecón between Prado and Capdevila, the prestigious Union Club, a favorite of Havana's politicians, offered poker, baccarat, and *monte de baraja*, a four-card game of Spanish origin, complete with chips bearing its insignia. (The club's founding members had paid an ounce of gold in 1889 for three months of membership. Its 1924 building, with its second story loggia supported by eight female caryatids, remains one of the most recognizable landmarks of the Malecón.) The rest of the population had only two legal options: the Casino Nacional in the Marianao Beach district and the Jockey Club at Oriental Park, Havana's racetrack. Both of these casinos had been built during the first two decades of the twentieth century (Oriental Park was founded in 1915 by Harry T. "Curly" Brown, who later sold his interest to Charles Stoneham, owner of the New York Giants, and John McGraw, the Giants' manager), and their license to operate had been secured anew in the revised Cuban Constitution of 1940. They were fashionable locations designed for the tourist used to playing in Deauville, Biarritz, and Monte Carlo, as well as the top echelon of Cuban white society. "The Casino Nacional during January and February is the smartest place on the American continent," wrote Basil Woon. Yet the annual period of operation of these casinos was limited to the six months of the tourist season. This might have been enough to satisfy the gambler who occasionally drifted over from New York or Miami, but it was hardly enough to quench the Cuban thirst for wagering.

Given the overwhelming demand for gaming, Martín and others like him stepped in to fill the void by supplying private, often roving casinos—usually hidden in homes—where players could bet a few pesos on dominoes, lay "a nickel on the butterfly," or hunker down for an all-night, high-stakes game of poker or monte. These makeshift casinos were illegal, but like the kiosks that sold bolita numbers, they were as much a fixture of Havana's landscape as street vendors, Chevrolets, and billboards. In backrooms throughout Old and Central Havana, men like Martín operated roulette and craps tables, plus an array of card games that, in addition to poker and monte, included blackjack and baccarat. The police were always on the lookout for these setups, but protection was purchased as easily as the whiskey and rum sold to the clients from the bars that were often in a family's kitchen. A friend who lives in Havana, whose father was a kingpin of the clandestine casino world in the 1940s and 1950s, recalled how this functioned:

> We lived in a three-story colonial house in Old Havana, with a large central courtyard and off of this a dining room, and several bedrooms where my father had his business. There was roulette, poker, blackjack, and dice. My father also ran bolita numbers and many of the people who came to the door just came to place their bets. The house was buzzing with men from morning to night. I would hear them talking, wagering, the smoke of their cigars pluming up to the third floor, where I would be trying to study and going crazy from all the noise. Our cook would prepare lunch and dinner for around thirty people each day and my mother would preside over the table as if this were just one giant family with dozens of uncles. My brothers and I knew what to do if my father gave us the signal. There was a safe in the wall where we would put the cash, the dice, the cards—anything incriminating, then we would block it with a large painted plaster statue of *la Virgen de la Caridad del Cobre*. No Cuban in his right mind was going to mess with one of the santos—that was the thought. But my father was usually warned before a raid anyway. I remember this police sergeant who was playing poker in our dining room turning to my father and saying: "*Oye*, they're scheduled sometime this afternoon."

The tip-off was generally reliable but, even if well paid for, not always foolproof. My friend's father was arrested several times during her youth. Usually released the same day, he would then go right on with his activities. "It wasn't just his livelihood, it was his world," she recalled. "It's like someone who grows up on a farm, or a jazz musician who thrives on the nightlife and the clubs. They can't conceive of any other life."

Martín Fox took to this milieu like a hothouse flower in the perfect greenhouse. He quickly made connections, using his bolita banquero status as a calling card. He began by offering a private poker game that roved between Niquita's house (which he eventually purchased for her) and the apartment of Oscar Echemendia. At first Martín would sit at the table with his guests, but soon he hired dealers so he could refrain from playing, and added monte and baccarat, because these were high-stakes card games favored by wealthier players. Martín knew that men who could risk their money without regard for a paycheck or the state of the economy would always be steady customers. This was a relatively small percentage of the populace compared to those who wagered on more popular games like dominoes, roulette, and craps, but Martín also had the lower rungs of society covered by la bolita. It was a winning strategy, which demonstrated that his brilliance as a gambler (the official term for someone whose living is made from organizing and running games of chance, as opposed to the "bettor") rivaled that of another occasional Havana resident, Meyer Lansky. Lansky and his partners, Benjamin "Bugsy" Siegel and Charles "Lucky" Luciano, had made a fortune from Cuban rum during Prohibition. In 1933, when the Twenty-First Amendment to the Constitution repealed Prohibition, before he began to be invited by the Cuban government to Havana for a series of high-level consulting positions (the first was in 1937, to clean up what had become unspeakably corrupt gaming conditions at Oriental Park), Lansky went back to running floating craps games in the back rooms of bars and hotel rooms in Manhattan and, later, at the glamorous casinos of Saratoga Springs, New York. "Gambling pulls at the core of a man," said Lansky to the Israeli reporter Uri Dan at the age of sixty-nine. Lansky's biographer, Robert Lacey, imagined that Meyer was talking of himself as he looked back on "a career spent in the rattle, click and murmur of the gaming room—the green felt, the dark wood, the glamorous, brightly colored chips" and "the men with their eyes and their hearts fixed on the table, losing themselves, and hoping to find something else in their contest with the dice or card or wheel." He could as easily have been describing Martín Fox.

CHAPTER 4

The Peanut Vendor

Mr. Van Chuba, came back from Cuba,
Playing his tuba,
That man is here again!

from Cab Calloway, Edgar Samson, and
Roy Collins's "That Man is Here Again"

There was trouble in Glendale. I could tell by the fact that after being let in by Rosa, I'd been waiting alone at the bar for fifteen minutes and no one had yet offered me a cocktail. Another clue was the stack of pages I had faxed the previous day, and which now sat before me on the poker table abundantly marked up in red, with the word "NO!" appearing frequently, followed by a row of exclamation points. The problem was my comparing Martín Fox to Meyer Lansky. Not long after we met, Ofelia had confessed to me that she wanted me to help her tell the story of Tropicana and her life with Martín. She had already begun to write the story, and the result was *Tropicana y Yo*—the short manuscript I had glanced at the night of my first visit to her house. The pages, which were full of anecdotes and ruminations about loss and destiny, had a specific purpose: "I want to set the record straight about my husband," she wrote. "He was not a gangster and Tropicana was never owned by the Mafia." The theme was one that she repeated often during my visits. Sitting there that night I realized that I'd probably offended her with the Lansky reference. My intention had been only to draw a parallel between two savvy businessmen whose passion for gambling went beyond the fortunes they made from it. I was ready to explain this when Ofelia sailed into the room, dressed in a beige linen pantsuit, perfectly coiffed, wearing makeup, and wafting the smoky floral perfume that she identified as Enigma, by Alexandra de Markhoff.

"Tonight's beer and tequila. Okay with you?" she said, heading straight for the bar. I nodded and she began to pour shots of Jimador and set out salt, Corona, and slices of lime—the ingredients for tequila boilermakers, which is what she drinks on alternate nights. (A few weeks earlier, when I had first asked about this back-and-forth with her cocktail choices, Ofelia said simply, "There's nothing scientific about it, it's just so I won't get bored.") I began to say something about the Lansky comparison. "Hold that thought until Rosa gets here," said Ofelia, then she launched into a series of pleasant questions about my parents, my son, my dog, and what kind of car I drive. As the drinks were served, Rosa finally came in and placed a worn-looking blue cardboard box in front of me. It had a Smith & Wesson label. "Open it," she said.

Inside was a .38-calibre Smith & Wesson with a gleaming blue-black metal barrel and a polished wooden handle. Ofelia watched me as she lit a long Benson & Hedges. "It was Martín's," she said. "He carried it everywhere because he always had large sums of cash with him. Pick it up."

I had never held a gun before, except in museums where I'd sometimes done restoration work on Civil War firearms. Martín's was heavy and smooth, invitingly sensuous and palpably dangerous. Once I made sure it wasn't loaded, I wrapped my finger around the trigger. The gun's weight strained my wrist.

"Oh, by the way," said Ofelia, handing me a beer and shot glass of tequila, "making your living off of gambling doesn't make you a gangster." She paused and I noted a sparkle of irony in her eyes. "Any more than owning a gun does."

I would have been hardpressed to imagine a more oblique method of addressing her concern about the Lansky and Martín comparison. On the other hand, I don't think I could have ever imagined myself drinking tequila boilermakers while holding a gun, let alone a sixty-year-old Smith & Wesson once packed by the man who owned Tropicana and was the kingpin of Havana's numbers game. Ofelia Fox, I was rapidly learning, had an unusual point of view about most matters. She believed unquestionably in fate, yet she was also the perfect pragmatist. This did not seem so unusual given all the highs and lows she'd been through, all the glamour followed by wrenching tumult. I was also learning other curious details about her. She took long, luxurious baths daily, always with bubbles, candles, and music. She was having her teeth straightened at the age of eighty, and she'd had a second set of holes pierced in her ears at the age of seventy. She lived with a woman, yet one day, after noting that I was wearing a new perfume, she told me that it was important for a man to always recognize a woman by her signature scent.

One of the most intriguing things about Ofelia was her forty-year relationship with Rosa Sanchez. The two women were inseparable. Since my second visit to Glendale, I had never seen Ofelia without Rosa. Rosa doted on Ofelia, insisting that she be allowed to enjoy her customary afternoon nap even when I was visiting. Sometimes, when we were about to look at a document whose content pertained to Martín's death or any other matter that she thought might upset Ofelia, Rosa, who was the one that kept the old letters, photographs, and newspaper clippings pertaining to Tropicana organized, would send her to the kitchen on a pretext. Ofelia always ate two full meals each day, including rice, beans, meat, and sometimes salad. At home, Rosa always cooked, and, to accommodate Ofelia's preference, dinner was never served before midnight. Ofelia likewise catered to Rosa's needs. She deferred to her on most practical matters and returned Rosa's care with a level of affection rarely seen in a couple together for so long. On the wall of the bar, near a trio of photographs depicting Tropicana's indoor and outdoor cabarets as well as the casino, were numerous pictures of Rosa and Ofelia arm in arm at costume parties, and a framed cigar box label that read *Rosa y Yo*. Despite this, when I once referred to them as "a couple," Ofelia sharply corrected me. "We are friends, Rosa. That's all. Comadres and friends."

"Okay, now that we showed her the gun you've got to tell her the story about Carmen Miranda," said Rosa.

Carmen Miranda performed at Tropicana for two weeks in 1955, part of a Brazilian production titled *Bahiondo*, which also starred Olga Guillot. At the time, Miranda was living in Hollywood, where she had been making movies like *That Night in Rio, Down Argentine Way, Weekend in Havana,* and the Marx Brothers' *Copacabana.* She was a popular, if somewhat kitschy performer, co-opted by Hollywood to play the role of Brazilian bombshell, and known more for wearing a turban hat bedecked with fruit than for the singing that had made her a household name in her native country. For her Tropicana appearance, however, Miranda went back to her samba roots. The cabaret brought in her Brazilian backup group, Bando da Lua, with whom she had not performed in ten years.

"At the time she was already feeling ill," began Ofelia. "We had a reclining armchair placed outside her dressing room so she could rest between shows. But onstage she was electrifying. Each night she brought the house down with her voice and movements. Olguita [Olga] Guillot performed in the shows, too. They were splendid together. At the end of each show she pulled off her trademark fruit hat, and unfurled this mane of hair that went down to her waist. And as if that was not enough, she carried a comb with her and she ran it through her hair so the public would see it was not false, as so many newspapers had speculated."

"Tell her about the night you guys got arrested," urged Rosa.

I'm getting to that. Let's see. I should begin by telling you that Carmen liked to go to after-hours clubs. No matter how tired she was after a show, she always wanted to see what was happening elsewhere in the city. Well, this one night we were headed to the cabarets down at the beach in Marianao. There was a whole string of these clubs. It was me, Martín, Carmen, and her husband, whose name I frankly can't remember. We were going to start off at Pennsylvania Club, I think, then move two blocks east to catch the sunrise either at the Panchín or the Rumba Palace. The way to get to the beach cabarets from Tropicana was by passing in front of Campamento Columbia, the headquarters of the Cuban army. At that hour there were no other cars on the road, and except for the crow of a cock in the distance, it was totally quiet. When we approached the edge of the military complex, a pair of lights shone through the back windshield. A car sped toward us, and it passed us and sharply cut us off. Martín hit the brakes on the Cadillac, and two men got out of the car and came towards us. They were in police uniform, but in Cuba you never knew who was who, and because Martín always carried the gun, he let his jacket fall open as he stepped out of the car, so the men could see that he was armed. Well, you can guess what happened next. We were taken to Campamento Columbia by the police. When we got there, Martín asked them to call [General] Fernandez Miranda. As you can imagine, they apologized and let us go. Martín invited the policeman to be his guests at Tropicana and Carmen signed autographs.

They were among the last autographs the samba star would ever sign. Two days after Miranda left Havana, she was rehearsing for an appearance on *The Jimmy Durante Show* in Hollywood, when, out of the blue, she decided to call Ofelia. "She had called to ask about her guayabera shirts," said Ofelia, recalling the traditional Cuban four-pocket linen shirts that Miranda was having made by Ofelia's dressmaker. A few hours later, the forty-six-year-old Miranda died of a heart attack.

While Miranda was in Cuba performing in *Bahiondo,* Ofelia and Martín gave her a party on the day of her santo, St. Carmen. The party was held at Johnny's Dream Club, a cabaret so after hours that it usually did not close until after dawn. The Foxes invited many of the friends Miranda had made during her stay in Cuba, including Olga Guillot, Mexican actress María Félix, and Cuban actress Lilia Lazo. For Ofelia, the party was memorable not only because of Miranda's presence or the meringue-covered sheet cake that she had specially made for the event, but because that night was one of the few times in her life that Ofelia danced with Martín.

Like many gamblers, Martín considered it undignified to whirl around on a dance floor, and a waste of time when there was a gaming table nearby. The horns, strings, and congas, and the melodic voices of Havana's troubadours and crooners were merely background music, the soundtrack to the more serious business of gambling. Yet music, more so than gambling, was the true lifeblood of Cuba. It was what lured the patrons through the doors of Tropicana. When Martín arrived in Havana in 1939, Cuban music was flourishing. It was being played all over the world, and its stars were becoming some of the country's hottest commodities.

Music had always been the essence of the island culture. Its earliest roots were based in African rhythms such as conga and rumba; but by the early twentieth century, these mixed and blended with Spanish and French melodic elements to create a variety of musical styles, like *son*—the precursor to what is now known as salsa; *guaracha,* a musical form that is characterized by the satiric content of its narrative lyrics; and a myriad of other styles: the romantic songs known as boleros, and the formal *danzón* that originated from European contradances in the coastal town of Matanzas. Much of this music stemmed from the countryside, and it was rich in percussive texture, with instruments such as bongos, maracas, claves (the two sticks that are played to set the one-two, one-two-three beat of most Cuban tunes), and *güiros,* which are made from gourds. As in all things, Havana had a more direct European connection. There were *danzas* based on classic orchestral music and a strong musical theater tradition imported from Spain and Italy.

In the early nineteen hundreds, the music of the countryside started mixing in elements from the city, and vice versa. String basses, pianos, trumpets, and clarinets were combined with bongos and the *tres,* a guitar-like instrument with three pairs of double strings. With the shifts in population in the 1920s and the migrations from the country to the city (all roads led to Havana), the capital resounded with septets, sextets, and smaller conjuntos that featured the percussive instruments of the countryside alongside the more traditional instruments of the city. There were hundreds of these groups, playing in bars and cafés. The music gave rise to local singing stars such as María Teresa Vera, the Trio Matamoros, Rita Montaner, "Bola de Nieve" (Ignacio Villa), Antonio Machín, and Miguelito Valdés, to name but a small number. These artists were the darlings of the cabarets and lyric theaters, and the new Cuban radio stations that opened in 1922, only two years after Pittsburgh's KDKA became the first commercial radio station in the United States. Their music was infectiously melodic, and the lyrics were at once sweet, plaintive, and bawdy, dealing with love, betrayal, and the assorted doubts and delights of courtship. With Havana at an international crossroads, these local stars soon began to play in the United States, South America, and Europe. In the New York clubs, the sounds of congas, maracas, and the *tres* were heard from Park Avenue to Harlem.

The American craze for Cuban music is often linked to a song called "El manisero," or "The Peanut Vendor," written by the Cuban composer Moisés Simons. The story behind "El manisero" goes like this: one sultry afternoon in 1928, Simons was sitting in an open-air Havana café, sipping coffee and watching the colorful parade of humanity. At the time, Cubans were partial to the café life, much like Parisians. The men, especially, would drink coffee throughout the day, sometimes pausing to sit, sometimes downing the small cups of strong, sweet brew on the run. That afternoon, Simons, a bandleader, composer, and a descendent of Jewish immigrants, was leisurely drinking coffee at his table when he was caught by the lyrical call of a vendor hawking peanuts: *"Maní! Maní!"* (Peanuts! Peanuts!) Simons scribbled the words on a napkin, added his own, and before he knew it, he had written a hit.

"El manisero" was first recorded in 1928 by Rita Montaner, a lyric opera singer who was the daughter of a white father and mixed-race mother. Though she was classically trained, Montaner was born and raised in Guanabacoa, a stronghold of Afro-Cuban religions, so she was also well versed in the Afro-Cuban songs and *comparsas* (dance processions) that were common in her neighborhood. By the time she recorded "El manisero," the feisty, politically outspoken Montaner was already one of Cuba's most beloved performers. She had sung on the historic first Cuban radio broadcast on October 10, 1922, had worked in Paris, and at New York's Plaza Hotel with Cuban bandleader and showman Xavier Cugat. A consummate professional who rehearsed religiously, Montaner studied local Havana peanut vendors to get the inflection of their calls before she recorded "El manisero." Later, in 1931, she performed the song in Al Jolson's show *Wonder Bar* at the Schubert Theater on Broadway. But "El manisero"'s great debut for the American public came earlier, on April 26, 1930, when the house orchestra of Havana's Casino Nacional led by Justo "Don" Azpiazu presented it at the Palace Theater on 47th Street and Broadway in New York. The song became an overnight hit with the American public. Azpiazu staged it again that year before a sellout crowd at the RKO Colisseum, with the band wearing ruffled-sleeved

Cuban shirts, using cocktail shakers filled with lead shot as maracas, and with his silky-voiced lead singer Antonio Machín making his entrance pushing a peanut cart. Probably few foreigners understood the double entendres of the lyrics, which urged housewives and young women not to go to bed without tasting the vendor's hot, salty nuts; nonetheless, the song's jaunty syncopation fired up audiences wherever it was performed. In November 1930, RCA Victor, which had been sending scouts to Cuba for a decade, released the first American recording of "El manisero." The record sold over a million copies. Louis Armstrong, Guy Lombardo, and Duke Ellington recorded later versions. The song was such a widespread hit that it was lampooned by Groucho Marx in one the first scenes of the Marx Brothers' classic 1933 comedy, *Duck Soup*.

"El manisero" launched a frenzy for Cuban music that quickly spread to all the major U.S. cities. Though the rhythm of "El manisero" was, in fact, a *son pregón* (a type of song that relies on the give and take of street vendors' cries), the music and the dance style that went along with it quickly became known as "rhumba." Actual Cuban rumba (in Cuba there is no *h* in the word) refers to a series of Afro-Cuban dances—the *yambú, guaguancó,* and *columbia*—which are danced to percussion. Cuban music historian Ned Sublette notes that rumba "can refer to the dance or to the music played. But, most importantly, it refers to the party where it all goes on, a collective, rum-fueled atmosphere." The U.S. clubs where the new dance craze took off were nothing like the Havana *solares* (tenement houses) and towns where the black population of Cuba developed real rumba out of traditions that originated in Africa. Places like the Waldorf-Astoria, which in 1931 snapped up Xavier Cugat for its chic Starlight Ballroom, were the more likely settings. "I have no doubt that the reason our music was so spontaneous a hit was our rhythm," wrote Cugat about rhumba in 1948. "It made those who usually only listened get up and dance." The Spanish-born Cuban had reason to know. When he first moved to

New York, Cugat had capitalized on the tango craze of the time. Later, when his orchestra became the Waldorf's house band, headlining in the elegant Sert Room for more than twenty years, he became one of rhumba's top spokesmen and proponents. "There is no popular song which cannot be played as a rhumba," noted Cugat. "I encouraged the dancing of the rumba by starting to play an American foxtrot, then suddenly changing to a rumba rhythm. This enabled the dancers to feel how easy it is to do." Cugat's easy approach to rhumba made it simple to learn and as fun for the American dancing public as swing. He also served as the springboard for the careers of other Cubans, like the vivacious showman Miguelito Valdés, who introduced the boisterous conga rhythm to the American stage and became the first to take up Margarita Lecuona's hit song, "Babalú." In 1935, his fourth year at the Sert Room, Cugat also introduced to America a "young, mild-mannered handsome Cuban from Santiago [de Cuba] named Desi Arnaz, who asked to join my band as a vocalist." Cugat auditioned Arnaz that day and hired him on the spot. Fifteen years later, Arnaz would also take up the cry of *"Babaluuu!"* to propel himself into the hearts of American television viewers as bandleader Ricky Ricardo on *I Love Lucy*.

In Harlem, where the jazz musicians hung out, Cugat was considered a musical lightweight and too much of a showman. Yet the jazz scene was also becoming rapidly Cubanized. The arrival of musicians such as composer and trumpet player Mario Bauzá, flute player Alberto Socarrás, Bauzá's brother-in-law, Frank Grillo (Machito), and a host of conjuntos with strong brass and percussion sections, were imbuing the big band sound with Afro-Cuban rhythms—the beginnings of what would become Latin jazz.

Throughout the '30s and '40s, New York, Paris, Los Angeles, and Chicago clamored for Cuban music. Meanwhile Havana heated up. "I was only a girl back then, but my sisters were always going out dancing," recalled Ofelia. "There were hundreds of cabarets and bars all over the city. I'd stand at the window, listening to the music, dying of envy as they went off. I taught myself to dance." Music emanated from the open doorways of bars and clubs, any place where people went to drink, eat, gamble, or have a generally good time. Pairs of Cuban dancers were hired to demonstrate the one-two, one-two-three beat of the rhumba to hopelessly hip-locked tourists who would flock down to Havana for the club scene. One such tourist was George Gershwin, who visited in 1932, and included four bars of composer Ignacio Piñeiro's hit song, "Echale Salsita," in his fifth symphonic work, *Cuban Overture*. Even more than tourists, the Cubans would pack the clubs, reveling in music that was wholly theirs, and which allowed them respite from their country's constant political turmoil.

During those years—the 1930s—one of the most popular of Havana's cabarets was a place called Edén Concert. Located at 228 Zulueta Street, in a bustling Central Havana commercial district near the Parque Central, Edén Concert was the brainchild of a Portuguese immigrant of Italian descent named Victor de Correa, who had arrived in Cuba in 1931 via Panama City, where he had been the cashier at a cabaret called the Overtop. Correa was a stout, bespectacled, neatly dressed businessman with a soft voice and a calm demeanor, a man who almost disappeared into the scenery around him. An unabashed *farandulero*—roughly translated as someone who likes mingling with show business people— Correa was also a man of burning ambition. At Edén Concert, his first solo cabaret venture, he set out to become the island's leading impresario.

He began with the setting. Correa rented a space on Zulueta Street that was an open-air ruin, consisting of half-dilapidated walls of charred brick, out of which had started to sprout small shrubs. The site, which had been the former headquarters of the Liberal Party, burnt down on the 20th of May, 1925, just as the so-called Liberal Party president, Gerardo Machado, was taking office. Correa set up a small raised stage under a red-tiled roof. Tables lined the periphery of the walls and the middle was cleared for dancing. It was a veritable Garden of Eden of palm trees and colored lights, giving the illusion of an outdoor tropical experience right in the heart of the city. And it was, most definitely, the heart. Edén Concert was within easy walking distance of many of the city's best hotels—the Inglaterra, Plaza, Parque Central, and the Sevilla Biltmore. Havana's most crowded watering holes—Sloppy Joe's, Dirty Vic's, and Ernest Hemingway's favorite daiquiri haunt, El Floridita—were just blocks away from Edén Concert. So were its most exclusive stores. Next door was a shop that sold perfume, alligator skin goods, and cigars to tourists, and down the street was the Abravanel Brothers' Oriental Bazaar, which also catered to the unquenchable thirst for souvenirs. Edén Concert was close to the Capitolio, which had opened only a year before the cabaret opened its doors; the presidential palace; and the headquarters of Bacardi, whose lit-up terra-cotta tower, crowned with the bronze fruit bat that was the symbol of the company, could be seen at night through the cabaret's open roof.

Correa's setting was inspired, but it was his eye for talent that made Edén Concert Havana's premier 1930s nightspot. To form the club's house orchestra, Correa hired Alfredo Brito, who had been the saxophonist and arranger for Don Azpiazu when the band recorded "El manisero" for RCA Victor in 1930. Brito's orchestra consisted of the best talent in the city, including Armando Romeu Jr., who was one of Havana's most versatile jazzmen, and the nephew of one of Cuba's venerated classical composers and bandleaders. The best singers of the day performed at Edén Concert. Rita Montaner and Cugat's lead singer, Miguelito Valdés, were fixtures at Edén Concert whenever they were not touring. Correa's choreographers staged elaborate revues around these stars, including Correa's wife, the flamenco dancer Teresita de España, a tall, lithe Dominican tango stylist who went by the name of Dinorah, and numerous lively Cuban dance pairs, including Roberto y Estela, who performed in the 1933 Chicago World's Fair and later went on to dance at New York's Cotton Club. "It was the country's respite from the violence of the Machado era," recalled bandleader Armando Romeu in one of his last interviews. "There we would be, with Rita [Montaner] onstage, singing, '*Mejor que me calle, que no diga nada, que tu sabes lo que yo se* [It's better that I shut up, that I say nothing, because you know what I know]' while outside the cabaret walls you could hear the shooting in the streets."

Olga Guillot, the bolero diva who went on to become a star of Tropicana and later, after leaving Cuba, had a career in the United States that has spanned four decades, began her career at Edén Concert when she was nineteen. "Correa was the master of his time," she said simply when I spoke with her in Miami.

One afternoon in 1939, when Edén Concert was at the peak of popularity, Correa was paid a visit by two men whom he had never met before. The men, who introduced themselves as Rafael Mascaró and Luis Bular, were from the underground gambling world, and they had come with an interesting proposition: they had plans to open a new casino out in the suburban Havana neighborhood known as Marianao and they wanted Victor de Correa to provide the food and entertainment. The property was ideal, they explained, because it was a six-acre estate with extensive tropical gardens that could house an outdoor cabaret. It was located in a fairly unpopulated part of the city where Mascaró and Bular had already secured police protection for the gaming, and practically its only neighbor was the Colegio de Belén, a Jesuit seminary where upper-class Catholic families sent their sons to study. Correa was immediately intrigued. At Edén Concert, he could have easily tripled his seating for two hundred people, but there was no room to expand. Secondly, unless Mascaró and Bular were pulling his leg, and they did not seem the type, the offer was beyond generous. They would cover the entire rent on the property, build him a stage, and purchase the furnishings for the cabaret. All Correa had to do was pay for the food and talent. And Mascaró was willing to be flexible about this as well: "If you find a big international act that would bring in the crowds, but that costs too much for you to cover, we'll underwrite the salary," he told Correa. The gamblers even suggested that if Correa managed to keep the house packed and if the casino took off, they would consider giving him a percentage of their own profits.

The next day, Correa called on the services of Emeterio López, one of his favorite chauffeurs from the taxi stands around the Edén Concert, and asked to be driven out to 72 Truffin Avenue in the municipality of Marianao. Truffin Avenue was a broad, sparsely populated street in what was then the outskirts of Havana. It had been named for Regino Du Rapaire Truffin, a Cuban-born descendent of French immigrants who had been president of both the Cuban Cane Sugar Corporation and the Havana Yacht Club. Upon his marriage to a high-society habanera named Guillermina Pérez Chaumont, Truffin had purchased a six-acre estate and named it Villa Mina, in her honor. After her husband's death in 1925, Mina, as Guillermina was known, continued to live at home with her son Marcial until she decided to remarry. Her second marriage, to a United States senator named Henry Walsh, never made it past the honeymoon: Walsh had a fatal heart attack on a train trip up the east coast of the United States. Widowed again, Mina moved with her son Marcial and one of her married daughters and put her Truffin Avenue property up for rent. She was asking for eight hundred pesos a month, equivalent to $10,000 today.

While Emeterio López waited for him in his brand-new 1939 Chevrolet, Correa walked the grounds of the estate. The afternoon was sweltering, insects buzzing in the dappled sunlight, the humid, verdant air making him dizzy. Villa Mina was like no place he had ever seen before. The house itself was fairly ordinary, which was fine, given that Mascaró planned to use it for gaming; but the grounds were something straight out of an impresario's imagination—dense, varied, and, at the same time, manicured to perfection.

Villa Mina's gardens offered the perfect jungle paradise—a natural yet magnified setting for the outdoor stage sets that Correa had toyed with at Edén Concert. Correa immediately saw the potential. Here was the tropical experience craved by Havana's tourists. Mascaró had proposed that the back patio might serve as the location for the cabaret, and Correa could already see how he would fit the tables in between the vine-choked royal palms and towering mamoncillo trees. He would have room to seat at least a thousand customers. He could build a generous-sized dance floor, dressing rooms, a bar, and an orchestra platform that would allow Alfredo Brito to expand, even double, the size of the orchestra if he wanted to.

Correa did not hesitate. That very afternoon, while Emeterio López patiently continued smoking cigarettes by the garages, Correa ironed out the terms of an agreement with Rafael Mascaró and Luis Bular in the mansion's chandeliered dining room. Mascaró did not waver from his original proposal: he would pay the rent, build the stage, buy the furnishings. Correa had simply to fill the place. The deal was sealed with a handshake.

Immediately afterward, Correa went to work. "I want you to put together the best orchestra in all of Cuba," he told Alfredo Brito. Brito got to work even as the carpenters were hammering the planks together for the stage. Less than six months later, on December 30, 1939, the new cabaret opened its doors under the name Beau Site. Mascaró and Bular set up four tables of roulette in the dining room of the mansion, including a private wheel for people who liked to play alone, and one table each of blackjack, craps, baccarat, and a big six wheel of fortune. The opening show, which was choreographed by Sergio Orta, received no particular mention in any of the papers of the day; but it most likely featured the Edén concert favorites, Teresita de España—Correa's wife— as well as the Brito Orchestra.

Then there was the matter of naming the cabaret. According to Cuban writer Rafael Lam, whose slender volume on Tropicana is the only existing history of the cabaret, the name used on its patent deed was Tropicals Night Club; but its name eventually was changed to the title of a song that Brito had composed for a revue at Edén Concert.

Tropicana	Tropicana
Diosa de amor,	Goddess of love,
Eres tú mi bien	You are my goodness
La que inspiró mi canción.	Which inspired my song.

The title of the song was "Tropicana," a word that suggested everything the new nightclub had to offer: exotic beauty, sensuous rhythms, and balmy nights under the stars.

CHAPTER 5

Valentín

O felia flipped the pages in Rafael Lam's paperback, furiously shaking her head. "Here it says I was a model of Chinese ancestry. There it says that Martín died of cancer in Chicago—the city of the Mafia! Where do they get these ideas? But this thing about Brito? Hmmm. I don't know. I never heard it before, but maybe." She called out to Rosa, who was in the bedroom, searching the Internet to determine which of the two Senator Walshes was Guillermina's second husband. "Rosa, what do we know about the name Tropicana coming from a song?" Ofelia continued poring through the book, now frowning while she read a description of herself and Martín aloud: "He was a brutish man, a pure Spaniard . . . She extracted from her husband everything she wanted—from precious jewels to a lion that was brought from the jungles of Africa directly to the patio of her house."

Ofelia slammed the book down on the poker table. "*Por favor!* What nonsense. Martín was more Cuban than the royal palms! And me, a model? I'll take the compliment but, really, they should try doing a little research before they say these things. Martín used to call me china. It was a common pet name in Cuba. And he didn't buy me the lion. Sunan was a gift from an African prince!"

"Hold on a second," I said. "You had a pet lion?"

Ofelia's demeanor softened. "Ah! He was the sweetest, most affectionate creature. How I hated to leave him when we had to go."

"I'm sure you did. But how did you get him to begin with? And did you keep him in the patio of your house?"

"Not in the patio. In the garage. We had a special cage with bars built for him. He was so tender. Once he escaped and the neighbors were petrified. We called the police but they were afraid of him also. I'm the one who found him. He was hiding in the grass behind the house, just like he would have done in the African savannah."

The story begged for a few more details. For example, who was this African prince? Why did he bring a lion with him to Cuba? And how did it wind up as a house pet in suburban Miramar?

"Oh, no, no. The Prince didn't bring the lion to Cuba," said Ofelia, laughing. "One night he came to Tropicana. I don't remember what country he was from. He was at my table. I was translating his conversation for Martín. At one point I made a comment on the beauty and majesty of the animals on his continent. And he asked me, 'Which animal is your favorite?' That was easy, because I've always been passionate about cats, especially lions. *Bueno,* one month later, this crate arrived for me at the port. Inside was a little baby *cachorrito* [cub], the cutest thing you've ever seen. It was love at first sight. I used to take him for rides in my convertible when he was a cub. Later he got too big and had to stay home. The nannies in the neighborhood would bring the children to see him."

For Ofelia, the quintessential animal lover, there was nothing odd about keeping a pet lion. In time I would learn how easy it was to bring any conversation with her back to her Cuban menagerie— her dog, Choni; her monkey, Tito; her cat, Negrita; and, of course,

Sunan, the king of all her beasts. Right then, however, she was locked onto the matter of Brito's Tropicana theme song. She stood and walked into the living room. "Rosa, did you hear me calling you?"

Nothing unnerves Ofelia like a piece of Tropicana information that conflicts either with her memory or that of the people she knew from the era and had come to trust as authorities. Tropicana is her past, her history, but also embedded in the collective memory of a million Cuban exiles and several more million who never left the island. Clearly it is impossible to master every detail involving the cabaret, to know every secret, to be privy to every deal. Nonetheless, I was learning how proprietary Ofelia felt about Tropicana. The cabaret is her life's subject matter, and she is always trying to unearth new details. Sometimes she is surprised by the depth of the emotion other Cubans harbor for Tropicana. In the mid 1970s, for example, when she and Rosa were active members of a local organization called the Cuban Cultural Club of Monterrey Park, she met fellow Cuban exiles Orlando and Fifi Ortega, who had brought a Tropicana cup and saucer in the one suitcase they took when they left Cuba. Orlando Ortega, who at the time was the director of the San Onofre nuclear power plant near San Diego, gave the cup and saucer to Ofelia. "Imagine what they must have experienced at Tropicana," said Rosa the day she and Ofelia pulled the delicate beige and green set out of their china closet to show me. "Of all the things this family could have taken, of all the photos, personal effects, and clothes, they chose a memory of this place."

It seemed equally amazing to me that this family chose to give their precious artifact away. It was an offering. Giving the cup and saucer to Ofelia was a way of expressing their pride in their Cuban heritage. This was something I was seeing repeatedly. People who know Ofelia want to help her archive information. They mail her clippings, books, letters, and videocassettes. The list of those people, most of them Tropicana staff and stars who have stayed in touch, shrinks with every passing year. The most recent losses were Martín's last remaining partner, Alberto Ardura; Martín's secretary, Gladys Torres; Dominguito Echemendia, the stepson of Martín's longtime partner and friend from Ciego de Avila, Oscar Echemendia; and Celia Cruz, who always got in touch with Ofelia around the Christmas holidays.

Yet though the passage of time had taken its toll, there remains a core of key figures who kept Tropicana's memory alive. Among the closest to Ofelia were Max Borges, the architect of all the renovations; Eddy Serra, a former member of the dance corps; and Leonela González, probably the most important dancer at the cabaret and one of the two most celebrated ballerinas in the history of Cuba. Models Alicia Figueroa and Jenny León, who lived in Merida, Mexico, and Azusa, California, respectively, were also her great friends, as was Jenny's musician husband, Frank Llopis, who played at the cabaret with his quartet. Olga Guillot remained in frequent contact with Ofelia; and acrobatic dancer Erna Grabler, who went by the stage name Chiquita, frequently invited Ofelia and Rosa to her Malibu home.

But among Ofelia's friends the only person still alive who knew the business side of the cabaret is Valentín Jodra.

Though I was still trying to get answers about Sunan the lion, Ofelia was dialing Valentín in Las Vegas. She was eager to ask about the Brito song and whether it had anything whatever to do with Tropicana's name. When he answered, she made small talk at first, asking about his family's health, clucking sympathetically about the desert heat. Then she got to the point: "Valentín, I have this book, and it says that the name Tropicana comes from a song—"

She stopped in mid-sentence. Nodding, she walked out onto the patio, where she put a dish of nuts out for the neighborhood squirrels. "*Claro,* that's exactly what I thought!" She called me over and handed me the telephone.

I heard a faint, raspy male voice: *"Buenas, mucho gusto . . ."*
Then without further introduction, Valentín launched into a long
explanation of the cabaret's name.

> Nothing to do with Brito. Correa made up the name Tropi-
> cana by combining the first part of the word *tropical* with the
> last syllable of *Mina*. See, it's Tropica with the *na* from
> *Mina*. She was the original owner of the *finca*, you know. A
> fine lady. Very elegant and proper, married to an American
> senator the second time. Dies [the senator, that is] right in the
> middle of the honeymoon, on a train trip up the East Coast
> of the United States. *Pero bueno,* everyone hits hard times,
> and after being widowed for a second time, she didn't want
> the upkeep on such a big place. So she rents it out to Mascaró
> and Bular and they bring in Correa. It's six acres, you know?
> But she was always coming over, taking walks, always look-
> ing out for the trees, which she loved, and that's why she had
> such respect for Martín . . .

Such is the nature of conversations with Valentín Jodra. At the
age of seventy-six, he is one of the last remaining Tropicana
casino dealers and probably the only person alive who remembers
Victor de Correa and Rafael Mascaró. At first it was hard for me
to understand him. He spoke in a whisper and his conversation was
full of names, stories, and inside gossip. "Luis Bular—a gigolo
with no money!" he said, laughing. "His girlfriend ran a house of
prostitution a few blocks down from Villa Mina. Correa—that
was *otro descarado* [another degenerate]. He had these two scruffy
dogs, and he was always trying to give Martín *la mala mano* [the
bad hand], but he didn't realize that El guajiro era bastante vivo
también [the Guajiro was pretty crafty himself]."

One day, when I was trying to get the bottom of the story of
how Martín managed to take over the Tropicana lease, what I got

was an avalanche of information and impressions. It all started further back, I learned. Valentín Jodra had been a pale-faced boy who had not yet finished the sixth grade when Rafael Mascaró and Victor de Correa hired him. It was 1941. Valentín's uncle, Emeterio López, the chauffeur who had taken Victor de Correa to see Villa Mina for the first time, had just done Correa a big favor and he wanted something in return. "Correa's head parking attendant at Edén Concert was named Rodolfo Cabeda, and they had a fight because Correa didn't pay on time—that was one of his great problems. He didn't manage the financial end of things too well . . ."

I gently prodded Valentín back to the original question. "How did you get a job at Tropicana?"

"*Bueno,*" he continued, "when Correa moved to Tropicana he said to my uncle, 'See if you can locate Rodolfito and get him to come back to work for me.' When he found him, Correa made him head of the parking attendants, and my uncle [Emeterio López] said, 'Can you put in a word for my nephew, who needs a job?'"

Valentín's first job at Tropicana was as a *botones* boy, a runner who worked for tips by going around to the tables in nightclubs and taking down the names of celebrities for press releases. The name *botones* (buttons) came from their bellhop-style uniforms, with jaunty caps and double-breasted jackets with silver buttons. In those early months, Valentín worked at a variety of odd jobs. He served coffee to the players between hands; he was responsible for giving the tips to the taxi drivers who brought tourists to the cabaret. "Correa had this deal with the chauffeurs since his days at Edén Concert," explained Valentín. "For every American client a driver brought, he would get a twenty-cent tip."

Before World War II effectively halted tourism in Cuba, according to Valentín, Mascaró tried hard to build up the casino portion of the cabaret. He brought in university students and organized workshops to train them in how to be dealers. Roulette was the favorite game among Cuban players and also one of the hardest to learn, because it required making rapid calculations on the payout even as the wheel was being spun again. Mascaró conducted training sessions in the afternoon in the casino, using the most remote roulette table in the room (Valentín remembered that it was table number three). One day, Valentín was standing on the sidelines watching Mascaró grow increasingly frustrated with his students. "They just couldn't get it. They couldn't finesse the chips, they had no speed whatsoever."

After the students left, Mascaró saw the young botones hanging around, watching. "*Muchacho,*" Mascaró called out, "are you interested in this?" Valentín shrugged. "*No sé,* I don't really know what it is." Mascaró called Valentín over to one of the roulette tables and showed him how to place the chips for the bets, how to run the wheel, how to collect the *fichas* [chips] after the play concluded. "Go ahead, you try it."

Valentín did his best. The hardest part was collecting the chips, palming them in groups of twenty so you did not have to waste time counting. When he looked up, Mascaró was running off, calling his partner. "*Oye,* Luis, check out this kid. He's a natural!"

Though Valentín was technically too young to be working in a casino, Mascaró immediately began the boy's training as a roulette dealer. Valentín was so short that Mascaró had him stand on a Coca-Cola crate to reach the wheel. Within a week Valentín had mastered the basics of the game, and his ability to palm those chips and make rapid payout calculations in his head were astonishing. He became a full-fledged roulette dealer before he was sixteen. From this vantage point, he became privy to all the goings-on at Tropicana and is probably the only living person to remember, for example, that Victor de Correa moved into the second floor of Villa Mina after separating from his wife, Teresita de España.

Valentín also happened to be around one day in late 1941, the first time a burly, affable guajiro with a strong provincial accent came to see Rafael Mascaró about renting a table for monte. "At the time Martín was running his *juegos* out of Concordia and Amistad," recalled Valentín. "He had the protection of the police, but he was looking for a better position, something with less risk and more long-term potential."

Martín found this through a fellow gambler, a man who Valentín remembered was named Pepito Bartarrachea. Bartarrachea told Martín about the new casino in Marianao and said that Mascaró was looking to rent space to other gamblers who had a specialty game that was not already covered. "Bartarrachea was a low-level guy, one of these front men in a nice suit with wide lapels who specialized in making contacts between people, brokering deals between gamblers and players." There were, apparently, many of these wheeler-dealers operating in Havana's gambling underground in the 1940s. They would hang around the pool halls, private gaming houses, the legal casinos, the racetrack, the jai alai *frontón*, or baseball stadium in their panama hats; they would shake hands, slap backs, buy drinks, introduce people to one another (for a price), always making sure they had an ear to the ground and their back to the wall. To men like Martín, these men were indispensable for keeping abreast of opportunities. Later, when he had his own casino empire, Martín relied on them for bringing in high rollers and for finding out what the competition might be planning.

Martín got to know Mascaró, and eventually rented two tables at Tropicana—"at first, one for monte only," recalled Valentín, "and later adding baccarat for his rich players from the Union Club." It was one of the savviest gambling moves of the decade. The next one came in 1943 or 1944 (Valentín would sometimes get the dates mixed up, but usually not the names), when U-boats prowled the depths of the Caribbean, sinking sugar carriers and passenger ships, making travel between Cuba and the United States unusually dangerous. Tourism plunged from 126,000 annual visitors in 1941 to a mere 12,500 in 1943. Sans Souci, one of the other cabarets in Marianao, had to close. Tropicana's gaming tables were practically empty.

"Mascaró was going out of his mind," remembered Valentín, then he launched into a recap of what was happening at Tropicana in those days. "No one was coming to the casino. And he had to make his rent payments, the payoffs to Colonel Raymundo Ferrer—he was the chief military officer for Santa Clara Province, the one who provided the police protection to operate. This Ferrer had a shill in the casino, a guy who plays, but for the house. His name was Manuel Ojeda. He hung around to collect the money for Ferrer, but he was also taking some for himself, putting his hand *en la caja* [in the till], where it didn't belong, and also *quemándole la cabeza a Mascaró* [frying Mascaró's mind], putting worries in his head."

Slowly, after much prodding on my part to get Valentín to unravel everyone's actions and intentions, the Tropicana casino's convoluted business dealings became clear. Manuel Ojeda was working on Mascaró because he wanted Mascaró to crack under the financial pressure and leave the Tropicana in his hands so he could manage it for Colonel Ferrer. But Mascaró had other ideas. In 1943, while Mascaró was struggling to bring in clients, Martín Fox's clientele of rich Cubans continued to play monte and baccarat at his two Tropicana tables. At a time when the Cuban peso and the U.S. dollar were of equal value, Martín's bolita bank, La Buena, was grossing six thousand pesos weekly, with about 9 percent of that being profit. One afternoon, after a week of losses that left him without enough even to pay the eight hundred pesos to Guillermina Perez Chaumont, Mascaró made Martín an offer that would change Cuban cabaret history. "Give me seven thousand [pesos] and take this over," said an exasperated Mascaró to Martín. Martín would assume the payment for the rent and, in turn, he would own the casino concession. Victor de Correa would continue to operate the cabaret portion.

Sixteen-year-old Valentín Jodra was standing in the carport with Martín's associate from Ciego de Avila, Oscar Echemendia, when he heard that Mascaró was leaving. "There goes my place at the roulette table," moaned the young dealer, thinking of the generous weekly salary of fifteen pesos that he was about to lose. Oscar Echemendia looked down at the baby-faced roulette dealer and clapped a hand on his shoulder.

"Don't you worry *chiquitico*," said Echemendia, using Martín's term of endearment for Valentín. *"Ahora es que empieza lo bueno."*—"Now's when things are really going to get going."

CHAPTER 6

Waiting Things Out

[Havana] was a place where the politician was boss.
—Charles "Lucky" Luciano

On October 17, 1944, the inhabitants of Havana woke to an eerie silence, broken only by the occasional honking of a car horn or the pounding of a hammer. Not even birds were chirping. Palm fronds hung phlegmatically in the stifling air, while overhead the clouds raced northward, as if running from something in hot pursuit. The "something" was a class five hurricane—five being the highest rating on the Saffir Simpson hurricane scale—that both Havana's National Weather Observatory and the Miami Weather Bureau had predicted would blow directly through the city sometime that night. Class five hurricanes are monstrous forces of destruction accompanied by winds of no less than 155 miles per hour and storm surges upward of eighteen feet. Throughout Havana, people had spent the days leading up to the storm boarding up windows, buying candles, stocking up on food, and tying down boats, cars, branches, and anything else that could be ripped up and thrown by the winds. The calm before the storm continued as the day wore on. "There was a strange stillness, a different quality to sound that makes one's voice seem changed in tone, an acute awareness of the silence of unmoving things," wrote *New York Times* reporter Ruby Hart Phillips.

By midnight everyone's worst fears had been realized. Wind and rain clawed at the city. Wind gusts measuring 260 miles per hour blew roofs to pieces, ripped ancient grillwork balconies from stucco anchoring, and snapped centuries-old trees by the dozens. When the storm's eye passed directly over the city, the scene already was one of colossal destruction. Cars were piled up against the sea wall of the Malecón, inundated under waves that had surged as far as twelve miles inland. In the countryside, the devastation was even worse. Most of the tobacco fields in western Cuba had been leveled. On the south coast, the entire shore village of El Cajio had been swallowed by the storm.

By early afternoon of the next day, when the winds had died down to about fifty miles per hour, Martín Fox drove his Cadillac through water and debris to Tropicana. He was expecting damage, but what he saw nearly brought him to tears. Apart from the royal palms and massive mamoncillos, almost every tree in Guillermina's glorious gardens had been either uprooted or snapped. The paths were knee-deep in mud. All of the shrubs and plants were flattened or choked by mud. Piles of fronds and branches were strewn throughout the cabaret area. The cabaret's stage had been destroyed; light fixtures dangled from torn wires.

Martín wasted no time. When Valentín Jodra arrived early the next day, his boss was in his shirtsleeves, spattered in mud, and working with a crew of ten who were staking whatever trees could be saved and hauling off those too mangled to be worth the trouble. "The wind was still blowing, but Martín already had a *carbonero* on the premises, drying out the wood and making vegetable charcoal to be sold," recalled Valentín. To the teenage roulette dealer, the task facing them seemed daunting. He looked up at his boss. "It will be years before we open, right?" Martín wiped his hands and put an arm around his protégé. "*Ay*, chiquitico," he said, shaking his head.

Valentín was right. Except that it wasn't the hurricane that would shut them down. It was Cuba's newly elected president, inaugurated a week before the hurricane amid great fanfare along the full length of the Paseo del Prado.

Ramón Grau San Martín had entered the quagmire of Cuban presidential politics a decade before his 1944 election. In 1933, following Gerardo Machado's resignation, he had served as interim president twice—first as part of a five-man team that served for six days and was called La Pentarquia, and then for a five-month stint that ended in January 1934. Grau was itching to be president. In 1940, he ran for the office, and was soundly defeated by Fulgencio Batista in what was the most expensive political campaign in the history of the republic. In 1944, Batista had decided not to run again; but no one in Cuba—not the press, nor the United States, which kept close watch on the politics of its closest trading partner in Latin America—expected Grau to win over Batista's hand-picked successor, Carlos Saladrigas. First of all, no opposition candidate since 1913 had won a Cuban election. Second, there were Grau's repeated failures at attaining the presidency. Third, there was Batista himself.

A charismatic career army officer from the eastern province of Oriente, Ruben Fulgencio Batista Zaldívar was the most unusual and powerful politician that Cuba had ever known. He was of mixed race, born in 1901 to a sugar worker near the town of Banes in northeast Cuba, where the American corporation United Fruit Company owned practically all of the centrales. Unlike all of Cuba's previous presidents since the beginning of the republic, Batista had no family connections and no wealth. He spent his youth working as a water boy, tailor's apprentice, brakeman on a train line, and the timekeeper for a work gang; he also did odd jobs for the army. Between jobs, he would always go back to work he had performed since his schoolboy days—cutting sugarcane, the backbreaking labor that was the backbone of his country's economy. At twenty, Batista joined the army, where he learned typing and stenography. These skills, modest as they seemed, led to his meteoric political ascent. After the resignation of Machado, when Cuba's government fell into violence and crisis, Batista became the secretary to the army sergeants who led the battle at the Hotel Nacional. By the time it was over, he was the indisputable leader of the group, the only person in the entire country who had any real power, according to U.S. Ambassador Welles. He promoted himself to the rank of colonel and from then on retained control of the army.

Yet neither the title of president, which Batista won in the 1940 elections, nor colonel, could begin to describe the extent of his influence. Throughout most the 1930s, the dashing Batista (so broad was his smile and so handsome his features that he was known, since youth, as *mulato lindo,* or "handsome mulatto") ran Cuban politics through a series of puppet presidents. It was no easy task, but Batista had an extraordinary gift for leadership and manipulation. "His mind works like lightning. He can practically convince one that a thing is true and that he is logical, which is extraordinary in a country whose idea of logic leaves one gasping," wrote Ruby Hart Phillips of Batista. "Boss Batista commands the biggest army in Cuba's history (12,000 regulars, 20,000 reserves and a national police force of 4,000)," reported *Time* magazine on April 26, 1937. That issue of *Time,* which had the Cuban strongman on the cover with the caption, "Boss Batista: paternalism begins at home," described Batista's methods of controlling the presidency, which involved spending vast sums on the army. With the army and trade unions solidly behind him, the office of president was de facto his, whether he was elected to it or not. When he ran in 1940, he had even received support from the Communist Party, which he then legalized at a time when other foreign or nationalist parties had been banned. In 1944, given that Batista flexed his political muscle on behalf of Saladrigas, no one had hopes for Ramón Grau San Martín's chances.

But that year an undercurrent of hope coursed through the Cuban electorate. Whether fueled by a stronger economy or Batista's gesture of stepping down, the people took to the polls in numbers not seen since the republic was born at the beginning of the century. In the cities and towns and at the train depots that served the great rural centrales, Cubans waited eagerly for the gaunt, dour-faced Grau—a respected professor of physiology at the University of Havana—to pass through in his rumpled white suit and panama hat. Grau's speeches were often eloquent diatribes against the American domination of Cuba's economy. "Cuba es para los cubanos!" he railed, promising raises for the workers and an end to corruption, graft, and payoffs to government officials. The people rallied behind him. British historian Hugh Thomas, whose book *Cuba: The Pursuit of Freedom* is perhaps the most complete political history of the country, noted that people in the countryside taught their parrots to say, "Viva Grau San Martín!" Grau was voted into office without incident. Yet more astonishing, and heartening to the Cuban electorate, was that Batista did not tamper with the voting. On election day, when it became clear that Batista was also going to allow the opposition to take power, spontaneous eruptions of joy broke out all over the country. It was like it was carnival time, reported *Time* on June 12, 1944: "By noon of counting day . . . the miracle dawned on the people of Havana. By afternoon they were milling in the parks and plazas, blowing horns, waving flags, beating bongo drums, dancing the conga down the magnificent Prado. Loudly they cheered for Grau San Martín. Even more loudly they cheered Fulgencio Batista, the strong man who had muscled democracy into Cuba."

Grau's inauguration proceedings began on October 10, 1944 and lasted three days. The worst hurricane in Cuba's history hit on the seventeenth. Even before the clouds began to race across the

sky ahead of the oncoming storm, those running the casinos—
Sans Souci, Montmartre, the Sevilla Biltmore, and Tropicana—
knew that the portent was ominous. "We already knew that if
Grau took office, we didn't stand a chance," said Valentín.
Grau's pledge to end corruption never singled out the gamblers, but as Valentín remarked, "Corruption is a term that we all understood. To
operate without incident you had to pay off the police, the inspectors . . . It's part of the cost of doing business. And we had sources
among Grau's people—Martín had courted the men who were his
top advisors. They had told him: 'If Grau gets elected, the casinos
will be shut down.'"

The post-hurricane cleanup at Tropicana was unfinished when
Grau's new government ordered the casinos closed. The only ones
permitted to remain open were those establishments with constitutional protection, meaning the Jockey Club at Oriental Park
and the Casino Nacional. At Tropicana, the cards and chips were
packed away in boxes, and the gaming felts dusted with a fine
brown powder, made from the vein of tobacco leaves, to repel termites and wood-boring beetles. The cabaret remained open, but
money was tight (Martín was barely making enough to cover the
rent on Villa Mina), and Victor de Correa had to scale the shows
back. "It was like turning back the clock," recalled Valentín, who
lovingly dusted each felt and inspected the equipment in storage
every week.

Reluctantly, Martín laid off all of his employees except Valentín, who remained at the reduced salary of twelve pesos a week.
Now Martín had only the men who, over the years, had been his
profit-sharing partners: his brother Pedro; his old friend from
Ciego de Avila, Oscar Echemendia; and a new associate named Alberto Ardura, who had originally been hired by Mascaró. Unlike
the others, Ardura was a debonair habanero, born to relative financial comfort. The world of gamblers would not have been his normal milieu except for the fact that his mother, a respected psychic

and tarot card reader, was also a lifelong and avid roulette player. Ardura often accompanied his mother to the gambling parlors. He met Martín in one, quite possibly Martín's old locale at Concordia and Amistad. When they encountered each other again at Tropicana, the two men quickly formed an alliance, though in personality they were as different as could be. Where Martín was gregarious and warm, Ardura was reticent and businesslike. Martín endeared himself to everyone with large gestures of friendship and was fond of using pet names such as *chiquitico, chinita, cariñito, negrita*, while Ardura remained aloof, leading some to wonder whether he had any friends at all. There was no question, however, that Martín was Ardura's friend. "He probably saw in Ardura qualities he did not have," said Ofelia. Ardura was tall, thin, urbane-looking, and strikingly handsome. He was a man of few words—a straight shooter, strict about his behavior and, added Rosa Sanchez, "the fact that he looked good, had contacts in the world of gambling, was trustworthy, but as shrewd about making a deal as Martín, most likely made them complement each other perfectly."

With his cadre of three loyal partners—Ardura, Echemendia, and Pedro—Martín weathered the Grau years, managing to hold on to the lease at Tropicana by running small-scale monte and baccarat games from the upstairs bedrooms in the mansion or at the Union Club. The former survived with the protection of the Marianao police, and the latter had the protection of its many politician members. Occasionally, Tropicana's roulette room would be opened for a single player or a private group. During the winter baseball season, Echemendia and Ardura would spend weekends at Tropical Stadium on Columbia Avenue in Marianao, taking bets on Cuban League games. And on Saturdays all five of the men (the four partners and Valentín Jodra) would be busy with the week's bolita game. "It was a small run, only six or seven thousand pesos every week, but it was all we could do during those Grau years," said Valentín. "Those were dark times. I never thought we'd get through it. But Martín never doubted. He said to me, 'chiquitico, nothing lasts forever. It's all a matter of patience and waiting things out.' "

MARTÍN'S PREDICTION proved correct. By the time Grau's term reached its midpoint, the rest of the Cuban population had joined the gamblers in their disillusionment. Despite his self-righteous patriotism, despite his diatribes against U.S. control of the island's economy, Grau's administration rapidly dissolved into a bacchanalia of theft. Contracts for public works projects were sold, false jobs were created for cronies. Lucrative lottery collectorships were awarded to his backers as well as to enemies he wished to silence. Anyone who held any official position, including mayors, submayors, school, housing and factory inspectors, judges, and even schoolteachers, was on the take. The price of sugar was high (the United States purchased the entire harvests of 1945, 1946, and 1947, to feed the war-devastated European nations) but so rampant was the pilfering that what should have been a prosperous economy teetered on ruin. There were severe food shortages. The army was ordered to seize cattle to supply Havana with beef. By 1946, the unions and revolutionary organizations that had backed Grau publicly withdrew their support. Revolutionary action groups that had fought for change ever since Machado's time dissolved into bands of gangsterish political splinter groups, with links to government, the trade unions, and the student body council of the University of Havana. By 1946, gangland-style political killings were common enough in Havana that a term, *gangsterismo,* "gangsterism," was coined, and stories were written about the violence in both *Time* and *Newsweek*.

Also in 1946, despite Grau's sanctimonious stance towards the Cuban gamblers, Havana's Hotel Nacional became the site of the first meeting of the American underworld since 1932. Charles

"Lucky" Luciano, who had been deported to Italy from the United States after serving ten years of a thirty-year sentence for aiding and abetting prostitution, arrived in October under enormous secrecy, to keep the American government from learning of his proximity to American shores. He was received by his old friend and boyhood colleague from the Lower East Side, Meyer Lansky, who arranged for a six-month extension of Luciano's visa with Grau's minister of the interior, and rented him a mansion in Miramar, the most elegant neighborhood in the city. In December, Lansky and Luciano were joined by Vito Genovese, Joe Adonis, Frank Costello, Albert Anastasia, Joe Bonanno, Tommy Lucchese, Joe Profaci, Giuseppe Magliocco, Willie Moretti, Augie Pisano, Mike Miranda, Tony Accardo, the brothers Fischetti, Phil Castell, and Santo Trafficante—essentially a who's who of the American Mafia—for a weeklong series of meetings that, according to Luciano's as-told-to biography, began with the men putting up the money so Luciano could purchase a $150,000 interest in the Hotel Nacional casino. At the time, the Nacional's casino was controlled by Lansky together with Fulgencio Batista, though the latter was in self-imposed exile in Daytona Beach, Florida. There was a rollicking Christmas Eve party, ostensibly in honor of Frank Sinatra, who joined the delegates at the Hotel Nacional. This took place right under the nose of Grau's government, but the newspapers reported nothing. "In them days, the word was around that what was goin' on at the Hotel Nacional was off limits," said Luciano to his biographers. "It was easy to lose a license to publish a paper if you ran something you wasn't supposed to."

Then there was the theft of the Capitolio Diamond. Since the opening of the majestic government building in 1929, the yellow diamond had been more than simply a symbolic decorative element; it was the fixed point from which all distances in Cuba were measured. On March 25, 1946, someone chiseled it and pried it out of the floor of the great hall. A week later it mysteriously appeared on Grau's desk in his office. The theft of the diamond became a bitter emblem of what had happened to the country under Grau. And though he had achieved some social reforms (in the area of pensions, in removing government from the control of the army), by 1948 Grau had so trampled the electorate's hopes that his own party didn't support him for reelection. "[Grau] did a great disservice to the cause of democratic reform, not only in Cuba but in the whole Western hemisphere," wrote Hugh Thomas. "His period of power is appropriately commemorated by the career of his old friend José Manuel Alemán, in 1944 a minor official at the Ministry of Education, who arrived in Miami in 1948 after two years as minister with twenty million dollars in notes in his suitcase, not to speak of thousands of *caballerias* of land, sugarmills, . . . and a chain of houses left behind."

"And these were the same people who were blaming the gamblers for corruption," Rosa Sanchez told me, laughing. "The gamblers were probably the only straight shooters in the country. They lived off their reputations. At least with them you knew what you were betting on."

CHAPTER 7

Covering Your Bets

Ofelia's life is charmed," said Rosa Sanchez. It was a Saturday afternoon and we were at Porto's Bakery in Glendale, waiting for a table to have lunch. This was my first time at what is widely considered the best Cuban bakery in Southern California. In Miami there are a dozen places as good as Porto's, but in Southern California people have been known to drive fifty miles for Porto's flan or *pasteles de guayaba*. On weekend afternoons the line to pick up wedding and birthday cakes snakes out the doors and around the corner into the parking lot. Most of Porto's cakes are not traditionally Cuban (they are frosted with buttercream instead of meringue) but they are nonetheless light, spongy, and filled either with creamy custard or a guava jelly that strikes the perfect balance between sweet and tart. They also make sublime Cuban sandwiches, which Rosa asked Ofelia to get for us while we staked out a table. Ofelia clearly knew this was a ruse so that Rosa could talk to me in confidence; but she obliged cheerfully and made her way through the crowds up to the counter.

"Look at her," continued Rosa, edging against a table where three women were about to get up. "She stands patiently in line and then the line just parts for her. Who said that life is a banquet and you take what you want? Well, except for that one dark period in her life after Martín got sick, Ofelia has always managed to turn life into a grand love affair. God gave her this gift. But I worry about her, because you can't always rely on that to work. Just the other day, I finally made a list of where all of our money is, in case something happens to me. I pay all the bills. I take care of everything related to our finances. It's the same as when she was with Martín. He did everything and she just trusted him. Yet, sometimes . . ." Rosa paused and looked towards the counter to make sure Ofelia was not coming back. "It's not that he took advantage of her. He adored her. But Martín's way was to use everyone. Let me give you an example. Back in fifty-nine, they went to Mexico to take some money out of Cuba. That was right after the revolution, and the military was patrolling the airports. The government was trying to keep people from taking valuables out of the country. As they're leaving the house, Martín hands Ofelia an envelope and casually says, 'china, put this in your makeup case.' The envelope contained fifty thousand dollars! Can you imagine that? It was true that they were more likely to search the men than women at the airport. But what if someone had stopped her? You think they would have believed she didn't know what was in the envelope?"

Ofelia was back with the first of our plates—a sandwich for me, another for them to share. "Don't forget the flan," Rosa called out as Ofelia returned for our coffees. The dessert was for my regenerate sweet tooth, a weakness that Ofelia and Rosa had begun to seriously indulge. Now every time I arrived at their house, in addition to the cocktails and snacks at the bar, I was treated to flaky guava pastries, creamy mango tarts, or whatever else happened to catch their eye at Porto's.

Rosa waited until Ofelia was out of earshot, then continued. "Martín began moving money out of the country long before the revolution. God knows how many bank accounts he had. The two of them went to Mexico in 1957 and he placed four hundred thousand dollars into two accounts in the Banco Mexicano. The accounts were in both of their names, but Ofelia can't remember which names he used." Perching her handbag on the back of a chair piled high with pink Porto's boxes, Rosa pulled out a piece of paper. "We've tried searching with no luck. They could be under any of the following: Martín Fox and/or Ofelia Suarez, Martín G. Fox, Martín Gabriel Fox, Martín Gabriel Fox Zamora, Ofelia Suarez de Fox, Ofelia Suarez González, Ofelia Fox."

The conversation about foreign bank accounts had come up several days earlier, when we were discussing Martín's business acumen and his gambler's ability to see a few moves ahead of others. In 1959, before most Cubans had had the slightest inkling that their country's businesses would be nationalized and all foreign currency would be confiscated, Martín began moving his money out of the country. Once it became more difficult for Cubans to get cash or valuables past revolutionary soldiers posted at the airport, Martín used American gamblers as his couriers, including several known members of the Mafia. Martín's modus operandi was to do these things in secret. Not even Ofelia knew where the money was kept or how much they had, though the majority of their accounts were in both their names. That was why in 1963, when Martín suffered a stroke that left him unable to communicate, Ofelia found herself suddenly destitute in Miami, with only three thousand dollars to her name. It was the amount Martín was carrying in his pocket.

"We scoured the earth looking for those accounts," said Rosa, shaking her head as we finally sat down. "Those were terrible days. Never before in her life had Ofelia been by herself. She had no way to take care of Martín. There was a household to maintain, doctor and hospital bills, and she knew for the rest of his life he would need constant nursing care, special food, medicines—"

Ofelia was approaching with my flan. "You know, I just remembered a story," she said brightly. "Martín once showed up at our house in Miramar with a scruffy little cat that had an eye infection. We took him to the vet several times, but he died after losing the eye. When we were about to bury him in the backyard, Martín said to me, 'Let's bury him standing straight up.' I asked, 'Why?' And he answered, 'Because he's a warrior. He fought for a home and he fought for his life. Y asi es como yo quiero que me entierren a mi'—'I want to be buried this same way.' And, you know, he made arrangements in Havana's Colon Cemetery to be buried upright. He had very strong beliefs. He wouldn't back his car up unless it was absolutely necessary."

"I think everyone in your house was superstitious," added Rosa as she quickly put away the pieces of paper. I unwrapped my sandwich and took a bite. "Good, eh?" said Ofelia, watching my expression. "Good" was quite the understatement. The Cuban sandwich consists of a layer of ham, roast pork, and Swiss cheese that is grilled on a press known as a *plancha* until the cheese melts and the bread flattens. The term is born of exile; in Cuba it is simply called *un sandwich*. No matter what it is called, however, the key to its taste lies in limiting the condiments to butter, mustard, and dill pickle slices (never lettuce and tomato), and in the quality of the bread, which comes in long loaves that are airy on the inside and mildly crusty on the outside, like French baguettes pumped full of beaten egg whites.

"There's nothing like the bread from Porto's," remarked Ofelia, taking a bite.

"Tell her more about Martín's superstitions," urged Rosa.

"*Ay dios*, he had so many! Let's see. He believed that invoking his dead mother's name would keep him out of trouble. And he never gave away any of his clothes. He thought his luck would go with the clothes. But if he had a bad night, if the casino lost a lot of money, you wouldn't catch him dead wearing those clothes again."

"He must have had a closetful of suits," I pointed out.

"No, no. The bad luck clothes were gone right away. Those had only *mala suerte.*"

Martín's luck changed with the next election. The presidency went to Carlos Prío Socarrás, a political ally of Ramón Grau San Martín, in an election as routine and uneventful as had ever taken place in Cuba. It was precisely the lack of incident that inspired optimism. Though Prío was not much more of a statesman than his predecessor (even before his election it had become common knowledge that the candidate was extraordinarily attracted to the financial possibilities afforded by political office), at least both men (and Batista before them) had been fairly elected. There were many who opposed the president, and they railed against him with all the vehemence and venom that the Cuban temperament was able to muster. In other sectors of the country, however, people rejoiced, though less enthusiastically than they had following the election of Grau. Democracy was dull and unexciting, but in and of itself that was reason for celebration.

Martín and his fellow gamblers—his partners and his competitors at other cabaret-casinos—were nonetheless wary of anyone associated with Grau, and they pulled out all the stops to influence Prío during the campaign. There were the usual payoffs, of course, and promises of future financial reward if the casinos were allowed to open. Martín now counted some of Prío's top advisors as well as other powerful politicians among his friends. Through men like Carlos Saladrigas, who had been Batista's candidate in the 1944 elections; Santiago Rey, a senator, and one of Martín's best *monte de baraja* clients; and Roberto Fernandez Miranda, a colonel and also Batista's brother-in-law, Martín was able to exert friendly pressure on the president to lift the ban on casino gambling. The Tropicana partners were also fortunate to have a supernatural method of influence. In Cuba, where conferring with a tarot card reader, *santero,* or *espiritista* is more acceptable than it might be elsewhere, Alberto Ardura's tarot-card-reading mother had become a phenomenon among the upper classes. Among those who consulted her frequently were many members of Prío's family. "When [a Prío] came for a reading," Valentín Jodra recalled, "suddenly the cards would have some positive message about gambling."

Given the extent of the spiritual and economic pressure bearing down on the candidate, it was no wonder that one of Prío's first acts as president was to lift Grau's four-year ban on gambling. The decree, which was handed down in 1949, could not have come at a better time. Postwar America was starting to vacation once again, and with its proximity to the United States, Cuba was positioned to reap the rewards like no other country. But unlike in the 1920s and '30s, when the majority of Americans visiting Cuba were businessmen, adventurers, rum runners, or high society, such as the racing set described in Basil Woon's book, ordinary middle-class Americans were now finding their way to Cuba. The men who had been stationed for training during the war in places like Miami or Fort Lauderdale felt inclined to migrate south every winter. Many were content to bask in the balmy winters of South Florida. The more adventurous went to Cuba, where the combination of legal, Las Vegas-style gambling and the tropical climate seemed to promise a national financial windfall.

By 1950, when tourism began in earnest, no one was in a better position to benefit than Martín Fox. To circumvent the suspicion of corruption, namely, that he had been unduly influenced by the gamblers, Prío had worked out a clever deal with the food and entertainment worker's union, one of Havana's most powerful. Officially, it was the union that lobbied for the opening of the casinos, hoping to bring more jobs to its members. The president, in turn, lifted the ban, but with the stipulation that only casinos that served food and offered entertainment, and therefore hired members of the union, would be licensed. When the law went into effect, new licenses were granted to but three establishments: Sans Souci, Montmartre, and Tropicana. Together with the venerable Jockey Club at Oriental Park and the Casino Nacional, which had constitutional permission to operate during the four months of the tourist season, there were merely five legal casinos in all of Cuba. But of those five, Tropicana alone was owned and operated by its Cuban owner. Sans Souci was nominally run by an American named Norman Rothman; however all signs indicate that it was under the general control of Santo Trafficante Jr., whose family ran the numbers game in Tampa. Montmartre was soon under the control of Trafficante's chief Havana rivals, Jake and Meyer Lansky. Tropicana, on the other hand, was wholly owned by Cubans: the property belonged to Guillermina Perez Chaumont; the cabaret concession was owned and operated by Victor de Correa; and the casino belonged to Martín Fox and his partners.

For Martín, it was as if everything that had happened after he left Ciego de Avila had been a prelude to this moment: success at la bolita, which gave him the capital to buy out Mascaró; and his penchant for high-stakes card games, which had propelled him into social circles he had never dreamed existed during his years at Central Jagüeyal. As a member of the Union Club, the guajiro from Ciego de Avila now regularly rubbed elbows with the country's elite. Industrialists like Domingo Mendez, owner of Regalias el Cuño, Cuba's largest cigarette factory, were among his new friends. Despite their difficulty, the Grau years had proven productive. The entire Marianao police department had been well paid to offer protection during those straitlaced times, and they were practically on Tropicana's payroll. This would continue to facilitate the running of the bolita, which remained illegal. It also boded well for any future problems that might arise. No matter who came to power, what leverage gangsters or Mafiosos might have, it was always good to have the police on your side.

There were just a few glitches in this seemingly perfect equation. The first was Martín's wife, Rosita, who continued to demand that he leave gambling and lead a more respectable life. "My father will bankroll any business you want," she continually begged her husband. Her pleas fell upon deaf ears. Martín did not need his father-in-law's money. By 1950 his bolita bank had become one of the five biggest in the city. Within two years of Grau's departure, La Buena's weekly gross had soared to a staggering 250,000 pesos, with 9 to 10 percent of that being profits. Martín's portion of the profit-sharing deal with his brother, Ardura, and Echemendia, was 44 percent, which came to roughly one hundred twenty thousand pesos a year, a good sum even by today's standards. According to Valentín, the bolita profits were calculated together with the casino profits at the end of the year. The payoff was made in early January. And that was only the beginning. Fueled by Victor de Correa's shows and Martín's reputation in the gambling world, Tropicana's casino was packed almost as soon as it opened its doors. Martín expanded the gaming, adding two tables of blackjack and one each of craps and roulette, to make a total of three blackjack tables, two of craps, one each of monte and baccarat, and four roulette wheels (a fifth was kept in a private salon for bigwigs like Senator Santiago Rey, who preferred to play alone). "It was astonishing," remembered Valentín. "The people rushed back to the casinos as if they had been starving for years and were finally allowed to come to the table to eat." A mere ten years after coming to the capital, Martín was the kingpin of what promised to become Havana's greatest gambling era.

Apart from his growing marital difficulties, Martín's other problems centered on the cabaret portion of Tropicana. One involved the layout. After the hurricane, the place had been restored to its original 1939 configuration. When Prío lifted the gambling ban, a few additional tables were added. Nonetheless, because Villa Mina offered no indoor performance space, Tropicana continued to be at the mercy of the elements. The shows were frequently

rained out, especially during the busy winter season. This translated into lost clientele among the free-spending tourists. Martín's
other, more pressing problem was Victor de Correa, the man in
charge of delivering the entertainment at Tropicana. Correa had
been a thorn in Martín's side since the moment he had taken over
the lease for the Villa Mina property from Mascaró. As Martín understood it, the deal between them was clear-cut: Martín would
pay the eight hundred pesos for the monthly lease on Villa Mina,
but each man was expected to cover expenses for his own portion
of the business and keep his own profits—Martín's from the casino,
and Correa's from the food and drink. This seemed straight-
forward enough. But Correa didn't see it this way. "He was always
demanding money, asking Martín to cover his costs for orchestras,
talent, things that Mascaró had sometimes paid for," remembered
Valentín.

In Martín's view, Correa was a bad businessman who could not
make ends meet and who refused to live up to his end of their bar-
gain. From Correa's point of view, it was Martín who was failing
to honor their arrangement. Mascaró had brought him aboard in
1939 to run the entertainment portion of his new cabaret, with the
understanding that there would be some financial fluidity between
the nightclub and casino. The problem was that this understanding, like most such agreements in the gambling world, was verbal.
There was nothing on paper to prove that Correa was entitled to
this or that amount of help, or any of the casino's profits. Yet it was
obvious—to Correa—that it was his cabaret, not the casino,
which had earned Tropicana its international reputation. Martín
was a newcomer. By the time he had joined Mascaró at Tropicana,
Correa had been a noted impresario for more than ten years. At
Tropicana, which he had named, his shows had gleaned continuously rave reviews. His 1941 spectacle *Conga Pantera*, a musical
reenactment of a panther being chased through the African jungle,
was a turning point in the Cuban music-hall world for its use of

narrative and classical ballet dancers in a cabaret show. The show, which was shaped by Edén Concert's choreographer Sergio Orta, included ballerina Tania Leskovia of the Ballet Russe de Monte Carlo in the title role of the panther. Cuban conga player Chano Pozo, who would later become one of the fathers of Latin jazz (he penned the jazz hit "Manteca" with bebop trumpet player Dizzy Gillespie) played the role of the hunter. Rita Montaner and her accompanist Bola de Nieve, as well as other members of the Ballet Russe, were also in the cast. The staging used the trees and foliage of the cabaret as part of the set, as well as a large and diverse group of modern and classical dancers, flamboyant costuming and choreography, and small musical combos in conjunction with larger orchestras, which all combined to attract big-name stars as headliners. And everyone knew that stars were the real draw for the tourist crowds that gambled in Martín's casino. By 1950 Tropicana regularly featured Montaner and Bola de Nieve, the popular Spanish singing orchestra Los Chavales de España, and Olga Guillot.

On the other hand, everyone in the cabaret business knew that the real money was made in the casinos. No matter how extravagant the shows, or how good the reviews, or how famous the stars, the entertainment was the lure for bringing in the gamblers. Mascaró had been up front about this but tried to smooth things over by being generous with Correa, despite constant financial difficulties. Mascaró was often late with the rent, or in paying Correa for some of the star salaries, but Correa attributed this to the hardships of the war years rather than to any fundamental difference in philosophy. Martín Fox was another matter. He was obviously a better businessman than Mascaró since he was making money hand over fist, but Martín was tight with money. He balked at covering costs and never once shared any of the casino's profits with Correa. "The truth was that Martín simply did not like Correa," said Valentín. "They were like oil and water, each always trying to get the better of the other."

Matters between Martín and Correa came to a head in the fall of 1950, when Correa came up with the idea of hiring Xavier Cugat and his orchestra for a two-week run at Tropicana. At the time, Cugat's records were a staple of most Cuban—and many American—households. He had recorded dozens of well-known Latin songs, including "El manisero" and "Perfidia," which he recorded with his lead singer, Miguelito Valdés. Cugat had also parlayed his musical fame at the Waldorf-Astoria into a Hollywood career. When Correa hired him at Tropicana, Cugat had already appeared in *You Were Never Lovelier* (1942) with Fred Astaire and Cugat's former lead singer, Rita Hayworth. He had also performed in six other films, including *Bathing Beauty* (1945) and *On an Island with You* with Esther Williams (1948), as well as *Weekend at the Waldorf* (1945) with Lana Turner and Ginger Rogers. Assisted by his beautiful wife, singer Abbe Lane, Cugat, with his elaborate costuming and jovial banter, provided just the type of showmanship that guaranteed a cabaret filled to capacity. Of course, an act of this caliber did not come cheap. Cugat was making four thousand dollars a week at the Waldorf. For Correa, the bandleader's reputation alone was worth the money. Martín, who was asked to foot the lion's share of the bill, agreed.

The night of Cugat's debut at Tropicana, the band's dozen or so musicians came early to set up their instruments, and then went back to the dressing rooms to eat, drink, and smoke before changing into their signature red and gold brocade costumes. Like the detail-oriented professional he was, Cugat was on hand early as well. He went over the arrangement of the instruments onstage and the lighting cues and did the sound checks on the microphones, all the while carrying his beloved pet Chihuahua, which traveled with him always. Just after Cugat went backstage to dress, it began to rain. The rain continued past the time of the eleven thirty curtain and the show had to be cancelled. The next day it began to rain earlier in the afternoon. By evening it had let up and the orchestra came out, but the house was nearly empty because rain was predicted for that night, also. Then, indeed, it began to rain again. It rained on and off almost every day for the next two weeks. The Cugat orchestra never once performed a full set during their entire contract at Tropicana. The sodden outdoor cabaret remained nearly empty every night, which annoyed the star bandleader nearly as much as it did Martín, who had to pay for his contract.

"I thought you said this place fills up. I've never seen it even half full," Cugat remarked snidely one night. The comment was directed towards Victor de Correa, but Martín, who was furious at the financial beating he was taking, had had enough. "You were supposed to bring in the public," he retorted. "But all you brought was rain and that stupid dog!"

After the problem with Cugat, Martín and Victor de Correa hardly spoke to each other. For Martín it was a wake-up call. Not only did it underscore his frustration with Correa (who should have known enough to include a cancellation clause in the contract), it proved again that without a proper indoor cabaret Tropicana would always be at the mercy of the weather gods. Within days of the Cugat washout, Martín decided to take action.

CHAPTER 8

Arcos de Cristal

*Soon a new magic room! Glass covered. A huge glass
shell will be the addition to Tropicana. Will insure
comfort in all kinds of weather. Our open air terrace
will continue as always.*

from an English-language Tropicana brochure, 1952

For months, Guillermina Perez Chaumont had been hinting
about selling the property that bore her name. She had been
renting it out for ten years, Valentín remembered, and she was
starting to wonder whether she, or her son, or anyone in her family would ever live there again. By 1950, Mina was sixty years old
and twice a widow. Her son, Marcial Truffin, spent his days culti-
vating orchids, giving them away to the cadre of socialite friends
that paraded endlessly through the mansion that he and his mother
shared with his sister and brother-in-law. Mina's daughter's house
was nowhere near as grand as Villa Mina, but it had the advantage
of being located directly across Truffin Avenue from the estate that
Regino Truffin had bought when he and Mina were married. When
it was not too hot, Mina would cross the street named for her former husband and take her mastiff on long afternoon walks through
the gardens. Valentín often talked with the widow on her walks,
and he could not imagine a happier face than hers as she wandered
among the vegetation of the estate. On her strolls Mina might

come across, for example, a forgotten stand of bamboo that she'd brought back from her travels with Regino, or some dwarf palm from China, or a rare orchid from the Amazon hidden among the towering acacias and the vine-choked royal palms. The gardens seemed to give her solace. There were more than seven species of mango on the property. Together with the array of orange, guava, creamy white anon, perfumed mamey, prickly guanabana, and the tart, glistening, lychee-like mamoncillos, they provided a year-round bounty of tropical fruit. Mina's walks through the orchards probably brought her back to the days when she was referred to by American as well as Cuban writers as "the social dictator" of Havana society. Villa Mina's garden paths were filled with wonderful memories of elegant parties, weekends at the races, and occasions when her home was constantly visited by the cream of Cuban and American upper classes. Selling it would surely be wrenching.

Still, it was clearly time to do so. Everything had changed. The house that had once been used for concerts and cotillions now resonated with loud laughter, the croupier's calls, and the clack of dice. The din of horns and raucous drumming that had led the adjacent Jesuit school to protest to the mayor of Marianao, almost causing the cabaret to close in 1942, bore no relation to the polished grace of the *danzónes* Mina had once known. And the gamblers and late-night partygoers who now frequented her estate were as removed from her world of Havana high society as the poor guajiros who lived in thatched roofed *bohíos* in the countryside.

Curiously, the one tenant of her estate with whom Mina felt the greatest affinity was the guajiro who held the lease to her property. Years later, when she attended her first and only performance at Tropicana, Mina told Ofelia that she had always truly admired Martín Fox. Much of it had to do with his respect for her gardens. On her walks, Mina noted that the place was being cared for with loving devotion. All the plants looked green and healthy, pruned to perfection, and nothing had been cut down or removed. Though she never ventured over at night, Mina had been told that the trees were lit in a way that magnified their splendor. She found it odd that a gambler would care this much about a garden, but this dapper yet slightly rough-at-the edges man was no ordinary individual. Mina had sensed this years earlier, during the war, when a near-broke Rafael Mascaró had come to inform her that he was turning the lease for the property over to someone who was having better luck in business, even during those tourist-lean times. Mina had spent her life surrounded by powerful men. These were generally men who had been born to wealth and privilege. Martín shared their intelligence, if not their education. What's more, he had a way of making you feel as if you were the most important person in the world—even when it was obvious he wanted something from you.

One of Martín Fox's other qualities was his quickness to act once he had made up his mind. And so it was that one day, shortly after the Xavier Cugat episode, that Mina found herself sitting across from Martín at her daughter's house, listening to him ask her to name a price for the property. This fateful meeting took place without witnesses, and over the years the tales about it have grown in the telling. One version has Martín driving his Cadillac rather than walking the two hundred yards across Truffin Avenue to avoid getting his white trousers and guayabera dusty. Another depicts the regal, white-haired Mina calmly smoking a pipe and refusing to sell unless Martín assured her that he would never cut down a single tree. Who eventually set the price of 300,000 pesos (equivalent to roughly 2.3 million dollars in 2005 currency) is still a matter of debate. Martín always claimed this was the widow's asking price, and that he accepted immediately and paid her off in three months with his own money. Other accounts have him bargaining her down and asking for a week to find the financing. The only things generally agreed upon by everyone are that the price was 300,000 pesos, and that Mina wept as she signed the sale documents in a Havana notary public's office. Yet the stories surrounding the purchase of the *finca* illustrate certain things about the way Martín conducted business. First of all, he approached Mina without consulting any of his partners. "He wanted to be the only owner," said Valentín Jodra. It was not as if his partners could not have afforded to be part of the deal. By 1950, Martín had already made them rich men. At a time when the peso was equal to the dollar and the average urban Cuban's annual salary was 2,000 pesos, the four men split a monthly draw of 15,000 pesos. Twenty-four percent, or 3,600 pesos, went to Oscar Echemendia; and 16 percent, or 2,560 pesos each went to Alberto Ardura and Pedro Fox. The annual profit sharing, which gave them each the same cut of the casino and bolita profits, yielded Echemendia roughly an additional 120,000 pesos a year (over $900,000 today), and 100,000 pesos apiece ($760,000 today) to Pedro and Ardura. "Martín was generous to a fault, but he wanted things on his own terms," said Valentín. Clearly they had the money to buy the property with Martín. Martín had his own agenda. And for this reason he did not inform anyone of his offer to Mina until he had an oral agreement, and papers had been drawn up.

Then there was the financing itself. Three hundred thousand pesos was a huge amount of money in 1950. However, given that the bolita alone was yielding about 25,000 pesos a week in profits, it seems plausible that Martín might have paid Mina off in three months using his own funds. Valentín Jodra remembered a different version of events. "The old man, his father-in-law [Leonardo García] loaned Martín 100,000 pesos—in a deal sealed with a handshake. The rest came out of Martín's own pocket." Under the terms of this agreement, Martín agreed to pay back his father-in-law at the end of two years—the time frame that he said it would take to pay Mina. Ofelia and others imagine a combination deal, with Martín paying the widow in three months, and using Leonardo's loan for the construction of the cabaret. There are no records to corroborate either version of events.

The stories illustrate how deeply people are fascinated with the legends of the Cuban cabaret world. As I pore over the photographs of Martín and the memories of those who knew him, the Guajiro comes alive as someone complex, shrewd, brash, secretive, and audacious—the quintessential Cuban of his day. Martín saw no limits, and he was willing to do whatever was necessary, to truck with whomever he needed to, in order to make Tropicana the number one tourist attraction in the country and to keep it in his hands alone. Undoubtedly, he was also protective of his lucrative bolita bank; but as with most illegal enterprises, little is known about its operation (and Valentín craftily skirted my direct questions). "Martín could be as subtle as a diplomat, but he always had his own agenda," said Rosa Sanchez. Martín's "agenda" would lead him, later, to court the heavy hitters of Havana's underworld, like Sans Souci's elusive Trafficante, a man so aware of his mobster status that he would refer to himself only as el Solitario, "the Solitary One," when he called Martín on the telephone. Trafficante would have certainly seen Martín as a competitor had they not been personal friends. To a lesser extent, Martín also cautiously courted the self-styled "Chairman of the Board," Meyer Lansky. "Martín hardly knew Lansky," Ofelia insisted repeatedly. Yet on several occasions she told me that she and Martín had paid Lansky a visit at Massachusetts General Hospital in 1957, when Martín was in Boston for his annual health checkup at Peter Bent Brigham Hospital.

"You don't usually visit someone in the hospital unless you know them well," I suggested carefully.

"You do if you're the owner of Tropicana and the man in the hospital is Meyer Lansky."

It was sometimes hard to see where Ofelia drew the line. At a certain point the separation between mobsters and people who regularly do business with them becomes irrelevant. It led me to wonder about the accusation that Martín was part of the underworld, and that Tropicana was owned by American gambling syndicates.

At times Martín himself encouraged this perception because, as Valentín put it, "the Americans were known for running clean casinos, so it made a good impression to have those connections." This may have been the reason why, beginning in 1956, Martín always made sure to have a credit manager who was connected to American mob interests on Tropicana's casino staff. Credit managers were able to quickly investigate the finances of American gamblers who needed extra cash and determine whether or not to accept their checks. Only men with the right connections had the means to run instant credit checks on high rollers and also enforce repayment of loans in the United States.

Records of Tropicana's ownership throughout the 1950s establish that Martín was sole owner of both Villa Mina and the Tropicana cabaret. "Martín was too obsessed with Tropicana to let anyone get a real foot in the door," insisted Ofelia. The fact that he did not even give his loyal partners a piece of the property supports her claim. Money did not seem to be the issue, for he routinely spread the wealth—among his partners, the police, and anyone else in government that needed to be paid off. But it was always on his own terms. Martín gave away apartments, houses, and cars. On one occasion, in 1956, he bought four red Corvettes and gave them away to the children of friends and associates, including the daughter of Alberto Ardura (who was fifteen years old at the time) and the son of a Havana zoning inspector who oversaw a residential area where Martín wanted to construct apartments. He regularly gave personal loans to Tropicana's workers who wanted to buy homes, a group that included Gladys Torres, his personal secretary; Ernesto Capote, the cabaret's lighting designer; Valentín; and a host of other kitchen staff and waiters. On the other hand, he'd always balk whenever his partners wanted him to put their profit-sharing percentages in writing. "He was a tough customer, but also the kind of person who treated the man who shined his shoes like his close friend," said Rosa. "He knew instinctively how much to give you and what would offend you. He had that sense, as probably all gamblers do, that sooner or later you might need a person, and god knows under what circumstances you would cross his path."

Martín may or may not have needed Leonardo García's 100,000 pesos to purchase Villa Mina in 1950. Whatever the case, by the time Martín paid him back, the man was no longer his father-in-law. On December 13, 1950, after he bought Villa Mina, Martín and Rosita Fox divorced. While we can't know whose idea it was, one thing is certain: Martín's decision to purchase Villa Mina was a sign that he was going even deeper into the gambling world.

WITH THE deed to the property in hand, Martín was now ready for his next move: building an indoor cabaret. This came at a moment when Havana was experiencing one of the biggest construction booms in its history. New houses, offices, and public buildings were springing up across the city as a result of the strong postwar economy. The archives of Havana's College of Architects record annual construction costs for registered projects totaling around forty-six million pesos in 1950, equivalent to approximately $260 million today. And what was being built was like nothing ever seen before in Cuba. Gone was the penchant for colonial-style stonework, or for the fanciful ornamentation of the city's eclectic and art deco structures. The new structures were bastions of unadulterated modernism. Spare, geometric, and light as air, Cuban architecture of the 1950s arose directly out of the international modernist style that was being touted by French architect Le Corbusier and embraced worldwide with almost religious fervor. But there was a difference: whereas many other Latin American architects stuck to the basic precepts of the style, the Cubans wasted no time in altering it. Taking advantage of engineering changes that offered support from the interior of a structure, allowing walls to be liberally pierced, perforated, encased in glass or louvers, or treated merely like curtains to keep out the elements, Havana's architects began opening their buildings to the tropical climate, curving them, making them as light filled, soft, and sensuous as the breeze off the Straits of Florida. Modernism, as the style was called, was playful, brash, utterly contemporary, and perfectly in tune with the mid-century Cuban zeitgeist. No architectural style that had reached the country in the previous four hundred years—not the baroque, neoclassical, neogothic, eclectic, art nouveau, or art deco—had ever been so deftly transformed into a Cuban mode of self-expression. It was as if the country were shedding layers of Spanish colonialism stone by stone and replacing the look of its freighted past with one built on transparency.

The construction boom spawned a passion for architecture as a profession, but for Martín only one man was worthy and capable of reinventing the face of Tropicana, and that was Max Borges Jr. In 1942, Martín had hired Borges to build his and Rosita's waterfront house in the Miramar district. Borges was barely twenty-two-years-old at the time. He had just returned from studying in the United States—first at Georgia Tech, and then at the Harvard Graduate School of Design—and he had gone into practice with his father, Max Borges Sr., a long-respected architect with engineering experience. In the ensuing nine years, the junior Borges had become something of an architectural boy wonder in Havana. He had secured several large-scale public commissions, including the Medical and Surgical Center in the Vedado neighborhood. His design had won him the 1948 gold medal from the Cuban College of Architects. In a city that was bursting with architectural innovation, Borges was considered a visionary—an architect who pushed the limits of modernism. His own residence, which he built in 1949 only ten blocks away from the home he built for Martín, is a purely modernist rectangular prism perched on tubular metal columns. (Though it has been altered somewhat, with new windows and a chain-link fence that disrupts the clean lines of the facade, the building, which faces a dilapidated oceanfront lot, still appears astonishingly contemporary today.)

"Martín hired me because he could rely on me," explained Borges modestly from his home in suburban Washington, D.C. "When I did his house it went exactly as he wanted it. Later, when he had a beach house built in Varadero, his wife [Rosita] insisted on another architect, and it went badly—not on schedule and over budget." Martín, the consummate gambler, wanted a known quantity for the indoor cabaret at Tropicana. He was not about to bet on anyone other than Borges for a project of this magnitude.

Victor de Correa thought differently. "Correa did not want me in the deal, he wanted Lin Arroyo," recalled Borges. Nicolas "Lin" Arroyo was another innovative young contemporary architect whose cutting-edge modernist houses were the rage in Havana's wealthiest neighborhoods. But whether he or Borges was the right man to design Tropicana, Correa was hardly one to have a say in the matter. Since the Cugat debacle, Martín hardly spoke to Correa unless he had to. Besides, Martín now owned Villa Mina, and he would foot the construction bill. Correa's opinions about the choice of architect were probably part of a last-ditch effort to exert control over Tropicana, for it was becoming increasingly evident that his days at the nightclub he founded and named were numbered. By buying Villa Mina, Martín had consolidated his power and made himself the sole arbiter of what—and who—would be tolerated on his property. Meanwhile, in the past few months, Ardura had started showing undue interest (from Correa's vantage point, anyway) in the workings of the nightclub. On more than one occasion, Correa had found him snooping around during rehearsals, talking with performers, musicians, even the choreographers. Correa did not need an interpreter to read the writing on the wall. He had already taken on an extra job as manager for the

Spanish singing orchestra Los Chavales de España, which had an offer to play the Waldorf-Astoria. Correa had made plans to join them on their New York tour.

Had Martín Fox offered Correa some payment for his years of work, which, actually, were the basis for the Tropicana cabaret's reputation, he might have considered it. Martín did not. For the Guajiro, the equation was simple: Correa had gambled and lost. Correa, on the other hand, was not about to let Martín take everything without a fight. While Martín focused on the building of the indoor cabaret, Correa worked out a plan to extract money from the Guajiro. "Extort is actually the word," insisted Valentín. The plan Valentín described seems worthy of a Shakespearean plot. It goes something like this: feeling trapped, Correa arranged to have a friend sue him for a fabricated debt of roughly 100,000 pesos and for a judge to rule against him. Correa would then fail to make the payment because he did not have that kind of money, and that person would put a lien on Correa's main source of income—namely, the Tropicana cabaret. As the main owner and financier, Martín would then be responsible for the debt. When the payment was made, the three participants—the so-called plaintiff, Correa, and the judge—would split the proceeds. It seemed like a foolproof plan. But, just to make sure that it went through without a glitch, Correa asked one of Cuba's most notorious and nefarious personalities to help him out.

The name Rolando Masferrer still elicits a shudder among Cubans of a certain age. Rarely does one hear a positive, even neutral word about the man. Masferrer's checkered history in Cuban politics began when he was a student at the University of Havana and fought to get rid of Machado. By the late 1940s, Masferrer's early idealism, which had led him to Spain in the '30s to fight against the Fascists (he was wounded at the battle of Ebro, whereupon he became known as el Cojo, "the Cripple"); to found the socialist political action group Movimiento Socialista Revolucionario

(MSR); and, in 1947, to join a failed expedition to the Dominican Republic to overthrow Rafael Trujillo, had devolved into gangsterismo. Since the election of Grau, Masferrer's MSR had become one of the most brutal and feared gangs in Havana. Years after Victor de Correa's phony lawsuit, Masferrer would become a staunch supporter of Batista and run a private army in Santiago de Cuba known as Los Tigres. After 1959, he would flee on a yacht for Miami, where he would become a virulent anti-Castroite who advocated the violent overthrow of the Cuban revolutionary government; and a journalist, whose October 1975 editorial encouraging Cuban exiles to plant bombs led to his being killed, a week later, by a bomb planted beneath his car. But in 1950, when he sued Victor de Correa for the sum of 92,000 pesos, Masferrer was still moderately respectable—a member of Cuba's senate, one of the country's ruling elite. "Correa probably met him at Tropicana," said Valentín Jodra. "All those men were always at the nightclubs."

The phony lawsuit was incubating when Martín hired Max Borges for the first of many projects at Tropicana. Martín proceeded cautiously. "That Christmas [1950], he had us do something quickly—*una bobería* [a little something] to the mansion [at Villa Mina]," recalled Borges. According to Borges, Martín was testing him, checking his approach. Apparently the Guajiro liked the small renovations, for early in 1951, as this first project neared completion, Martín asked the thirty-year-old architect to come up with ideas for an indoor cabaret. Martín's instructions were minimal, but they respected Guillermina's wishes. "All he said was that we were not to cut down any trees unless absolutely necessary," remembered Borges. Though not much of a directive, it was a tall order to fulfill, considering the lushness of the property. Most of Arcos would fit in the land formerly occupied by Villa Mina's tennis courts, but there were several towering mamoncillo trees on the periphery that would need to be addressed. Borges used this restriction as the springboard for a daring design. His building, which eventually required the removal of only one tree, was designed to incorporate the other trees inside the cabaret. The design itself was a soaring open space enclosed by nothing more than a framework of six concrete arches with sheets of glass hung in between them. The arches (or vaults, as they are more aptly called) were to be slender, two-and-a-half-inch-thick ribbons of concrete, set off center from each other and decreasing in height as they approached the stage. This would create a telescopic effect, drawing attention to the cabaret's focal point. During the day, the cabaret would look like not much more than a giant dusky cave with many windows; but at night, when it was meant to be seen, the dark paint of the ceiling, the pinpoint lights, the illumination of the outdoor trees, and the presence of those incorporated trees, their trunks and branches piercing the framework, would create the illusion of being out in the open.

The day Borges came to Tropicana to present initial perspective drawings for Arcos de Cristal, or "Arches of Glass," the name eventually given to the building by Oscar Echemendia, he was more than a little nervous. Though initially the idea for using arches had "popped into [his] head one day," as it came to life in color pencil, the young architect became more and more excited by it. Using parabolic concrete arches and glass walls was the perfect complement for this garden setting, the perfect marriage of form and function—the credo of contemporary modernism. It was also a completely Cuban adaptation of the style, a space designed for the luxuriance of the tropics. But how would the Guajiro react to something this unusual?

As it turns out, he loved it. "Martín's excitement was instant," recalled Borges. Martín pored over the documents, as fascinated as a child with a new toy. Nonetheless, even someone as decisive as Martín knew the importance of a second opinion. He called in his brother Pedro and Oscar Echemendia, to see the drawing. "Oye, Max, te la comiste," said Echemendia, which means, roughly, "You outdid yourself."

Now there was the question of cost. The design was basically quite simple, but Borges foresaw some tricky technical issues in the construction: pouring the concrete arches in place, hanging the glass, installing a stage that rose up from the level of the dance floor. Martín also wanted the project completed as quickly as possible, and though Borges and his father worked with an excellent crew (at the time architects in both Cuba and the United States doubled as contractors), this project would require hiring extra people from among the best construction workers in Havana. Borges laid the bad news on the table: 82,000 pesos for their fee and the basic construction, equivalent to $630,000 today. There would be additional costs: for carpeting, which Martín sent Borges and his wife to purchase in New York; for lighting, which was done by a team of engineers from Broadway; for the specially designed furniture; and for additional theatre technology, including what Olga Guillot remembered were the first wireless microphones in Cuba. The total cost of Arcos de Cristal would come in at around 300,000 pesos—roughly what Martín had paid for the entire property.

Martín did not even take a moment to think about it. He slapped the table. "*Métele mano*, Borges!" he said, which means, roughly, "Go for it." The young architect stood rigidly without speaking, not sure he had heard correctly. Then he asked if he might use the telephone. He still remembers trembling as he dialed his office and spoke with his father.

Within the month, the Borges team was ready to break ground. The elder Borges made the engineering calculations for the sweeping arches, and the younger Borges arrived with a battalion of workers who prepared the terrain, poured the foundation, and set up thick-walled wooden molds for the concrete pour on what had once been Villa Mina's tennis courts. The casting went quickly. In less than two months, the arches began to grow up from each end of the foundation, looking like curved coconut palms as they joined up in the middle.

Shortly before they were completed, Rolando Masferrer stormed into Tropicana with his private army, demanding that Victor de Correa hand over the money that he had been awarded in the phony lawsuit judgment. For three days, Martín and his partners watched helplessly while a dozen armed thugs prowled through Tropicana's cabaret and kitchens, interrogating staff and performers, opening drawers and storage cabinets, propping their feet up on the tables, and acting as if they owned the place. Victor de Correa ran around like a hapless victim, but Martín was not fooled. And, being no fool, Martín was careful to steer clear of any direct confrontation with Masferrer and his men, though he made sure to let his jacket flap open to reveal the Smith & Wesson .38 in his waistband.

On the fourth day of the occupation, Masferrer's men upped the ante. "They started coming into the casino, asking questions of the dealers," recalled Valentín. "Everyone grew tense. They were pressuring us to hand over the house's money." For Martín it was the last straw. Storming out of Tropicana in his Cadillac, he sped towards downtown Havana, where he paid a call on his Union Club friend, Senator Santiago Rey. Rey returned to Tropicana with Martín, and the three men—Martín, Masferrer, and Rey— sat in Martín's office to negotiate a settlement. "They were in there for hours," said Valentín. "Outside we all waited around anxiously. [Masferrer's] soldiers were on alert, and we were sweating." Like most of the financial deals in Martín Fox's world, the one negotiated on that afternoon in 1951 left behind no written records or outside witnesses. Those in the know, most notably Santiago Rey, maintained that Correa's little scheme cost Martín 90,000 pesos, and this was split between Correa, Masferrer, and the Marianao judge who ordered the bogus judgment. It was a huge sum to extort, equivalent to $750,000 today.

Still, by the time Senator Rey returned to his Vedado mansion, the guajiro from Ciego de Avila had once again turned adversity into advantage. For less than a quarter of his annual bolita profits Martín had finally gotten rid of Victor de Correa and now had complete control of Tropicana—the casino, the nightclub, and most importantly, the huge, stunning parcel of urban property on which he was constructing the most striking contemporary building in Cuba. He would have his indoor stage. Now all he needed was the choreographer who could bring it to life.

PART II

CHAPTER 9

The Santos and the Song-and-Dance Man

A long, long time ago, before men and women walked the earth, Olodumare, the Supreme Being of the Yoruba pantheon, decided to bless his children, the orishas, with his powers. He called them all together to his house. "*Mis hijos,*" he said, "I am going to distribute my *aché* among you, so you will be able to take responsibility for the world." According to the Afro-Cuban myth, the orishas were both nervous and excited to receive their father's *aché*, or spiritual power. They lined up, and his daughter Ochún went first. "My beautiful daughter," said Olodumare, "I am going to make you mistress of the rivers." Ochún thanked her father and stepped demurely back. The next in line was his son Changó. "To you, my powerful son, I give thunder." "Thank you, Father," replied Changó, and he made way for another sister, Yemayá. Olodumare next gave the sea to Yemayá; metals to Oggun; the wind to Oyá; and entrusted their mischievous baby brother, Eleggua, with entrances and paths.

When it was Babalu-Ayé's turn, Olodumare was nearly at the end of his blessings. So he asked, "Babalu-Ayé, are you partial to any special gift?" Babalu-Ayé was a tall, strapping youth with shiny hair and smooth brown muscles, which made him nearly irresistible to women. "Father," he said, "I want the power to be every woman's lover." Olodumare paused. This was a frivolous request, a waste of his *aché*. His son would have to learn the hard way. "Your wish is granted, but there is one condition: you can love as many women as you like, except on the Thursday of Easter week."

For years, Babalu-Ayé observed his father's condition, remaining indoors during Easter week to avoid temptation. But one Ash Wednesday he was working in his garden when he looked up and saw the loveliest wide-hipped beauty he had ever seen. Forgetting his father's admonition, he kissed her, touching her sumptuous body, and the next day—the forbidden Thursday—he took her to bed.

Babalu-Ayé awoke in agony the following morning to find he was covered with oozing, leprous lesions. The woman screamed and fled in horror as Babalu-Ayé's once-gorgeous body began to disintegrate. He tried soothing baths, prayers, and sacrifices. Finally, he crawled back to his father. Olodumare slammed the door on him. Babalu-Ayé collapsed and, convulsed with pain, died on the spot.

A few days after Babalu-Ayé's death, all the women who had loved him went to Ochún and asked her to go to Olodumare to plead on behalf of her brother. Ochún complied, and after much persuading, Olodumare agreed to bring Babalu-Ayé back—like Lazarus in the New Testament. But he would remain forever a leprous cripple and be given power over the most terrible diseases that afflict humanity.

TWENTY MILES south of Havana, in a rural town of sinuous streets called El Rincón, a small church dedicated to San Lazaro sits on a neatly trimmed lawn, surrounded by trees and flowering hibiscus shrubs. The air inside the sanctuary is thick with the scent of burning candles. Bouquets of purple and yellow flowers crowd the tall mahogany altars. Offerings of pesos, gourd rattles, mangoes, and brooms made from the fruit clusters of the palmetto surround the statue of the santo, or orisha as they are called in Yoruba. San Lazaro, the Catholic synchretizaton of Babalu-Ayé, is always depicted with gnarled, sore limbs, bent over crutches, two faithful little dogs at his side. During the years of slavery, Africans, forbidden to worship their deities, matched the orishas to Catholic saints. Thus cloaked in piety, they continued practicing their own religion, while also slowly absorbing Roman Catholic doctrine. This mix, whose most widely practiced version is known as Santería, slowly became the unofficial religion of Cuba. In every neighborhood of Cuba are practitioners, both full-fledged *santeros* and novice initiates, walking in their pristine white clothes and colorful beaded necklaces, each particular to a specific santo. The island's ceiba (silkfloss) trees and *palmas* (royal palms), both of which are sacred to *santeros*, are popular places to leave offerings— coconuts, apples, or paper-wrapped bundles containing the remains of some evil one is trying to discard. Though Santería originated in Afro-Cuban culture, over the centuries it has become popular among the white population as well. In many Cuban homes one sees altars festooned with candles, sweets, fruits, and flowers, especially on the santo's day of celebration. Changó, who is syncretized with Saint Barbara, is feasted on December 4; his colors are red and white and his favorite foods are cornmeal, okra, apples, and bananas. Ochún, mistress of rivers, love, and sexuality (her Catholic counterpart is the Virgin of Charity, Cuba's patron saint) celebrates September 8 as her day, and likes yellow offerings such as honey, oranges, pumpkins, and sunflowers. Even Cubans who don't openly profess belief in Santería observe some of its rituals. Watch a Cuban open a new bottle of rum. Before anyone is served, a few drops are spilled on the floor *"para los santos."*

According to several former Tropicana dancers, at Tropicana, there was so much *brujería* (casting of spells), "you had to visit a *santero* just to keep from breaking your leg walking through the door."

Behind the church at El Rincón is a craggy rock-faced fountain from whose hollow center drips holy water. Now that religious practice is again tolerated in Cuba, the faithful have returned to bathe their faces, hands, and feet at the mossy, slick fountain. On December 17—San Lazaro's day—tens of thousands in need of healing, or those who have recovered from an illness and are fulfilling a promise they made to San Lazaro, make the trip on foot from Havana, many crawling over the last mile. San Lazaro's colors are purple and yellow. Though the actual saint was named after a bishop who was beatified at Marseilles in 407 A.C., the two Lazaruses of the New Testament—the one who rose from the dead (John, 11), and the beggar who sat at the gates of a rich man, wracked by leprosy (Luke, 16)—are the ones being worshipped along with their Yoruba counterpart.

San Lazaro may be the spiritual source of health, but religion does not preclude medical care. Today a hospital dedicated mainly to the care of AIDS patients is located behind the church. In the years of Correa's Edén Concert cabaret and the heyday of Tropicana, the hospital served as a leprosarium, a place for people with contagious diseases such as syphilis, smallpox, and leprosy, one of the world's most feared afflictions and one of the most misunderstood. Leprosy's stigma arises from the Bible, where it is associated with uncleanliness, ostracism, and death, a punishment against those who defied God's will. The leper was deemed spiritually as well as physically diseased, and buried separately. Actually, the disease does not usually kill its victims and, contrary to popular belief, is only mildly contagious (and only if there is repeated contact). The main symptoms are raised red lesions on the skin and superficial nerves that, if left untreated, will lead to loss of sensation and severe deformity, especially to the feet and hands. Leprosy also attacks the vocal chords, nose, and eyes, in the latter case causing blindness. In 1873, the Norwegian doctor Armauer Hansen was the first person to identify the leprosy germ (*Mycobacterium leprae* is its scientific name, and it was the first bacteria to be identified as causing disease in man) under the microscope. Hansen's discovery eased some of the leper's social burden; the disease was no longer seen as a divine scourge. Nor was it hereditary. But symptoms of leprosy were not medically ameliorated until the 1940s, when doctors began treating it with sulfone drugs. Today, "Hansen's Disease"—the preferred term—is almost completely curable through either drug therapy, chemotherapy, or a combination. Epidemiologists estimate there are eleven million cases worldwide (two million have been reported). The disease is most prevalent in tropical countries, with seventy percent of cases occurring in India, Indonesia, and Myanmar; however, recent cases have also been reported in the United States, particularly in Hawaii, Texas, and Louisiana.

In 1900, during the American occupation of Cuba, journalist Dorothy Stanhope wrote a piece on Havana's leper colony that was printed in the *New York Times*. Stanhope noted that the San Lazaro leprosarium had ninety-six inmates, mostly from poor families. However, "Wealthy victims are in their own homes shielded from an asylum life, and in more than one apparently happy family in Havana there is a skeleton in the closet . . . So well is the secret guarded that the presence of leprosy in that home can at most only be suspected, and it does not get to the ears of the authorities, who would probably enforce the law which Gen. Brooke [acting military governor of Cuba] issued, that all lepers should be confined within the asylum and not remain in their homes—a menace to the health of the family."

In turn-of-the-century America the fear of leprosy became linked to the fear of expansionism. A February 4, 1900 article in the

New York Times reported that New York physician Albert Ashmead (who attended the first international conference on leprosy
in Berlin in 1897 and was instrumental in the detention of cargo
ships in New York harbor that were suspected of contamination
with bubonic plague) was contacted by anti-expansionists concerned that the U.S. occupation of the Philippines (as a condition
of Spain's withdrawing from Cuba, the U.S. insisted on control of
the Philippines) would increase the number of American cases of
leprosy. Dr. Ashmead, however, was more concerned about "our
closer relations with Cuba, for there are five hundred lepers, he de-
clares, walking the streets of Havana at the present time."

In the 1930s and '40s, the police in Havana would round up
known lepers and send them to El Rincón. One such patient was a
song-and-dance man named Roderico Neyra. Roderico would
sometimes check himself in to the leprosarium. But often, when he
was going home from a singing gig at CMQ Radio or the Alkazar
Theater (where he was a member of the all-star cast of the *Mara-
villosa* revue that included Rita Montaner), he would be detained
by a policeman who would spot the leprous lesions on his gnarled
hands, then send him to El Rincón against his will. Roderico was
a short, round-faced, impish-looking, light-skinned mulatto with a
perpetually wicked grin. Originally from Santiago de Cuba, he
had been kicking around Havana's cabaret and music hall world
since the early 1930s. He was as versatile a performer as could be
found. He could act, sing, dance tango and traditional Cuban
dances, do vaudeville-style stand-up routines, and perform any
type of musical comedy, including traditional Italian *comedia del
arte*. But Roderico was hindred by his affliction and haunted by its
inevitable outcome.

None of Roderico's friends in show business—not Celia Cruz,
Olga Guillot, Bola de Nieve, or his closest pal, Rita de Cuba
(Montaner)—knew where he had contracted leprosy. Some had
heard that it was in Uruguay, while on a South American tour with

a Havana dance troupe. No one thought to ask him what he might have been doing to pick up something so terrible, or with whom. His disease was becoming more obvious all the time; yet his show business friends didn't seem to notice. They adored Roderico. Whenever he was present, there was constant laughter. He had a way of seeing straight through to the core of a person, and his observations, delivered in a deadpan growl, made him the center of attention. He was a song-and-dance man with a huge stage presence. But outside of show business (or *la farándula,* as showbiz folks and hangers-on are known in Cuba), he was just one more leper, an object of revulsion who often missed performances when he was hauled off to the leprosarium by the police. Days afterward he would be bailed out by Rita Montaner.

One of Roderico's first regular gigs was at a burlesque theatre called the Shanghai, on Zanja Street in Havana's Chinatown. The Shanghai was a strip joint in the old fashioned sense of the term. There were full-out shows, with dancers, comedians, and a live band, the main difference being that at the Shanghai the chorus of wasp-waisted girls would eventually strip down to nothing and perform their act nude, often behind provocatively positioned feathers and fans that would ultimately be discarded. Roderico was one of the Shanghai's most versatile male performers. Not only was he a great dance foil for the ladies, but his quick delivery of naughty double entendres while surrounded by completely nude women made him a favorite with the Cuban men who frequented the Shanghai, and with the Spanish-speaking tourists and sailors who slipped in to partake of Havana's seedy underside. Roderico saw nothing seedy about the blend of sex, music, and comedy offered up at the Shanghai. For him, a certain degree of bawdiness was key to stimulating the senses. And that is exactly what Roderico believed a person expected from a night on the town.

By the early 1940s, Roderico was touring Cuba and Venezuela with one of the top musical theater troupes of the day. Back in

Havana, he did a stint as the rumba partner of the lovely Celina Reinoso at a number of cabarets in town. Devotees of radio heard him frequently on CMQ as a singer with the station's house band, Orquesta Broadway, and—amazingly, to friends familiar with his profane side—as an actor on a weekly show called "Youth Hour." He counted many friends among the artists of the cabaret set. Pianist Felo Bergaza, soprano Ester Borja, and declaimer of Afro-Cuban poetry Luis Carbonell tended to him when he was in pain and brought him food when he was so down and out that he could hardly get out of bed. Despite a varied career that by 1945 spanned nearly two decades in the capital, Roderico had trouble achieving any real success. His disease began to get the better of his performance skills. His hands became so deformed that he would try to hide them under his shirt cuffs. Being picked up by the police and hauled off to the leprosarium was humiliating and depressing to no end, though apparently his leprosy had responded to treatment and was stable. When he was at El Rincón, he was close to San Lazaro.

Like many natives of Cuba, especially those from Santiago, Roderico was a *creyente*, a believer. The power of the santos moved him. Though he never admitted to being possessed by a spirit, he had seen others at *bembés* and *toques de santos* rituals collapse on the floor, convulsing, tearing at their clothes, and speaking in tongues. For Roderico, *Lucumí* (the term used by adherents of Santería to refer to their practice) ritual was a form of meditative therapy, a way to relieve the stress of work and illness. At the leprosarium Roderico felt closer to the santo who watched over him. And he needed watching. By the mid 1940s, his disease had advanced to the point that he could no longer perform. His deformed feet made dancing painful; some moves were simply too excruciating. Even more excruciating was the thought that he might have to quit show business. Roderico loved the stage, the spotlights, the late-night performances, and then hitting the town until long after the sun had risen. Without it, he felt empty and miserable. What's more, he knew, deep down, that he could be one of the greatest cabaret stars Cuba had ever known. All he needed was health and an opportunity to shine.

WEARING A dark blue satin shirt, gilded vest, dark pants with satin side stripes, and a rakishly tilted white panama hat, the dancer launched himself onto the dance floor with a sudden surge of energy. His head was high, his back ramrod straight, arms spread wide, palms facing his audience. He took his partner's hand and swept her forcefully against his chest. No one could see his shoes because he moved too quickly: *uno-dos, uno-dos-tres.* The crowd was spellbound, feet tapping, some—like me—feeling envious at the grace, the movement, the *sandunga,* a word with no English equivalent that refers to an indefinable sexiness marked by fluidity of movement. The dancer was performing a *son montuno,* a traditional Cuban country dance that is a precursor of what is now known as salsa. Hips and shoulders moved in unison, then he cut loose and started to rumba solo. His knees were bent, his arms pumping. Beads of sweat rolled down from his cheeks and forehead, settling in his neatly trimmed white beard and mustache. The dancer's name is Eddy Serra. At the time of this performance, which took place at a birthday celebration for the owner of the Copacabana, a sprawling Latin-themed cabaret-restaurant in Pomona, California, he was sixty-three. When he was seventeen years old, in 1958, he joined the cast of the Tropicana cabaret.

Like Roderico, his mentor, Eddy planned the performance down to the smallest detail. Copacabana was no Tropicana, of course. Hanging above the stage was a sparkly tropical-themed mural he made bearing the name COPACABANA flanked by conga drums, maracas, and guitars. There were potted paper-maché palm trees and centerpieces filled with lemons, limes, and oranges. Eddy had choreographed the floor show, which was performed by a group of local Cuban youths who took classes in traditional Cuban dance. The kids moved well to the beat of the music; but their teacher was the star. When he stepped out onto the dance floor, he drew every eye. Every move seemed effortless, executed with elegance and precision.

"Nothing was the *sueño* [dream] that Tropicana was," said Eddy, mopping his brow and sipping ice cold Coca-Cola after his set. "If you worked at another cabaret it was fine, but Tropicana was the maximum. Whether you were a principal or in the chorus, you felt like royalty." I was seated at Eddy's table, the one reserved for friends like Rosa and Ofelia, as well as former Tropicana model Jenny León and her husband, Frank Llopis, a musician who had played the cabaret four times, first as part of a quartet which he had founded with Cuban jazz pianist Felipe Dulzaides; and later, with a combo that did interpretations of American rock-and-roll. (Llopis translated the lyrics to such tunes as "Chantilly Lace" and "I'm All Shook Up"; he also played the Hawaiian guitar, a steel-strung guitar that is played lap-style and uses a movable bar to create a glissando effect.) Onstage, the Cuban band was playing a rapid *son montuno*, and the Tropicana table was rocking. Jenny, a live wire as lithe as a twenty-year-old (she would not say her age, but it was in the range of seventy), was shimmying in her seat, trying to get Frank onto the dance floor. Ofelia was already dancing—and quite well—with Miguel Paneque, the thirty-seven-year-old host of the Los Angeles Spanish-language dating show, *"Buscando Amor."* (Paneque's mother, Cecilia, and his aunt, Mabel, were both former Tropicana showgirls.) "She is an equal opportunity social butterfly," said Rosa Sanchez, sighing.

Copacabana partygoers stopped to offer Eddy their congratulations. His mind, however, was focused on the questions I was asking about the choreographer who taught him. "All of this I owe to Rodney," said Eddy, using the stage name that Roderico created for himself by melding the first syllables of his first and last name.

"He was like no one you could ever imagine. He was tough, mind you. Always had a biting word. If a dancer got her costume dirty, for example—" Eddy lowered his voice and growled in imitation of his mentor: "'Pepito, take a look at Amy's clothes. She looks like a cook who's spent her day frying plantains.' One girl's mother used to send her soup every day for lunch so he called her Potaje."

By the time Eddy met Rodney, the choreographer was known throughout Havana as a tough if mercurial boss.

I met him for the first time one afternoon when I went to Tropicana to pick up a payment for a film called *Tami, la reina del mar.* I had been at the Riviera and I'd worked on the film with some of the Tropicana dancers. I was practically just out of dance school. They were rehearsing a new show called *Luisa Fernanda en Chemise,* a comic piece based on zarzuelas [a Spanish form of popular operetta]. Roderico had mixed in mambo and cha-cha-cha with the traditional Spanish dances. In the middle of the show, I see that Roderico is fighting with one of the principal dancers, a guy named Tomasito Morales. I don't know what happened but Roderico just threw Tomasito out, and the show *se quedo cojo* [was crippled] for the lack of a soloist, and there were only three days to go before the opening. But then one of the guys I knew in the chorus said *"Mira,* there's Eddy Serra, he can fill in." Roderico turned to me. With that stare of his he looked me up and down and said, *"Dale, muchacho,* get up on stage and see what you can learn." I learned about six dances in two hours. Then Roderico said, "Go up to wardrobe and see which of Tomás's costumes fit you." They took another of the guys for [Tomás's] lead role and put me in the chorus.

When I met him later in Cuba, Tomás Morales laughed heartily when reminded of the incident. The soft-spoken, white-haired dancer, who now serves as Tropicana's artistic director, arranged to meet me one afternoon while he rehearsed with the cast. It had been nearly five years since the last show had opened; in the 1950s the shows were changed every three months. All around us tall, slender dancers stretched and drank from plastic water bottles as the man they referred to as "Maestro" talked about his predecessor's mercurial temper and his genius. "Roderico got angry with me," said Morales, switching back and forth, as Tropicana's dancers often do, between Rodney's given and stage names, "because I was at the time also working with Luis Trapaga [a ballet dancer who had been a star at Tropicana and now headed his own conjunto to perform on television]. I wanted to continue with Luis because he was teaching me technique. Rodney was a genius at the production values and the choreography, but he was not much of a dancer. Luis opened my eyes to what a *bailarín* should be. And I wanted to learn and be the best dancer I could be."

Despite Rodney's volatility, no dancer turned down a chance to work with him at Tropicana. "There was an aura to him that was like the maximum artistic expression," Eddy told me at the Copacabana. "When he designed a show he paid attention to every detail— from the types of beads that were on the costumes to the exact way that a dancer turned her foot when doing a pirouette. His illness was hard on him, but in some ways it led to his genius, because he had something to overcome. And if not for his illness he might have continued dancing and not have ever turned to choreography."

By 1945, Rodney had finally accepted that he could not dance anymore. His feet were beginning to get numb, his hands were too gnarled, his fingers too red and twisted to expose in performance. But though his limbs were beginning to resemble those of his patron saint, Roderico's reputation as a dancer and comedian, coupled with his extensive connections in the entertainment world, helped him get a job at the Teatro Fausto, an art deco theatrical palace in the heart of the Paseo del Prado. There he came up with the first signature piece of his career as choreographer, a revue based on rumba dance and music called *Las Mulatas de Fuego,* or "The Fiery Mulattas." Performed by six tawny-skinned dancers with spectacular bodies, and three female singers, including Elena Burke (who later became one of the country's greatest bolero singers), and a young *guarachera* with a perfectly pitched alto voice named Celia Cruz, the original 1947 production of *Las Mulatas de Fuego* was based on what Rodney had picked up while working at the Shanghai—cleaned up for public consumption. His dancers included future Tropicana models Marta Castillo and Sandra Taylor. The women performed the rumba, *son,* and *guaracha* in the skimpiest bikinis allowed on popular stages. Both the tourists and locals loved it: it was standing room only at the Fausto for the entire run of the show. Later *Las Mulatas* went on to play at other venues, including the Hotel Nacional and the Radiocentro theater, located in the heart of Vedado, and toured throughout Mexico and Central and South America. The cast changed several times as its performers became stars in their own right, but the raw energy and raciness imbued by its choreographer kept the show going for years. The cult of Rodney had begun.

ONE NIGHT in early 1952, while Arcos de Cristal was in its final days of construction, Alberto Ardura decided to go over to Sans Souci to see the current show. Sans Souci was Tropicana's most direct competition. Located even further out of town in quasi-suburban Marianao, the cabaret featured many of the same attributes, such as an outdoor setting under clusters of royal palms and a multi-level proscenium that could accommodate a cast of hundreds. Sans Souci's casino had an advantage over Tropicana's: it was managed by Santo Trafficante's close associate Norman Rothman, giving it a certain allure for serious gamblers, especially the coveted group of American high rollers.

But lately, Sans Souci had also been attracting a Cuban clientele, and in droves. The reason was a show that was getting the best press anyone had ever read. The show, which had been given the Afro-Cuban title *Sun Sun Babae*, was Rodney's brainchild. Ardura was a huge fan of Havana's dance and music scene and had been among the lucky ones to catch the first run of the original *Las Mulatas de Fuego* at the Fausto. It was one of the best shows he had ever seen, and the dancers were enough to make any man forget himself. The word around town was that Rodney himself was not interested in women. But no one could question that he knew how to show them off.

Ardura drove his car through the entrance gate to Sans Souci and down the long driveway to the cabaret entrance. "In his opinion," Ofelia explained, remembering the story told to her by Martín, "it was unthinkable for Sans Souci to be doing better than Tropicana. Its grounds were luxuriant, but there was not the same abundance of trees, and the architecture was a Spanish hacienda, no match for the cabaret that Martín was building." Ardura gave his car over to the valet attendant and slipped in quietly without even stopping to greet Norman Rothman. He hoped no one would notice him.

At eleven thirty, which was also when Tropicana's first show began, the lights at Sans Souci began to lower. Out of the darkness came the sound of drumming—loud, resonant, overwhelming. The lights came up on three black drummers, the same number as in *bembé* ceremonies. Dressed entirely in white and wearing colorful beaded necklaces, the men did not look like cabaret performers. They were pounding out the rhythms on actual *batá* drums, the ones used in the *bembés* and *toques de santos*, in which initiates dance and are possessed by the spirit of the orishas to whom they are consecrated. Ardura was no *creyente*, but the sight of the tall, two-headed drums, which were not normally brought out except for sacred ritual, made him shudder. From either side of Sans Souci's stage emerged a pair of dancers who moved slowly to the rhythm. A singer started chanting in high-pitched Yoruba. A chorus of singers responded. Six male dancers came out dressed in colorful striped pants and straw hats adorned with green feathers and proceeded to sit down, sprawling comfortably on either side of the drummers. Ardura couldn't believe his eyes. Was Rodney staging real *bembés* for the cabaret public? Would the community of *santeros* let him get away with this? And would this sustain the interest of a cabaret public that wanted to see skimpily clad showgirls and hear the latest Cuban music?

A woman came out, dressed in the traditional yellow garb of the orisha Ochún. She moved suggestively to the *batá* rhythm. The male dancers got up and encircled her. Slowly everyone seemed to become enthralled by the spirit of the orishas. The faces of the dancers glowed, their eyes fixed on something in the distance. Suddenly, the men came down from the stage and into the audience. The spotlights followed them as they approached one of the tables. A striking blond woman—a foreigner, Ardura assumed—was sitting there, nursing a cocktail. The beam of spotlight caught her face. The woman was clearly engrossed in the experience. Suddenly, the woman stood. The dancers turned to her. She beckoned to them, her arms held out. Is this for real, or is it part of the show? wondered Ardura. The dancers seized the woman by the arms and swept her toward the stage. The drumming mounted in intensity, the singing grew louder. The woman seemed in shock. Then, without warning, she ripped off her black satin cocktail dress and began dancing in her black lace underwear and garter belt.

Ardura slapped the table, laughing, as the dancer—an American hoofer named Skippy, as it turned out—began to shake and shimmy like the voluptuous *cubanas* that surrounded her. The men grabbed her, tossing her around the stage while the music alternated between traditional Afro-Cuban rhythms and a more moderate rumba. Skippy's movements became more frenzied the more she succumbed to the spirit of the santos. Then amid heightening music and movement, she abruptly snapped out of her trance, let out a bloodcurdling shriek, grabbed her clothes, and hurried off the stage and out the back door of the cabaret. The crowd was ecstatic. But the show was not finished. Celia Cruz and Afro-Cuban singer Mercedita Valdés now came out. Backed by a chorus, they began singing the anthem of the show, which was written by Rogelio Martínez: "Sun sun sun sun-sun babaé / Sun sun sun sun-sun babaé / Pajaro lindo de la madruga / Pajaro lindo de la madruga (beautiful bird of the night / beautiful bird of the night)."

When the performance was over, the reserved Ardura was on his feet and clapping as madly as the rest of the audience. The cast, including Celia Cruz and Skippy (still wearing only bra, panties, and garter belt) graciously accepted their ovation and performed an encore. But Ardura did not wait for this. He had seen enough. He was too preoccupied thinking, first, about what he would say to Martín, and, second, how much it would take to bring Rodney to Tropicana.

CHAPTER 10

The Two Loves of Martín Fox

*My goal is to construct two grand cabarets in one—
to bring joy to all Cubans, and make us the pride
of the world.*

—Martín Fox, September 1952

After spending a month in Cuba and Miami, I was back in Glendale, mounting the thirty steps to Ofelia's front door, with exciting new Tropicana stories and loaded down with old magazines and photographs. In Miami I had spent several hours with Ofelia's good friend Olga Guillot. In Havana I had met a range of ex-Tropicana dancers, musicians, and staff. In both cities I had tried to learn more about Rita Longa's ballerina sculpture, which still sits at the entrance to the cabaret and remains its most recognizable emblem. Max Borges only remembered commissioning the piece in 1950, though in Rafael Lam's book on Tropicana, Longa is quoted as recalling that the architect took his inspiration from the 1948 film *The Red Shoes*, a dark fairytale about a ballerina who is forced to choose between her imperious ballet teacher and love. Borges laughed when he was told this, saying that he had no memory of such a thing. Then he admitted that, following open-heart surgery the previous year, his memory faltered on many matters. Longa's personal inspiration for *Bailarina* has long been the subject of gossip. The opinion among several artists who knew Longa is that she modeled it after a ballerina she was in love with. Indeed, the sculpture's long curved neck and arms resemble Cuban ballerinas Carlisse Novo and Leonela González. Nonetheless, Longa vigorously denied to Lam that she based her signature piece on any dancer in particular.

It was December, and Ofelia and Rosa's porch was ablaze with Christmas lights. The mood, however, seemed somber. "Ofelia's having a tough time tonight," Rosa told me when she answered the door. Rosa looked pretty weary herself. "There's been a lot of bad news since you left," she murmured as we entered the house. I nodded, recalling how my interview in Olga Guillot's condominium was suddenly shattered by a phone call announcing Celia Cruz's stroke. Olga was barely able to continue talking about Tropicana. "It's more than Celia," whispered Rosa. "Everyone seems to be sick or dying. Max Borges is healing way too slowly from his heart surgery. Carmelina Ardura seems to be slipping away"—I knew she had Alzheimer's disease—"and then there's the illness of Santiago Rey ... Valentín's wife ... Chiquita ..."

It was easy to forget, around the lively duo of Ofelia and Rosa, that advanced age inevitably brings illness. "Is it better if I go?" I asked.

"No, no. Talking about Tropicana makes her feel good. She has missed your conversations. Just don't touch on depressing topics—like Martín's death or their time in exile."

Martín's death was not on my mind that night. If anything, I wanted to ask Ofelia about her life with Martín, specifically, how they fell in love. Ofelia had mentioned it several times, but only in fragments. She always ended by telling me that marrying him was her destiny. "If anyone believes that we are sovereigns of our own future, they are sorely mistaken," she frequently told me. "The life we lead is all part of a big design. Call it fate, call it God—it doesn't matter. The only thing to know is that your choices are not yours. We're all marionettes who play a part in a greater plan."

Under the cozy amber lights of the Bar and Grill, I questioned what sounded like fatalism.

"It isn't fatalistic," Ofelia responded, shrugging, as she poured tequila. "Look, it's obvious. Martín smashes his finger at the Central Jagüeyal and this sets off a chain of events. Roderico contracts leprosy and this keeps him from dancing and sets off another chain. You and I both come to live in Los Angeles, yet we don't meet for over ten years, until the time was right."

And if not for other, painful and enigmatic aspects of this story—losing Tropicana, going into exile, losing her wealth, and Martín's eventual death—she probably would have never wound up here in Glendale, in what seemed to be a lovely relationship with Rosa Sanchez. I asked Ofelia about her and Rosa. "How was it that you two happened to decide to leave Miami and come here together?"

"Those were terrible days," she replied curtly. "Martín had had a stroke. There were family problems. I had no money, no way to take care of him. And Rosa was my dear friend. She came to my rescue." The message was loud and clear: probe no further. And I didn't. Instead I gave Ofelia an early Christmas present—two boxes of Cuban cigars. Her mood instantly brightened. "*¡Ay, tabacos cubanos. Qué rico!*" I'd brought a small box of Partagas panatelas and a larger one of Romeo y Julietas. Ofelia opened the Partagas box and pulled out one of the thin medium-length cigars. She cut the tip and lit it expertly, twirling it to get a complete burn. Soon the room filled with its pungent, smoky perfume. "Nothing quite like a Cuban cigar, is there?" Ofelia said. Indeed, they were the perfect complement to the bar, cocktails, and poker table.

"I worried about buying them for you," I said. "Because they come from Cuba."

Ofelia nodded thoughtfully and inspected the column of ash forming on the cigar's end. "*Bueno,* normally I don't like the idea of giving money to Castro. But one does have to honor the Cuban cigar."

Most cigar connoisseurs acknowledge that the best tobacco in the world is grown in the province of Pinar del Rio in western Cuba, especially in the rich, red soil of the Vuelta Abajo, a ninety-mile-long valley that runs south of the Sierra de los Organos mountains, about two hours from Havana. Tobacco is native to the Americas. According to legend, when Christopher Columbus landed in Cuba, he sent two emissaries with letters from the king and queen of Spain to the emperor of China, which is where he thought he had landed. Instead of Asians, Columbus's men were greeted by natives who were smoking rolled *Nicotiana tabacum* leaves, the chief commercial species of tobacco. Two centuries later, tobacco cultivation was widespread in Cuba. By 1845, it had even surpassed sugar as the island colony's most important cash crop.

Cigars are hand-rolled works of art that use three different kinds of leaves: wrappers, fillers, and binders. The wrapper plants, which are grown in furrows on flat ground, are often covered in cheesecloth as they grow, to protect them from the hot tropical sun and imbue them with a milder flavor. Both of Ofelia's parents were born and raised among the tobacco fields of Pinar del Rio. Victor Suarez came from San Cristobal. Ofelia's mother, Francisca González, or Cuca, as she was known, was born in Rio Seco, but raised in the Vuelta Abajo town of San Juan y Martínez, after an outbreak of plague that coincided with the War of Independence left her orphaned. When Ofelia was a girl, her family would often make the long trip into *el campo*, "the countryside," to visit relatives. The visits left a strong impression. "My uncle and aunt would roll cigars on their bellies. And the fields themselves were amazing. When we'd approach Pinar del Rio, my father would stop at a lookout point. There would be all those miles of tall tobacco plants, some seven feet high and draped in cheesecloth. It looked like a giant snowfield."

Ofelia grew up in the middle-class Havana neighborhood of Santo Suarez, the youngest of four siblings. She had a brother, Osvaldo, and two sisters, Fara and Hildebranda. Though Ofelia was sixteen years younger than Fara, and ten years younger than Hildebranda, or La Niña, as she was called, the Suarez girls were close knit. Fara and La Niña treated Ofelia like their baby. They doted on her and protected her. Ofelia, however, did not think she needed babying and was fiercely independent. As a teenager, she was not as obsessed with dating, boyfriends, and the whole ritual of social engagements that characterized middle-class Havana life. It wasn't that she didn't like to go out to the dances, the nightclubs, or the endless parties; on the contrary, to the mild dismay of her mother and sisters, Ofelia seemed to relish the nightlife more than any other young woman of her social class. When she went out with one of her string of suitors, her mother, who would often serve as chaperone (at other times it was La Niña, when she was between one of her four marriages), could not help but notice how much her youngest daughter loved music and dancing, as well as the carefree carousing that went with all the cocktails. Ofelia seemed more taken with the venues and music than with any of the young men who asked her out. They were a rather lackluster collection. There was René, son of Ofelia's godmother, who turned out to be an alcoholic. There was Manolo, a government employee twenty years her senior, whom Ofelia's mother could not stand and, indeed, could not even bear to see *en pintura,* "in a painting," as the saying goes, so she dropped him.

Lacking serious marriage prospects when she turned seventeen in 1940, Ofelia enrolled at the Havana Business Academy. She studied English for three years and taught for several months, then landed a job with Cuba Motor Car, a firm that sold truck parts. Like many Havana companies at the time, Cuba Motor Car did a brisk business with American suppliers. It was Ofelia's job to manage these contacts. She enjoyed the work, which made her feel productive and fulfilled, though she always had to fend off the annoying amorous attention of her portly, pockmarked supervisor. By then it was 1948. She was twenty-five years old and unmarried. Though Fara, Ofelia's eldest sister, was beside herself with worry about what she saw as Ofelia's looming spinsterhood, Ofelia was truly unconcerned. When people would say, *"Ay,* you're still not married!" with that note of incredulity that was part alarm and part indicative of their relief that they or their daughters had fared better, Ofelia would retort with a phrase worthy of a Jane Austen heroine: "The day the world permits women to court men instead of having to wait to be courted, there will be far fewer single women walking around." There was no bitterness behind her feistiness. Though at the time she had not yet verbalized her belief in fate, she was confident that one day the right person would come along.

In 1949, Ofelia was offered a job in the United States by one of Cuba Motor Car's chief suppliers, the Evans Trucking Company of Sumter, South Carolina. Mr. and Mrs. Evans had met her while on a trip to Cuba. She had done all their translating, and now they wanted her help in expanding their Latin American business. At first she turned it down. Her father had died only two months before of kidney failure, and she didn't want to leave her mother. But the Evanses continued to insist. They upped the ante, raised the salary, offered to have her live in their home with them. In the end, Ofelia went off to Sumter, but she lasted only eight months in the States. "I couldn't get used to the customs. The Evanses were nice, but once, when I was out late with a boy, I called home thinking they might be worried about me, and they were both asleep. I needed to come home to people who would take care of me!"

Back in Cuba, Ofelia was without work, so Fara arranged for her to meet a friend of her husband's named Manuel who was starting a decal company. Fara was undoubtedly hoping that Ofelia would find more in common with Manuel than their business, which they named Blue Star. That did not happen. ("He was so nondescript, I can hardly remember what he looked like," said Ofelia.) However, the decal business finally kicked fate into action.

One day in the fall of 1951, while Martín was busy with the construction of Arcos de Cristal, he was invited to a dinner party at the Vedado apartment of an old friend from Ciego de Avila. Normally Martín did not leave Tropicana in the evenings, but tonight his sisters Angela and Domitila were also going with their husbands, and Martín, who despite his nocturnal lifestyle was a family man, graciously complied on the condition that he could leave sometime around midnight and return to the cabaret. What Martín did not realize was that the dinner was part of a matchmaking scheme orchestrated by his and Ofelia's sisters. There were to be twelve guests in total—the quartet of plotting sisters and their spouses; the prospective couple, who were the only ones not in on the evening's plan; and the hosts, remembered only by their first names, Mirta, and Domingo, who, like Martín, was known as El guajiro. (In Cuba, many people are known by a nickname, or *nombrete*. Most Josés, for example, are called Pepe. The youngest in any family is usually *el niño* or *la niña*. Blonds are almost always *rubio* or *rubia*. Anyone with Asian features is *chino* or *china*. President Ramón Grau San Martín was called *el pollito*, the chick, because the hand gesture he used when he spoke seemed to mimick a chicken pecking at the ground.)

Each family had its own reasons for piloting the amorous course of their sibling. The Suarez sisters, Fara especially, were continually on the search for an eligible bachelor for Ofelia. Angela and Domitila Fox had a different reason. After his divorce from Rosita, Martín had been too immersed in the cabaret expansion to make much time for women. Women, however, made time for him. The owner of the Tropicana was as attractive a catch as could be found in Havana. It mattered little that he was now fifty-five years old and a guajiro from the provinces without much family social standing. Martín was personable, funny, handsome in that rough, garrulous way that women tend to find irresistible, and rich, powerful, and a welcome figure at all of Havana's night spots. In short, the city's single women were at Martín Fox's feet, from the middle-class society girls who came to Tropicana for birthday and engagement parties with their chaperones in tow, to the showgirls who were the objects of every Cuban man's fantasies.

When Martín finally chose to get involved, it was with the sister of one of his employees, a man named Dario, known to all as Kunkún, who was one of the cashiers in Tropicana's baccarat lounge. Kunkún's sister was neither a society girl nor a showgirl, though she certainly had the raw material to be the latter. Tall, long-legged, with provocatively slanted eyes and a figure that, to borrow from the pages of one of the decade's most popular entertainment magazines, *Show*, "had more curves than Cuba's central highway," Pucha, as she was known, was considered either *tremendo pollo* (a bombshell) or *tremenda puta* (a prostitute), depending on one's gender and outlook. For Angela and Domitila Fox, there was no question which she was. Frankly, they believed, had Pucha been an official prostitute, she would have made them much more comfortable. At least then Martín could simply pay for her services, instead of showering her with clothes, jewels, and gifts, as well as money. Even worse than Martín's generosity was his growing obsession with this woman. Lately he had started calling her at all hours to find out where she was. He would ask people to trail her and report on her activities. And Pucha played him like a violin. She would flirt in public, purposely disappearing for whole days without calling. Pucha planted tiny seeds of doubt in Martín's mind to keep him hooked. Now the seeds had started blooming into full-blown desperation that was becoming a matter of concern to his family and business partners.

A few weeks before the dinner party, the Pucha situation almost came to a tragic conclusion. Anxious over one of her absences, Martín had her trailed one afternoon. He got a telephone call at Tropicana with the information that he feared: his doe-eyed girlfriend was at a beach house in the company of a common *chulo* (gigolo) whom Martín had been suspicious of for a long time. Choking with rage, the normally level-headed Martín threw his Smith & Wesson .38 into the glove compartment of his Cadillac and sped towards Santa María del Mar, one of the fashionable beaches east of the city. He parked his car a block away from where Pucha had been spotted and, like a crazed stalker in white linen trousers and a soaked guayabera, he trudged up and down the soggy dunes that ran behind the line of modern beach houses. When he found the couple, half dressed and in each other's arms, Martín yanked out the loaded .38, fully intending to blast them both into oblivion. But then, as he later told Ofelia, "*Tilita, mi mamá,* looked down on me from heaven and kept me from making a terrible mistake."

Whether they believed in it or not, Martín's sisters could no longer rely on the supernatural intervention of their mother. And the fact that Martín refused to have anything more to do with Pucha (he even fired Kunkún from his job at the casino) made no difference. Something had to be done to steer their brother toward better company.

The dinner party was held on a Sunday night, the traditional evening for family gatherings in Cuba. As was his custom, Martín arrived punctually, dressed in a yellow suit, yellow shirt, and yellow tie, socks, and shoes. A crisply folded yellow handkerchief protruded from his pocket. To Ofelia Suarez y González, the only other single person at the table, Tropicana's owner looked like a large canary. Still, he seemed nice enough. Ofelia had been lured to the dinner party on the pretext that it had nothing to do with romance. "Think how great it would be for the decal business if you were to land the Tropicana account," Fara had told her.

At the dinner table, Martín was his usual gregarious self. Over rice, black beans, yucca with *mojo,* salad, and roasted chicken smothered with garlic and onions, he regaled the group with stories about Tropicana. He told anecdotes about the stars who played at the cabaret—the jovial rowdiness of Bola de Nieve, the smoldering sexuality of Josephine Baker. Martín boasted about the gardens and his plans to remodel all of the buildings in order to make Tropicana the most beautiful cabaret in the world. "Martín really used terms like 'best in the world,'" recalled Ofelia. "Medium-size goals meant nothing to him." His greatest enthusiasm was reserved for Arcos de Cristal. "The indoor cabaret was like his favorite child, his pride and joy," said Ofelia. Like a parent intent on sharing details about his children, Martín discussed the construction minutiae with those at the dinner table. He told them how Max Borges himself would sit at the top of the arches and measure the vibration of the nearby train line, how the carpets and drapes were being brought in from New York, and how Max was designing a stage that would rise up from the dance floor with the push of a button.

Ofelia listened raptly. She had never been to Tropicana, but as a devotee of Havana nightlife she would have given anything for the chance. Martín made it sound even more appealing than she had ever imagined. Despite his boasts, his outfit, and his heft, he was gentle and soft spoken. Far from making it seem as if Tropicana was an exclusive place, a playground purely for society's elite or tourists from the States, Martín gave the impression that everyone at the table was welcome at Tropicana. Indeed, the way he talked, he made it sound as if he was inviting everyone in Cuba.

As the evening wore on, the cadre of sisters turned away from Martín and Ofelia, forcing them to focus on each other. After a few more minutes of Tropicana this and that, Martín finally asked Ofelia about herself. "Do you work?"

"I'm in the decal business," replied Ofelia.

"Hmmm, decals. What are they for?"

Ofelia put her fork beside her plate and wiped her mouth with her napkin. "Decals are used for advertising."

"*Ah, sí?* How does that work?"

"Well, the decals can be printed with a picture—or the name of a business. Like Tropicana, for example." Ofelia waited for him to take the bait. Martín just nodded and looked at her. "Have you ever thought about producing a decal for the cabaret?"

Martín shrugged. "Never thought about it."

Now Ofelia leaned in, ready with her sales pitch. "*Bueno,* you should. You could sell them as souvenirs. Or give them away. They only cost pennies, but people will put them on their windshields, and the advertising benefit is immeasurable."

Martín shrugged, not sure what to say. "I guess I would need to see a drawing . . ."

Without missing a beat, Ofelia offered to get a drawing ready in a few days. "Should I call you at the cabaret?"

Martín leaned back and observed the young businesswoman. Something about her eagerness was at once charming and compelling. She reminded him of himself. "Why don't you call me when you have a drawing? I'll put you in touch with the advertising manager, see what he says."

The next morning, Ofelia rushed to her partner's house and practically chained him to his drafting table. Martín Fox had been affable about discussing the decals and had spent the remainder of the evening talking with her exclusively. She was certain that if they came up with a good design quickly, he would place an order. Manuel labored under Ofelia's scrutiny, and by the end of the day the pair had devised a design that seemed to convey the mood of Tropicana. Ofelia laughed as she recalled the decal. "It was a total cliché, with all the typical tropical motifs—a woman dancing rumba, a pair of maracas, a palm tree . . ." The next day she called Martín. He invited her to Tropicana. She went accompanied by her sister Fara and Fara's husband, Atilano Taladrid.

Entering the Tropicana cabaret for the first time, Ofelia was overwhelmed. "Even as we pulled into the driveway, I felt like it was another world. It was not just the beauty of the gardens, or the elegance of all the details—from the uniforms of the parking attendants to the crystal champagne glasses at the tables—it was an air of perfection that hung over everything. And everyone was having a good time. A paradise under the stars—like Martín always said."

Ofelia has little memory of what show played that night. She remembered that Martín came over to their table several times, and that, sometime before the show, she was summoned to the office of Miguelín, the marketing director and Martín's nephew, to show her design for the decals. Ofelia was not sure how to read Miguelín's expression as he looked at the drawing. When he concluded the meeting with the words, "Let me look into our needs, and I will get back to you," she was almost sure that the design had fallen flat.

She was wrong. The following afternoon, Miguelín placed an order for four hundred pesos' worth of decals. "It was a huge amount, much bigger than anything we could have expected," said Ofelia. The partners agreed to have the order ready in a week. Two days later, Martín called Ofelia. He spoke hesitantly. "There's another show opening this weekend, and I was wondering . . . well, would you like to see it?"

"Why don't we wait until the decals are ready?"

"Just come and see the show," said Martín. "You can come again when you have the decals."

That second night at Tropicana, Ofelia noticed that Martín's interest had shifted. "He kept coming around to our table. He would sit with us, then get up and go off, but he came back repeatedly." The headliners that night were Los Chavales de España, one of Ofelia's favorite orchestras. Just before the second show, which Martín insisted that she stay to see, he pulled Ofelia aside and asked her out on an official date.

Martín and Ofelia's first date was at another cabaret. "We saw Bola de Nieve at the Parisien. Martín was not the type to go to movies or the theater. I never saw a movie with him. He liked casinos, cabarets, and everything associated with them. Later, in our married life, we would go to after-hours clubs occasionally, or if we had out-of-town guests we might go to Varadero, where he rented a fishing yacht named *Mar Afuera*, 'Open Sea.' We would spend the day on board. I generally slept the morning and then socialized for a few hours before we left. We always headed back in time to make it to Tropicana."

After the evening at the Hotel Nacional's Parisien, Martín began inviting Ofelia out for lunch at his regular haunt, the posh Miami Restaurant on the corner of Prado and Neptuno boulevards in Central Havana, one of the busiest corners in the city. The Miami was a tropical version of a New York bistro, with tiled floors, mahogany tables, potted palms, and starched white tablecloths and napkins. Martín and Ofelia sat at his regular table, close to the mahogany bar, and Ofelia watched the full parade of Cuban life through the glass windows. Even during those early lunches, when nothing romantic was ever said, she sensed that destiny was in motion, and that her life was about to change. Martín received guests like a godfather. People came by to ask for favors or just say hello. "This was all part of his courtship plan," said Ofelia. "I think he not only wanted to impress me, he also wanted me to see him in his element."

Between the handshakes and the backslaps, Martín would talk to Ofelia about the cabaret, the shows they were going to have, the rehearsals, the stars they were lining up. His focus, even when courting, was primarily on Tropicana. "But I found this endearing. He was so obviously in love with something other than me that I could not help but be drawn to his passion."

Two months after their first date, Martín ended lunch by telling Ofelia that he wanted to speak with her mother. Ofelia carefully folded her napkin. "What do you want to talk to her about?" Martín's response was vague, something about wanting to get to know Ofelia's mother better so that she would feel comfortable with the man her daughter was dating. For a moment, Ofelia was convinced. Attention to her mother, Cuca, was one of the things that most endeared her to a man. Once, several years before she had met Martín, she had dumped a boyfriend on the spot for failing to bring her mother a chair at a dance where she was chaperoning. With Martín, Ofelia never had to worry. Though he was not much younger than Cuca herself, he treated her with the deference and respect he would have given his own beloved, departed mother, Tilita.

The following afternoon, as the sun sloped down toward the horizon, tinging the palms and sidewalks with a rosy winter pink, Martín pulled up to Ofelia's apartment in the middle-class neighborhood of Santo Suarez. The local children scurried toward the polished Cadillac, craning their necks to look at the creamy leather interior. Martín said something that made all the children laugh. Ofelia, who was watching from the window, could not hear what it was. Once he was seated in a mahogany rocker opposite Ofelia's mother, Martín got right down to business. "I wanted to speak with you, señora, because I want to marry Ofelia."

Ofelia almost dropped the glass of water she was bringing to him. "Why didn't you ask me first?"

Martín shrugged and fumbled with something in his pocket. "The truth is, that I know that if she says no, you'll say no, so I figured I'd save myself the trouble and ask her first."

Martín's first gift to Ofelia was a band, as is customary in Cuban engagements. ("We would get the *solitario*—the solitary diamond—at the wedding," Ofelia explained.) The band had six .5-carat oval diamonds set in platinum. During the day, when Ofelia drove around town in Martín's second engagement gift—a powder-blue Cadillac Eldorado convertible—she was often startled when the sun flashed off the ring. Overnight she had become a Cuban Cinderella. Her engagement to Martín was reported in all of the major newspapers except the ultra-conservative, Catholic-

slanted *Diario de la Marina,* which would not report a divorced
man's second engagement even if said man ran a full-page ad
every Saturday in that paper, announcing the shows at his world-
famous cabaret. Ofelia became a minor celebrity in her neighborhood. The children would scuffle with each other when she pulled
up, vying for the best spot to watch the marvelous, touch-of-a-
button closure of the Cadillac's electric roof. Fara and La Niña
rushed over to see each new present from Martín, which came almost weekly. After the Cadillac there was a five-inch diamond pin
encrusted with bluish-white baguettes. The pin was made in two
sections so it could be pulled apart for more subdued occasions,
such as when they went to lunch at the Miami Restaurant. Otherwise Martín liked Ofelia to wear the entire pin. He also liked her
to wear diamond earrings instead of the small drop pearls she was
used to. "He adorned me like he adorned Tropicana," remembered
Ofelia wistfully. She was thinking of the two pairs of diamond earrings that he gave her that Christmas they were engaged. There
were the 3-carat studs (six in total) for going out during the day.
For evenings at Tropicana there were inch-long baguette-encrusted,
pear-shaped earrings. It was a king's ransom in jewels. And to be at
Tropicana every night, sitting at a table near the stage and listening
to Olga Guillot sing; watching mambo whiz kids Ana Gloria and
Rolando execute the most complicated moves she'd ever seen; or
tapping her feet to the big band sound of the Armando Romeu orchestra, while Martín roamed like a lion through his kingdom,
shaking a hand, slapping a back, bringing a dizzying number of
socialites, business associates, politicians, actors, and writers (Errol
Flynn! Ernest Hemingway!) to meet his lovely, English-speaking
bride to be—all this was the most extravagant gift of all.

Sometime in early 1952, while Arcos de Cristal was in the
last stages of construction, and while most of Havana was gear-
ing up for the annual carnival, which that year began in March,
Martín asked Ofelia an unusual question. They were at the Miami

Restaurant. He was talking animatedly about the last details of the gala opening of Arcos de Cristal planned for early March, when he abruptly changed the subject. "Ofelia, why do you want to marry me?" Ofelia hesitated. She did not want to lie to him. "I feel great admiration for you. We get along very well . . ." She hesitated, then added, "I am not in love with you, Martín. But I feel that we could have an excellent marriage."

Martín took Ofelia's hand and squeezed it lovingly. "*Gracias, china,*" he said. "I think we're going to get along just fine. Honesty is the one thing I expect from everyone around me."

Martín then waited for her to ask the same of him. But Ofelia was not about to inquire into what she already knew.

BACK IN Glendale, on that balmy night when we were drinking Jimador and talking about destiny and predetermination, Ofelia explained her silence of fifty years ago. "At the time, Martín felt the same way I did. But there was another matter also. Pucha. I already knew about her, and I knew that he was still embroiled in that obsession."

"How did you know?"

She blew a plume of cigar smoke towards the ceiling before answering. "Sometimes he would take me out to see this other woman—*una mulata* of roughly his age—and insist that I dress up and wear my best jewels. I learned that it was a friend of Pucha's. He was trying to get even with her by showing me off."

We were outdoors, under a multi-colored awning. A tray of votive candles sat on the table next to the tequila and beer. Ofelia put down her cigar and picked up her lime and her shot glass. She bit into one of the fiery pickled jalapeños that she had prepared (and which are too hot for both Rosa Sanchez and me). I was right behind her on the tequila. I had more questions. "Why were you willing to marry a man who was in love with someone else?"

She paused, looking at me as if she were about to reveal something profound. The largest of the four cats, named Yellow, sidled up to the glass den doors followed by Rosa Sanchez. "Sometimes you just know what you have to do. Life's full of strange surprises."

CHAPTER 11

The Coup

Early in March 1952, just as the tourist season was ending, the Cuban food and entertainment workers' union went out on strike. Though it came at a time of maximum inconvenience, few were surprised by the walkout. Strikes were a constant feature of the Grau and Prío presidencies. Whether it was the railroad workers, the longshoremen, the bus drivers' union, or the powerful, broad-based labor coalition known as the *Confederación de Trabajadores de Cuba* (CTC), almost once a week the morning paper heralded some new breakdown in labor negotiations, some other union that was threatening to walk if they weren't cut a bigger slice of Cuba's booming postwar economy.

The food workers' strike was aimed specifically at Tropicana, Montmartre, and Sans Souci, by then known as the Big Three of Havana's cabarets. Earlier in his presidency, Prío had used the union's lobbying efforts to justify legalizing casino gambling. Now the union wanted their share of the profits that had accrued because of their efforts. Not that anyone who worked at the Big

Three was doing poorly. The salaries of everyone from the lowliest custodian to the most experienced casino pit boss ranked among the highest in the country. At Tropicana, even the pot scrubbers and prep cooks were making one hundred sixty pesos a month, which was more than a schoolteacher. And this did not include either free meals or tips, which the tourists lavished on everyone from the botones boys who got a few centavos to light cigarettes, to the croupiers, whose weekly gratuities frequently tripled their paychecks.

The cabaret owners, Martín included, argued that the tips generated by the increased business constituted ample enough raise for anyone, but union leaders scoffed at this. The owners were making the kind of money that in Cuba had previously solely been reserved for bankers, sugar barons, and the most rapacious politicians. One only had to consider the sprawling modern homes they were building for themselves on the priciest real estate in Miramar and Marianao, or the latest model Cadillacs and Oldsmobiles they traded in yearly, or their frequent trips to Miami and New York, or the jewels and furs they gave their wives and mistresses (most had both), and, above all, the extravagant cabaret shows they were staging and the capital improvements they were making to their properties.

Though both Sans Souci and Montmartre were in the process of planning renovations at the time of the strike, without question the grandest of the building campaigns was taking place at Tropicana. In those first weeks of March, Arcos de Cristal was in the final days of construction. The building itself had been completed, but there were still plenty of technical and interior-design details to work out before the scheduled March 15, 1952 opening. When the workers walked out, the carpeting had been installed; the furniture (also imported from the United States) waited in containers at the dock. Tropicana's ballerina sculpture had yet to be moved from its location outside the casino to the pool that had been built next to a mamoncillo tree at the entrance of Arcos de Cristal. And there were countless other unfinished details: tiny starlight bulbs that would be set into the vaulted ceiling, and the dramatic lighting in the outdoor trees that would complete the illusion that one was actually outside under the stars rather than in the air-conditioned comfort of an indoor cabaret.

Martín had spared no expense in the construction of Arcos; even in its unfinished state, however, it was obvious that the expenditure was going to pay off. The structure was a masterpiece. The pinnacle of modernity, it also possessed airy sensuality, and there was something thrillingly primeval about all the jungle foliage encroaching on its walls and penetrating its roofline. Arcos already had grandeur. It was going to be the stage for a new level of artistic accomplishment.

"It had the feeling of a great concert hall, the music resonating in the architecture," Ofelia described of the first time she walked through Arcos, when Martín took her on a tour during those early weeks of March. The workers were already striking. She didn't yet know this but she sensed Martín's anxiety. He hurried down the tiers toward the dance floor. Tropicana's chief lighting designer, Ernesto Capote (managers were not required to be a member of any union), was standing on a scaffold, adjusting stage lights. Ofelia watched as Martín stormed over to Max Borges. Two of Borges's technicians were making the final adjustments on the mechanism that would lift the stage above the level of the dance floor. (To cut costs Borges created his own, using four hydraulic lifts of the sort employed in garage bays to repair cars. When initial tests failed—the stage rose, but the movement was jerky and uneven—Borges contacted a friend from his Georgia Tech days who now worked at General Motors, and was advised to increase the width of the tubing that ran the lubricant to the lifts. The stage worked perfectly. To this day the same system remains in place, though it is no longer used.) Martín was impatient with the slowness of the work. "*¿Qué está pasando aquí?* Capote, what's with that giant yellow bulb?" It was the moon, rising early in the winter twilight.

Ofelia had never heard Martín speak like this. "What about those wires dangling from the trees? Can't we hire other people? Aren't there other electricians in this country?" Ofelia sat quietly as Martín raged, watching the silhouetted trees pressed close against the windows. She was concerned for his health. After their engagement he had informed her that he had diabetes, which he managed through careful diet and daily shots of insulin. Earlier, when he had walked past the closed doors of the casino, he had had to sit down. His housekeeper, Pancha, had told Ofelia that Martín's blood sugar had been spiking lately, and that at night he wandered around the house, sleeping barely two hours at a time. Few members of the striking staff had much to do with the actual construction process; that was not the point. Martín liked things to go smoothly. He was used to getting his way. He took the walkout personally, for as he saw it, he had always looked after his employees, and now, when he most needed them, when it was critical that the cabaret stay open and make money to pay for all of the construction, they had deserted him. Originally estimated at around 300,000 pesos, the budget for Arcos had mushroomed to over 500,000, equivalent to $3.4 million today. Martín did not mind spending the money. He was a gambler, after all, and he remained convinced that Arcos de Cristal was the best gamble he had made since he had bought Villa Mina. But he needed the revenue from the casino to accomplish his plans. If things kept going well, Arcos would be only the first of many construction projects at Tropicana that he was determined would live up to what his advertising team was now billing as "The Jewel of the Americas" and "A Paradise Under the Stars." In the press, Martín explained his position. "Many Cubans invest their pesos in buildings and apartments in Miami," he told reporter Edgar Lescano Abella later that year. "I have put everything I have right here, to manage a business that four hundred families depend on, and to build something that my compatriots can feel proud of. And the setting alone is not what makes it. There is comfort and service for the public, a show of the highest quality that gets better every day . . . in the interest of good, healthy competition, I encourage all of my competitors to also do great things for the benefit of Cuba."

CUBA, HOWEVER, had only days to go before it was knocked off course by the most audacious political maneuver since Gerardo Machado seized a second term of office in 1928. In early March of 1952 there were no rumblings of any upcoming calamity. But what a month it had been! Presidential elections were to be held in May. It was also *carnaval* time in Havana, a nonstop partying season that begins on Ash Wednesday (February 27th that year) and continues until Easter. The boulevards of Central Havana were lined with posters for political candidates, strewn with streamers and confetti, and reeking of stale beer. The conga rhythms of Afro-Cuban *comparsa* dance troupes lingered over the Paseo del Prado, mixing with the modern mambo of *cuartetos* and *septetos* that filed past on floats looking like meringue-covered houses. Tropicana's 1952 float featured the Senén Suarez conjunto, a group that played regularly at the club and was known for its danceable *sones*, mambos, cha-chachas, and *guarachas*, aboard a glittering float bedecked with cardboard versions of the Arcos de Cristal arches. The band was flanked by the Tropicana Girls—twelve showgirls dressed relatively modestly in beaded chiffon carnival attire, exposing only a little midriff and cleavage to the winter breezes that blew up from the Straits of Florida. Each weekend of *los carnavales*, floats sponsored by all of the major cabarets and large companies, such as the Polar and Cristal beer companies and Bacardi, and government ministries including the armed forces and the Department of Public Works, shared the same stretch of Prado, from the Capitolio building to the Malecón. The upper echelons of Cuban society retired afterward to private balls given at the Biltmore Yacht Club, Havana Country Club or the Vedado Tennis Club. But the spirit of the season was to be found on the streets. During *los carnavales* the differences between tony Sans Souci, the favorite cabaret of the upper classes, and third-rung rum-and-music clubs—such as the Las Vegas and Tokio in Central Havana, or the Two Brothers Bar, a favorite among American sailors—were unimportant. People wanted to forget about the country's constant problems. Strikes were the least of those problems. Though the price of sugar remained high, there were inexplicable shortages, as well as fluctuations in the price of meat and housing; there were random killings, the culprits often linked to a government in which there was rampant corruption. But a Cuban, as Ofelia says, can always be counted on to put these matters aside for a few days to have a good time watching the floats and *comparsas* down the Prado.

Even the upcoming presidential election failed to stir the emotion that it had several months earlier, when Prío announced that he would not run again. And it was nothing compared to the previous August, when the leading opposition candidate, the ardent, rabble-rousing leader of the Ortodoxo Party, Eduardo "Eddy" Chibás, took out a gun and shot himself in a radio station just after completing a live broadcast. The country was stunned. An avowed reformer (his party's symbol was a broom), Chibás had been considered the leading threat to the Auténticos—the discredited party of Prío and Grau. Every Sunday night people would gather around radios in cafés and hotels to hear him on CMQ railing against what had become an orgy of government graft, mismanagement, and rampant gangsterismo. Whether or not Chibás would have won the 1952 election or not will always be a matter of speculation. For many he was the nation's next great hope, and his funeral drew the biggest crowds in Cuban history. To others, he was simply a spoiler.

Still other Cubans considered him unstable (he frequently challenged opponents to duels) and a demagogue in the making—yet
another politician who said one thing and did another. What is certain is that a Chibás victory would have wreaked havoc on the
gamblers. "Chibás would come to Tropicana every few months,
each time there was a new show," recalled Valentín. "He'd arrive
in a red sports car with a bunch of girls. He never came into the
casino. But he would stand by the door, and when it opened he
would shake his finger at us, to let us know that if he got to power
we were through."

Feared by some, revered by others, Chibás was a Cuban
through and through and therefore a devoted fan of shows such as
the ones at Tropicana. But like so many others before him, and like
the revolutionaries who would eventually take up and further his
reformist ideology, he failed to see that without the casino revenues there would have been no Tropicana showgirls, no orchestras playing until dawn, and certainly no Arcos de Cristal. Chibás's
on-air suicide was precipitated by his failure to produce the hard
evidence that he promised would prove the extent of government
graft once and for all. In the grand scheme of things, stealing from
the nation's coffers would seem far more destructive to the public
welfare than the payoffs made by gamblers to police and other officials. Nevertheless, because they were all part of the same apparatus, gamblers were always targeted when populist politicians
took aim at corruption. The gamblers themselves knew this better
than anyone. "Martín always kept track of the views of the candidates," said Valentín. The Ortodoxo Party candidate who suc-
ceeded Chibás, Dr. Roberto Agramonte, was not going to glean
many votes from Martín and his colleagues. Neither, ultimately,
would Carlos Hevia, the forty-eight-year-old engineer of reportedly scrupulous morals (he was a graduate of the U.S. Naval
Academy at Annapolis) who was selected by the beleaguered Auténticos to bring a modicum of respectability back to Grau and

Prío's party. "The Auténticos were never enthusiastic about gambling," Valentín added. "They gave us the permission, but if it became politically expedient they would have wasted no time retiring it."

But there was a third candidate in 1952, one who gave hope to the gamblers. Former president Fulgencio Batista was back in the presidential race, and he understood the value of casino gambling to Cuba better than any other politician. In the 1930s, when he controlled the country by controlling the army, Batista actively cultivated gambling interests, transferring oversight of the casinos and the lottery to the military. One of his first moves was to change the national lottery from a weekly to a daily draw. He also encouraged Meyer Lansky, whom he had befriended in Prohibition days, to return to Havana and make sure the gambling at the Casino Nacional was clean enough to keep the tourists coming. Batista and his cohorts made fortunes from gambling. Thousands of lottery tickets passed into the hands of favored politicians for resale or to hold for possible winnings. When the winners were announced at nine thirty every night, it was not unusual for the wife or brother of a member of the senate to hold a winning ticket. Unfortunately, many Cubans rationalize this corruption. "It was logical to imagine that the money for the lottery would not exactly go to the place it's supposed to go," remarked Rosa Sanchez. "Anywhere that there's a politician there's going to be corruption. It's just a matter of degree." There were, of course, no written records of these transactions, or of payoffs like the ones Martín made weekly to the Marianao police department as well as to the Havana chief of police. Nonetheless, when Batista decided to temporarily retire in 1944, he was able to do so in luxury, at a gated estate in Daytona Beach. By 1948, when he was elected to the senate—in absentia—his renewed presidential aspirations were more than clear. And the gamblers could not have been happier.

THERE IS no better place on earth to talk about the merits of casino gambling than Las Vegas. Here in the white Nevada desert, among the middle-class ranch houses inhabited by croupiers and cocktail waitresses, it feels practically sacrilegious to question the benefits of legalized gambling. Las Vegas streets bear the names of casinos and entertainers—Jimmy Durante Boulevard, Frank Sinatra Drive, Flamingo Road, Duke Ellington Way—and the entire city was created to satisfy the craving for fun and games, for pleasures licit and licentious. Gambling, wagering, *juegos de azar* (games of chance, as Valentín Jodra calls them) are perfectly acceptable forms of pleasure so long as one engages in them in moderation and realizes that the house eventually always wins.

I met Valentín Jodra one morning at his neat grey ranch house, located a few miles from the Strip, where every new casino-hotel is a colossus that could easily engulf half a dozen of the old Havana nightclubs. Over the months that we'd been talking on the phone, Valentín had grown increasingly eager to tell me stories about Tropicana. "Doña Mina's dog once tried to eat me," he announced as he led me to a table in his spic-and-span kitchen that was piled with photographs. "Mina was very refined. She always tried to teach me English. She was widowed twice, and the *malas lenguas* (literally, "bad tongues") used to say she killed both husbands. Rita Montaner was with us from forty-four to forty-eight. Boy did she have a temper! Once she had a fight with the head of the kitchens and she pulled a knife on him."

The walls of Valentín's house were covered with reminders of his past—for example, a photo of his 1936 elementary school class from Las Alturas de Belén, a poor neighborhood on the outskirts of Havana; and an employee of the year plaque from Caesar's Palace, where Valentín worked as a roulette dealer for twenty years. His wife of fifty years, Ailsa, served us sweet, delicious coffee while he took me around to see the Tropicana pictures. A slightly blurry one from 1955 shows Valentín, by then the *jefe* of the roulette ring, standing beside a roulette wheel adorned with a bronze replica of Rita Longa's *Ballerina*. In another photo, taken in 1949, Valentín smiles broadly among Tropicana's three other roulette dealers. The four croupiers are dressed in black trousers, white dinner jackets, and bow ties. A smiling Alberto Ardura poses between them in a white suit and white shoes, every inch the proud bandleader. Valentín was then twenty-two years old. "Tropicana was run like a family," he said, pointing out Ardura's brother in the picture and the uncle of his own wife, Ailsa. Emeterio López, Valentín's taxi driving uncle, who had originally taken Victor de Correa to see Villa Mina with Mascaró and Bular, was eventually hired to be a shill (a player who works for the house) in the casino. Valentín's brother, Paco, was hired to be the man in the casino who made change for the slot machine players. "If you worked at Tropicana, it was a windfall for the rest of your people. Martín liked to have relatives there together. It gave more of a sense of loyalty."

In 1952, however, Valentín Jodra also went out on strike even though the strike made little sense to him. "I was a union man, involved in union politics. But my loyalty was to Martín." Each day Valentín was out he counted his losses. How much of a raise would he need in order to make up those days? "Usually these things wound up being a wash," he admitted, as we looked at the trio of Tropicana architectural photographs that are identical to the ones that hang opposite Ofelia's bar. "There's Arcos de Cristal, there's the outdoor cabaret, and the casino after the renovation," he said, with the same paternal tone he used earlier, when he took me through a roomful of photos of his children and grandchildren. Valentín continued talking about union issues, strikes, and the differences between working at a big corporation like Caesar's Palace and the family business where he got his start as a roulette dealer. Though he framed some of the comparisons in terms of financial gain—"In Las Vegas you have to share the tips among all the dealers, whereas at Tropicana I would often go home with two, three hundred pesos a night"—the photos on the wall betrayed him. Valentín may have been a committed union man but, like Martín—and like Ofelia—Tropicana meant everything to him.

By 1952, Valentín's daily routine was dictated by the moment at which he put on his tuxedo. He would wake up in the early afternoon, read his paper, spend time with Ailsa and his children, eat a late breakfast, then bide his time until it was time to head for the casino. When he crossed beneath the arching neon sign and between the flanking acacia trees, his world opened up. He told me he felt he was joining the great rhythm that made Havana the liveliest nocturnal city in the Western Hemisphere. He was a vital part of what fueled it all, as key as a musician or a dancer. On a typical night, after greeting Rodolfo Cabeda at the valet drop-off, he would be accosted by Martín: "*Oye,* chiquitico, keep your eye out for a fat *Americano* with a beard. The word is that he cheats"; or, "Don't forget that Don Jesús is coming. Make sure he doesn't exceed the ten thousand peso credit limit." No matter how busy the club was, Martín always managed to seek Valentín out—to ask after his family, to see how the house was doing that night, to have a word with him about Saturday's bolita run, to share any number of confidences with the roulette dealer to whose child he was godfather.

Striking against Tropicana was therefore anathema to Valentín. In March of 1952, he did not have to wait long to get back to work.

JUST AFTER midnight on March 10, 1952, less than a week after the strike began, three black Buick sedans rolled out of a luxurious country villa located on the outskirts of Havana. The cars were packed with army officers—eleven in all. Each sped off in a different direction to avoid arousing suspicion. Within the hour, the Buicks convened at the gates of Campamento Columbia, the

Marianao-based headquarters of the Cuban army. The officer on duty waved the cars through the checkpoint. Armed men stepped out of the first two cars. Fulgencio Batista stepped out of the third sedan, flanked by two high-ranking officers.

The presidential election was only two months away, but on this particular evening Batista was not campaigning. In full military uniform, he strode across the manicured grounds of Campamento Columbia, stopping first at the headquarters of the Sixth Regiment. The officer in charge handed over control to Batista without a word of protest. The rest happened with alarming alacrity and surgical precision. The troops at Columbia were mobilized, their officers—those who opposed the *golpe de estado*, "coup d'etat"—placed under arrest. Other Batista loyalists took command of the army, the navy, the Havana police department, and La Cabaña, the largest Spanish garrison in the Americas. They also commandeered the telephone exchange, which allowed them to monitor their opposition as word of the *golpe* spread.

By dawn, President Prío, who had been at his own country estate (his brother, Antonio, had been dancing at Sans Souci when he received word of the coup) was back at the presidential palace, desperately, if ineffectually, trying to deal with a fait accompli. Later that morning, the radio stations began to broadcast news that Batista had taken control in order to save the country from "chaotic conditions which endangered lives and property." The streets were deserted. Tanks surrounded the presidential palace. Scores of university students gathered outside to protest and to demand that their elected president, who was packing his family to leave for Mexico, mount more than a tepid response to Batista's audacity. Eventually, inevitably, there was a bit of bloodshed, but it was minor considering the magnitude of what had happened. On March 10, 1952, constitutional rule was revoked on the island of Cuba. As of this writing, more than fifty years later, it has not been restored.

"Within a day of the *golpe*, we were ordered back to work. No raise, no change in benefits. But for me it was a relief." Valentín rubbed his eyes beneath his heavy black-rimmed glasses. I had been asking questions about March 10, and he was weary and unusually reticent. Here was a man who could wax enthusiastically for hours on the telephone, sometimes making Ailsa hold his dinner while he described the workings of roulette and the ins and outs of financing the bolita, or shared a tidbit of gossip about Victor de Correa or the Tropicana partners. Politics, on the other hand, tired him out. In the solarium of his Las Vegas ranch house—an air-conditioned patio that allowed the outdoors in ("Something like Arcos," I said, though Valentín dismissed this with a gesture)—I began to understand the reasons for this.

I had a tough time leaving Cuba. I sent Ailsa and the girls ahead in 1961. I was trying to leave with some money and that couldn't be done with a visa waiver. So I got together with nine guys leaving on a boat from Santiago de Cuba. But one morning, when we stopped to have breakfast, I saw one of the men make a phone call. It made me suspicious. When we got to the city of Holguin we were apprehended. I had about seventeen hundred dollars and another six thousand in jewelry. Also three hundred hidden in my passport. At my trial the prosecutor asked why I was trying to leave and I just said I missed my wife and kids terribly. I said, "Look, I would've left on a piece of eggshell if that's all that was available." I was in jail for about four months. They gave me electric shock treatments. I was so depressed. In the press they said I was crazy and an assassin. When they let me go and I returned to Havana I was desperate. I had no passport and no means to leave Cuba. My brother went to the secret police and spoke with people there. They hadn't recorded the fact that they'd found money in the passport, which means that someone had kept it. So my brother mentioned this, and under threat of this accusation he got the passport back. I applied to leave the country again, but I learned that the file was placed in what they call *el cementerio* [the dead zone]. There was this guy that owed me a big favor. He was an old *communista* who had no work and four kids, and earlier I'd gotten him a job at El Panchín [a cabaret]. The guy was now working for the government. I don't want to say his name because he might still have family in Cuba. We met in some dark bushes at the beach at Santa Fe. The guy said, "I'll do it, but you know this can cost me the firing squad." Three days later, I got a telegram saying that my application was accepted. What the guy did was take out someone's file from the active drawer and replace it with mine. I owe this man my life. Not long ago he called me from Mexico. I sent him two hundred dollars.

After telling me the story, Valentín pointed out a photographic list on the solarium wall bearing the title *"Los Presidentes Electos de Cuba,"* the elected presidents of Cuba. It showed every Cuban president elected from 1902 to 1952, the period of the republic. In fifty years, Cuba had seventeen presidents, without counting the five of the Pentarquia who served concurrently for a few days following the ouster of Machado. Batista's smiling face fills the 1944 slot. Valentín pointed this out to me, adding quickly, "Prío was the last elected president. After 1952, there is no one."

It is hard to tell the Tropicana story and avoid politics. The history of the cabaret is entwined with the history of a very young republic. Cuba's experiment with democracy was deeply flawed and lasted only fifty years. During those years, the aspirations of young middle-class Cubans, particularly in Havana, resembled those of their neighbors to the north. This was especially true in the early 1950s, when the latest American products were as readily available in Havana as they were in Chicago and New York, and more quickly than they were in Peoria, Spokane, Akron, and Indianapolis.

When Valentín began working as a botones boy at Tropicana it was for one reason only: to make enough money to feed his mother and his siblings. Becoming a roulette dealer was his way up and out. It allowed him, in 1951, to marry and provide well for his children. Eventually he even bought a house. "Only Martín Fox made it a reality," said Valentín, his voice filled with emotion. Martín paid for the house, taking his repayment, interest free, in small monthly installments. That was a practice Martín would repeat with numerous devoted employees, including Ernesto Capote, Tropicana's lighting designer; Gladys Torres, Martín's personal secretary; and Armando Freyre, one of Tropicana's attorneys. Here was the American dream, Cuban style. Nonetheless, in Havana, one always had to be ready for sudden disturbances. Strikes, shortages, random violence, graft that seemed never ending. You'd wake up in the morning and, while drinking your *café con leche,* read in *El Mundo* or *El País* that the markets were out of beef and the army was commandeering cattle from the provinces. You might wonder how this could this happen given that the price of sugar was so high and that tourists were coming down in droves. Then your eye might catch another article telling you that three youths had been gunned down outside the Café Carmelo in broad daylight. The assailants had fled in a black Oldsmobile; no one saw the license plate. You might sigh wearily, bite into your buttered toast, and wonder if you knew the murdered boys. Probably you didn't. The boys were probably radicals, most likely members of one of the gangster groups like MSR, whose leader, Masferrer, "rode around Cuba in his Cadillac like a pirate king, surrounded by bodyguards," according to historian Hugh Thomas. Maybe they were union agitators, communists, members of the rabble-rousing Ortodoxos. There were many reasons to get killed in Cuba in the 1940s and 1950s. In late 1951, a month after Eddy Chibás's suicide, masked gunmen shot up the office of the editor of the Communist Party newspaper. But one did not necessarily have to be a communist to be a target. A note, in *Newsweek*'s Pan American Week section, dated September 23, 1946, described the situation perfectly:

CUBA: Killers Beware

In Havana last week the toughest high-ranking officer in the Cuban Army tackled the biggest job of his career. General Abelardo Gómez, formerly second in command of the army and newly appointed chief of the National police set about stemming Cuba's frightening murder wave.

Since President Ramón Grau San Martín took office in 1944, 48 Cubans have been shot to death in the streets. Until last week not one killer had been caught. The murder pattern is always the same. A speeding automobile draws up behind the victim's car or overtakes him as he walks along the street. Its occupants open fire with pistols, machine guns or sawed-off shotguns. Then they speed away. Most of the victims have been former officials of the pre-Grau Machado or Batista dictatorships who were brutally active against revolutionary organizations. Cubans believe the killers are paying off old scores.

Hugh Thomas described dozens of murders during the Grau and Prío administrations. Many were the result of private feuds or internal power struggles within gangster groups. Grau's adopted son, Gustavo Ortíz Faes, was implicated in the death of Manolo Castro, Grau's own state secretary of sports. The leader of the university's student union, Justo Fuentes, was shot in 1949 by an assailant who then hid in the home of Senator "Paco" Prío, the president's brother. Jesús Menendez, the Negro sugar workers' leader and a prominent Communist, was killed by an army captain. And Aracelio Iglesias Díaz, the secretary of the communist maritime workers' union, was gunned down by an old rival. The list goes on and on. Finally, there is this item from Ruby Hart Phillips, the *New York Times* correspondent:

> On July 4th, a group of gunmen invaded the court where the case against former President Ramón Grau San Martín for misappropriation of $174,000,000 was being investigated and stole all the documents of the proceedings. This was to become the famous Case No. 82 against Grau, but it never came to trial and it did not deter Grau from running for President in 1954. No one was ever arrested for the stealing of the documents and none of the documents was ever found.

In the wake of all this violence, Batista's return was, for many Cubans, just another chapter in the country's never-ending drama. *Diario de la Marina* welcomed back the strongman as a prodigal son. *Time* put him on its cover again, this time on April 21, 1952. Batista stands in front of a Cuban flag above the caption: "Cuba's Batista: He got past democracy's sentinels." There was deep outrage over the *golpe*, but it came primarily from students at the University of Havana. On the morning of March 10, anti-Batista student groups—many of them rivals who had been murdering each other prior to the *golpe de estado*—mobilized and headed for the presidential palace. They asked for arms and offered to defend the country against Batista and the army. Their efforts fizzled out in the frenzy of Prío's departure and the general public's acquiescence. Instead, they protested, ending their vigils on April 4 with a mock funeral in which a copy of Cuba's Constitution of 1940 was interred before a bust of José Martí in Vedado.

In the rural town of Sancti Spiritus, where Rosa Sanchez was a student intern at a radio station, March 10 was followed by several days of protest. Then the outrage sputtered out, and things settled back to normal. "The Auténticos were all a collection of corrupt losers and the country was inundated with killings during their time," explained Rosa. "So after a few days we just shrugged and accepted that Batista was back to get things in order, and that eventually he would hold elections. No one expected the power to take hold of him the way it did. And as we say, '*mas vale malo conocido que bueno por conocer,*'" which essentially translates as going with the devil you know rather than the one you don't.

At Tropicana, the staff got back to work and readied for the opening of Arcos de Cristal.

CHAPTER 12

Mambo a la Tropicana

What the heck is a Mambo?
from Vaughn Monroe's "They Were Doin' the Mambo"

March 15, 1952: the ceiling sparkled with incandescent pinpoint lights. The men were in black tie, the women in evening gowns designed in Paris and New York (some of them imitations done by Havana's savvy dressmakers). March breezes rippled through Villa Mina's jungle foliage. Leaves pressed against the glass. Champagne flowed, the flashbulbs popped. Though it was still early on Arcos de Cristal's opening night, Armando Romeu's Tropicana orchestra already had the dance floor packed.

Now in its tenth year, the orchestra played a steady catalog of all the latest Cuban dance trends—mambo, rhumba, and the brand-new cha-cha-cha that had become the rage with Americans who could manage its moderate one-two, one-two-three beat. Its strength, however, was its interpretations of American big band music. Count Basie, Duke Ellington, Les Brown, Ray Anthony, Fletcher Henderson, and Stan Kenton were the bread and butter of Romeu's repertoire. The handsome blond conductor transcribed their arrangements off of records that were brought to him as soon as they were released in the United States. Often working in collaboration with the orchestra's drummer, Guillermo Barreto, and lead trumpeter, Arturo "Chico" O'Farrill, Romeu would pore over the records for hours, deciphering notes and phrasing with the rigor of a doctoral candidate.

There was a steady flow of jazz talent between New York and Havana. The Cubans went north, looking for work and the authentic sounds of swing and bebop. They might spend an entire month of nights watching their compatriot Machito and his Afro-Cuban All Stars fire up the dance crowds at New York's Palladium. They would seek out other Cubans, like *congüero* and former Tropicana star Chano Pozo, or the composer and arranger Mario Bauzá, the consummate musician's musician, whose credits included writing "Tanga," the first Latin jazz tune. (Bauzá also introduced Chano Pozo to Dizzy Gillespie, and Gillespie to Cab Calloway, and possibly most important of all, he was one of the musicians who urged the big band conductor Chick Webb to hire, in 1934, a then-unknown seventeen-year-old singer named Ella Fitzgerald.) When one of the American greats, or even near-greats, came to Cuba for a visit or a gig, local musicians would spread the word among themselves and hope for an opportunity to talk jazz and *descargar* (jam) at a jazz bar like the Tokio in Central Havana, or at a private home in Marianao. The Americans who came south to Havana eventually found Armando Romeu.

Born in 1911 into what was Cuba's most important musical family, Romeu's career as a musician was assured before his birth. His uncle, Antonio María Romeu, was Cuba's first piano soloist for dance music and a well-known composer of *danzones*. The Antonio María Romeu *danzón* orchestra, a favorite of Cuba's top social set, cut dozens of records before World War I and toured New York in the 1920s (bringing the then-seventeen-year-old Mario Bauzá to play clarinet). Romeu's father, Armando Romeu Marrero, was a radio music pioneer in Cuba and the leader of a popular *charanga* band, consisting of piano, bass, percussion, flute, and violins. By the time the young Armando was thirteen years old, he had learned to play flute, clarinet, and piano from his father and uncle and was playing clarinet with both of their bands. In 1924 he heard his first swing band, and everything changed for him. It happened at the Jockey Club, where his father's *charanga* band was alternating sets with American saxophonist Ted Naddy's orchestra. Armando bought a tenor saxophone from Naddy and soon he was listening to nothing but jazz on the radio. He began seeking out the jazz bands in Havana, playing at all of the small clubs as well as with the Casino Nacional and Montmartre house orchestras. He devoured the music. He followed it and sometimes the music seemed to find him as well. In 1932, Alfredo Brito, the first leader of the Edén Concert and Tropicana orchestras, sought the young tenor saxophonist for a tour of Spain with his celebrated Siboney Orchestra. A year later, Romeu formed his own small jazz band at Victor de Correa's Edén Concert. He began poring over the music of American greats. He heard them in Havana, where they came looking for inspiration and, sometimes, musicians. He met them in the bars and saw them at the cabarets—Chuck Howard, Paul Whiteman, and the jazz conductor and showman Cab Calloway. In 1940, nearly a decade before Montmartre first brought the "hi-de-ho" man, as Calloway was known, to its stage, Romeu had already formed what was then the best jazz band in the country, the Bellamar Orchestra at Sans Souci. It was a short-lived gig—the outbreak of World War II forced the swanky cabaret to temporarily close in 1942. After that, Correa, who had parted ways with Alfredo Brito, called Romeu and asked him to assemble a new house orchestra for Tropicana. Since then, the Tropicana orchestra had featured the greatest talent in the country, jazzmen who took the big band and bebop sound of their North American counterparts and fused it to their country's native folk music to create the sound known as Latin jazz. Havana brimmed with great musical talent—sextets, septets, troubadors, combos, all-girl rumba bands—but the jazzmen were the vanguard. They searched out new trends and new sounds, and when they found them, in New York especially, they bathed the notes in rum and sugar and served them to a public that craved novelty and lived to dance.

Jazz and Cuban music have been intertwined since the onset of the twentieth century. Jelly Roll Morton, one of the undisputed fathers of jazz, believed that "if you can't manage to put tinges of Spanish in your tunes, you will never be able to get the right seasoning, I call it, for jazz." By 1910, *danzón* bands were playing in New Orleans, and all-black ragtime bands were coming down to play in Havana. There are also reports of jazz being brought down earlier to Santiago de Cuba by American troops who fought in the ironically named Spanish-American War. By the mid-1940s, the migration of Cubans and, more importantly, Puerto Ricans, to New York had completely "Latinized" jazz. Jazz phrasing and improvisation had also transformed Cuban music. In New York, Machito and his Afro-Cubans, led by Mario Bauzá together with his brother-in-law Frank "Machito" Grillo, blended jazz phrasing with the upbeat *son montunos* of the Cuban countryside. The Afro-Cubans recorded prodigiously and played all over New York: uptown and downtown; in the Puerto Rican clubs of Spanish Harlem; and most notably, at the Palladium, where they were the main house band from 1946 into the 1960s.

At the time, the most popular of the new rhythms was mambo—a music and dance style with rapid-fire syncopation and jazz-fueled improvisation. The word *mambo* comes from the Bantu African dialect. Arsenio Rodríguez, one of the early founders of the genre, whose grandfather was a slave from the Congo, claimed that the word came from the phrase, *abre cuto güirí mambo*, which means "open your ears and listen up." "It's hard to give a precise definition for the mambo," writes musicologist Ned Sublette. "It can be instrumental or vocal. It's an up-tempo, horn-driven music, but there are slower mambos. It's big band music, but you can play it with a combo if you must. It was the biggest musical craze in the United States in the days immediately preceding rock-and-roll, peaking around 1953, and it has been fabulously recycled as nostalgia."

Mambo began in the mid-1940s. By the early 1950s, American dance charts were filled with mambo, many recorded by American artists such as Perry Como ("Papa Loves Mambo," 1954) and Rosemary Clooney ("Mambo Italiano," 1955). Vaughn Monroe's "They Were Doin' the Mambo" was reported to be RCA Victor's biggest-selling record in 1954, the same year that *Newsweek, Time,* and the *New York Times Magazine* featured articles on "mambomania." The dance academies were filled with mambo novices and dozens of books were published trying to explain the impossibly complex moves, simplifying them for Americans. Even Bill Haley and the Comets got into the mambo mood with "Mambo Rock."

There has been much debate about who originated the mambo. Among Cubans, especially of the "mambo generation," the subject is as vital as politics—but generally, Dámaso Pérez Prado, a pianist who was a native of Matanzas, the colonial port town in north-central Cuba near Martín Fox's birthplace, is credited with popularizing the rhythm. Musicologist Helio Orovio, author of half a dozen books on Cuban music including the weighty tome *Diccionario de la música cubana,* has probably given more thought to the subject than anyone else. "The mambo rhythm originates from two separate traditions," he explained to me one damp October afternoon in Havana. "The earliest mambos come from the López brothers, Orestes, and Israel, who's known as Cachao. As early as 1929, the brothers' band was pulling the sound out of the formal *danzones* that they played, using mainly the bass and the piano for the syncopation and the violins to hold the melody. Separately, around 1940, Arsenio Rodríguez begins to introduce a similar syncopation in the livelier *son montunos* that he was playing with his group. But it was Dámaso," added Orovio, speaking of the leading Cuban musician of his generation as if he were a neighbor, "who gave the complete structure to the new Caribbean genre. Dámaso's saxophones took on the syncopation. The trumpets held the melody. Dámaso gave it speed and swing, he jazzed it up."

Orovio and I talked about music while sitting at a table on the patio of the Union of Artists and Writers building (UNEAC), located in a mansion built in 1920 for Juan Gelats, a banker who reaped huge benefits during the "dance of the millions." UNEAC is a place of constant movement. Sculptors, poets, experimental filmmakers, and pianists who had come to meet about projects, or seek permission for travel milled around the marble entryway of the mansion. Cuba still affords few luxuries to most of its residents, but artists enjoy the privilege of travel. In the 1990s the island again turned into the artistic mecca it was in the mambo heyday. Cuban dancers, musicians, and singers performed regularly on American and European stages. The work of Cuban sculptors, painters, and video artists became a standard feature of international museum exhibits, biennials, and galleries. The rage for Cuban visual art reached a pinnacle during the seventh Havana Biennial in 2000, when groups of collectors, on tours organized by almost every major museum in the United States, vied with each other to purchase work directly from the studios of Havana's top artists.

The talk on the UNEAC patio is sometimes of travel, but mostly it is of music. The union often hosts *descargas*, jam sessions, here. The musicians use the mansion's porte cochere as a stage, and the audience sits around white plastic tables, nursing drinks from a nearby bar. Even when there is no show, the patio is filled in the afternoons, mostly with musicians. Often the conversations wind up drifting over to the lively, white-haired Orovio, who is a fixture in the patio every afternoon.

"Like many musicians of his generation, Dámaso was obsessed with jazz, and that's what led him to these heights of improvisation," explained Orovio to me over shots of rum with lime. ("Don't order the *mojitos* here, they're overpriced," he counseled, referring to the Cuban national cocktail, a mix of rum, lime, sugar, a minty herb called *yerba buena,* and sparkling water.) Orovio's uncle was a trombonist with the Tropicana orchestra and he spent his teen-age years there, hanging around musicians. The day we met he drummed his fingers on the plastic tabletop to illustrate how Pérez Prado's mambo took a jazz-fueled leap from the scheme that had been developed by both the López brothers and the Arsenio Ro-dríguez band. The subtleties were lost on me, but soon a crowd formed around us and the scholar was transformed into a musician. "*Claro, Maestro,* it was *el jazz!*" affirmed a lanky, deep-voiced bass player whom Orovio introduced as the stepson of one of Tropi-cana's 1950s prep cooks and the brother of César Pedrozo, the vir-tuoso pianist for the salsa band Los Van Van. "*Pero, Maestro,* wasn't it like this?" said a drummer, slapping the table and begin-ning to play. A third musician joined in, the conversation heated up, and I picked up our cups to keep them from jumping off the table.

ROMEU'S FORTE was American big band music, and his orchestra played a list of standards that were favorites on both sides of the Straits of Florida—"Blue Skies," "I've Got Rhythm," "I Can't Get Started," "One O'clock Jump"—mixed in with the mambos that were now being written by all Cuban composers, including members of the band. Few of the patrons on the Arcos de Cristal dance floor probably knew this, but the musicians in the pit were all jazz stars, with a following that extended from Havana to Harlem and Paris. Barreto was the island's first real bebop drum-mer. Pianist Ramón "Bebo" Valdés was one of the island's best improvisationalists and a composer of mambos whose output rivaled that of Pérez Prado. Chico O'Farrill was, by 1952, a legend in his own right: before his stint with Romeu, he had played with Benny Goodman in New York, and composed "Undercurrent Blues" for Goodman as well as "Cuban Episode" for Stan Kenton. O'Farrill's works of Afro-Cuban jazz, written for Machito and Dizzy Gillespie, were so impressive that when he finally met his idol, Count Basie, the great bandleader expressed his amazement that a white person could write such arrangements. Romeu himself penned "Mambo a la Kenton" based on the tunes of his idol, bandleader Stan Kenton. The band's sound was full, yet effervescent. "You could barely stay in your seat when they played," said Ofelia. Of course, Ofelia rarely made it onto Tropicana's dance floor; she was usually by Martín's side, or at her table, entertaining Martín's guests while he worked.

On the night of the opening of Arcos de Cristal, those guests consisted of the crème de la crème of Cuba's press and *farándula*. Tropicana's public relations office had made sure that anyone who was anyone in Cuba received a personal invitation with their name engraved, in the Tropicana font, next to the ballerina logo. Ofelia's memory was murky about many of these names, but she recalled Don Galaor, the entertainment columnist for *Bohemia*, one of the nation's most popular magazines, and her and Martín's close friends Senator Santiago Rey and his wife, Berta. "Even President Batista was invited," said Ofelia. Batista declined to come, however, the opening taking place a mere week after the *golpe de estado*. But he sent his good wishes with General Fernandez Miranda, who communicated them to Ardura on behalf of his brother-in-law.

Ardura was the other reason why, by 1952, Tropicana was *the* place for jazz in Cuba. No one with a superficial knowledge of Martín Fox's dour-faced partner could have imagined that Ardura was a jazz lover. ("*Cómo?* Are you sure?" exclaimed Ofelia and

Rosa incredulously, when I showed them a note to that effect in
Cubano Be, Cubano Bop, a history of jazz in Cuba written by musicologist and alto saxophonist Leonardo Acosta.) But Bebo Valdés
echoed the sentiment. "One day I was at Rita Montaner's house rehearsing and I heard this clarinet playing [Cole Porter's] 'Begin the
Beguine,'" explained the pianist recently. "I looked out and saw
this young man playing. When I left we said hello to each other.
Another day I saw him and we waved. The next time I saw him
was in 1948 when I began at Tropicana. Alberto Ardura was that
young man."

I spoke with Valdés in the lobby of the Meridien Hotel in Los
Angeles two days after he had won a Latin Grammy award for *Lágrimas Negras,* an album of Cuban boleros he had recorded together with Spanish flamenco singer Diego "El Cigala." Though
it was early on a Saturday morning, the tall and lanky eighty-five-
year-old pianist was smartly dressed in a grey suit, white shirt with
cuff links, and a purple silk tie. Like the Buena Vista Social Club's
Compay Segundo, Ibrahim Ferrer, and Omara Portuondo, Valdés
was in the middle of a major late-in-life career surge. *Lágrimas
Negras* had been nominated in four Latin Grammy categories, and
it was selling well in Europe, Mexico, and the United States. The
night before our meeting I heard Bebo and Cigala in concert at Los
Angeles's Conga Room. Valdés's piano playing was clean and
forceful, a beautiful backdrop for the flamenco singer's raspy, ex-
pressive voice. The near-sellout crowd clapped wildly after every
number.

Though his Grammy win was still fresh, Bebo (as Valdés insisted I call him) was most animated when talking about Tropicana. "The music would start at nine with the conjunto Senén
Suarez. We'd come in later at ten thirty and play until four. Unless there was a need for us to stay later, then we'd stay until whenever. Armando [Romeu] was only interested in international
music, the big band sound. So when it came to the Cuban stuff for

the shows, I did the arrangements. Rodney had a piano player for the rehearsals. I'd go and watch as the show progressed and work out the arrangements for the band." Bebo began at Tropicana in 1948 and left in 1958 to form his own full-time conjunto at the Sevilla Biltmore. "Victor de Correa's checks couldn't be cashed for fifteen days, and when it rained he didn't pay," he told me conspiratorially.

If I had learned anything by this point, it's that former Tropicana regulars loved the gossip and the inside stories. "The most famous mambo dancer—I'm not going to say her name, but you know who I mean—was actually the daughter of Miguel Matamoros," said Bebo, nodding and putting a tapered finger to his lips. Matamoros, composer of the beautiful *son bolero*, *"Lágrimas Negras,"* which Bebo and Cigala had just recorded, was one of the most important singers and composers in Cuban history. The implication in Bebo's story was that Matamoros's life itself resembled a bolero. But the most deliciously ribald tale Bebo told me pertained to a 1952 mambo he composed in honor of Miguel Angel Blanco, Tropicana's notoriously rakish master of ceremonies. I had heard many times the story of this mambo, titled "Güempa," based on Cuban slang for "good lay." Yet there was nothing like hearing it from Bebo himself.

Miguel Angel liked to brag about his conquests. He was always coming in and saying, "I slept with that one, and with that one." *Vaya,* to hear him talk, there wasn't a single girl that didn't pass through his hands. One day this *guapo* [tough guy] came to see him at the club. Apparently he'd messed with the guy's wife, and the man was itching for a fight. While this was happening, I walked by him and said, *"Oye, Güempa,* don't take them all for yourself, leave some for us." *Güempa,* of course, comes from *buen palo,* and you know what that means. And even with the guy standing there,

[Blanco] responded, *"Mientras que el caballo se enderece me
meto todas las que yo quiera* [As long as the horse straightens
up I'll take as many as I can get]."

Bebo was thrilled to hear that Ofelia was alive and writing a
book about Tropicana. "Martín Fox was the best boss I ever had,"
he exclaimed. "He'd sometimes be around while we rehearsed.
He'd just stare at the trees, the mangoes, like a man in love. I've
never met a man as good in business as he was. But Alberto Ardura was like my brother. He was my boss but he treated me like
family. He was a man who really loved music—a musician in his
own right."

Ardura's love of jazz might have been one reason Tropicana
hired Woody Herman's octet in 1950, and Cab Calloway, right
after Calloway had finished his contract at Montmartre. Given that
he was in charge of entertainment at Tropicana, Ardura was probably aware of the vast tourist marketing appeal of a Cab Calloway
or a Josephine Baker. But this could not explain why he was instrumental in opening Tropicana on Sunday afternoons so that jazz
musicians, Cuban and American, could jam together in a free, un-
structured environment. Those legendary sessions, which were the
brainchild of Guillermo Barreto, were among the first meetings of
the Club Cubano de Jazz. Every Sunday afternoon, a quintet that
featured Barreto on drums, Bebo on piano, tenor saxophonist
Rafael "Tata" Palau (who, according to Leonardo Acosta, "was
heavily into the cool style started by Lester Young"), trumpeter
Alejandro "el Negro" Vivar, and his brother Fernando Vivar on
bass, would get together to play bebop classics and to jam with all
comers. Tropicana was the place where everyone played together.
Members of Romeu's orchestra would mix with those of the Sans
Souci orchestra; or the house bands from Radio Kramer or Radio
Artalejo, which specialized in jazz; or the dozens of smaller com-
bos that could be heard at El Faraon, La Gruta, Tokio Bar, El Gato
Tuerto, or El Atelier, to name a few of the clubs. Big name Amer-

icans came also—Woody Herman was there; Sarah Vaughan joined in when she was in Havana, appearing at Sans Souci.

"We asked her to sing 'How High the Moon,' but she said, *"No puedo,* that's Mama's song!" recalled Gilberto Torres, a seventy-five-year-old self-proclaimed *jazzista* whose home in the Santa Amalia district of Havana has been, for the past thirty years, the gathering place of a spirited, almost all-black private dance club called *La esquina del jazz,* "The Jazz Corner." To *jazzistas* in the know, "Mama" is Ella Fitzgerald. Vaughan was reluctant to sing her colleague's signature material, though in the end she did. On a recent Saturday night meeting of the dance club, an ebullient Gilberto, shouting above Louis Armstrong's rendition of "What a Wonderful World" and the sound of expert dancers' swishing feet, said of Vaughan's performance that night, "She kept on going for an hour, with us clapping, barely able to stay seated."

In that remote corner of Havana, located a twenty-minute taxi ride from the bustling tourist sections and a half hour from Tropicana, I had found the mirror image to Ofelia's Bar and Grill in Glendale. Gilberto's house was smaller, and it possessed few of the amenities of Glendale, but the basics were all there: a bar with 1950s tiki brass lights, a shelf lined with whiskey, rum, and vodka bottles (empty and used purely as adornment), a wall of photographs of the jazz greats who had visited, and a good sound system, which was the reason for everyone's coming together the first Saturday of every month to dance. Right then the tune was "Don't Mean a Thing if it Ain't Got that Swing," as played by Sonny Rollins. As at Ofelia's, the music was present, urgent, more than a nostalgic background. The dancers, who were mainly in their seventies (some were also in their sixties and eighties, but of the twenty people present, only one was under forty) moved expertly across the cracked tile floor. Those sitting the number out sipped industrial-strength rum from coffee cups and shot glasses. At Ofelia's the crowd was generally made up of white Cuban-Americans who listened to Olga Guillot, Celia Cruz, Pérez Prado, and Benny Moré. Those gathered in Santa Amalia were black Cubans, and the music was American swing and bebop. "We live for jazz," explained Roberto Cabrera, another eager raconteur who worked as a tennis instructor when he was not dancing. "We followed it [in the '50s] from bar to bodega to radio station. When the Club Cubano de Jazz met at Tropicana, you would find us there en masse, every Sunday afternoon, in Arcos de Cristal."

Arcos de Cristal sits dark most nights now. The contemporary show at Tropicana tends to be performed in Bajo las Estrellas, the outdoor portion of the cabaret, where the drama of the trees and starlit catwalks plays to the expectation of the tourist public. On a recent trip to Cuba—the same one in which I visited La esquina del jazz—I snuck over to peer through Arcos' glass windows while my tour group settled into their seats. A thick-trunked mamoncillo blocked my view of the stage. I realized that this was the same tree used for an opening night publicity shot with las Mamboletas de Gustavo Roig, a troupe of ten young dancers wearing strapless, shirred bathing suits, fishnet stockings, ballet slippers, and boxy mesh hats, who posed on the gnarled trunks and branches for Muñiz, the official Tropicana photographer. Las Mamboletas headlined the opening night show, together with comedian Harry Mimo and mambo dancers Ana Gloria and Rolando. But the real star of that evening was Arcos itself, a modern masterpiece. The building would earn Max Borges his second medal from the College of Architects and lead to more work with the Guajiro. The next project would be the expansion of Tropicana's outdoor cabaret space to increase seating capacity and extend the proscenium stage.

"That night is a blur for me," said Ofelia of the opening of Arcos de Cristal. "I remember the music, I remember Max. I remember Martín walking here and there, and me trying to keep up with all the names, all the people. You have to realize this was my first official stepping out as Martín's fiancée. That's when I realized that being Martín's wife was not just going to be glamorous, it was going to be work."

"In what way?" I asked.

"It was a public relations job," interjected Rosa Sanchez. "Ofelia had to entertain his guests. She had to dress up every night, wear heels and makeup, look stunning, and make conversation with people that she did not know, sometimes—often—in English. Try speaking a foreign language, even one you know well, for a few hours at a time. And she did this night after night for nine years. I'll tell you this, I could not have done it."

"Oh, come on, Rosa," said Ofelia, getting up and going—so gracefully, I thought—to the bar to refill her martini glass. "It was a life set to music. What could be better?"

The only thing I could think of was a life where she occasionally got to dance. That only happened once at Tropicana—on October 5, 1952. On a gusty autumn evening, with several late-season hurricanes threatening the celebration, Martín Fox Zamora and Ofelia Suarez y González were married after an eight-month engagement. Because of Martín's divorce, the wedding was a civil affair, performed in Martín's office by notary public and lawyer Carlos Saladrigas. Saladrigas had once been supported by Batista in his run for the presidency against Grau, and now served as president of the Consultative Council, a Batista-appointed panel that replaced the elected Congress and was intended to bestow the military junta with a semblance of legislative respectability. There were eight witnesses to the nuptials, including Atilano Taladrid, Ofelia's brother-in-law, Max Borges, Alberto Ardura, Oscar Echemendia, and Armando Freyre. It was a Saturday evening at six. Before Tropicana opened for the night, the tables at Arcos de Cristal were set with white linens and decorated with enormous bouquets of white orchids. One hundred of Martín and Ofelia's friends,

including General Fernandez Miranda and several other government officials who were friendly to gambling, feasted on lobster
thermidor and filet mignon and danced to Armando Romeu's
music. The bride wore a cap-sleeved lavender chiffon dress with
an orchid corsage. In her ears were the inch-long baguette-encrusted
earrings, and on her finger, in addition to the band with six .5-carat
diamonds, was her wedding ring—a 5.2-carat blue French-cut
solitary diamond. For the couple's first dance the bandleader
played *"Noche de Ronda,"* by Augustín Lara. It was (and continues to be) Ofelia's favorite bolero. Muñiz snapped dozens of photographs. In the ones that remain in Ofelia's album, she is smiling
dreamily at Martín, or at some faraway place. Martín beams his
crooked half-smile directly at the camera.

By eight o'clock it was all over. The white orchids were removed and distributed among the staff, the soiled tablecloths
replaced with clean ones to await the evening's patrons. Meanwhile, the happy couple went off to celebrate their first hours of
marriage at Havana's Casino Deportivo, the national sports complex where Kid Gavilan, the Cuban-born world welterweight
champion, was defending his title against Billy Graham, a contender from New York. When asked about this most unusual start
to her honeymoon, Ofelia shrugged. "I didn't really enjoy it, but
then again, I'm not much of a boxing fan. Neither was Martín.
We went because there were people to see there. There was business to be done." Among those people was Lou Walters, manager
of New York's swanky Latin Quarter cabaret and the father of
a future journalist named Barbara Walters. "Lou had been to
Tropicana several days before," recalled Ofelia. "He was sitting
near us at ringside. He came up to Martín, looking almost annoyed, and said, 'Listen, Martín, you've created a big problem for
me. The Latin Quarter's motto used to be the Most Beautiful
Cabaret in the World, but now that I've seen Tropicana, we have
to change it.'"

Kid Gavilan retained his title in fifteen rounds. Afterward, Martín drove his weary bride back to the house at the corner of 14th Street and 1st Avenue in Miramar. Ofelia finished packing for their trip to New York the following morning, and Martín went back to the cabaret—just for an hour. Ofelia soon learned that he would never sleep unless he knew that all was well at Tropicana.

CHAPTER 13

The Leap

The morning's conversation inside Ofelia and Rosa's Chrysler Cirrus was tense but spirited. Rosa was driving, Ofelia next to her. I was in the back seat, asking them about a man named Frankie Carbo, a boxing promoter who had hosted Martín and Ofelia during their four-day New York honeymoon. What I already knew about Carbo was fairly troubling. According to *The Last Testament of Lucky Luciano,* Martin Gosch and Richard Hammers's as-told-to biography of the notorious mobster, Frankie Carbo, a.k.a "Jimmy the Wop," was a hit man who worked with Bugsy Siegel in the late 1930s. The two men were indicted, arrested, and, according to Luciano, responsible for the 1939 Los Angeles contract killing of Harry "Big Greenie" Greenberg, a mob enforcer who had threatened to talk to New York Special Prosecutor Thomas Dewey. Frankie Carbo's name appears frequently in biographies of mob figures and on Internet mob and boxing history websites. He was known as a member of Murder, Inc., the media's title for the enforcement arm of the Unione Siciliana that was run by Albert Anastasia and Louis "Lepke" Buchalter and responsible, according to authorities in New York, for at least sixty-three murders. After World War II, Carbo cleaned up his act—somewhat. Though he had been already arrested eighteen times, including five times for murder, he became a boxing manager and promoter, controlling the sport from behind the respectable facade of the International Boxing Club.

It was during those years, 1945 to 1960, that Carbo met Martín Fox. On the morning of October 6, 1952, he sent a limousine to pick him and Ofelia up at Idlewild Airport and deliver them to New York's Essex House on Central Park South; he had made sure they would be given one of the best suites. During their four-day stay, he arranged for them to be escorted up and down Fifth Avenue so Ofelia could shop. He gave Ofelia pear-shaped diamond earrings and hosted dinners for them at his home and at the 21 Club. Ofelia still recalled the sublime excellence of their martinis. When one day Carbo asked what else they might like to do, and Ofelia expressed a desire to see *The King and I* on Broadway, Carbo got center orchestra seats, though the musical was sold out for the next three years.

After I shared my information about Carbo's past, Ofelia turned to face me. "So what's your question? Did I know that he was in the Mafia? Of course I did. Before we got to New York, Martín told me that some of the people we were going to see were in the Mafia. But there was nothing to worry about. They would look and act just like regular people, and they were very important in gambling."

"Gambling is not the issue here," I said. "This man was a known murderer."

"*Mira,*" said Ofelia, her voice tightening a tiny bit. "People say and write a lot of things. I didn't know about him killing anyone, and if Martín did, he couldn't do anything about it, either. These men were part of his business world. Carbo treated us like royalty in New York. The next time we went, he got us tickets to *My Fair Lady.* Wherever we went with him, everyone, and I mean everyone, rolled over to please him."

I hardly knew how to respond to that.

"And what did you expect Martín to do?" Ofelia continued. "Offend him? Tell him not to host us? *Por favor,* Rosa, you can't be that naive!"

There was a modicum of truth to Ofelia's position, but in my opinion she was truly being naive. Her blithe dismissal of Carbo's reputation underscored the very notion that she had been trying so hard to dispel, that all of Cuba's casinos, Tropicana included, were rife with mobsters. This was more than a matter of perception. Meyer Lansky, Santo Trafficante, Wilbur Clark, and the host of lesser-known Americans who ran most of Havana's other casinos were at different times under investigation by the U.S. Treasury Department, the New York Crime Commission, and, most notably, the Senate Special Committee on Organized Crime organized by Tennessee senator Estes Kefauver. During the Kefauver Committee hearings, which began in 1950, these and other so-called mobsters were brought before Congress and questioned about the existence of a widespread organization known as the Mafia or Cosa Nostra, which originated in Sicily and controlled crime across the United States. The hearings were televised, thus popularizing the idea that in America there was a well-organized, nation-wide crime syndicate composed mainly of Italians and Jews. The Kefauver Committee, the FBI, the Immigration and Naturalization Service, and the commissioner of U.S. Customs were very interested in the activities of American mobsters in Cuba. Amletto Battisti, a Cuban of Italian ancestry who controlled the casino at the Sevilla Biltmore, was described in a March 27, 1958 letter by the commissioner of customs as "capable of anything." To Ofelia's idealized way of thinking, Tropicana was the stalwart Cuban schooner in a sea of pirate craft. But evidence pointed to the contrary. Beginning in late 1956, posters for Tropicana, and advertisements—in *Diario de la Marina,* as well as the Cuban English-language publications *Cuba Airguide* and *Havana Post*—read: "Visit Lefty Clark's Casino." The commissioner of customs' 1958 letter suspects Clark of narcotics trafficking in Cuba and links him to both Lansky and Trafficante.

Naturally, both Ofelia and Valentín tried to dismiss the Lefty issue. "Clark was hired on in 1956," explained Valentín. "It was a time when Martín and his partners took over the running of Sans Souci for a few months, because Rothman had run it into the ground and Santo asked for a hand. In the end it didn't work out well, but Lefty Clark came over to Tropicana as credit manager of a few tables, because having an American with those connections was good for business."

It was a neat explanation—and one I had heard before—but a "few tables" hardly justified the poster ads that trumpeted "Lefty Clark's Casino" at Tropicana. Moreover, when Clark was fired (according to Valentín) and went back to his original position at Sans Souci ("Visit Lefty Clark's Sans Souci!") Tropicana hired a succession of other figures with unsavory connections. One of these was Dino Cellini, a close associate of Meyer Lansky, who ran the croupier school at the Hotel Riviera and later, after the Cuban revolution, Lansky's casinos in London and Freeport, Grand Bahama. Another was Lewis McWillie, a close associate not only of Santo Trafficante, but of Jack Ruby, the killer of JFK assassin Lee Harvey Oswald. Transcripts of McWillie's 1978 deposition by the U.S. House of Representatives Select Committee on Assassinations (investigating the assassination of John F. Kennedy), which grilled him about Ruby's connection to him and other mobsters, mention Martín Fox repeatedly:

> MR. MCWILLIE: I managed the Tropicana some time and then the government took it over and I was sent to the Hotel Capri by Martín who said you can get a job up there so go there.

CHAIRMAN STOKES: Who is Martín?

MR. MCWILLIE: He owned the Tropicana, Martín Fox. . . .

CHAIRMAN STOKES: Well, isn't it true that you made trips to Miami?

MR. MCWILLIE: To take money for Fox.

CHAIRMAN STOKES: From Cuba to deposit money?

MR. MCWILLIE: Yes, sir.

CHAIRMAN STOKES: Explain that to us, tell us what you were doing.

MR. MCWILLIE: They would ask me to, if I would go to Miami and deposit some money for them, and I would do it.

CHAIRMAN STOKES: By what you were doing, you were sort of running for them is that right?

MR. MCWILLIE: Well, I was a casino manager, and if they wanted me to do that for them, I did it.

CHAIRMAN STOKES: The effect of what they were doing is they were getting their money out of Cuba into banks or deposit boxes here in the States, is that right?

MR. MCWILLIE: Well, the money I took over there was—I took it to a teller and she put it in their account.

CHAIRMAN STOKES: Was this for the Fox brothers?

MR. MCWILLIE: This was both the Fox brothers and Cheninder [Echemendia], too. Cheninder was one of the partners.

There were also warm personal relations between the Foxes and known mafiosi. I had seen the photos of Mr. and Mrs. Cellini at the Foxes' Tropicana table, of Valentín and "Mack," as McWillie was known, posing in bathing trunks at the beach in Guanabo. In one of those family-style photos of the period, Ofelia stands with the Trafficante women in front of their neat ranch house in Tampa, Florida. On October 5, 1954, Santo sent her a grey mink stole by messenger with a note that read, "Wishing you a very happy second anniversary." After the Cuban revolution, Martín and Ofelia were among the few non-family guests who attended Santo's daughter's wedding in the chapel of the Trescornia Detention Center, where he was in jail. (Two published accounts note that Trafficante was allowed out of detention to attend the wedding at the Havana Hilton; but Ofelia repeatedly insisted that it was not so. "I remember it as if it took place yesterday. The wedding took place at the jail. The bride wore a simple short wedding dress with a veil and gifts were all in cash.") Either way, those relations extended well beyond the perfunctory. I said so in the car, and triggered an argument.

"It was precisely Martín's wheeling and dealing around these men that kept them from getting control of Tropicana," said Ofelia, now annoyed with me. "Do you have any idea what these people are like? They're sharks, always waiting for the opportunity to take a bite. Martín kept them off his back by letting this one have the linen concession, by hiring that one's man as credit manager. It was a constant juggling act. But in the end it kept Tropicana out of their hands."

"Did it really? If Meyer Lansky's man was Tropicana's credit manager, and one of Santo's men was doing Tropicana's linens and running Martín's money to Miami, it's pretty safe to say that Tropicana was riddled with mobsters."

"Let me tell you a few things about the gambling business, Rosa. Not just gambling. Business in general. There's always someone out there that you have to deal with who is less than—how to put this—morally intact. Martín made a payoff every month of five thousand pesos to the chief of police in Havana. His name was José Salas Cañizares. It was for protection of la bolita. One time I went with him. We drove up to the station, Martín said who he was, and they said, '*Pase, pase*'—'Come in, come in.' And they were very cordial. He asked us to sit, and they were going to make coffee. But Martín said, 'No, *gracias compadre*, we have to get to the cabaret.' Martín gave the chief the envelope and he slipped it into a drawer without even acknowledging what had transpired."

"That comparison only demonstrates that the police in Cuba were as corrupt as the Mafia."

Ofelia stopped herself and sighed, exasperated with what she perceived as willful obtusiveness on my part. "Look, if you think that there's no Mafia involvement in so-called legitimate business in this country—, my point is only that Martín's line of work required him to finesse all sorts of people. But when it came to the running of Tropicana, he was the one in charge. He was pulling the strings."

It all seemed too tidy an excuse. Luckily, Rosa Sanchez interjected from the driver's seat, "You know, guys, no one ever said that Cuba in the 1950s was a convent. And guess what, no place is! But this is all the juicy stuff that people love to read. Think *The Godfather*! Think *The Sopranos*! The whole idea is that these people look like your next-door neighbor. In the pictures Santo looks like a college professor. Martín's the one who looks like he's got a gun hidden in his pocket."

"*Ay*, Rosa, Martín didn't carry the gun in his pocket!" said Ofelia. Then for my benefit, she added, "He needed it because he always walked around loaded with cash. And he did have a permit."

The talk of guns and gangsters now dwindled as we emerged from a freeway tunnel on the I-10 into a sparkling panorama. We were on the Pacific Coast Highway, heading north toward Malibu. It was a crystalline winter morning. The mountains were green and sharply outlined, a few clouds drifted in the sky, the silvery water was dotted with surfboards straddled by wet-suited riders. Our destination was the home of one of the first great Tropicana stars to emerge during Rodney's tenure. The woman now used her real name, Erna Grabler, but as a youth, when she was part of Tropicana's acrobatic dance team, she was called Chiquita. Her partner, a man who went by the name of Johnson and who was twenty years her senior, coined her stage name in the late 1940s, when they began to work together in their native Prague. It was a reference to the then-twelve-year-old acrobat's size and amazing flexibility.

Chiquita's home sat on a high white bluff with terraces of succulents and bougainvillea clustered among the native coastal chaparral, and dozens of aromatic eucalyptus trees flanking a turquoise grotto pool. The house itself had all the qualities of a residence fit for a star: two levels of picture windows overlooking the Pacific, pale beige carpeting and matching overstuffed couches, an airy bedroom with a white lace canopy above a California king-sized bed, and a kitchen with enough space and appliances to allow two chefs to work without having to cross each other's path. But lovely as Chiquita's house appeared, it was actually a killer. Some years before our visit, the walls were found to harbor a toxic mold beneath the plaster surface. The former acrobatic dancer began to feel constant fatigue, nausea, and terrible vertigo. She visited a number of doctors, but each one was stumped by her symptoms. They told her that it might all be psychological. They told her that they could do nothing for her. Her health deteriorated rapidly. She developed jaundice and liver ailments; her immune system began to fail, her white blood cell count soared. Finally, on her own, she began to suspect that the damp places on her walls might have something to do with what was happening to her. She hired experts to investigate. They discovered several types of mold growing in the walls, including a particularly virulent species of the aspergillus family. By the time she got her insurance company to agree to pay for the cleanup and her relocation costs (it did not cover her medical bills) she had become gravely ill.

Ofelia, Rosa, and I stepped gingerly into the carpeted study where Erna, as she insisted on being called—"I'm not a little girl anymore," she stated flatly when Ofelia told me to please call her

Erna—kept her photographs and press clippings. She moved
slowly, as if her bones might collapse. Though only sixty-three
years old, her face was deeply lined and there was a yellow cast to
the whites of her eyes. Angry purple bruises showed through skin
that looked as thin as tracing paper. When she greeted me, I feared
I'd snap her fingers with too vigorous a handshake.

"This is the way I used to be," Chiquita said somberly. She
pointed to a photograph of herself executing a one-handed handstand against Johnson's upturned palm. It was a startling feat of
strength and gymnastic ability. Chiquita's body pointed effortlessly
up into the air, a human arrow. In other photos she is performing
equally gravity-defying moves. Johnson holds her by one foot and
she spins straight out in a horizontal line, parallel to the stage.
Johnson is a perch from which she hangs upside down, with her
legs wrapped around his waist, her head inches from the floor. In
all of the pictures, but especially in the studio shots, in which she
gazes directly at the camera, Chiquita seems as striking as a movie
star. Her heart-shaped, almond-eyed face bears a startling resem-
blance to Audrey Hepburn. And her body is at once athletic and
voluptuous. No wonder her stardom spanned three decades and included post-Tropicana contracts at Radio City Music Hall and Lou
Walters' Latin Quarter cabaret in New York; appearances on the
Ed Sullivan Show and the *Colgate Comedy Hour*, where she performed with Frank Sinatra; at Frank Sennes's Moulin Rouge in
Hollywood; and at the White House, where, in 1957, she and Johnson performed for President Dwight Eisenhower.

It had been over twenty years since Chiquita's retirement from
show business, and it was a mold-weakened Erna Grabler who led
us to the alcove of the paneled Malibu kitchen. With careful delib-
eration, she untied the knot around a pink pastry box that Ofelia
had brought as a gift. Inside were two thick Cuban sandwiches
and four glistening pastries oozing cream and chocolate. "Oooh,
Ofelia, you remembered my favorites," she exclaimed in English
accented with the hard consonants of her native Czech.

"They're from Porto's," replied Ofelia. "I know you have diet restrictions, but I thought that maybe once in a while you cheat." Erna squeezed Ofelia's hand in gratitude. Her eyes glistened as she lowered herself carefully into a breakfast booth. "My body was always my source of strength," she said. "And now look at me." Ever since she was a child in Prague, Chiquita's body dictated her life decisions. "As soon as I knew how to walk I walked on my toes, from the time I was three years old I knew I would be a ballerina." Chiquita studied classical ballet in Prague. At the age of twelve, she was offered a scholarship to Russia to study at the Bolshoi, but she declined it. "I was starting to feel that ballet was too regimented. I was light as a bird and I loved to be lifted. That was when I met Johnny."

John von Kralik entered Erna's life through her father, a Viennese furniture manufacturer who was a frequenter of Prague's cabaret nightlife. Von Kralik led an acrobatic troupe made up of two men and two women. But he had never seen agility and grace like that displayed by Herr Grabler's twelve-year-old daughter. For her part, Erna was thrilled by the chance to do something more exciting than ballet without giving dance up altogether. The pair began rehearsing almost immediately after meeting. Soon, with Herr Grabler's enthusiastic approval, von Kralik, who was already performing under the stage name Johnson, abandoned his acrobatic troupe and began working exclusively with his young new partner. This was in 1948, when Europe was still devastated from the war. (Von Kralik had lost his wife and daughter to an Allied bomb while he was working in Germany.) Chiquita's radiant stylishness and Johnson's mix of acrobatics and ballet, coupled with the girl's nearly unnatural agility, brought them rapid fame in Prague. This was followed by tours through Germany, Greece, the Middle East, and finally Mexico, where they arrived in late 1951. It was there, when she began to speak Spanish, that Chiquita learned that her stage name meant "little one." "I was horrified," she said. "I thought it was a name, but it was no name at all." Unfortunately,

Chiquita's disapproval of her stage name came after Chiquita and Johnson had become a marketable commodity. Their show in Mexico City was drawing record crowds. The audiences would gasp in a mix of delight and horror as Johnny, as Erna referred to her partner, lifted her into the one-handed handstand, then dropped her, catching her by her legs when her face was an inch from the ground.

In the kitchen of the Malibu house, Erna recalled, laughing, how this once led to a terrible incident involving an obese woman who kept leaping out of her seat and gasping each time she did one of her daredevil tricks. "There was this commotion after the show, and they were taking her out and later they told me she had died of a heart attack. I felt terribly guilty. But the management assured me that I had done nothing. After all, no one else had died in the entire run."

In mid-1952, a few months before Martín and Ofelia's wedding, Chiquita and Johnson's act was spotted in Mexico by a scout for Tropicana. Chiquita was sixteen, so Johnson, who had been named her legal guardian by Herr Grabler to facilitate their travels, took care of all their arrangements. It was for this reason that Erna did not remember who approached them about working in Cuba. But Ofelia was sure it was Ardura. "He was in charge of the contracts. He had a private plane and he was always flying off to different places—always looking for new acts." No matter who it was that spotted them, Ardura eventually made them the offer to come to Tropicana for the 1952–1953 winter season. They arrived in October. "Up until then we had traveled all over the world, performed for kings and queens and presidents, but nothing prepared me for the spectacular grandeur of the Tropicana," wrote Erna in a 1999 note to Ofelia entitled, "My Year at Tropicana." Excited as she was to see this glamorous cabaret, Chiquita was still concerned about how she would manage so far from home and with still few language skills to help her communicate. Happily, she found a kindred spirit in Tropicana's new choreographer.

After much persuasion from Ardura and an initial salary that was reported to be three hundred pesos a week, Rodney began at Tropicana in June of 1952. His first shows were *Chinos en la Habana*, a revue based on Cuba's Chinatown; *Prende la Vela* (Light the Candle), inspired by Afro-Cuban customs; and *Orquideas Para Usted* (Orchids for You), a floral fanfare of traditional Cuban music that ended with the entire Tropicana dance corps, the men in white tuxedos and the women in lilac satin dresses, wandering through the audience with armfuls of purple orchids. The three shows were performed nightly in Arcos de Cristal—at ten, midnight, and two, although the outdoor cabaret was also used on holidays and busy weekends. Just as Ardura had predicted, the number of reservations doubled. "Production and Choreography by Rodney," proclaimed the ads in *Diario de la Marina* beginning in August 1952. In September, Rodney added to his revolving repertoire of productions *Las Viudas Alegres*, a show based on Franz Lehár's *The Merry Widow*. "Next Friday: Sensational Debut of International Stars, Chiquita and Johnson," announced the October 4th advertisement for *Las Viudas*.

Rodney incorporated the pair into *Las Viudas Alegres* and *Orquideas Para Usted*, which played throughout November and into the first weeks of December. He observed the acrobatic beauty whom Ardura had hired. Though by far the youngest performer he had ever worked with, Chiquita was an astonishing artist. Her physical ability was only half of it. The sixteen-year-old dancer also displayed an emotional maturity that was beyond her years. Rodney had an intuition that she would be able to act as well as dance. This gave him an idea: what if he were to use this acrobatic performer in creating a new, improved version of the *toque de santo* (the Yoruba ritual that is a kind of baptism, intended to rid a child or initiate of impurities) that had been staged in *Sun Sun Babae*?

One afternoon while Chiquita and Johnson were rehearsing for the evening's performance, Rodney approached her. "I had seen him sitting there, watching me while we rehearsed," recalled

Erna wistfully. "When we were finished he waddled up to me—because of his illness he had this awkward way of walking, like a penguin—and he said, 'I have an idea for something special we can do together.' Now you must understand that Johnny did not like change. But Rodney was a genius—we both saw it even after working with him just a few weeks. And this idea he had was so intriguing that I made [Johnny] agree to do it."

The proposal that Rodney made to Chiquita was to create a contemporary ballet based on an authentic Santería ritual, putting her at the center of the action. "I was to play this foreign white woman who goes slumming one night and finds herself at a *bembé*. I start to move to the music and suddenly I am possessed by the spirit of the santo." It was the same idea behind *Sun Sun Babae*, but with two key differences: Chiquita's acrobatic range, which would allow for far greater possibilities once the woman in the show became possessed; and Ardura's promise to Rodney that he could have a nearly unlimited production budget.

Two weeks after Chiquita and Johnson arrived in Cuba, Rodney began rehearsing the new revue. In the afternoons, barely twelve hours after Tropicana's performers had completed the previous night's show, the cast would gather to listen to Rodney's concept on the broad new stage of Bajo las Estrellas, the outdoor portion of the cabaret, which was in the final stages of renovation by Max Borges. The idea was far more complex than anything done before at any cabaret in Cuba. Rodney planned to go full out in his staging of the *toque de santo*. The actual religious event takes place over a number of days. Rodney planned to represent this through different scenes within the ballet. The first part, in which the religious ceremonies are performed and the Santería priests (*los babalaos*) read the *Itá*, which evokes the past, present, and future, would be performed by authentic practitioners—men and women whom Rodney had known from his days at the leprosarium. There would be offerings of animals and fruit to the santos. This would set the stage for the next part of the ceremony, in which the family is allowed to receive well-wishers. One of the visitors would be Chiquita, a white woman who is not an initiate. Upon entering the space of ritual, Chiquita would find herself possessed by a free-floating spirit of the dead. From there on, the show would center on Chiquita's frenetic dance of possession, and the frantic efforts of those present to free her from this state.

Except for Chiquita and Johnson, all of the dancers and musicians in the show were Cubans, and therefore familiar with the basic concept of *Sun Sun Babae,* as well as its success. Being Cuban, they could also perform the undulating movement and the syncopated swaying required by the drumming. For Chiquita, on the other hand, it was not quite as easy. "The Cuban rhythm is very unique," Erna recalled in Malibu. "The motions conflict. You have the upper body doing one thing and the lower body something else. It's like trying to play the piano with each hand doing a different song. It was hard for me because ballet is very precise and this is all instinctual."

Rodney noticed his young star struggling with the Cuban dance moves. One day early on in the rehearsal process, when Chiquita arrived at the club after her morning ballet lessons, he said to her, "Tonight we're going someplace." At around eight that evening, Rodney picked Chiquita up and they drove across the entirety of Havana, skirting the port with its illuminated cruise ships, and the long line of warehouses that dotted the outskirts of the city. Johnson had stayed home, but Rodney had brought two of the other male dancers. The group joked and laughed with Chiquita as the driver wound through the dark streets. After what seemed like hours, they came to a stop in front of a ramshackle stucco house that looked hundreds of years old. From the street, Chiquita heard powerful drumming.

We walked into an ordinary room, like someone's living room. There was a table in the corner piled with food— bananas, mangoes, cakes. People were coming in, bringing more food, while these two guys played the bongos [the drums were actually two-headed *batá* drums]. The place was crowded. People were sitting on the floor. Rodney told me to sit down, and I did. Some people were up and dancing, but mostly people sat in their places, swaying to the music, moving so naturally. As I listened and listened I became transfixed by the sound. The sound got into my bones and without even being aware of it, I started swaying also. Suddenly I felt someone tapping me. It was Rodney. He said, "Okay you got it. Now we can go."

Taking his performers to an authentic *bembé* was nothing new for Rodney. According to dancer Hector Leal, who had been at Sans Souci before being hired at Tropicana, Rodney had done the same with the entire cast of *Sun Sun Babae*. In both cases he had gone to a house in Guanabacoa, an old hill town on the outskirts of Havana that was a center for the practice of Afro-Cuban religions, and where a family of *batá* drummers, led by patriarch Trinidad Torregrosa, were among the most venerated in the entire country. Three generations of Torregrosa family men had played onstage for *Sun Sun Babae*. To do so, they first had to ask for special permission from the santos. Rodney asked them again to ask for permission to play in his new version of the cabaret-based *toque de santo*. The title of the piece was to be *Omelen-ko*, a Yoruba expression that appears to be based on the words *omele enko*, which means "the music of your drum companion," or "drum comrade."

Now that Chiquita had the rhythm, the rehearsal process for *Omelen-ko* leapt into overdrive. Her fluid acrobatics became steeped in sexy syncopation. The Tropicana dancers sensed the change and became more daring in their lifts, jumps, and tosses. Inspired by the extraordinary agility of his young star, Rodney began to propose ever more complicated combinations. The male principals lifted Chiquita by the hands and feet; they swung her 360 degrees, tossing her among themselves like a ninety-pound sack of guavas. "Johnny was scared to death," remembered Erna, laughing. "He considered himself the only person that knew how to handle me carefully. He would tell them, *'Cuidado, cuidado!'* [Careful, careful!] in the little Spanish that he knew."

For his part, Rodney told them to keep throwing her. *"Tírenla entre ustedes, así, así,"* he would croak out in a voice made raspy by his illness, drawing the movements in the air with his gnarled hands and letting his ballet stars, Argentine Henry Boyer and Cuban Miguelito Checki, block them out for the company. For Rodney, rehearsals were always fraught with as much tension as excitement. "It was frustrating to him that he could not show us the moves himself," said Eddy Serra. When Serra joined the cast of Tropicana in 1958, Rodney was already famous, but during that first season, in 1952, the choreographer's reputation was on the line. *Omelen-ko* was his trial by fire: it had to outdo not only all of Tropicana's previous productions, but everything Rodney had done up to that point.

One afternoon, in the middle of the rehearsals for *Omelen-ko,* Chiquita came up with an interesting idea. "We were rehearsing the final scene, where I wake up from the possession and am shocked to find myself half naked in that place, and Rodney was trying to come up with what I was going to do at that moment. I was thinking too—he was very good about collaboration—when I looked up and saw the metal sculpture that is the focal point of the outdoor stage. I said, 'Why don't I climb up to the top in my state of trance, and when I wake up at the top, I'll scream and jump down into Johnny's arms?'"

Chiquita's idea seemed preposterous to everyone except Rodney. The metal sculpture, which Max Borges had designed for Bajo las Estrellas, based, according to him, on paintings of mathematical formulas that he had seen in an exhibit in Milan, was over twenty feet high. The opening of the outdoor cabaret was set to take place on December 22 with *Omelen-ko* and a second show titled *Caribbean Island* that showcased the dance and music of each of Cuba's six provinces. When no one seemed to heed her suggestion, Chiquita began scaling the polished stainless steel tubes that formed the sculpture. Johnson sharply vetoed the idea. "He almost forbade me to do it," recalled Erna. "But Roderico was hooked on the idea from the start." Before Chiquita reached the top, Rodney could tell that this was a rare moment of inspiration. "To calm Johnny's agitation he suggested using a few of the other boys to spot him." Johnson continued to object, but it was no use. While he was arguing with Rodney, she was at the top, ready to leap.

"How about if I try it from halfway?" Chiquita called out, to placate her partner. Knowing her willfulness, Johnson nodded reluctantly. Chiquita climbed halfway down again as Johnson positioned himself. "Miguelito, Henry, get on either side of him," said Rodney in his throaty growl. The two male dance stars stood beside Johnson, making a lattice of six arms to catch Chiquita as she swan dived. Chiquita leaned out from the metal sculpture, holding on with one hand. Then, carefully gauging the angle of her fall, she jumped. The landing was perfect.

Now it was time to see if they could pull this off when she jumped from the top. "First go up another five feet," suggested Johnson. But Chiquita was tired of the arduous climb; anyway, she knew that she could do this. She dashed up to the top of Max Borges's elliptical structure before her partner could protest. To those below she looked like a spider in her black rehearsal leotard. She remembered feeling like a monkey at the top of a jungle canopy. She could look out over the roof of the mansion where Martín operated his casino, and the tropical panorama that was Villa Mina. Again, she held onto the metal tubing and leaned out. Without taking his eyes off of her, Johnson clasped wrists once again with Henry and Miguelito. No one moved. Even the custodians who were sweeping and setting up the chairs and tables stopped what they were doing to look up. At the top of the sun-dappled sculpture, the tiny leotarded dancer unleashed the bloodcurdling scream of her *Omelen-ko* character, then plunged into the lattice of waiting arms.

Tropicana crackled with anticipation the night Bajo las Estrellas opened. The place was packed with press and dignitaries—much like the night of the opening of Arcos except that tonight the excitement was as much about Rodney's new production as the outdoor cabaret. The public was also buzzing about Martin's recent acquisition of a famous Cuban landmark—the multi-figure marble fountain that for years had sat at the entrance to the Casino Nacional. Known as *La Fuente de las Musas*, or "Fountain of the Muses," the early twentieth century marble sculpture by the Italian Aldo Gamba consisted of a round basin topped by eight life-size nude nymphs. When the casino closed its doors in 1952, reportedly because it could not compete with the success of Tropicana, Montmartre, and Sans Souci, Martín rushed over and purchased the fountain for 30,000 pesos ($200,000 today), and spent another 10,000 to have the fountain sectioned and reinstalled in a grassy patch opposite the carport and entrance to the casino.

Backstage, no one was thinking about Martin's expenditures. The cast was palpably tense as they put on their costumes. Erna recalled that the dancers joked nervously about her dive as they put on their costumes. "*Oye*, better make sure your nose doesn't itch when it's time to catch her," she remembered someone saying to the dancers. "Don't worry, if you drop me, Johnny will come after you," Chiquita retorted. Rodney, who was his usual cantankerous opening-night self, relaxed and laughed. But only for a moment. "The place is jammed," he warned his cast. "All of the press is out there. If we mess up, they'll be calling us amateurs for months to come."

Bajo las Estrellas was indeed filled to capacity. Tropicana's publicity department had capitalized on the buzz that had been rolling through the city's entertainment sector since the show went into rehearsal. "*Omelen-ko*—a negro baptism," they wrote, "will be the most fascinating production ever performed at the world famous cabaret. The frenetic rhythms of a *Lucumí* ritual, exemplified by the tam-tam of the *batá* drums, the *ilia*, the *okonkolo* and the *itolele*, will be played by real members of the African faith." At Ofelia's table, the level of expectancy was even higher than normal. In honor of the evening's stars, Martín had invited members of the Austrian and Czech diplomatic corps in Cuba. Ofelia's role was to host the dignitaries while Martín worked the room and made his nightly rounds of the casino. He was becoming increasingly reliant on his wife's social skills, as well as her ability to speak English. Though he understood much more than he let on, he found it most convenient to have a translator handy whenever he needed to be specific about a point, or to really understand what people were saying. Ofelia was the ideal addition to the staff of his cabaret emporium. Naturally, he would never have put it in those terms. Her manners, her years at business school, and her eye for detail were serving Martín well in all aspects of his business. She had updated his wardrobe, insisting that he wear only finely tailored suits or tuxedos to Tropicana, instead of the more casual white pants and guayabera shirts that he had favored, or—heaven forbid—the canary-yellow ensemble he had sported the night they had met. She had also insisted on their having a fixed table in each of the two cabarets, and attended to his family. Whenever Martín's sisters and sister-in-law came to Tropicana, Ofelia would seat them at their table, together with her sisters, Fara and Hildebranda. She would see to them all night long, leaving Martín free to work.

But the main reason that Martín was finding her indispensable was that he was falling in love with her. This took them both by surprise. Even during their New York honeymoon, they had both felt more like good friends than passionate lovers. But something had changed. It began the day they got home from the honeymoon. "It was afternoon and I unpacked our things, then we took a nap," recalled Ofelia. "At eight, when we awoke, I began to dress for the evening without his saying a word, or my asking. I could tell he was moved that I was ready to go to Tropicana. And I continued going every night."

Thus began the ritual that would go on until the day Ofelia and Martín left Cuba. In the mornings, Ofelia slept and Martín ran errands. In the afternoons they napped in separate bedrooms, so that if the house staff needed her, Martín would not be disturbed. Most days they lunched at the Miami Restaurant, where Martín received visitors at his table by the bar during their drinks; but when the meal came, it was the signal for everyone to leave Tropicana's owner alone with his wife. This was their time together to converse about family and planned trips, which were mainly for business, or to Boston, where Martín had a complete physical once a year. (Early on in their marriage, it became apparent to Ofelia that traveling for pleasure gave no pleasure at all to Martín. Even on their belated three-week honeymoon to South and Central America, a trip which ended in a luxury cruise from Rio de Janeiro to New Orleans, Martín was miserable away from Tropicana.) They would always talk about Tropicana.

The Miami Restaurant was also where, a year after they were married, Martín told Ofelia that he had received two anonymous letters telling him to watch out for her.

"Watch out for what?" Ofelia calmly asked.

Martín fixed his gambler's gaze upon his young wife. Ofelia stared right back, chin high, hands folded in front of her. "The first one was a general warning, china. It said to watch out for your youth, that I'm rich, and that I should not expect you to be faithful."

"And the second letter?"

Martín paused and pursed his lips. "That one arrived the day we came back from Varadero. They wrote that you are seeing the bearded man who sat in the bar at the Hotel Internacional."

Ofelia let his words hang in the air. Martín waited. They were like two gamblers at that moment, each waiting for the other to show his hand. Finally Ofelia spoke. "Let's analyze this, Martín. I am always with you. When I go to the beauty parlor or the stores, I go with your sister or mine. At home I'm with the maids. Tell me now, when do I have the time or place to meet a man—in Varadero or Havana?"

Martín looked away briefly. The sending of anonymous letters was a common tactic in Cuba, and he was angry with himself for being so easily duped by the ruse to separate them.

"By the way, I've never told you, but I receive letters about you," continued Ofelia calmly. "I usually throw them away. But I kept one in my night table. When we get home, I'll show it to you."

Martín's mouth unfurled into its crooked grin. He had met his match.

OMELEN-KO began with the deep, powerful drumming of the Torregrosa family. Bajo las Estrellas seemed to shudder, and the audience was transfixed by sounds that seemed primeval. The jungle setting had something to do with it. "You felt that you were right in the middle of things," Ofelia told me. "The separation between the audience and the stage was lost in the music. By the time the dancers came out, no one in the audience was moving. No one was even picking up a glass or fork." The night was balmy and the stars were out. Apart from the music, the only sound was the wind in the trees.

The first scenes of *Omelen-ko* were much like those of *Sun Sun Babae,* featuring successive pairs of dancers performing the authentic ritual dances for each santo. As always in Yoruba ritual, the first to be summoned was Elegguá, the orisha who opens the path to fortune and holds the keys to destiny. Then a woman dressed in yellow came out to dance for Ochún, the orisha who governs love and sexuality. Here Rodney took liberties with costuming. The women showed midriffs and lots of thigh; some of the men were bare chested, sitting onstage or stomping out the rhythm while a chorus sang in Yoruba. Sitting in the audience, Chiquita wore a sleek black evening dress and real black-and-white fox furs slung over each shoulder. Like her counterpart in *Sun Sun Babae*, she did her first dance in the dress, but that's where the similarity between the two shows ended. Rodney deepened Chiquita's dreamlike state by later having her wear a short, fringed outfit, sort of a fantastically "native" look. "The outfit had all these colors that were picked up by the [ultraviolet] lights overhead," recalled Erna. "When this happens I start dancing and dancing and everything gets more frenetic until finally, this guy dressed up as death, bids me to start climbing the sculpture."

When Chiquita began her trance-like ascent up the sculpture, there was a collective intake of breath from the audience. "There was so much going on onstage. Rodney had asked for animals and there were pigeons, goats, the usual things that get sacrificed in these rituals," said Ofelia. "And then you have this little woman climbing up this sculpture, and the men line up beneath her. You know what's coming but you can't believe it's going to happen." Of course, everyone in the cast knew what was going to happen also, yet when the moment came and Chiquita jumped, Henry and Miguelito balked. "They cowered and loosened their grip," Erna said. "Johnny caught me, but since he was expecting help, I slipped out and I hit the ground." Because she fell in a swan dive, Chiquita's hip took the impact. Henry and Miguelito were so shaken that they could hardly concentrate on the timing of later moves. "There was this moment when they threw me to another dancer, and he draped me on his shoulder—by then my hip was the size of a piece of steak, and hurting so bad I couldn't even think—then Miguelito came and took me by the legs again, but I could tell he wasn't ready when the dancer started tossing me. I tried to shout, 'Not yet! Not yet!' But the drumming was so loud, he couldn't hear me, and I fell on my head. Luckily I had a tight chignon that braced the fall."

Despite the tumult onstage, the show was a thundering success. The ovations lasted half an hour. "I remember someone saying it was the first time the club made more money than the casino," remarked Erna proudly. One person who was not convinced that everything was fine, however, was Trinidad Torregrosa. The day after the opening of *Omelen-ko*, the family of drummers apparently arrived at Tropicana in a somber mood and told Rodney that the orishas had not been fully appeased by the preparations. Some offense had been taken and Chiquita was the one absorbing the *mala suerte*—bad luck. For a split second, recalled Chiquita, Rodney looked like he would faint. If the Torregrosa drummers walked out, *Omelen-ko* was finished. Then Trinidad Torregrosa pulled out a small beaded bracelet and pointed to Chiquita. "She needs to wear this, to make sure nothing else happens." The bracelet, a small delicate band, consisted of ten groups of five red and white beads— an amulet to Changó, who rules thunder and male power.

"I have kept these sacred beads with me always, everywhere I have traveled, and from then on I was never hurt again," said Erna as she pulled them out to show them to me. The interview had clearly exhausted her. She ran the five largest white beads along her fingers then slipped the bracelet onto her bony wrist. Around the Malibu kitchen, the silence was palpable.

CHAPTER 14

The Circus

*Leonela González Pérez was born in Havana. She's
22 years old. Weighs 120 pounds. Measures 5 feet 5
inches. Waist: 23½ inches. Thighs: 22 inches each.
And to her greatest satisfaction, as a statuesque
woman, her bust and hips are both 36 inches—the
very measurements of Miss Universe.*

from *Show* magazine, April, 1955

*I warn you, I am just getting started! If there is in
your hearts a vestige of love for your country, love
for humanity, love for justice, listen carefully.*

—Fidel Castro, "History Will Absolve Me"

A story from the Tropicana mythology, one that Ofelia swears
is true: In the late spring of 1953, when Tropicana's gardens
were at their most lush, Alberto Ardura was walking past the
entrance to the casino when he chanced upon a strange sight.
Standing in the marble basin of *La fuente de las musas* was a
woman whose beauty eclipsed the statues. The woman had dark
hair, almond-shaped eyes, and sweeping eyebrows, and was wearing ballet slippers and a short black leotard that showed off her
spectacular curvature. She posed for photographers with one leg
raised, as if one of the eight nude muses that surrounded her had
been brought to full-blooded and very sensual life.

"Who is that girl?" asked Ardura of the crew assisting the photographer, trying to sound offhanded.

"That's Leonela González, the ballet star."

When the photo shoot—part of a publicity interview for *Diario de la Marina*—was over, Ardura approached the woman and introduced himself. Leonela smiled demurely, slipping a skirt over her leotard.

"Have you ever thought about dancing in a cabaret?"

"*Por favor!* I am a classical ballerina!"

"I know that, but we are thinking of using a classical dancer for our next show, and we can pay you two hundred pesos a week." Ardura let his words hang in the air. He waved a botones boy over and asked him to bring a tray of sodas and ice for the ballerina and her photographers.

Leonela hesitated. "I've never danced anywhere but in the ballet. And you'd have to talk to my mother."

Ardura popped open a bottle of ginger ale and poured her a glass. "Have her call me, okay?"

A few days later, the ballerina and her mother, who worked as a mid-level assistant for the Cuban foreign ministry, sat across from Ardura in his office. Leonela seemed even lovelier in street clothes than in her leotard.

"My daughter is no showgirl or *rumbera*," said Leonela's mother sternly. "She has been a student at Pro-Arte Musical since she was eight years old, and is a charter member of Alicia Alonso's ballet company."

Ardura tried to interject, but Leonela's mother continued.

"Besides, her father is a pediatrician, so she does not need to work in a cabaret."

Ardura tried to control his impatience. "Señora, Tropicana is a family place. Here we have weddings, anniversaries and *quinces* all the time."

"But Leonela is a classical ballerina!"

"And that's all she will dance," said Ardura.

"And she'll make two hundred pesos a week?"

Ardura nodded once. "Está bien explicado?" he said, using his signature phrase when a conversation was finished.

And so it was that two months later, Leonela González was starring as Marie Antoinette in *Europa Año Cero* (Europe, Year Zero), a three-part production described by Tropicana's marketing department as "a parade of the most interesting European personalities throughout the centuries." After the opening, Ardura called her back into his office. Her mother came as well. Leonela Perez de Cardelle attended all of her daughter's shows. With Ardura was Rodney, who had scripted the dancer's performance with ballet star Luis Trapaga (billed as "the lover" in *Europa Año Cero*). Their scene began with Leonela wearing a French court hoop dress made of lace and a two-foot-high eighteenth-century wig, and ended with the dress coming off to reveal a pink and white tutu for her pas de deux in Arcos de Cristal.

Ardura got right to the point. "We think Leonela is terrific. And we'd like to offer her a regular contract. Given this we were wondering if we could not agree to a discount in her salary."

"If she's so terrific," replied Leonela's mother, "you should pay her more than two hundred a week."

Ardura flashed one of his rare smiles. "We were thinking of one hundred fifty. That's more than three times what she makes at the ballet."

Leonela's mother began to shake her head. The ballerina could not stand it any longer. "*Ay, sí, mama! Por favor!* I love it here at Tropicana."

NEARLY A half century had passed since Leonela González began her cabaret career. The ballerina embraced Ofelia, smothering her in masses of platinum blond hair. "*Ay, qué tiempo mas bello!*

Mira, how wonderful you look! Me, I've gained weight, I don't feel like myself, I've talked to my doctor but he says I'm crazy to worry."

The doctor was right. At seventy-three, Leonela still had somehow retained the twenty-three-inch waist of her dancer days. She had lost neither her voluptuousness nor the dancer's tautness that a woman half her age could covet. Leonela was in Los Angeles to visit old friends from the Tropicana days. There was Ofelia, of course; also dancer Eddy Serra, Jenny León, and Frank Llopis. Leonela and her friends sat around the Llopis kitchen table in Azusa, California, a town twenty minutes east of Glendale, eating hors d'oeuvres (and Cuban sandwiches that Ofelia and Rosa had brought from Porto's bakery), laughing, reminiscing, and sharing photos of plump grandchildren and Latin-lover-handsome sons. The Llopis house was as cheerful as the conversation. The furniture gleamed (including a white piano on which was some sheet music of Frank's composition), as did the floral upholstery, artificial flower arrangements, and glass knickknacks. Even the gunite ceiling was flecked with silver sparkles.

Cubans in groups tend to be loud. Table pounding and joyous laughter resonated off the mirror-bright appliances. "Remember the night Joan Crawford came?" said Jenny laughing. "Tyrone Power was also there, with Cesar Romero. Frank, you said to her husband, 'Aren't you someone important too?' and the man was Alfred Steele, chairman of Pepsi-Cola!"

As with Valentín's Las Vegas home, there was not a speck of dust in Frank and Jenny's house, not a fingerprint smudge. Jenny, as slender and youthful-looking as Leonela and with hair so red it was impossible not to simply stare at it, offered up a constant barrage of one-liners as she filled frosted glasses with soda and beer. The Llopises had a garage full of beer, a perquisite from Frank's old job with the Miller Brewing Company. After arriving in the United States, he abandoned music as a career and worked as a chemical engineer, settling in Azusa because it was just a few miles from the West Coast's largest Miller plant.

I wondered how people who went off in so many directions— Ofelia to Miami, then Glendale; Frank and Jenny to Europe, then Mexico, Miami and finally Azusa; Eddy to Las Vegas, then Glendale; Leonela, to Miami, then Puerto Rico, then eventually to Jackson Heights, Queens—managed to find each other. "How did you all meet up again?" I asked.

Everyone thought for a moment. "*Bueno,*" said Jenny finally. "We've always been in touch with Leonela, and with Eddy . . . but Ofelia and Rosa . . . Didn't we meet up at that show of Olga Chaviano's?"

Ofelia nodded. "*Ah, si,* that showcase for her son. Across from the House of Blues."

"*Pobrecito!*" Jenny sighed, rolling her eyes dramatically. "But a mother can't judge. She has to do those things."

"The boy is not a very good dancer, but he was Olga's son with Norman Rothman," explained Rosa. "Olga Chaviano was a striking dark-haired woman—very voluptuous, and a pretty good dancer. She was with Rothman and, *tu sabes,* he was the head guy at Sans Souci. So he made her career."

There was a brief silence as the others absorbed this. Illicit love is a touchy subject, especially with Ofelia. In addition to being a cultural mecca, an icon, a locus for all that was glamorous in 1950s Havana, Tropicana was a place where powerful, rich, married men chased after the country's most exquisite women. Many Cubans— my parents included—had told me that you could go to Tropicana and watch the show for the price of a drink if you sat at the bar (and arrived properly dressed). This made it an attractive pick-up place for young people of both sexes, and all predilections. Havana's top-tier call girls also knew they could count on receiving a substantial cash gift if they brought in a high roller who lost heavily in the casino. Ofelia admitted to all of this. Nonetheless, both she and lots of former showgirls vigorously refuted the accusations made in stories about Tropicana—like the novel *Muñecas de cristal* (Glass Dolls) written by Cuban journalist Orlando Quiroga; and *Mob Lawyer*, the memoirs of Santo Trafficante's attorney, Frank Ragano—that the girls were made available to any rich client who wanted them. At some casinos, showgirls would be asked to *fichar*, which meant to sit at the gaming tables after the show and attract male customers by pretending to gamble with chips provided by the house. Ofelia claims that it was strictly prohibited at Tropicana. "We weren't allowed to have anything to do with patrons," said model Alicia Figueroa. "Even if one of our friends was in the audience, we had to ask permission of management to approach the tables."

Still, Tropicana's atmosphere simmered with sexuality. When I talked with pianist Bebo Valdés, he recounted tales of being approached by American tourists who were looking for prostitutes. For a five-peso tip, Valdés would take them to one of two famous houses—either the Casa de Marina in the barrio of Colón (the largest and most well-known whorehouse in Havana, according to my mother) or Casa de Violeta on Virtudes Street, which specialized in black women. "The Americans from the south wanted only black girls," remarked Valdés who is of African ancestry himself, chuckling wryly at the hypocrisy of that situation. Like most habaneros, Ofelia knew about these places. She and everyone at Tropicana—not to mention most of Cuba—also knew the story behind Valdés's mambo "Güempa." Nightly from her table she witnessed the behavior of men who came with their wives one night and with their mistresses the following night. ("I could always tell the difference. With their wives they'd sit glumly at the table, and with the mistresses they were animated and drinking champagne.") From her friends among the showgirls she had heard of the bouquets of flowers that crowded their dressing rooms, orchids and roses being the favorites of the industrialists

Entrance to Villa Mina, with Tropicana sign. *Courtesy of the Vicki Gold Levi Collection*

Ofelia Fox in Bajo las Estrellas, September 1955.

Martín and Ofelia Fox, February 13, 1958. Ofelia is wearing the mink stole given to her by Santo Trafficante.

Liberace onstage in Bajo las Estrellas with Ana Gloria Varona, August 1956.

Liberace with Ofelia and Martín Fox in August 1956 at the piano table designed in Liberace's honor. *Inset:* An aerial view of the table.

Santo Trafficante (standing) with Martín's sister, Angela (Lita) Fox; Martín and Ofelia Fox; and Ofelia's mother, Cuca González.

Martín Fox and Lefty Clark in front of the Fountain of the Muses, 1956.

Valentín Jodra (left) at his post at the roulette wheel.

Rodney and Alberto Ardura signing a contract on October 17, 1954.
Courtesy of the Vicki Gold Levi Collection

At Martín and Ofelia's house on 1st Street in Miramar. Left to right, back row:
Ofelia's brother, Osvaldo Suarez; his wife, Diana Palacio; Raúl Taladrid; Fara
Suarez; Atilano Taladrid. Seated: Hildebranda (La Niña) Suarez, Cuca González,
Martín Fox, and Ofelia Fox with Osvaldo and Diana's infant.

Front row, left to right: Lilia Lazo, María Félix, Olga Guillot, Carmen Miranda, Ñica Fox, and Ofelia Fox. Back row, left to right: two unidentified journalists, Martín Fox, and Pedro Fox, July 1955.

Olga Guillot and Carmen Miranda in the finale of *Bahiondo*, July 1955.

Ofelia and Martín Fox with Joan Crawford (holding Ofelia's hand) and Crawford's husband, Pepsi-Cola Chairman Alfred Steele.

Tropicana makeup artist Carlos Gomery with Celia Cruz.
Courtesy of the Vicki Gold Levi Collection

Tropicana's choreographer, Rodney (Roderico Neyra), with two *modelos*.
Courtesy of the Vicki Gold Levi Collection

Diosas de Carne (Goddesses of the Flesh) performed April 28, 1958. Back row: Las Hermanas Lago with Berta Dupuy (singing). Standing (center): Hector Leal. Seated (center): Clarita Castillo. *Modelo* on right is Sandra Taylor.
Courtesy of the Vicki Gold Levi Collection

Chiquita and
Johnson.

Chiquita and Johnson perform in *Orquideas Para Usted* in Arcos de
Cristal, October 1952.

Ballet stars Leonela González and Eduardo Perovani.
Courtesy of Leonela González

Música del Alma, a show with a rock 'n' roll theme, performed in Bajo las Estrellas in June 1957 and starring Leonela González and Henry Boyer (center). Male dancers (left to right) Jorge Martínez, Miguelito Checki, and Hugo Romero. Max Borges's elliptical sculpture is in background. *Courtesy of Leonela González*

Ana Gloria Varona on the cover of *Show* magazine, February 1958.

Alicia Figueroa.

Fulgencio Batista (third from left) at the 1954 Anti-Cancer League Dinner at Tropicana. (Martín Fox is in the white jacket.)

Emilia "La China" Villamíl. *Courtesy of Emilia Villamíl*

An ad in the June 1, 1957, issue of *Diario de la Marina*. Includes the Cuarteto Llopis (misspelled in the ad). Frank Llopis is to the right of the accordion player. *Courtesy of Frank Llopis*

Jenny León in *Show* magazine, September 1957.

Steve Allen, Ofelia Fox, Martín Fox, and Jayne Meadows.

Nat "King" Cole and Maria Cole at Tropicana's bar.

Nat "King" Cole
performing at Tropicana,
February 1958.

Sunan, Ofelia's pet lion.

Rumbo al Waldorf, November 1958. Left to right: Emilia Villamíl, Leonela González, Eddy Serra, Henry Boyer, an unidentified dancer, Bobby Carcases, Miguelito Checki, Marcelo Bosa. *Courtesy of Emilia Villamíl*

and government officials wooing them. Some of the married men who sent flowers were Martín's friends and partners, and Ofelia was concerned that their wives and children would be embarrassed by any public mention of past indiscretions. In the case of Rothman and Olga Chaviano, however, there was no problem, because Rothman was an American gangster, and Olga was deceased ("*Concho,* a brain aneurysm, same as Celia [Cruz]," said Jenny when Rosa and Ofelia told her their old friend's cause of death). Moreover, Chaviano had been open about her relationship with Rothman. But there were other stories, other so-called *mundos secretos*—"secret worlds"—that were about much more delicate subjects; and although they were about as secret as the fact that la bolita was played at Tropicana every Saturday, my merely mentioning them alarmed Ofelia. "*Por favor,* you cannot even think of telling that story. The man's wife is still alive! His daughters will be reading what you write!"

I assured Ofelia that we would not divulge the name of the Tropicana partner who was the lover of a certain Tropicana mambo dance star (even forty years later, his widow couldn't bear to hear the dancer's name mentioned). Nor would I speculate on whether said partner kept up his affair with the mambo star after he laid eyes on another Tropicana dark-haired dancer and became smitten with her. "I still think too much has been said," remarked Ofelia. I wondered whether it was enough.

By the time Leonela González left Cuba in June 1959, she had been Tropicana's top dance headliner for seven years. She was an island legend, more recognizable than any other dancer except prima ballerina Alicia Alonso and mambo star Ana Gloria Varona, both of whom remained in Cuba after the revolution. Alonso, who later went on to become the first (and as of this writing, the only) director of the Ballet Nacional de Cuba, was a bona fide international ballet star. Together with her husband, Fernando Alonso (unlike most Cuban women, Alicia took her husband's last name), she had worked in the 1940s and 1950s with Jerome Robbins and George Balanchine. She was also a principal dancer with the companies that would later become the New York City Ballet and American Ballet Theatre. Both Leonela and the Alonsos were taught at the school associated with a cultural organization known as Pro-Arte Musical.

I learned about Pro-Arte from its former secretary, Célida Villalón, whose book *Pro-Arte Musical y su divulgación de cultura en Cuba* (Pro-Arte Musical and the Promulgation of Culture in Cuba) is a history of Havana's cultural life between the 1920s and the 1950s. "Ballet is one of the great marks of culture and in Cuba we always saw the greatest dancers," said Villalón with great zeal and Valentín-like speed over the telephone. "This begins way, way back—before independence from Spain. In 1841, [Austrian] Fanny Elssler, one of the four greatest ballerinas of her day, came to Havana. Anna Pavlova danced three times in the Teatro Nacional—in 1914, 1917, and 1918. All sorts of star performers came. Caruso toured the island in 1920. Pro-Arte brought Serge Prokofiev in 1930 and Serge Rachmaninov in 1922 and 1940."

World-class opera, ballet, and theater were staples in Havana, and for the same reason that it boasted great architecture: the city was a crossroads between continents, and everyone there kept abreast of artistic trends in Europe and North and South America. In the era before airplane travel, artists' itineraries often had them passing through Havana on their way to other ports. "The ballet companies came during their off-season, and usually through New Orleans," said Villalón. In 1918, María Teresa García Montes de Giberga, a wealthy Havana socialite, founded the Sociedad Pro-Arte Musical to provide habaneros with a program of music and dance that was not solely dependent on travel schedules and seasonal commitments. Pro-Arte's efforts exposed Cubans to the world's finest dance companies, such as the Ballet Russe de Monte Carlo in 1936, Martha Graham in 1941, and American Ballet Theater in 1948. Pro-Arte also brought orchestras, such as Eugene Ormandy and the Philadelphia Orchestra, to perform at its ornate theatre on D and Calzada Streets in Vedado; opera stars Rosa Ponselle, Renata Tebaldi, and Richard Tucker; and soloists Arthur Rubinstein, Isaac Stern, and Jascha Heifetz.

In 1931, Pro-Arte hired Russian immigrant Nikolai Yavorsky to open Cuba's first ballet academy. Yavorsky and his Russian successor, George Milenoff, trained Alicia Rodríguez and her future husband, Fernando Alonso. Another student was Fernando's brother Alberto, who joined the Ballet Russe de Monte Carlo in 1935, and later became the Pro-Arte school's third and last director. The professional ballet school was one of only two in all of Latin America (the other was at the Teatro Colón in Buenos Aires) and it signified an increased commitment to classical dance in Cuba. This was underscored in 1948, when Alicia and Fernando Alonso returned from New York to found what eventually became the Ballet Nacional de Cuba. Nearly sixty years later, the company continues to produce world-class ballet dancers. Many wind up defecting (like Cuban sisters Lorna and Lorena Feijoo, who, as of this writing, are principals with the Boston and San Francisco ballets respectively); Alonso nonetheless remains a revered figure of the classical dance world, as evidenced by the wide attendance at her annual Festival Internacional de Ballet. (In October 2004, the New York City Ballet was scheduled to perform an all-Balanchine program at the nineteenth annual ballet festival; however the company's application to travel to Cuba was denied by the U.S. Treasury Department, the agency that oversees the embargo, as a means of "enforc[ing] the Cuba sanction program to ensure [that] hard U.S. currency doesn't flow into the hands of Castro and his cronies.")

Leonela's training had begun with Milenoff when she was eight and continued with Alberto Alonso. She then went on to become a charter member of Alicia Alonso's ballet company. But there were problems from the start. "Alicia was not easy to work with," said Leonela. "She did not tolerate competition. As an artist you want a chance to shine. And there was often no money to pay us." At that pivotal moment when Ardura spotted Leonela posing for her photo shoot, she was ready for a change. She became a rare species of dancer: one whose pirouettes and pas de deux were showcased nightly in the world of mambo. "I would dance to the same music as the rest of the cast, but in a classical style—on pointe. I could also dance rumba and congas, but Rodney kept my performances separate, and the people saw me with a different eye than most other performers," explained Leonela, sitting in the Llopis's living room. (Ofelia was videotaping an interview with Leonela, and at one point, the dancer—ever the star—asked her to change seats so she would have a more direct angle to the camera.) Over the years, Leonela's partners alternated between Henry Boyer, Luis Trapaga, and Raul Díaz, all three acclaimed dancers with classical training and who, together with Miguelito Checki, formed the core of Tropicana's male chorus. In keeping with the cabaret's exacting insistence on the highest quality costuming, her tutus and headpieces were made by the same seamstresses who sewed for the Ballet Alicia Alonso. Eventually, both Montmartre and Sans Souci began inviting Alberto Alonso to choreograph performances. But only Tropicana featured a performer of Leonela's caliber nightly.

By mid-1953, Rodney was exploring the potential afforded by an environment with almost no boundaries. In April, several months before Ardura hired Leonela, Rodney had followed *Omelen-ko* with a series of shows that evoked, as the advertisements proclaimed, "the gay and picaresque 1800s." One of them featured Celeste Mendoza, the undisputed queen of a popular type of song inspired by the *guaguancó*, a type of rumba wherein the male dancer performs a distinctive pelvic thrust called the *vacunao* on his partner. Mendoza's deep voice and her brazen delivery of popular songs and boleros in a *guaguancó* style had little to do with what the advertisements chastely proclaimed. Then again, neither did the "Dance of the Fans," performed in the same shows by Chiquita and Johnson. The costumes, on the other hand, were detailed period pieces made at Tropicana in what was beginning to be the country's top costume shop.

"Rodney could spend whatever money he wanted because Martín was obsessed with Tropicana," Olga Guillot told me during a visit to Miami Beach. "When I worked with Miguelito Valdés they made me a dress that cost twenty-five hundred dollars. The dress had yards and yards of handkerchief linen and it was totally decorated with silk ribbons. In another show, I came out wearing a black velvet cape that was thirty-six feet wide. Inside it was completely embroidered with beads, like a backdrop—all done at Tropicana. You should have heard the gasp when the musicians opened it up."

On the bright December day I visited Guillot in her sun-drenched condominium, she waxed eloquent for several hours on the subject of the Paradise Under the Stars.

"I never saw a place with so many seamstresses," she proclaimed. Guillot's speaking voice is rotund and deep, like that of her signature, emotionally charged recordings. In her early years her sound was also passionate, but there was always a light, silvery quality to it as well. "If a dancer had a loose thread, you had to report it immediately and have it fixed before you went on stage. If your heel broke, you'd have to change it before going out or you'd be fined twenty-five pesos. It was considered a *falta de respeto* (lack of respect) to go out with a pin or a tear in your bra. There was a room full of fishnet stockings, shoes in all sizes and colors, all brought in from the United States. Are you getting this? Do you understand what I'm saying?" As she spoke, Guillot swept through her all-white living room in a floor-length orange robe, occasionally stopping to pet one of her two toy dogs and complain of back pain from her performance the night before. Before meeting Guillot, I had no idea what it meant to be in the presence of a true diva. After spending an hour with her, I could imagine no one more suited to her style of song, the bolero, an unabashedly sentimental type of rhythmic ballad with despondent lyrics. At seventy-nine, Guillot was still statuesque and beautiful. She gestured broadly, leaned in closely, rolled her *r*'s and made her *s*'s more sibilant than required by normal conversation as she told me how Martín built a mini-cabaret just for the performers, so they would have a place to gather by themselves before and after the show. "We'd stay there for hours, eating and drinking, talking among ourselves," she said, her voice thick with nostalgia. "*Ay,* how that guajiro loved his Tropicana." It was not hard to imagine Guillot conveying the same emotion when singing "*Mienteme, dime que me quiere, aunque sepa que no es verdad* (Lie to me, tell me you love me, even if I know you don't)," the plaintive refrain to her signature bolero, "*Miénteme*" (Lie to Me).

Guillot's career was linked to Tropicana almost more than that of any other artist. She got her start with Victor de Correa at Edén Concert. Later she performed at Tropicana in half a dozen shows, including the 1954 productions *Canciones de Ayer* (Songs of Yesterday) and *Ritmo en Fantasía* (Rhythm in Fantasy) together with Miguelito Valdés. In 1955 she was in *Bahiondo* and *Flamingo Rhapsody* with Carmen Miranda. By the time she began appearing in Rodney's productions she was one of the most famous female singers in Cuba—even more so than her close friend Celia Cruz, who later had a meteoric crossover career singing salsa in the United States. Guillot's fame reached the United States in 1946, when she recorded a Spanish-language version of Ted Koehler and Harold Arlen's "Stormy Weather." After leaving Cuba, she performed all over the world. On October 31, 1964 she became the first Latin singer to appear onstage at Carnegie Hall. At Tropicana she became close to Ofelia. "She is like a sister to me," Guillot said, "and Tropicana, the cabaret that her husband, Martín Fox, built was the glory of our nation."

In October and November of 1953, Rodney staged two Spanish-themed productions. *Majas de Toro* and *Patio Andaluz* featured a flamenco troupe performing with Paulina Alvarez, a popular singer of *danzonetes,* a type of song which is more or less a formal *danzón* with lyrics. Both the Armando Romeu orchestra and the Senén Suárez conjunto accompanied the productions. At the same time, Martín and his partners began other renovations to Villa Mina, converting the mansion's garages into a smaller, more rustic version of the main casino. Now, less affluent habaneros—the people who would never spend the four pesos for dinner and a show at Tropicana—would also have a place to gamble. Because the work seemed too mundane to relegate to someone of Max Borges's stature, Martín left it to his godson, Hector Carrillo, a man who looked so much like Martín that there was a rumor afloat that he was Martín's son from a previous liaison. (When I mentioned this to Ofelia she sighed and said, "You're going to hear and read a lot of rumors about everyone connected with Tropicana. Especially me and Martín.") The place, which became known as the Casino Popular, was also a boon for the taxi drivers, who were getting tips of a peso apiece for every tourist they brought, plus, in an ingenious marketing ploy that served to redirect many a client away from Sans Souci and Montmartre, a percentage of the house's profit each time their tourist lost in the casino. Instead of waiting up to five hours in their cars while their clients danced and gambled, the drivers could now play dominoes, roulette, and cards in a venue that cost Martín 200,000 pesos to renovate. In other words, they could send their tip and percent right back into Martín's pocket. If they were not gambling men, they could enjoy drinks while listening to a three-piece combo and eat light meals that cost only pennies. Or they could watch the show. In December, for the official opening of the winter tourist season, Rodney staged his second full-out Afro-Cuban production. *Mayombe* maintained the basic structure of *Omelen-ko,* but in place of Chiquita, it was Emilia "La China" Villamíl, one of Tropicana's core group of dancers, who performed the death-defying jump, her waist-length hair sweeping the stage of Arcos de Cristal on her landing, which, as with Chiquita's, was botched by her spotter on opening night.

"I owe this scar on my chin to *Mayombe,*" La China, as she is known to everyone, told me the day I first visited her home in Guanabacoa, the same colonial hilltown on the outskirts of Havana where the Torregrosa family of drummers once lived. It remains a stronghold of Afro-Cuban practice. La China's house was fronted by a long grassy yard, which was bordered by a tall chain-link fence that was padlocked even during the day to protect her from thieves. Huge rosebushes were in need of pruning; a small ginger shrub was in riotous bloom. On the day I arrived it had been raining and La China skipped to the door holding a huge black umbrella that dwarfed her. She commanded her dog, a brown and white mongrel with as bouncy a personality as its mistress, to stay indoors, while she came around to lead me in. La China's modest whitewashed living room was a world away from Guillot's stylish oceanfront condominium. Yet both were animated by their connection to Tropicana. If Guillot's home was that of a diva's, La China's was that of a hardworking dancer, a veteran of the grind of rehearsals (which stars, like Guillot, did not have to attend). Rodney was the main figure in her conversations and his productions the source of most of the photographs in her huge scrapbooks. A collection of brightly colored Santería necklaces hung from nails on the walls of her otherwise bare living room. "Rodney used to buy boxes of these," explained the elfin-looking seventy-year-old as she served me coffee. "On the first night of *Mayombe* I ripped all of my necklaces off after the jump, scattering beads across the stage. I was panicked that they would fire me, but from then on, Rodney said, 'Rip them, rip them! They cost only centavos.' He had such talent. But such a temper! He was always cursing. Were we afraid of him! One summer day I was up a tree, swiping some mamoncillos, when suddenly Rodney stormed in and shouted, 'Rehearsal!' I jumped down so fast I fell onto a glass and cut my foot."

La China's career at Tropicana began in 1951 as a member of las Mamboletas de Gustavo Roig, the dance troupe that performed at the Arcos de Cristal opening. The daughter of a circus magician of Asturian descent and a French and Cantonese mother, her Asian heritage defined her looks. "Rodney liked to feature me because I would really go into the trance in the Afro-Cuban productions," she said. To demonstrate, La China swayed around her living room, imitating the dreamy portion of her role in *Mayombe*. The Afro-Cuban show was the hallmark of the Tropicana winter season. *Mayombe*'s lead singer, Celia Cruz, was accompanied by *danzonete* singer Paulina Alvarez, Mano López, and Kiko González (interestingly Cruz, who was a much bigger star than the others, did not get special billing). The show also featured performances by Italian comic Nazaro; the Solera de España, a grand singing orchestra in the tradition of Los Chavales ("the most applauded orchestra in all of Europe," declared the ad in *Diario de la Marina*); and of course, Leonela and Henry's ballet centerpiece. "They had special giant cigars made for Paulina's performance so you could see them from the audience," said La China. "We would light them for her backstage, but they were so good we kept smoking them and smoking them, until Rodney would yell at us to stop."

The next Afro-Cuban show was *Karabalí*, which opened in December of 1954. It featured China Villamíl again, doing an undulating pelvic dance that embarrassed her slightly. "I was wearing this little bikini, and I had the feeling I was naked. Then I heard Rodney barking at me from offstage, 'Pretend you're pressing

against your boyfriend in a dark corner!' " The show included performances by the Cuarteto D'Aida, Cuba's most popular female
vocal group, which included the bolero singer Elena Burke; Moraima
Secada, the aunt of future Latin-pop singer, Jon Secada; Haydee
Portuondo; and Haydee's sister Omara Portuondo, who years later,
as a grandmother would see a dramatic resurgence of her popularity after she was selected by Ry Cooder to be part of the Buena Vista
Social Club. Other elements in *Karabalí* included a new brother-
sister, Chiquita-and-Johnson-style acrobatic dance pair that went by
the name Julia y Darvas. Julia also became great friends with Ofelia.
"She would come to see me at my table," Ofelia recalled. "She gave
me a lovely ring I had admired on her hand. And even though she
didn't sing, when she found out that my favorite song was 'Noche
de ronda,' she learned it and had an arrangement made to sing it for
me every night. She always looked directly at me when she sang it.
And one night, when I was not at my table—maybe we had taken
someone to another cabaret . . . who knows!—she forgot the words.
They told me this the next day."

Ofelia's friendship with Julia was the source of an anonymous
letter to Martín. "Be careful of the friendship between Julia Darvas and your wife," it warned. The anonymous author reported
that Ofelia had been spotted at the Hotel Nacional with Julia Darvas. "I don't want you to be friends with her," demanded Martín
when he confronted Ofelia. "Tell her not to come around to our
table between shows."

Ofelia would have none of it. "Martin, if you want that, you
are going to have to tell her yourself. She's your employee." Martín
did no such thing. Soon Julia y Darvas's contract was up and the
matter never came up again.

THOUGH THE AFRO-CUBAN spectacle was the crowning feature
of each year's tourist season, several months before *Karabalí*'s
opening Rodney came up with an idea that proved that either he

was out of his mind or a bona fide genius. "I'll never forget when Martín told me they were bringing lions and an elephant to Tropicana," said Ofelia about the show that would be titled *El Circo*. Rodney's circus show was going to feature two lions, a leopard, six monkeys, several miniature horses, a pygmy elephant, and an entire crew of acrobats, trapeze artists, contortionists, clowns, and magicians. The performers were hired en masse from the Cuban circus. Among them were La China Villamíl's magician father and a young makeup artist named Carlos Gomery, who had worked on a staging of the Broadway musical *The Greatest Show on Earth* at Havana's Biltmore Country Club. La China (who had gotten her training in the circus) was put to work with the lion tamers, dancing between animal acts. If all this was not sufficiently diverting, there were also Armando Romeu's musical selections. *Show* magazine, a new monthly founded by attorney Carlos Palma that was billed "*La revista de los espectáculos*" (by coincidence, Palma was the lawyer who represented Victor de Correa in a 1941 battle with neighbors over noise at Villa Mina) described the show's music in a three-page spread devoted to *El Circo* when it opened in July 1954: "In the first show of the evening, that of *El Circo*, [Romeu] selects a medley of rapturous numbers: 'Lover,' 'The Charge of the Light Brigade,' 'Black Magic,' 'Caravan,' 'Tea for Two,' 'Artistry in Bolero,' 'Temptation'—arranged by Julio Gutierrez—'Mazucamba,' 'Stardust,' 'In the Mood,' and for the finale, the march from the film *Show Business*."

FOR THE one thirty A.M. show, called *Luna de Tropicana*, Romeu's musical selections included: "Stranger in Paradise" and "Moonlight Serenade." The finale, which was danced to George Gershwin's "Rhapsody in Blue," featured all the performers—the models, the dance corps, a few trapeze artists, and the soloists—dressed in black outfits with fluorescent blue threads visible only under ultraviolet light. They even wore a blue makeup base on their faces which Gomery the makeup man had specially produced by Max Factor in Hollywood.

This Tropicana night didn't end there. While *El Circo's* elephants galumphed across the stage (on opening night, *Show* reported, the dancer Zonia panicked while mounting the elephant, causing "the greatest of the mammals" to drop to the ground, tumbling her off and into Rodney, who had come to her rescue); and Leonela pranced along the top of a cage containing two full-grown male lions; and Marta Véliz, an aspirant in the upcoming Miss Cuba contest and the reported mistress of General Fernandez Miranda ("What a body on that woman!" exclaimed Bebo Valdés, when I showed him a photograph of Véliz) performed a Zsa Zsa Gabor-style number wearing only a bikini and an eye patch; a gala dinner was in process at a ringside table. The honoree was Carmen Franco, daughter of "el Generalisimo," Francisco Franco, who was then fifteen years into what would eventually become a thirty-five-year dictatorship of Spain.

Ofelia had no recollection of playing host to the Spanish strongman's family. "They were there like anyone else," she said, shrugging. Yet there is an irresistible parallel in this event. At roughly the same time that Franco's daughter was being feted at Tropicana, the streets of Havana were buzzing about an anti-Batista manifesto that was circulating clandestinely. *La historia me absolverá* (*History Will Absolve Me*) was a recompilation of a speech that a fervent thirty-year-old lawyer named Fidel Castro had made in his own defense during his October 1953 trial for leading a bloody assault on Santiago de Cuba's Moncada military barracks and on the army's barracks in the historic interior town of Bayamo. When the pamphlet began to turn up in Havana, Castro was in jail on the Isle of Pines, as was his brother, Raúl. Most of his other men had been killed in the aftermath of the attack, which had taken place in the early hours of July 26, 1953, while most of the soldiers on duty at the barracks were sleeping off the drunkenness of Santiago de Cuba's rowdy *carnavales*. Castro's plan to topple Batista had failed. But the viciousness of the government's response (many of his men were brutally tortured, some dragged behind cars to their deaths) brought him widespread sympathy from those opposed to Batista. His group garnered for itself a following and a name—the 26th of July Movement. The pamphlet was seen as a sign that a revolutionary movement against Batista's military government was beginning to take root.

One night in Glendale, as Ofelia prepared cocktails, I asked whether she had seen *La historia me absolverá* when it came out. She calmly continued pouring ice over brandy and vermouth. Rosa, I noticed, was eyeing her and deliberately not saying anything.

"Of course we knew what happened at Moncada," said Ofelia dryly, "but I never heard a thing about that pamphlet."

"I was already in New York," added Rosa carefully. "But I heard about it. *Vaya*, as far as I knew, even the cat knew about *La historia me absolverá*. And . . ." Rosa hesitated, looking at Ofelia, then at me. "Personally, I was against Batista, because he just took over. And you know me. Freedom is not even my middle name, it's my birthday—July fourth. I don't care about political parties. I believe in freedom. Let the people choose what they want. Batista wasn't giving us a choice. Fidel was a possibility. At that point, anyway."

"What did Martín say about the pamphlet?" I asked.

"Martín was too busy running a business that employed more than four hundred people," said Ofelia. She handed each of us an Omelenko, a drink she had invented in honor of the show of the same name. "Come on, let's toast. To Tropicana."

CHAPTER 15

On Diamonds, Razzle, and Goddesses of the Flesh

It was mid-November and ninety degrees in Havana, but I was as cool as *coco-glacé* inside the air-conditioned bedroom of the former Tropicana model, Alicia Figueroa. This was our first meeting and Alicia paced as she talked on the telephone to a representative from Cubacel, the state-run cell phone company. She had just come in from Merida, where she lived with her husband, Mario Menendez, publisher of a popular leftist daily, as part of a delegation that was to attend Cuba's yearly Havana International Exposition. The *feria*, as this trade show was called, seemed an ironic thing for a country that supposedly allows no private enterprise. It was a standard capitalist showcase for food products, furniture, cars, and electronics from Cuba's trading partners, as well as items like lamps, handbags, and shoes that were manufactured locally. The *feria* opened the day after my meeting with Alicia, and she had many things to arrange and many old friends to contact before she had to appear at the convention center, a sprawling late-1970s complex set among the mansions of Havana's Siboney neighborhood.

"Forgive me for this, but if I don't activate my cellular, I'll be stuck out there incommunicado," said Alicia of the glamorous but remote neighborhood where Alberto Ardura built himself a house in 1958 (it now serves as a government guest house). An expert multi-tasker, the former model flitted around the bedroom of the apartment she still kept in Havana as she was put on hold, applying eyeliner, drinking coffee, chatting with a friend and former Tropicana dancer, Leowaldo Fornieles, who had dropped by to say hello.

I had much to do that morning; but doing anything in Cuba generally involves a great deal of waiting. So I entertained myself by talking to Fornieles, a rail-thin, red-cheeked chatterbox whose carriage unmistakably denoted him as a former dancer. Like most Tropicana old-timers, Fornieles had a treasure trove of impressions and almost-forgotten tales. "Marlon Brando was at the bar one night and in the dressing room all the girls were going crazy," he told me. "Rodney told them, 'Dejenlo tranquilo putas! [Leave him alone, whores!]' He called the girls '*putas,*' but he meant it without ill will. He loved the girls. Brando had already won the Oscar [in 1954, for *On the Waterfront*], but he was crazy for Cuban music and he flew down to find a *tumbadora*. That night he even tried to buy one off of Armando Romeu! In the end he left Tropicana without the drum, but he left for Club 21 with two of the most beautiful *modelos,* Berta Rosen and Sandra Taylor." (Ofelia had forgotten about the Brando event until her memory was jostled by Fornieles's recollection. When I told her about it, she said that she and Martín had failed to see Brando that night, but they had heard that the star had come to Tropicana dressed in a flowered shirt and casual slacks. "We had a closet full of men's jackets and ties for that purpose. But I don't think anyone went up to Marlon Brando and told him to improve his outfit.")

"Oh, those were such beautiful days! We had so much fun," said Fornieles, sighing. From a frayed blue airline shoulder bag he produced photographs of himself beside Leonela González. "That was the party after we returned from performing at the Waldorf-Astoria in New York. It went on all afternoon and into the evening. When we got on the plane to go, Rodney offered a prize to the person who was best dressed for the airplane ride. Leonela was wearing a suit with two fur pieces, one on each shoulder—of course she won."

In the days to come Fornieles would introduce me to several other Tropicana performers, such as Gladys González, a member of the dance pair Gladys and Fredy, as well as a male hustler who used to hang around the bar and pick up tourists and asked to be identified only as Pepe. Pepe's stories ranged from the titillating ("the house knew what we were up to, and they encouraged us to be there") to the positively scandalous. ("The one guy you had to watch out for was Papo Batista, the president's son. If he took a shine to you, *te ponía en candela!*" which roughly means, "you'd be in big trouble.") But those and other tales of gossip were still days away when I sat on Alicia's leopard-print bedspread. Then Fornieles was eager to talk about himself.

"I was in the chorus for . . . oh, had to be five years, or more! I worked with Roderico, with Tomás [Morales]. I was in the show that went to the Waldorf-Astoria in New York, I worked with Rosita Fornés, also with Celia Cruz in *Bongo Congo*, which went to the Miami auditorium after the revolution in fifty-nine. My brother was there at the time, he was a pitcher with the Red Sox, and I called him in Boston, because you know in those days"—he lowered his voice—"everyone was staying. It was the time. So I asked my brother what to do and he said, 'Don't be crazy! Now that Batista's gone is when we should go back. I'm returning after the baseball season.'" Fornieles seemed to disappear into his chair as he talked of his brother, right-handed pitcher José Miguel "Mike" Fornieles, who was with the Boston Red Sox at the time, but began his major league career in September 1952 by pitching a one-hit game for the Washington Senators. Fornieles played next for the

White Sox and then the Orioles, finally joining the Red Sox in 1957. This was at a time when the sheer number of Cuban players in the majors, and the number of American pros who played in Cuba during the winter season, made the difference between the two countries' baseball leagues practically inconsequential. America's national pastime is also Cuba's obsession. For nearly a century it joined the two countries more than anything else.

Baseball made its way to Cuba sometime around the mid-1860s or the 1870s, roughly thirty years after it was supposed to have begun in the United States. It was brought to Havana by middle- and upper-class Cubans who were studying in the United States. Both Estéban Bellán, who played on Fordham University's baseball team in 1871, and Nemiso Guillo, who was at the University of Alabama roughly ten years earlier, are anecdotally credited with being the first to return to the island with bats and balls in their suitcases. The presence of American sailors and businessmen led to the game's rapid dissemination across the island. According to historian Roberto González Echevarría, whose book *The Pride of Havana: A History of Cuban Baseball* provides a thorough account of the subject, so popular was baseball in Cuba in the 1890s that guides for visitors included the location of the baseball clubs, complete with ballrooms for dancing the *danzón*. By the time of the war with Spain in 1898 and the four subsequent years of United States occupation, there already existed a Cuban baseball league (official statistics were kept as of the 1885–86 season); Cuban players were in the major leagues; and American teams like the Negro Leagues' Cuban X-Giants (González Echevarría reports that the use of the word *Cuban* in the name of this most famous of the Negro League teams is a sign of the early influence of Cuba on United States baseball) and a barnstorming team of major leaguers called the All Americans were coming to Havana to play against the Cubans.

By 1920, the two nations' baseball communities were as inextricably intertwined as the cork and rubber inside a baseball.

Regular visits to Havana by Negro and major league teams such as the Cuban X-Giants, Brooklyn Dodgers, Pittsburgh Pirates, and both the Philadelphia Phillies and Athletics continued. Charles Stoneham and John McGraw brought the New York Giants down regularly, possibly so they could spend time at Havana's Oriental Park, which they had purchased in 1919. Babe Ruth arrived in October of 1920 for the beginning of the Liga Nacional de Base Ball de la República de Cuba's regular season—it was the year that he had hit fifty-four home runs for the New York Yankees—and made two thousand dollars a game playing with the Giants against the Havana teams Habana and Almendares. (It was reported that "the Babe," an avid gambler, lost most of his earnings betting on jai alai.)

Because Cuban teams were not racially segregated, when American players began regularly going south for la Liga's winter season, Havana became the first arena for integrated baseball. Years before Jackie Robinson broke through the color line in Brooklyn, players such as Ty Cobb and Carl Hubbell faced Cubans of all races and members of the Negro Leagues in Havana. "If a proving ground was necessary to show that blacks could compete with whites, that the two could co-exist on the same squad, or to dispel any racial shibboleth," wrote Rob Ruck in the fifth edition of *Total Baseball: The Official Encyclopedia of Major League Baseball*, "Caribbean baseball was just that." Nonetheless, Cuban players who played together in the winter season suddenly found themselves segregated when they went north. The contradiction, wrote Ruck, was not lost on the American public.

In the 1930s and 1940s, both the Major League and the Negro League were filled with Cubans. Some were exceptional athletes, heroes on both sides of the Straits of Florida. Matanzas native Martín Dihigo, who played in the Negro Leagues for twelve years, became a member of the halls of fame of the United States, Cuba, and Mexico. The website of the National Baseball Hall of Fame in

Cooperstown, New York, names Dihigo "perhaps the most versatile player in baseball history." Almendares pitcher Adolfo Luque had twenty seasons with teams such as the Cincinnati Reds, where in 1923 he had a 27 and 8 record and a 1.93 ERA, considered to be one of the best records of any pitcher in major league history. In the United States he was known as both the "Havana perfecto" and "The Pride of Havana." (Ofelia also remembered that he was the subject of a rumba entitled "Papa Montero," and that he was famous in Cuba for losing his temper and breaking Casey Stengel's nose during a Giants-Reds game.) In addition to these standouts, there was a constant flow of players between the countries. The Washington Senators actively began recruiting in Havana following the 1933 World Series, when Luque's relief stint at the mound shut out the Senators in the seventh game.

Yet perhaps the most important connection between Cuban and American baseball was eventually formed in the minor leagues. In 1954, the Havana Sugar Kings were established as a AAA International League team affiliated with the Cincinnati Reds. It was considered by many to be the first step towards the establishment of a Cuban-based major league franchise. Though the Sugar Kings' roster included many Americans as well as players from Puerto Rico, Venezuela, Mexico, and Panama, the team reveled in the association with Cuba. On the road in their first season, it brought along its own eleven-piece *charanga* band, which played whenever the team was at bat. In October of 1959, almost ten months after Batista had fled the island, the Sugar Kings won the Minor League World Series in Havana. Fidel Castro threw out the first ball in front of thirty thousand cheering supporters who gave him a standing ovation.

"After baseball was nationalized, the American teams stopped coming down, and my brother never returned," said Leowaldo Fornieles wistfully. Meanwhile Alicia Figueroa breezed toward us, phone at her ear, offering little porcelain cups of coffee prepared by her Havana housekeeper. Fornieles handed me my cup then sipped elegantly from his. "Three times I applied for United States visas," he said, "but the Americans denied me every time."

Hearing Fornieles say this, Alicia cupped her hand over the receiver and pointed out the window. *"Mira, la sección de interés,"* she whispered slyly. Indeed, within a stone's throw of her balcony stood the imposing stone and glass rectangle that houses the United States Interests Section in Havana. Up until that moment I had somehow not noticed it, but there it was—the hub of the exile drama, the symbol of the conflict between Cuba and the United States, or more aptly, between Cubans in Cuba and Cubans in the United States.

La sección de interés, "the interests section" as it is called in Cuba, was a United States embassy until January 3, 1961, when the outgoing U.S. president, Eisenhower, broke off diplomatic relations with Cuba. It was turned over to the Swiss Embassy, which represented American interests in Cuba and Cuban matters in Washington until 1977, when President Jimmy Carter established limited diplomatic relations with Cuba once again, in part to facilitate visits by Cuban exiles to their relatives on the island. Henceforth, the interests section has effectively become an embassy, with a chief officer whose diplomatic status is equal to that of an ambassador.

You can't miss the interests section when you walk along the Malecón. The building is ringed by a series of guard kiosks and a forbidding-looking steel-post fence painted beige, presumably to blend visually with the local Jaimanitas stone that now covers the facade (originally it was clad in travertine). The structure is an austere rectangle of glass and stone that would fit in at Lincoln Center in New York or on the Mall in Washington. In fact, the building's architects, the New York firm of Harrison & Abramovitz, later went on to design Avery Fisher Hall and the Metropolitan Opera House at Lincoln Center, as well as Empire State Plaza in Albany,

New York; the firm had already designed the United Nations head-quarters in New York and CIA headquarters in Langley, Virginia. According to Eduardo Luis Rodríguez, Cuba's leading authority on modernist architecture, the prestige of Harrison & Abramovitz and the building's prime location on the Malecón caused something of a sensation in 1953. Yet, writes Rodríguez, "The architects failed to take into account the Cuban climate, to which the building exposes an excessive amount of glass."

From Alicia's window it was hard not to see this as symbolic. I watched the slow-moving, long queue of visa applicants that formed every morning before dawn. Dour Cuban soldiers checked names off an appointment list. When an applicant reached the entrance gate, a uniformed United States Marine inspected his application documents before allowing him inside, usually to wait at least another hour. The process was grueling and often humiliating. In late 2003—the time of my first visit to Alicia's apartment—Cuba had been placed on the United States Office of Homeland Security's list of terrorist nations, and as a result, the response was frequently negative. Even artists, filmmakers, and educators who had traveled repeatedly to the United States by invitation of the Museum of Modern Art or the Grammy Awards committee were routinely denied visas on the grounds that their presence was detrimental to the interests of the United States—the same language used to keep potential terrorists out of the country.

In mid-2005, hopes of reconciliation between the two countries remain dim. That was a fact hard to imagine in 1953, when the building first opened its doors. Back then there was almost no border between the two countries. Americans flocked to Cuba, and tens of thousands of Cubans visited the United States annually. Among the many Cubans who honeymooned in Miami were Fidel Castro and his first wife, Mirta Díaz Balart, in 1948; and my parents, who were married in 1954. Pan American averaged twenty-eight daily flights between Miami and Havana. In 1948, roundtrip airfare cost thirty dollars. In spring and summer, Havana's newspapers were filled with advertisements for hotels and shops in Miami. The Peninsular & Occidental Steamship Company, with offices at municipal pier #2 in Miami and on the Paseo del Prado in Havana, published guidebooks in Spanish for the Cubans who went to Miami for weekend shopping trips, advertising everything from Burdine's department stores to Wolfie's Jewish delicatessen. Martín Fox was liberal about sending his staff to the United States for anything that was needed. Pedro Fox and Ernesto Capote, Tropicana's lighting designer, went several times a year to purchase meat and alcohol, as well as lightbulbs and electrical cable. Rodney and the costume designers went to New York annually to buy fabric, shoes, sequins, and feathers.

Nineteen fifty-three, the year that Alicia Figueroa began dancing with Alberto Alonso's conjunto at Montmartre, was also the year that Meyer Lansky left the county jail in Saratoga after serving a two-month sentence and made what was to be a permanent move to Cuba. Lansky had pleaded guilty to conspiracy, forgery, and gambling charges brought against him by New York State under pressure from the Kefauver Committee. Despite this, Lansky was back on the nation's payroll as a gambling advisor, courtesy of his old pal Batista, as soon as he made it back down to Havana. Lansky might seem a poor choice for a nation trying to maintain good relations with the United States, but gambling was Lansky's business, and he had a reputation for scrupulousness among both his peers and enemies. At the time Cuba desperately needed someone who could restore the reputation of the casinos after a cheating scandal that had threatened its growing tourist industry.

The scandal was sparked by a fast-paced and tricky combination dice-and-card game known as razzle or razzle-dazzle. According to Valentín, who told me what he knew about it, razzle-dazzle is a game with shifting rules that only the dealers seem to understand. ("Don't even talk to me about it," he said, when I asked him to explain how it was played. "Those guys were crooks. And what's worse, they wouldn't teach any of us how to run the game.") Razzle would be offered to a client by a smooth-talking dealer—always an American—who would insist that it was easy, that the odds were stupendous, and that there was no way to lose. In truth, there was no way to win. Under the thrall of the lights and the music, with a few rum-and-Cokes under his or her belt, and the dealer shuffling cards and rolling dice rapidly, promising double or nothing as a way to make up losses, a player was a sitting duck. "Among the victims was a honeymoon couple who lost the five hundred dollars they had saved towards furnishing their apartment. Another was a mother of four children who paid her losses with five checks, predated against her husband's salary," wrote *Saturday Evening Post* reporter Lester Velie, in an exposé that appeared in the widely read March 1953 issue. Velie's article, "Suckers in Paradise, How Americans Lose Their Shirts in Caribbean Gambling Joints," identified Tropicana as the operating place of Billie Bloom, "the most expert of the razzle pitchmen." And it would have been disastrous for tourism had Batista not taken action before the article even appeared.

Complaints had been filtering in to the embassy in Havana, and these were being transmitted to Marcial Facio, president of Cuba's tourism commission. Then, one day in 1952, a Pasadena lawyer named Dana Smith fell victim to a razzle scheme at Sans Souci while on vacation in Cuba. Smith lost four thousand dollars to the razzle dealer in a matter of minutes. He wrote a check to cover the losses, but upon his return to the United States he cancelled payment and was subsequently sued by Norman Rothman, San Souci's manager. But Smith had powerful political connections, most notably Senator and Vice President–elect Richard M. Nixon. In fact, Smith was one of the organizers of a private fund that had put Nixon's candidacy in jeopardy when it was made public by the *New York Post*, and that eventually led to Nixon's famous "Checkers" speech. Smith's complaint to Nixon set off a chain of phone calls to the state department, to the embassy in Cuba, and the Cuban tourism commission. When word reached Batista himself, he acted swiftly. A brief note in the March 31, 1953 issue of the *New York Times* announced the ouster of thirteen Americans who were "employees of the Sans Souci and the Tropicana night clubs." Velie reported that "helmeted and bayonet-wielding Cuban troops marched into the gambling joints and ordered the [razzle] games out. Gun [*sic*] in hand, they patrolled the casino entrances to keep the games banished."

"*Na', na',* there weren't any soldiers," scoffed Valentín when I read to him from the article. "But *si*, I remember our guy. Dino Cellini brought him by for Martín. He would post himself at the door, to get people as they were coming in. Once this young couple lost like a hundred dollars before they even set foot in the casino, and that's when a hundred dollars was something. When Salas Cañizares [Havana's chief of police] came to arrest him he took off running into the fields behind the cabaret."

"*CHICA,* I WAS working at Sans Souci back then, but I don't recall anything about that razzle scandal," said Alicia, breezing by on three-inch platform mules, her pink tunic rustling against brown gabardine slacks as I discussed the matter with Fornieles. I had been waiting just under an hour for her, not bad by Cuban standards. Besides, watching her walk around with the phone glued to her ear was like getting a lesson in regalness. Her voice was even-toned and musical, even as she explained her cell phone situation for the umpteenth time to someone who was evidently still unable to solve her problem. Anyone else would have been exasperated at this point, but Alicia's only sign of impatience was the occasional tapping of her terracotta-colored nails against a tabletop. She was tall and long-limbed, with the robust sensuality of Sofia Loren, and a wide, perfect smile. Her skin was flawless. She was sixty-six years old, but if not for her white hair, which she wore cropped and swept off her face, she could have passed for forty. Not that she was trying to. Like Ofelia, Alicia seemed completely comfortable with age. She did not agonize over it; when asked, she told the truth.

Our mission that morning—our first day together, after weeks of talking on the phone and e-mailing from Los Angeles to the Yucatan—was to visit Ana Gloria Varona. Alicia had tried calling the former mambo star on my behalf but had gotten no answer. "Let's just go to her house, we've got a car." As I watched her step outside her building, I immediately wondered how she'd manage on those three-inch platform heels. In this windswept part of Vedado, where Alicia still retained the apartment she had lived in before marrying the Mexican publisher and leaving Cuba, there were so many holes and chunks of lifted sidewalk that breaking one's ankle wearing running shoes would have been a distinct possibility; but she gingerly stepped around mud and pools of water from a morning rainstorm without so much as a downward look. We got into her brand-new rented Nissan. "It's another world in here," quipped a Cuban artist who was joining us this morning. Indeed, there was no comparing the world of cell phones, new-car upholstery, and powerful air-conditioning with the general difficulties—broken sidewalks, blackouts, and shortages—one faced in the rest of Havana. Alicia laughed, then without a trace of irony put on Yves Saint Laurent sunglasses and started the engine.

While we sped along Vedado's wet streets, Alicia made suggestions about whom else I should meet. "You've got to see Rosita Fornés," she said, referring to the country's most beloved *vedette,* a term for a cabaret singer-dancer, similar to a musical theater performer. The blond Fornés starred in only one of Tropicana's shows—Rodney's 1955 version of the opera *The Merry Widow,* titled *Las Viudas Alegres*—but her name was forever linked to

Tropicana, possibly because *Las Viudas* was such a huge favorite with the Cuban public. It was first staged in 1952, starring *vedette* Zoraida Marrero as well as Ana Gloria and Rolando, and then a third time in 1957, with Jenny León in the starring role.

"Tomorrow we'll drive out to Guanabacoa to see La China Villamíl," Alicia continued. "And you also must meet my great friend Santiago Alfonso. He's not from the period you're working on, but he has been the choreographer for the last fifteen years. You should also see Tomás Morales, who has taken over the position in the last few months. Both men are very important to the Tropicana story."

Unlike many other Tropicana performers who either left right after the revolution or stayed in Cuba and lost contact with their colleagues in exile, Alicia remains a bridge between the old and new Tropicana. Until 1957, she was one of the cabaret's top models and dancers. She left for a higher paying job at another cabaret, and eventually landed the lucrative job of spokesperson for Trinidad y Hermanos, one of the island's most popular brands of cigarettes. In 1967, after almost a decade in retirement, Alicia began working again, as the mistress of ceremonies in an artistic brigade the government sent around the island to perform in factories and other *centros de trabajo* (workplaces). Those were tough times for performers. "Some *burro* [ass] had decided to close the cabarets and all the artists were left without work," wrote Alicia to Ofelia years later.

They turned Sans Souci into a military school and made plans to do the same with Tropicana. But here let me tell you a lovely story about a worker of Martín's. His name was Miliki, and he worked in the kitchen. He was a staunch supporter of the revolution, but when he heard what they were going to do to Tropicana, he became very distressed. Somehow he had access to Raúl Castro [brother of Fidel Castro and head of the army] and he asked for an interview with him. Miliki told him that Tropicana had been created by a man who'd dedicated his entire life to that place. That he personally tended to every plant, every flower, every corner of that paradise. He'd go every day and if a plant was sick, he'd personally nurse it back, etc. The story of Martín's utter dedication somehow convinced [Raúl Castro] that Tropicana should be preserved for the future and that the Cuban government would never regret it.

Miliki's determination spared Tropicana the fate of Sans Souci. And six years later, Alicia Figueroa, then thirty-seven, became Tropicana's new mistress of ceremonies. In her apartment, Alicia showed me a small black diary she kept during those years. The pages were full of the transliterated names of Eastern bloc dignitaries. "I had to welcome them as guests of honor, and if I didn't write the names out who could possibly pronounce them?" The idea of statuesque Alicia Figueroa greeting Cosmonaut Yuri Gagarin, the first man to circle the earth, to the Paradise Under the Stars sounds like it could be the opening line of a Cuban joke. Indeed, after the Soviets left Cuba, the country abounded with jokes about the Russians. In private, among Cubans, they were known as *bolos* (balls) because, as one friend put it, "Have you ever looked at them?" Cubans are fastidious—no man loves cologne more than a Cuban—and mercilessly funny when it comes to people's physical characteristics. The Eastern Europeans, who were not accustomed to the relentless heat of the tropics, were the butt of many private jokes that in part masked a terrible resentment. In the '70s and '80s, Eastern bloc technocrats and their families were given many privileges not available to the average Cuban; they could have foreign currency (for Cubans this was punishable by ten years in prison) and buy in special stores that had products not available on the open market. Often those products, like canned tuna and cooking oil, were later resold to ordinary Cubans at astronomical black market prices.

"What was it like to work at Tropicana in those days?" I asked Alicia.

"My son's father would not let me take the boy out of the country," she replied, skirting the actual question and justifying why she stayed on after the revolution. "I tried to sneak him out in secret, using false papers. I even had a person who was going to come to the airport and pretend he was the boy's father. But I couldn't go through with it. Once I decided to stay, I chose to incorporate myself into the system. I didn't want my son to grow up the child of a dissident."

Though Alicia tended to be matter-of-fact about her life's choices, the how and why of her decision to stay in Cuba was a subject of some delicacy, largely because it alienated her from some who chose to leave at the beginning. As the car entered the tunnel under the Almendares River, she recounted a story of a trip to Miami the previous year, which coincided with dancer Miguelito Checki's visit from Spain, where he now lives. A party was thrown for Checki at the home of a well-known Tropicana dancer, but Alicia, a dear friend of his, was not invited. Reportedly she was thought to be "too pink" because she did not leave Cuba immediately. It didn't help that, like me, she traveled back and forth to Cuba. "It's inexplicable to me," she lamented, as the car headed back into the open sunshine of Miramar's Fifth Avenue. "Everyone makes their decisions for their own reasons. None of my friends here make me justify to them why I eventually left for Mexico."

There was truth to her argument but it also harbored an obvious blind spot. In Cuba, no one questions why a person leaves because the reasons are so obvious. Economic opportunity is just one reason. Times are hard in Cuba. Whether or not one subscribes to the Cuban government's reasons for the hardship, namely, that the tightening of the United States embargo is placing undue stress on the nation, or the point of view shared by Cuban exiles and many residents within the country who don't want to leave but who want the chance to open a bodega or shoe repair, it is no secret that daily life grows ever more difficult. "Without the few dollars that —— brings me, I wouldn't be able to survive," said a former Tropicana dancer, who insisted I not name him or his benefactor. In some ways, that's no different than anywhere else. Without money, it is also hard to manage in New York, Sao Paolo, and New Delhi. But Cubans were given another type of expectation, and life was radically upended to support this vision.

We reached glamorous Miramar and pulled up beside Ana Gloria Varona's yellow stucco mansion. Things here did not look so very different than they must have in 1953, when the tunnel under the Almendares River was opened, allowing for swifter access to the suburbs and the Marianao casinos. Except for the flapping embassy flags, satellite dishes, and the numbers of late-model cars belonging to the embassy personnel who occupy the mansions that once belonged to Cuba's wealthiest families, this could have been just another sultry fall day in the 1950s when Alicia was making her way to Tropicana for an afternoon rehearsal, or when Martín Fox set out to see General Fernandez Miranda about securing zoning variances for a series of apartment houses he was trying to build next door to his and Ofelia's seaside home. In contrast to the rest of Havana, Fifth Avenue boasted fresh paint and clipped shrubbery. Along the center divider of the boulevard, the trees were trimmed into bell-shaped topiary, as they had been in the 1950s. Ringed by high hedges, Ana Gloria's home was a square two-story Spanish-style house that would not have looked out of place in Beverly Hills. She had shared it for years with her late and last husband, the high-ranking revolutionary general, Jorge "Yoyo" García Bando.

Alicia asked me to wait for her in the car. Behind the hedges, two gardeners were pruning trees. Alicia rang Ana Gloria's doorbell. A big white German shepherd trotted out when the door was opened, then trotted back in after Alicia.

While she was gone, my artist friend furtively snapped pictures of embassy sentinels and some children roller-skating around the topiary. I watched the cars on Fifth Avenue, imagining Ofelia whizzing past the mansions in her blue Eldorado convertible, with Sunan, the lion cub, riding shotgun. (Rosa now does most of their driving, but when Ofelia used to drive regularly she was a speed demon.) I pictured Martín in his white trousers and guayabera, overseeing the construction of the four seaside buildings a few blocks further north. Once they were completed, Martín rented out one of the four-story apartment houses, gave each of his sisters one, and gave another to Ofelia.

For Ofelia this was the greatest gift, better than all the jewelry Martín ever bought for her, because it enabled her family to move in next door to her. Ofelia's nephew—Fara and Atilano Taladrid's son, Raúl—still lives in an apartment that Martín and Ofelia had rented to him when he was first married. His son, Reinaldo, the man who originally gave me Ofelia's phone number, has settled into his late Grandmother Fara's apartment. I thought about going over to the buildings but held back because of the bad blood between the relatives. I also worried that the two men, who were both high-level members of the present government, might not have taken kindly to my probing, especially if they knew I was now close with Ofelia and writing about Tropicana. As of this writing, Ofelia's nephew Raúl Taladrid is deputy minister for foreign investment and economic collaboration; his son Reinaldo is a television newscaster and member of the "Mesa Redonda," a political roundtable that airs several times a week to discuss issues, ranging from the foreign policy views of the 2004 American presidential candidates to the fate of five Cubans who were convicted of spying in the United States in 2001. My fear was that one of the Taladrids would try to thwart future attempts of mine to get back into the country. Though I had had no run-ins with either of them, it was not a far-fetched worry. The Cuban government is hypersensitive about the written word. Two art historian colleagues of mine were barred from entering Cuba after writing books—in both cases seemingly benign art texts with only tangential political content—that still managed to offend the authorities. So instead of visiting Ofelia's relatives, I imagined her and Rosa with me waiting for Ana Gloria, enjoying the sunny morning in her old neighborhood. I daydreamed about us having our nightly cocktail under the mamoncillo trees at Tropicana. It was a lovely thought, but impossible. For decades a dividing line has existed between those Cuban exiles who travel to Cuba and those who refuse to go there while Fidel Castro stays in power. I sometimes felt Ofelia was tempted to return, but Rosa Sanchez, who left Cuba well before the revolution, was a broken record on the matter: "I will not go anywhere where I am not free to speak my mind!"

After nearly forty minutes, Alicia was back, with the weary countenance of someone returning from a particularly tough diplomatic mission. "Ana Gloria was worried about the way she looked," she said, slipping back into the driver's seat. "She's going to fix herself up, then meet us for lunch."

Now that I had spent so much time with former Tropicana showgirls, both in person and by leafing through the pages of the magazines that are a record of their glamorous past, I realized the mistake we made in simply showing up at Ana Gloria's unannounced. The women of Tropicana do not face the public without looking their best; even now, when most of them are grandmothers. Cabaret women were revered for their beauty. Their looks earned them the name of *diosas*, "goddesses," whose sequin-clad bodies were the quintessential expression of their country's celebrated sensuality. At the larger cabarets, such as Tropicana, Sans Souci, and Montmartre, and even at many of the smaller ones, like the Cabaret Nacional at the corner of Prado and San Rafael in

Central Havana, or the rustic Bambú on the road to the airport, production numbers included scores of dancers, singers, and *vedettes*. There were also *modelos*—models whose job consisted mainly of sashaying along the stage and, at Tropicana, on catwalks in the trees, wearing outfits designed to show them off. Jenny León was a modelo. So was Alicia Figueroa, though she had been trained as a dancer. Ana Gloria Varona was strictly a dancer. She was Cuba's leading performer of *baile típico*, the term used for traditional Cuban dances like mambo, cha-cha-cha, *guaracha*, and *son*. Her fame came more from what she did than what she looked like. But her appearance contributed. Ana Gloria was small, shapely, with dark features and a rosebud mouth that was pursed in perpetual coquettishness. In October 1955, when she returned to Tropicana after a hiatus to appear in the Asian-themed show *Casa de Té*, *Show* magazine ran a photo of her with the caption *"bella entre bellas"* (a beauty among beauties). Actually, Ana Gloria was not as striking physically as Leonela González, Jenny León, or Alicia Figueroa; but she emanated playful sexuality. She oozed it and winked it from the pages of the February 1958 *Show*, where she is pictured crouching in a leotard on the cover, and smoldering in a black halter bikini on the pages inside. She was twenty-two then, and had been a star for seven years. The article in *Show* describes her body almost as much as it does the spice and speed of the mambos she performed with her longtime partner, Rolando. But this was the 1950s, when such things were applauded without reservation. More importantly, this was Cuba, where, even now, broad hips, a well-formed pair of legs, and most of all, full, round *nalgas* (the most elegant term used to describe a woman's bottom) can still elicit block after block of heartfelt, if disingenuous, marriage proposals.

In Cuban argot, the comments that men deliver to women on the street are known as *piropos*. *Piropos* are not lewd and aggressive. They are usually uttered softly, unlike a catcall. The classic *piropo* is affectionate, expressing joy at what the Cuban man considers God's greatest creation. Sexist? Absolutely. But when you walk down the streets of Havana and someone murmurs, *"Mami, me estás matando* (Baby, you're killing me)"; *"Voy a soñar con esos ojos* (I'm going to dream of those eyes)"; or the most famous *piropo* of all, *"Si cocinas como caminas, me como hasta la raspa* (If you cook the way you walk, I'll eat even what sticks to the pan)," it is hard not to feel your step grow a little lighter. It's a good idea to keep going, but you might find yourself tossing a smile over your shoulder, moving a little slower, with more subtle bounce and rhythm. Right there, on the streets of Havana, you become a Tropicana modelo, strutting for an appreciative public, showing off what you have to offer.

Nowadays at Tropicana, most of the modelos are attenuated, medium-to-dark-skinned black women. ("Where do these beauties hide? I've never run into a single one!" lamented my artist friend the first time he went to the cabaret.) But in the 1950s, the women were all white or at least had pale skin. "No one could imagine *una negra* as a standard of beauty back then," said a former dancer who asked not to be named. It was unfortunate, for then, as now, the country teemed with stunning women of all skin colors. Tropicana was not alone in this policy of only picking white, or white-looking models and dancers. The pages of *Show* reveal hardly any black women at all, the exception being the singers. On the other hand, there are many, many light-skinned women of mixed race, for the problem was not race itself, but appearance. "There was a standard," said dancer Eddy Serra. "If you were reasonably light-skinned, tall, and shaped like *una guitarra*, you had a chance at stardom."

Still, the general dearth of blacks at Tropicana, both onstage and in the audience, has led some to say that the club had a whites-only policy. It is an accusation Ofelia rejects with even greater vehemence than she does the one about Tropicana being owned by the Mafia.

"That's an absurd point and I want to make sure we address it directly," she insisted during one of our earliest meetings. I had asked the question in response to a 1996 *Los Angeles Times* article titled "Legendary Cuban Hot Spot is Newly Hot," in which the reporter published an account of racism told to her by a former Tropicana parking attendant, Policarpo Fajardo Suarez. "When [a group of African-Americans] got to the lobby, the owner refused to let them in," wrote reporter Juanita Darling, specifically stating that it was "Tropicana's owner" who was at the door enforcing the club's alleged whites-only policy.

"Can you imagine something more ridiculous than Martín working the door?" demanded Ofelia when we discussed the article. As it turned out, she had also seen the article and had responded with a terse and pointedly acerbic letter to the *Times:*

> Gentlemen:
>
> This is to let you know that Juanita Darling's article about Havana's nightclub Tropicana . . . erroneously states that the establishment had a whites-only policy in the 1950s.
>
> I am the widow of Martín Fox, owner of Tropicana, and I can assure you that while my husband ran his casino-night club, everyone was welcome if they could pay the tab and wore proper attire (we had a collection of jackets and ties for those who came unprepared.)
>
> Sincerely Yours,
> Ofelia Fox

Ofelia accompanied her letter with photographs that showed her and Martín laughing with Nat "King" Cole and his wife at the bar at Arcos de Cristal. In another picture, she and Martín are standing with a group of Haitians at her table, one of whom, she said, was the president of the country. As with so many matters involving Tropicana, I found myself caught between conflicting positions. On the one hand, the pictures supported Ofelia's statement; on the other, the presence of diplomats and singing legends hardly indicated racial tolerance. But as I looked at those pictures of the Haitian delegation the whole racial question temporarily faded as I wondered whether I was looking at the face of François "Papa Doc" Duvalier, one of the most brutal dictators of the era. The men were, in fact, the country's foreign minister and cultural attaché to Cuba, both of whom had been invited with their wives and assistants to the opening of *Vodú Ritual*, a 1958 Rodney production based on Haitian ritual.

Given that in Glendale there was such adamance but little concrete fact to illuminate the matter of racial tolerance in 1950s Tropicana, I made a point of frequently asking the question in Cuba. When I visited La esquina del jazz, the all-black *jazzista* club in the neighborhood of Santa Amalia, I asked the members if they felt any racial tension when they used to go to the weekend jam sessions. *"Claro que no!"* said Gilberto, the owner of the house. The crowd that surrounded us echoed the sentiment. "But what about the cabaret itself?" I pressed. "Were any of you ever there at night, for the shows?"

"Bueno, not really," said Gilberto uneasily, shrugging. "But that's because it was expensive."

"And most of it wasn't our music," echoed Roberto Cabrera. "We were mainly interested in jazz."

On the patio of the UNEAC, I asked musicologist Helio Orovio to elaborate on the matter. Orovio laughed and stroked his chin as he pondered the question. *"Mira,* it's very complex. Remember that this country had *un mulato* as president, but that man couldn't become a member of the Havana Country Club. And sure, there were all sorts of racial separations here, but remember that here we've always been more liberal about mixed-race couples.

And there were black dance clubs where whites were not admitted. In the cabarets, things were a little different."

"That's right," murmured someone in the all-black crowd of musicians that had gathered around Orovio.

"You have to realize that all our music is black. And many of the musicians were black, without question. And Rodney *era mulato también* . . . But to go as a guest . . ." Orovio pursed his lips, his bushy white brows crowding his eyes, then seeming to scatter across his entire forehead. "It wasn't really about being turned away . . . It was more about spending time where you felt comfortable. In Havana there were dozens of cabarets. Why would you need to go to a place that merely tolerated your presence, if you could go someplace where the music was just as good and where you could be with your own *gente*?"

In his 1930 essay "Cuban Color Lines," American poet and author Langston Hughes described the specifics of the racial question in Cuba:

> In spite of the fact that Cuba is distinctly a Negroid country, there exists there a sort of triple color line. At the bottom of the color scale are the pure-blooded Negroes, black or dark brown in color. In the middle are the mixed bloods . . . Then come the pure white of skin. In Cuba, although these three distinct divisions exist, the lines are not so tightly drawn as in some of the other islands of the Caribbean. The British Islands are the worst in this respect . . .
>
> Occasionally a dark Negro occupies a very high position in Cuba. That is what misleads many visitors from the United States—particularly colored visitors who are looking anxiously for a country where they can say there is no color line—for Cuba's color line is much more flexible than that of the United States, and much more subtle. There are, of course, no Jim Crow cars, and at official state gatherings and

less official carnivals and celebrations, citizens of all colors meet and mingle. But there are definite social divisions based on color—and the darker a man is, the richer and more celebrated he has to be to crash those divisions.

The issue of race at Tropicana was summed up for me by two stories, told to me by former employees of Tropicana. The first was recounted by Pedro Antonio Calvo, a prep cook known as *Goyito*, who spent years in Tropicana's kitchens brewing huge urns of coffee and chopping hundreds of heads of lettuce. "One night this black guy came, wearing a tux, his wife with beautiful clothes, but he came on a Saturday night and there was no table," recalled Goyito, who is himself of African ancestry. "So the guy pulled out a huge tip for the maitre d' and they found him a table but it was behind a tree, and he couldn't see. Then he went into the casino and started losing. He wrote some checks. When they checked on his credit, Martín asked, 'Where is this guy seated?' When he found out, Martín just about hit the roof. 'Find this guy a good table!' he said. 'Make sure he's happy and keeps spending money.'"

The story confirms what Langston Hughes noted about wealth allowing individuals to crash through the racial divide. But a second, more disturbing story was told to me by Bebo Valdés.

One night these four black *peloteros* [ball players] came to the cabaret. They'd come all the time. I knew them. But that night there was a table of about sixty Americans from Mississippi and they complained to the management about the presence of the *peloteros*. Next thing I know, Martín and Ardura call me over. They say, "Bebo, this is happening. What do you think we should do?" They wanted the *peloteros* to leave so the people from Mississippi would not leave. But they didn't want to insult them. Or me. So I said, "Look *gente*, you're my bosses and you do what you think is right.

But in my opinion, you have to do what's good for business." Martín and Ardura went over to the table and asked the *peloteros* to please come back another day. They let them in for free that second time as their guests.

In essence, the ball players were asked to leave.

BLACK OR white, rich or poor, capitalist or communist, there is one thing Cubans on both sides of the Straits of Florida have always agreed upon: a woman's beauty depends upon fullness—especially of the thighs and *nalgas*. Later that day, as I waited with Alicia outside the crowded Cubacel offices, I found myself paying special attention to the constant nonverbal dialogue among men and women. There was plenty to take in: stares, whispers, demure, and some not-so-demure body language. The streets of Havana are mini-theaters, an ongoing *telenovela* (soap opera) *a lo cubano*, actually, and as I watched two young guys jabbing each other furtively as they glanced at the thigh-high hem of someone else's bottom-heavy girlfriend (she was obviously aware and working it, in my opinion), I couldn't help but recall the lyrics of Enrique Jorrín's song, *"La engañadora"* (The Deceiver), which is considered the first cha-cha-cha ever written. The song, which starts off with the phrase, *"A Prado y Neptuno iba una Chiquita...,"* tells the story of a girl who was walking near a busy corner in Central Havana (the corner where the Miami Restaurant was situated). The girl was so well-formed and plump, the song says, that all of the men had to stare at her. However, when they learned that her plumpness was achieved with padding, and that she was deceiving them about her fullness, they stopped staring.

And in Havana, the idea has always been to keep them staring. Rodney looked for that quality directly when he scouted for modelos on the streets and in *el campo*, where he could spot a *guajirita* with the proper raw material a mile away. "He chose them mainly for their bodies, not their faces," remarked Gomery, Tropicana's former makeup man, when I visited him in Miami. "An ugly face can be disguised with makeup, but you can't fake a tiny waist that blossoms into colossal thighs and hips or monumental height. *Por dios*, those women were magnificent!" he cried, looking at photos of Sandra Taylor and Zita Coalla, two of Tropicana's most celebrated modelos.

Raw material was only the beginning of the process of becoming a Tropicana modelo. "The women had to carry themselves regally, like true *diosas de carne*," said dancer Hector Leal, referring to Rodney's April 1958 production, *Diosas de Carne* (Goddesses of the Flesh)—a tribute to female sexuality that was based on the women of Greek literature and mythology. (Of course, Rodney conjured Greece in his own way. One of the production numbers featured model Clarita Castillo bathing in champagne in a gigantic goblet.) If gracefulness did not come naturally to a woman, as it did to a dancer like Alicia Figueroa, there were grueling lessons, and these were in addition to the dance classes that were mandatory for the entire cast and held three mornings a week at Tropicana, where they were taught by either Henry Boyer or Eduardo Perovani, two of the cast's male ballet stars.

Hair was cut short. Rodney felt it added chicness and stature. Dancers Gladys Robau and Monica Castell, and modelos Rosalia Fernandez and the almond-eyed Nora Osorio, who showed up for her audition as a *guajirita* wearing a long ponytail and lopsided beret and went on to become one of the most celebrated modelos in Cuba (and the obsession of singer Miguelito Valdés), were among the stars of Tropicana whose short hairstyles were almost identical. China Villamíl's long hair used to so dramatically sweep the floor in the production of *Mayombe*, was also gone by 1957.

Show magazine featured the women monthly in their saucy "Ensalada de pollos" (chick, or chicken salad) pages. The *pollos electrizantes* (electrifying chicks) were posed in bikinis, shorts, and garter belts, crouching in the sand, sprawling across the deck of a yacht, one leg hitched up, knees crossed, gazing at the viewer from the back, over pointedly provocative captions: "Monica Castell—with that anatomy one can never lose a battle"; "The sculptural Mitsuko Miguel—a splendid invitation to life"; "The sweet and spectacular Sarah Corona—few women in this world can offer the characteristic of a twenty-three inch waist and thirty-nine inch hips . . . upon her graceful gait one can hear unanimous murmurs of exaltation among the public."

Then there was the beloved Leonela, the darling of all Cubans, who graced the covers of both the April 1955 and June 1957 issues. Leonela's pictures reveal a fullness that would normally be anathema to any other ballerina. "Speaking of Leonela's legs," reports the 1955 article, "we recently learned that the first lady among our dancers has had the foresight to insure them against accident. The sum? Not more nor less than $30,000. And a small sum it is indeed, given that the secret to her success is in those shapely lovely legs." The accompanying photographs beg the question—as *Show* would have so dramatically asked: what about the rest of her?

AT EXACTLY two in the afternoon, Alicia and I stepped into the garden patio of La Fontana, a *paladar* where we were to meet Ana Gloria for lunch. *Paladares* are a type of house-based restaurant in Cuba, one of the few businesses that can be privately owned and operated. There are many rules and, of late, many restrictions to the operation of these restaurants, but in the verdant surroundings of the business that is half-owned by Ana Gloria's son-in-law, you sensed nothing but abundance. It had been raining, and all of the dense foliage, the vines that crawled up the thatched roof of the waiting area, the fragrant hibiscus, gardenia, and bougainvillea blossoms that surrounded the cast iron café tables sparkled as if dotted with jewels. A pair of box turtles lifted their heads languidly out of a bubbling turquoise-tiled fountain, looking for us to feed them bits of ceviche, crab, or calamari. La Fontana is known for its seafood, and in the cozy basement-level bar where we were eventually seated, a room decorated like an old-fashioned Spanish *taberna*, there was a full wine list to complement the selections. We ordered *mojitos* from a waiter who stared at Alicia Figueroa. Did he know her, or was it just this thing that she possessed, this legacy of beauty that was as fresh that day as when she was onstage in a garter belt and stockings? I'd been noticing this happening all day, even when we stopped off in the crowded Cubacel offices, where the atmosphere was charged with tension and frustration.

Alicia leaned towards me and whispered, "I think that's Ana Gloria's son-in-law."

The strapping dark-haired man looked too young to be the owner of a restaurant, but then again, in Cuba it is mostly the young who have the will and verve to start a business. Most older people—forty-something and up—either find it too hard to work around, within, and through a system that discourages private enterprise, or are unalterably locked into the old ways, where the state owns everything and takes care of everyone.

Ana Gloria's son-in-law stopped to say something to his bartender. His body language and demeanor bespoke self-confidence. I knew nothing of him, but it was evident that he knew all the right people, and his success was a foregone conclusion.

"These *paladar* owners are like the Martín Foxes of their era," I said to Alicia.

The music of Alicia Figueroa's laughter turned every male head in the room. Ana Gloria's son-in-law strode towards us, full of entrepreneurial affability.

"Ana Gloria called," he said. "Unfortunately, she won't be able to make it after all."

PART III

CHAPTER 16

"The Guajiro has gone crazy!"

We were what Las Vegas is now. No, much more!
We were Vegas and Broadway mixed together, and
everyone in the world used to go down to Havana to
see us.

—Olga Guillot

The scene on the stage of Arcos de Cristal was of a winter won-
derland: sleighs with bells ringing, svelte "Santa Clauses"
dancing in white tights and cinched red-velvet jackets, and shapely
ice-skaters in white boots, fur-trimmed hats, and short skirts. The
"reindeer" were none other than modelos Nora Osorio and Sonia
Marrero dressed in bikinis, wearing tall feathered headdresses and
fishnet stockings trimmed with sequined appliqués of snowflakes.
Rodney's version of *White Christmas,* a show based (very) loosely
on the 1954 Hollywood film of the same title that starred Bing
Crosby and Danny Kaye, opened Tropicana's 1954–55 tourist season only two months after the film had played at Havana's Payret
Theater. Rodney had cubanized a New England-style Christmas
with Leonela dancing ballet, the Armando Romeu orchestra performing mamboized versions of popular American Christmas
music (*Show* reported the tune of the finale as "Ginger Bell"), and
the Cuarteto Rufino and the Tex Mex Trio singing Cuban and

Mexican love songs. "The luxury of the costumes, the rapturous music, and Rodney's choreography," wrote Carlos Palma in the January 1955 issue of *Show*, "combine in the proposal that Tropicana, jewel of the Americas, offers its cosmopolitan public—that Cuba can compete with any other country in the presentation of dazzling musical revues."

Christmas 1954. Decorated pine trees stood in most of Havana's department store windows and hotel lobbies. Christmas carols played on radio stations. Santa Claus appeared in orphanages to hand out toys to children. Christmas Eve, or *nochebuena*, is a Cuban holiday celebrated with a roast suckling pork dinner (Cuban jokes about pigs hiding in December are similar to American turkey jokes around Thanksgiving). Cuban gift-giving, however, traditionally takes place on January 6—*El día de los reyes magos*, or Epiphany. The island was rapidly absorbing the customs of its neighbor to the north, adapting itself to the tourists, settling into a dreamy self-satisfaction. With the world price of sugar rising since the onset of the Korean War in 1950, Cuba's economy was becoming as ripe as mangoes in August, and more and more diversified. Two hundred fifty thousand Americans were visiting Cuba annually, spending approximately $80 million. There were new joint ventures with foreign companies in industries like nickel, paper, cement, steel, glass, rubber, and food production. Construction boomed as well: by early 1955, new permits were being issued to the private sector at the rate of 300 a month. Among the many projects were my grandfather Alberto Lowinger's twelve-unit apartment building in Vedado, and Martín's four seaside apartment buildings. The government made plans to spend $350 million building roads, sewers, aqueducts, and even a tunnel under Havana Bay that would facilitate access to the powder-sand beaches fifteen minutes east of the city. There, a series of grand casino-hotels were about to be built, so that Havana could compete with beachfront resorts in Puerto Rico and Acapulco.

The strong economy notwithstanding, the nation's political landscape was as fraught as ever, and as farcical. On November 1, around the time that *White Christmas* opened at Tropicana, Batista finally held elections. Of course, once he declared his own candidacy, no one wanted to run against him. The exception was Ramón Grau San Martín, the perpetual opponent; but even Grau withdrew days before the vote, when the government insisted on having complete control of the election boards. Batista was returned as president unopposed, with only half the electorate casting ballots. Public indignation was sporadic and limited to occasional bombings in outlying cities and demonstrations at the University of Havana. Perhaps it was simple exhaustion—a half-century's worth of outrage quelled by an economy that seemed to have no limits. As my father said, "You can't always worry about politics. In Latin America there's always corruption in elections. If things are basically functioning, you have to move on and keep making money."

And was there money to be made. For the gamblers these were golden years. So much money passed through Tropicana that management began to pay for everything (except salaries) in cash. Martín and his partners ventured into so many new business deals that sometimes all he did to keep track of money that he had lent or invested was scribble some figures on a piece of paper. (He also had a steel-trap memory when it came to these minor loans—and people always paid him back, even if it took them several years.) Thanks to Alberto Ardura's connections, they went into the highly lucrative slot machine rental business, forging a partnership with Fernandez Miranda that made Tropicana the sole source in Havana for rental *traganickels*, as the one-armed bandits were called. The traganickels were purchased in Chicago and rented out to the smaller cabarets, like Johnny's Dream Club. Through Fernandez Miranda's political connections, the partners even managed to place dozens of slots in bars and corner bodegas, making them a fixture of Havana's urban landscape. The partners charged a percentage of the take for the rentals and were the only ones allowed to empty the machines. Valentín would usually make the rounds with an associate named Efrain Hernandez, who had been sent to Chicago to learn how to service the traganickels; and with Ardura, who received 2 percent of the profits, an amount equal to roughly half a million dollars a year, for bringing this business to Martín through his childhood friend. Fernandez Miranda himself was reported to receive a whopping 50 percent of the profits, which amounted to almost $1 million a month.

As a measure of charity, the traganickel business also committed a portion of its earnings to First Lady Marta Fernandez de Batista's *comedores populares,* a series of soup kitchens that she created to feed the poor of Havana. The donation was a shrewd move, designed to keep popular opinion favorable to the ever-growing presence of gambling in the nation. It was an act worthy of Evita Perón (wife of Batista's contemporary and fellow dictator, Juan Perón of Argentina) who was adored by the poor because of her very visible charitable work. Her charity notwithstanding, Evita owned a king's ransom in jewels, which, through a gambling debt, once wound up in Ofelia's hands. "I forget the date, but it was probably in 1957," she recalled one rainy night in Glendale.

Un argentino named Jorge Antonio spent a night playing baccarat at Tropicana and lost badly. Turns out that this Jorge Antonio had been Eva Perón's secretary. He had no money to pay his debt. But he had this small bag of Evita's jewels that he left as collateral. Probably he stole them, who knows? Or maybe it was payment for something. By then Evita was deceased and this man was living in Spain. Martín took the bag of jewels home for safekeeping, and I had *un banquete* [a feast] poring through that bag. There were necklaces, diamonds, rings with emeralds, stones the size of almonds. It all seemed make believe. They sparkled like a treasure chest you see in the movies.

Jorge Antonio eventually paid his baccarat debt to Tropicana; and Armando Freyre, Tropicana's lawyer, returned the bag of jewels to him in Spain. "I'll tell you, when I was holding those jewels I could not help but remember that time Martín and I went to Argentina during our honeymoon," said Ofelia on that rainy night. "Things were so bad in that country that even the taxi doors were held together with rope. And I wondered, if Evita was able to buy all those jewels, why couldn't she do more for Argentina's poor?"

I was tempted to point out that Cuba in the 1950s was also a place of poverty, yet there was no shortage of jewels in the lives of the rich women. Martín, for example, continually showered Ofelia with jewelry, cars, and exotic pets. For their third anniversary he gave her a four-inch, diamond-encrusted crucifix pendant. For her thirty-fourth birthday, in 1957, he gave her a new cream-colored Eldorado with a 14-carat-gold key. He himself took to wearing a 13-carat diamond ring. "The stone was the size of a cooked garbanzo," remarked Ofelia, admitting that it was somewhat extravagant. Though she already had a dog and cat, Martín bought Ofelia a pet rhesus monkey that she named Tito. Another time he came home with a pair of tiny spider monkeys that she told him to return because they were too ferocious. In 1956, a year before the Kenyan tribal prince sent Ofelia the lion cub that irrevocably stole her heart, Martín presented her with a pair of chimpanzees. "I rejected them also because they were already grown and I would not be able to train them."

ONE OF the results of Cuba's booming 1950s economy was that the island suddenly found itself with a dire shortage of hotel rooms. Havana had fewer than half the rooms it needed to accommodate the influx of tourists. To address this, Batista's tourist-friendly government devised an incentive to encourage would-be developers. A new law, known as Ley Hotelera (Hotel Law) 2074, granted tax exemption to any hotel or motel providing tourist accommodations and allowed for any hotel with more than one million pesos of new investment to apply for a gaming license. The official fee for licenses was merely 25,000 pesos; however the real price included a kickback to Batista amounting to somewhere around 250,000 pesos, equivalent to $1.6 million today. Over and above, there was a monthly operating fee of 2,000 pesos, plus a profit percentage—usually a fee paid directly to Batista or a member of his family. The size of these payoffs was staggering; several accounts place the annual totals at $10 million. The government also provided loans through Cuba's state-controlled banks as a further stimulus to construction. Those most aware of the potential, most notably the American gambling syndicates that ran Cuba's casinos at Sans Souci and Montmartre, rushed to come up with new projects. In December, the Hotel Nacional, still the grandest of Cuban tourist installations, opened the new Casino Parisien as part of a full set of renovations that were undertaken by the hotel's new management, International Hotels, a subsidiary of Pan American airlines. Managed by the former front man for Las Vegas's Desert Inn casino, Wilbur Clark, the true power behind the Parisien was Meyer Lansky. Thus began what would become the 1950s version of the danza de los millones. This time, however, the avalanche of moneymaking would be accompanied by actual dancing: all the proposed hotel-casinos were going to feature cabarets with all-night music, big-name headliners, and showgirl-studded dance revues that rivaled those at Tropicana.

Although there were plans in the works for at least five new hotels by early 1956, including a $25 million Hilton at the top of la Rampa (the portion of 23rd Street in Vedado that slopes towards the Malecón and is one of the centers of modern Havana) and a $14 million Las Vegas-style hotel-casino on the Malecón that was the dream project of Meyer Lansky, no cabaret in Cuba came close to rivaling Tropicana. Rodney's boundless imagination had hit its stride. In addition to the mainstay winter Afro-Cuban spectacles, now el Mago, "the Magician," as he was referred to with increasing frequency in the press, was producing shows with themes as far-flung as Hawaiian hula dance (*Polynesia*, October 1954); Chinese opera (*Casa de Té*, August 1955); Broadway musicals (*Hello Broadway*, December 1955); and Italian romantic music (*Madonnas de Capri*, December 1955). The productions grew ever more extravagant. For *Casa de Té*—"Tea House"—real silk kimonos were brought in from Hong Kong and a group of sword-wielding martial artists performed with the dancers. As his fame and Tropicana's fortunes grew, Rodney became tempestuous. During a rehearsal for *Copacabana*, a 1957 Brazilian show, Rodney battled Alberto Ardura—Jenny León recalled that he stormed out of the production—until he was allowed to include a miniature zeppelin that would "fly" in on wires and land on the catwalk. Rodney traveled widely, at Tropicana's expense, to gather sheet music for Armando Romeu and to hire dancers. Yet no matter how outrageous the production was, the main elements were exquisite music and flawless dance numbers. "Part of the fun was seeing how he created this big vision, but still managed to showcase the greats of Cuban music, like the Cuarteto D'Aida, Olguita Guillot or Miguelito Valdés," said Ofelia.

One Cuban musical giant who was conspicuously absent from Tropicana's roster of stars was Benny Moré. By 1955, El bárbaro del ritmo, as he was called, was considered one of the most talented and versatile singers in the country, quite possibly the best musician Cuba has ever produced, according to listeners as well as critics. A self-taught musician who never learned to read notes, Moré was born Bartolomé Maximiliano Moré in Santa Isabel de las Lajas, a rural town near the southern coastal city of Cienfuegos, in Las Villas Province. Like Armando Romeu, Moré's musical talent came with his birthright. His great-great-grandfather had been a slave brought to Cuba from the Congo. Upon emancipation, Ta Ramón Gundo Moré became the first "king" of a *casino*, or society, to maintain Congo traditions in Santa Isabel de las Lajas. Foremost among those traditions was music. Young Bartolomé was welcomed into the Casino de los Congos from an early age. By the time he was six he was adept at playing the *tres* and singing and dancing rumba, *son, guaracha,* and all manner of Afro-Cuban music. He was also an expert improviser and could make up verses on the spot in the best tradition of guajiro country music.

After a childhood of cutting sugarcane and singing with his brothers, Moré went to Havana in 1936. He kicked around the bars and clubs of the era and eventually wound up singing with the Trio Matamoros, one of the best known and most beloved of Cuban troubadour groups headed by Miguel Matamoros. With the trio he traveled to Mexico where he met Pérez Prado. Moré's multi-octave voice, his talent for improvisation in any style of Cuban music (he was adept at everything from *guarachas* to the most tender boleros), and his dynamic, sexy stage presence, catapulted him to stardom. He recorded several numbers with Prado and acted in Mexican films. Onstage, Moré carried a cane and wore dapper suits, a guajiro's straw hat tipped at a rakish angle. When he returned to Havana, he worked with several orchestras, including one that Bebo Valdés formed in 1953, before assembling his own group.

Moré and his group found a regular gig at the Ali Bar, a second-tier cabaret on the Avenida de Dolores, off the highway to the airport. "It was one of Martín and my favorite places," recalled Ofelia. "It was open really late and it was rustic, with a thatched palm roof, red and green lights around rough wood columns, and plank tables for only about twenty parties." Moré had a great rapport with Martín and Ofelia. "Whenever we were there, he would stop by our table and joke with Martín. He'd say, '*Chico,* when are you going to give me work at Tropicana? I need it bad. I've got to buy a lot of *malanga* for my *negritos!*'"

One day Ofelia did ask Martín why Tropicana never hired the man who was unquestionably the greatest Cuban singer of his era.

Martín told her to see about it with Ardura, who made those decisions. "The reason Ardura gave me," said Ofelia, "was Benny's drinking. He was unreliable. He'd miss performances or show up late." Other cabarets, including Sans Souci, were willing to work around Moré's weaknesses. Rodney, on the other hand, was not. He demanded rigor and professionalism from his cast. At Tropicana the concept was the star of the show, not any individual performer.

Cuba's other top-flight choreographers—Gustavo Roig, Alberto Alonso, and Carlyle, an American whose 1954 Christmas production at Montmartre included Tropicana regulars Henry Boyer and the Llopis-Dulzaides quartet—tried copying Rodney's formula. But no one had el Mago's prolific imagination. By 1955 he was coming up with eight different shows a year, bringing them from concept to opening night in three months. The schedule was grueling for the cast. A month after a set of shows opened, preparations for two new productions would begin. Performers were expected to rehearse for three hours every afternoon ("and we were not paid for that time," remarked Jenny León), then they were due back at eight sharp for the night's performance. Because a new set of productions would begin the night after the old ones closed, dress rehearsals took place in the middle of the night. "You had to have nerves of steel," said Jenny. "It would be three in the morning, right after we'd finished working. The old set was struck while we changed costumes. Rodney was stressed, he swore at us if we messed up. Ardura was stressed too. But everyone knew when Tropicana had a dress rehearsal. Dancers from other cabarets would pass the word among themselves and try to sneak in and watch us. That's when Rodney would really freak out."

The payoff to all this work was evident in the reactions of the public. Recalled Ofelia, "I'll never forget when Joan Crawford came with her husband, Alfred Steele. She grabbed my hand and held it, telling me over and over how the show had been the best thing that she'd ever seen and how the architecture and setting were magnificent. She asked to be taken backstage, and all the cast went crazy. The models were still in their gingham costumes with ribbons. [Crawford] was a legend, and she had her picture taken with the cast and told them that she had never seen anything as exciting or beautiful."

America was drawn irresistibly to Tropicana. "Tomorrow, the cameras of CMQ-TV will take the beauties of Tropicana to more than 30 million American viewers," announced the cabaret's ad in the December 17, 1955 issue of *Diario de la Marina*. The following afternoon, the hefty kinescope cameras of Cuba's premier television station beamed live images of Tropicana's floor show on the Sunday NBC show *Wide, Wide World*. With its forty cameras and twelve mobile vans, *Wide, Wide World* was an innovative soft news show watched by millions of Americans and hosted by Dave Garroway, the low-key, intellectual host of the *Today Show* and one of the pioneers of talk-show television. *Wide, Wide World* specialized in live segments from around the United States and the world. In June of 1955 it aired its first live broadcast from a foreign country—Mexico. Its Christmas 1955 program (touted in a *New York Times* ad as "the first four-nation live telecast in history!") featured the Tropicana floorshow of the moment (*Hello Broadway!*); along with clips of the Posada festival from Juarez, Mexico; a traditional Christmas party in Quebec; and the choir of the Cathedral of St. John the Divine, in New York. The program ended with a message of peace from President Eisenhower.

Straitlaced 1950s America already had a vision of Cubanness, via the comic, family-style *cubanidad* depicted every Monday night on the *I Love Lucy* show. Tens of millions tuned in weekly to watch Xavier Cugat's former protégé, Desi Arnaz, play the foil to his ditsy but devoted American wife. The half-hour show was by far the most popular in America. The fictional couple, Lucy and Ricky Ricardo, played by Arnaz and Lucille Ball, a real-life couple, was a mirror of the average married American couple—up to a point. Lucy comically pushed the limits of acceptable behavior; Ricky played the all-knowing husband, whose English pronunciation was a source of hilarity. The Cubanness depicted on *Wide, Wide World*'s Tropicana show was the titillating side. It took little effort for the typical American to make a mental leap from the sultry music, leafy catwalks, and sashaying *diosas de carne*, to Havana's other offerings, such as the houses of prostitution, live sex shows, and Chinatown-based opium dens that American travel writer W. Adolphe Roberts described in his 1953 book, *Havana: The Portrait of a City*. "Here is one [show] that earned a grin from me," wrote Roberts of a show that was most likely performed at the Shanghai, though he does not name the place.

> The scene was a deserted city square at night, indicated by backdrops with street lamps painted in and the silhouettes of houses. There sauntered on stage a woman totally nude except for her hat and shoes, and swinging a handbag. Her implied calling was unmistakable. She produced a mirror from her bag and went through the motions of making up her face under a lamp. Presently she was joined by half a dozen sisters of the pavement, all in similar state of undress. They talked by means of grimaces and shrugs which established the fact that business was poor indeed. Then appeared a tall and robust female, naked too except for a policeman's cap, brogans and baton. The newcomer scowled at the harlots, menaced them with her nightstick, lined them up and proceeded to search them for concealed weapons. The comedy of this last operation was broad. I need say no more.

When presented with this perception of Cuba as a place of licentiousness, Ofelia laughed. "Everyone complains about prostitution, but tell me where in the world it doesn't exist. Wherever there are men there are prostitutes. And it also serves a practical purpose. In Cuba, fathers would often take their sons to houses of prostitution for their first sexual encounter. Not a bad thing, so they can learn what to do."

Wide, Wide World assured Tropicana its place as the premier nightlife destination for American tourists. Not only could they watch a Rodney show, but gamble in the newly renovated casino. In mid-1954, against the objections of his partners, who were tired of spending money on construction (after all, the money came from their profits, yet went into property wholly owned by Martín), Martín had Max Borges open up the roof of what had been Villa Mina's living room, adding an extension that was sheathed in glass. Gamblers—key patrons of "Martín Fox's Emporium," as the press now frequently referred to Tropicana— were now able to continue sitting "under the stars" while they played roulette, baccarat, craps, and 21, or tried their luck at the long rows of traganickels. There was a separate room for high-stakes monte and roulette players, such as Santiago Rey and Papo Batista, the president's son. The tile floors were thickly carpeted and the old crystal pendant fixtures replaced with slender brushed-brass ceiling lamps that cost a thousand dollars apiece. (Remembering that the wife of General Díaz Tamayo had once admired the original chandeliers, Martín, the consummate businessman, had one boxed up and sent to her as a gift.) Miniature bronze replicas of Rita Longa's ballerina crowned the roulette wheels. There was also all-night music provided by groups like renowned jazz pianist Felipe Dulzaides's band Los Armonicos, and a bar that sent drinks to players on a little brass cart on which were piled free roast pork or ham-and-cheese sandwiches.

"*El Guajiro se volvió loco!* (The Guajiro has gone crazy)" exclaimed none other than Fulgencio Batista himself. It was the night of the 1954 gala for La liga contra el cáncer (Cuba's anti-cancer league), and Batista and his wife were the guests of honor. His admiring comment, made within earshot of Valentín Jodra, referred to the millions that Martín and his partners had lavished on the renovations. Total expenditures to date on Tropicana were now in the neighborhood of two million pesos—roughly $14 million today, including Martín's purchase of the property. He was making a fortune with both the casino and la bolita, but his obsession with Tropicana went beyond money. Martín wanted his Jewel of the Americas to obliterate the competition. He wanted gamblers to forget that any other nightclub even existed. Americans were now thinking of Tropicana as synonymous with Cuba itself: brash, elegant, and sexy. For Martín it was equally important that Cubans feel the same.

That he had achieved this as early as 1954 was apparent by the presence of Batista and his wife at the charity event. Though other top members of Batista's government were also there that night— Sports Director Fernandez Miranda, Minister of the Interior Santiago Rey, and Foreign Minister Carlos Saladrigas—these men were friends of Ardura's and Martín's and regular Tropicana patrons. Batista, on the other hand, normally shunned cabaret venues. One key reason was safety. Though the election had brought a measure of calm to Cuba, Batista was still opposed by almost all of Cuba's student, political, and labor leaders. (In a surprising show of anti-Batista camaraderie, most of them, including Prío, Grau San Martín, Raúl Chibás—the leader of the Ortodoxos— and José Antonio Echevarría—the newly elected president of the Federation of University Students, or FEU—attended a huge anti-Batista meeting at Havana's docks in November 1955.) Most vociferous among Batista's enemies was the jailed Fidel Castro. From his cell, where he communicated to his supporters regularly through letters, Castro expressed continual indignation over the March 10, 1952 *golpe de estado* and the killing of his followers after Moncada. Despite this, Batista decided he would declare amnesty for all political prisoners. In May 1955, six months after the election, almost a year since the publication of Castro's *La historia me absolverá*, Batista made good on his offer. As part of that amnesty, Fidel Castro, his brother, Raúl, and eighteen of the Moncada attack participants walked out of the prison on the Isle of Pines where they had been held for two years. Within the month, Castro left for Mexico to form the nucleus of a guerrilla army to overthrow the very government that had granted him amnesty. He never once masked his intention to topple the man he had referred to in a letter to his friend, the journalist Luis Conte Agüero, as "[the only] man who in all these centuries has stained with blood two separate periods of our historic existence and has dug his claws into the flesh of two generations of Cubans." But though the nation had been convulsed by the coup (historian Hugh Thomas likened its effect on Cuba's political system to "a nervous breakdown after years of chronic illness"), at the time no one could imagine that Castro's threat was serious. For the violence-weary average Cuban, there was still a shred of hope that the nation's problems would be resolved eventually at the ballot box.

CHAPTER 17

Cabaret in the Sky

Our idiosyncrasies . . . were divine!
—Eddy Serra

O felia has something to say," said Rosa Sanchez. We were
driving south along the I-15. It was one of Ofelia's lucky
days again, this time according to the *Los Angeles Times* horoscope, and I had been invited to accompany her and Rosa for a day
of gambling at Harrah's El Rincón casino. Actually we were going
to begin our day at Harrah's and then head over to nearby Pala, another casino-hotel on the Indian reservation. According to Ofelia,
it had a simpler approach to craps and a better buffet lunch.

I had noticed something a little odd about Ofelia's demeanor
that morning. I was about to learn what it was.

"I'm not sure I like where you are headed with this story," she
said from the passenger's seat. "That business about unfair elections, about Batista being a dictator—"

"Are you trying to say he wasn't?" I interrupted, not able to let
this comment pass.

She turned around and fixed me with that stare that looked
like it could melt iron. "If you are going to say that Batista is a

dictator, then you'd better say the same thing about Fidel Castro. And I know you aren't going to put that in the book, because otherwise you'll never get back into Cuba."

She had touched a raw nerve. I had told her about my friends who had been banned from Cuba after writing books. It was already hard enough dealing with U.S. restrictions. In mid-2004, the Treasury Department's Office of Foreign Assets Control, the governmental agency overseeing economic embargoes, had instituted severe new travel restrictions that made it almost impossible for American citizens to go to Cuba. Cultural travel had been completely eliminated. There were no more American tour groups, no further people-to-people exchanges. Even Cuban-Americans were barred from visiting their families more than once every three years. The Treasury only authorized visits to parents, children, siblings, and grandparents—not cousins, uncles, or aunts. I still had nominal permission to travel because I qualified under a research license, but that, too, was under threat of elimination. What's more, Cuban artists, like my friend who had accompanied Alicia Figueroa and me through Miramar, were now automatically being denied visas to enter the United States. The Homeland Security Act deemed all Cubans, even the elderly singer and Grammy winner of Buena Vista Social Club fame Ibrahim Ferrer, a threat to our country. The thought of also being kept out of Cuba by the Cuban government made me think twice about broaching political subjects.

"You say a lot about unfair elections," continued Ofelia. "But at least we had elections! What do people in Cuba have now? Anyway, elections are manipulated all over the world. You think Mexico was any different than Cuba? Even Florida—," Ofelia stopped herself.

"Yes?" I urged.

"You get my point," she said curtly. "But if you write about this, I want to go on record. I think that the counts and recounts in 2000 were fair and, as far as I am concerned, the outcome in the 2004 election put that whole subject to rest. And now I'm going to quote Rita Montaner: *'Mejor que me calle'* [I'd better shut up], because almost the same thing happened with Kennedy and Nixon. But Nixon didn't want any recounts. He just let Kennedy be president. Anyway, it doesn't matter anymore. The last election proved that."

The stories weren't quite parallel. In 1960 John F. Kennedy had received both a popular and electoral majority, which was not the case in 2000. Still, to have Ofelia come so close to admitting that there might have been irregularities in a United States presidential election felt like a minor victory in our endless political debate. Our politics are very different. Whenever I'd go down to Cuba, Ofelia would express more worry for my safety than Cuban-exile indignation; nonetheless I knew she disapproved of travel to the island and was pleased when the new restrictions went into effect. I tried to avoid direct political confrontation, though sometimes it was difficult, such as on the night after the 2004 presidential election when I sat glumly at the poker table while Ofelia danced around the room and poured celebratory cocktails. I hadn't seen her this happy since Arnold Schwarznegger had been elected governor of California.

"It's always easy to look back and talk about how bad things were," Ofelia continued. She had turned fully around in her seat. "We're looking back in history, judging things I lived before you were born. Sure we had poverty! What country doesn't? But one thing I know is that the communists inherited a prosperous country with a large middle class, and hardly anyone wanted to emigrate. On the contrary, people from all over came to Cuba and stayed, like your grandfather."

"All that is true, Ofelia, but there were serious problems that should have been dealt with earlier."

"For example?"

I hesitated, not wanting to get into the full-blown argument that I'd felt brewing over the previous months. Despite the fact that Batista's tyranny and thievery were legendary (so colossal was his corruption that even the nation's top sugar barons and industrialists supported his ouster) and that the American embargo has not only failed to unseat Castro, but has instead helped him to stay in power by giving him a concrete enemy on which to blame his country's economic failures, Ofelia was intractable on both subjects. I was in no mood to hear rationalizations, however.

"Rural poverty," I said, bringing up a subject I thought had no argument. "The great economic conditions that you and Rosa are always telling me about didn't exist in the countryside. The cities had excellent hospitals and free education, but the same wasn't true *en el campo.* There was extensive seasonal unemployment. There were very few hospitals. A majority of guajiros lived in houses with dirt floors, without electricity, plumbing, or bathrooms."

"Do you think Mexico and Brazil took better care of their rural populations?" Ofelia countered. "If I understand correctly, now there isn't even running water in Havana. Doesn't everyone have water tanks because of shortages? My sister, La Niña, had one installed in her Vedado apartment in the seventies. We're talking about Havana, once one of the most beautiful and modern cities in the world. How can you justify that?"

I wasn't trying to justify it. And I hated being put in the position of apologist for Castro, which I am not. I often feel equally frustrated by left-leaning Americans and Europeans who discount what Cuba had achieved before the revolution and romanticize the communist regime.

"All I'm trying to say is that there were huge discrepancies," I told Ofelia. "People ignored the poor. Batista was a dictator and the United States helped keep him there to serve its own economic and political purposes."

"*Ay, por favor!* Let's not always blame the Americans. Like any other country, we created our own problems. Anyway, there's no way the United States could not have had influence in Cuba. We're only ninety miles apart. The two countries were joined at the hip."

"Did you know that even the term *guajiro* comes from the Americans?" added Rosa Sanchez.

That statement halted the argument. "It does?"

"Yeah. When Roosevelt's men came to fight in our War of Independence, they began calling the Mambises 'war heroes.' Well, you can imagine that no Cuban could pronounce that, so it simply became *guajiro*."

It was startling to learn that the name for the quintessential Cuban, the backbone of the nation's agriculture, came from the United States. It underscored Ofelia's assertion that our two countries were "joined at the hip" for nearly a century, but that only intensified the tragedy of rupture. It seemed profoundly absurd after so many years, like a love affair gone awry. This becomes particularly poignant when one visits Cuba and sees how much American culture is still widely embraced by the populace. Among Havana's youth, the hunger for music, movies, video games, and fashion from the United States is as keen as it was in the 1950s. The regime does what it can to suppress that hunger by, for example, making it difficult to use public venues for events where house or techno music might be played. (Arcos de Cristal was a popular late-night dance locale before this ban went into effect.) There are no video-rental stores in Cuba, and it is illegal for Cubans to rent their own videotapes to each other. The laws change all the time, but not too long ago even owning a large number of videotapes or DVDs was considered suspect. There are also proscriptions against opening Internet accounts (except in the workplace, where e-mail can be monitored) or getting satellite television. Those caught breaking the law often have their possessions—televisions, computers, and DJ equipment—impounded. There have even been many cases where a person's home is confiscated for these offenses, a draconian punishment in a country with a severe housing shortage. Despite these threats, Cubans expertly skirt the restrictions on a daily basis. In the 1950s, everyone played the bolita. Today, anyone with expendable income can purchase satellite television and Internet service on the black market.

We continued to debate the political issues as we wound through the chaparral-covered hills of the reservation. I expressed my point of view that if it's freedom we want for Cuba, we should drop the embargo. Ofelia disagreed. Rosa, who hardly ever contradicted Ofelia, was on my side. "I'd send so much business and dollars down there, and so fast, that the communists wouldn't know what hit them. Let's see them try to put that genie back in the bottle!" Then we got to Harrah's El Rincón, and the subject turned to gambling.

"We'll start you off with a simple game," said Ofelia while we ordered Bloody Marys with salt on the rim of the glass. She slipped a twenty-dollar bill into a video poker machine built into the bartop. The monitor swirled with color. Blips and bells sounded. She bet the maximum number of credits. A five-card hand appeared.

"Hmmm . . . two queens." Ofelia nodded pensively. "But look. I've got a jack, king, and ten of hearts as well. A shot at a royal flush." She touched the screen and the queen of spades became a six of spades. "*Bueno* . . . easy come, easy go." The next hand came up loaded with diamonds. There was a ten, a jack, a seven . . . and then there was an eight of spades and jack of clubs. "Go ahead, you choose."

I knew the basic rules of poker. I knew that a full house beats a flush, which beats a straight, and so forth. I kept the jacks.

"Now why did you do that?"

"Because the jacks assure me a win, no?"

"It just means you don't lose. You should've gone for the straight, kept the ten and the jack."

"What are the odds of getting a straight?"

Ofelia shook her head. "Odds are odds. We're here to gamble!" The words took on a philosophical overtone. I succumbed and lost fifteen dollars in ten minutes. "Ah, too bad!" She patted me on the back approvingly and ordered a pack of Marlboro menthols from the bartender.

Next we headed toward the tables, drinks in hand. En route Ofelia played some quarter slots and made back twelve of the eighteen dollars she had lost at video poker. We stopped at electronic roulette, where Rosa was concentrating on a monitor, and then we sat at the actual roulette table, which, because of the laws that govern the California casinos, consists not of the traditional wheel but a glass tube where the numbers pop up like in a lottery.

I put five dollars on red. I won and left it there. Then I lost. "Bet again," Ofelia urged, but I declined, preferring to watch her bet a whole array of numbers, some of her chips placed on the corners between numbers to hedge her options. Next to us, a pair of men wearing ratty T-shirts and identical World Series 2002 caps were discussing public education in America.

"When I was in school the teachers were these mean old broads, but this girl's twenty-five, twenty-eight, tops. Looks like she could be on television. I mean, how's a teenage boy s'posed to concentrate?"

"Yeah. It bears thinking. Not that you can do anything about it in this day and age."

Ofelia calmly sipped her Bloody Mary, seeming to tune out everything except the clatter of her chips as they were being stacked up. Within ten minutes the pile began dwindling inexorably. Then it was time for lunch and we got back in the car. We passed cows, organic-produce markets, and fields of wildflowers, until we reached a monolithic casino that around these parts is known simply as Pala.

Indian reservation gambling has been a hot political issue in California. The governor tries to extract state taxes from the hundreds of millions generated by the casinos, and the tribes attempt to maintain their monopoly on this most lucrative business. Just the day before I had been stopped at the door of my local supermarket by someone asking me to sign a petition to protect the Native Americans' rights to autonomy in this matter. Not being a gambler, I had no idea what was at stake, as it were. Now, entering the rose-colored concrete complex landscaped with tiers of fountains and tennis court-sized beds of impatiens, an electronic billboard announcing appearances by James Brown, Julio Iglesias, and Olivia Newton-John towering over the entrance, I began to understand. Were it not ringed by the sage-colored hills of the California coastal range, this hotel could easily have been mistaken for one in Las Vegas, albeit one off the Strip. Today's casinos cater to a clientele that one might describe as casual. Typical attire at both Harrah's and Pala is a T-shirt for men and sweat suits for women (Ofelia was elegantly turned out in pressed black trousers with a matching embroidered jacket, crimson silk sweater, and a felt fedora). Nonetheless, the interior of Pala was opulently decorated with stained glass, colored lights, and mirrors, all designed to set off the rows of slot machines—gleaming, singing, exhibiting the latest in video and audio technology, so as to induce sensory overload as quickly as possible.

We ate until we could eat no more, then Rosa went off to electronic roulette and Ofelia and I went to craps. Here Ofelia was completely in her element. She tossed a wad of bills onto the tables as her neighbor, a white-haired cowboy in a light blue shirt and straw hat, threw the dice across the felt. "Hard ten!" shouted one of the croupiers. There were about four attendants at the table, and one of them raked the dice back over to the thrower. Ofelia placed a chip along the pass line. "On six, and hard eight," she said, and tossed two five-dollar chips to the dealer. "That's sort of a sucker's bet," she explained to me, then proceeded to deliver, in a perfunctory fashion—her focus never wavering from the dice—the rules of craps. I absorbed almost nothing except that the bets remain active until a seven is rolled, and that a "hard" number is one composed of two equal parts, such as four and four for hard eight, three and three for hard six, and so forth. When it was Ofelia's turn to roll, she removed her hat and gave it to me to hold. "I have better luck this way."

The California gaming laws allow only for card and lottery games. Craps is therefore played using dice whose colors match two decks of cards. The cards are imprinted with pairs of dice, and the die with the higher number signals the dealer which card to turn over. "It's a pretty clever way of getting around the law," I said to Ofelia as she continued to roll. "Worthy of Martín himself," she replied, as the croupiers egged her on. She kept the game alive for about twenty rolls of the dice. People clapped each time the dealer turned over a card and it did not show seven. "Alrighty, Miss *Ofeelia*, keep it going!" said the white-haired cowboy as his chips accumulated. The enthusiasm was infectious. To Ofelia's delight, I even placed a bet myself. I lost immediately.

On our way out to the car, Ofelia chided me gently for not betting more. "I really have no luck in these games," I explained. Rosa Sanchez laughed and put an arm around my shoulder. "Ask Ofelia how *she* did today."

"Not so bad," Ofelia said dryly.

"Come on, how much did you lose?" insisted Rosa.

"A hundred and twenty. Which is under my limit."

"Her luck is much better on cruise ships," Rosa added.

HEADING HOME to Los Angeles, I was struck again by how close Rosa and Ofelia were. In the casino I sensed that Rosa could only relax at her roulette machine because Ofelia was being taken care of. A few weeks earlier, Rosa had confessed that in 1988 she had refused the opportunity to be staff writer on a sitcom because it would have meant often working until midnight. By then she and Ofelia had bought the house in Glendale. Rosa's son, Ralph, who had been raised by the two women, was grown and out on his own.

Ofelia, who had a heart condition, had retired from her job at a bank in 1980, and Rosa worried about her constantly. "In 1982 she fell and hit her head, and after that I had a full-time housekeeper to be with her," she told me. "But the thought that something might happen to her nagged at me, and I couldn't imagine such long hours away from home."

I often wondered at what point this extraordinary devotion had begun: was Martín alive when they got together? They were obviously a couple, but the topic of their relationship seemed to be off limits. "Is it so impossible to imagine a long-term friendship between two women?" said Ofelia testily the last time I had gently broached the subject. I'd also noticed that the décor in the home bar had changed. The photos of Ofelia and Rosa arm in arm in costume were gone, as was the framed "Rosa y Yo" cigar box label. Their friends—Chiquita, Jenny and Frank, Eddy, Leonela—never referred to them as a couple, either. In New Jersey an old friend of Ofelia's named Julieta, the widow of Don Galaor, the 1950s entertainment columnist for *Bohemia*, told me, "Ofelia was not gay, but she had that inside of her. She had her adventures. Once she told me, 'Cuba was different. You could have your *amiguita*.' She would go off with a woman named Coralia." After Ofelia read the notes of that interview, I received a late-night phone call.

"Julieta's my good friend, but I think she thought you wanted to hear *algún escándalo* [some scandal] about my life," said Ofelia, chuckling. "I don't know where she got the idea. As a matter of fact, that poor woman she was talking about was known to be pretty loose with men. Her husband was a friend of Martín. One of those low-level gangsters. All she did was sit with me at Tropicana if her husband was talking business with Martín."

It seemed a reasonable explanation, but I was not convinced. There was also the question of the *anónimo* that Martín had received in 1955, about Ofelia and the dancer Julia Darvas. When I asked about that, Ofelia brushed me off by saying that anonymous

letters were the order of the day in Cuba. "You can read about
anónimos in the old *Show* and *Confidencial* magazines. Stirring up
trouble was a Cuban pastime. People sent them to each other all
the time."

"Did it stir up trouble for you?" I asked, hoping she would finally come clean about this aspect of her life.

"Not really. Martín knew it was absurd."

"What about his family?"

Ofelia paused to consider the question. "Martín's family was
pretty obsessed with him. Particularly the sisters. Pedro, his
brother, didn't get half the attention. *Imagínate*, Martín was the
one with the money. It was constantly, 'Martincito this, Martincito
that.' Did I tell you that he gave each of his sisters an apartment
building?"

I tried to steer her back to the question. "But did they give you
trouble because of the anónimos?"

"No, no. But I am sure he didn't discuss that with them. And
Martín and I had no problems. The only problem I remember in
Cuba with the family was this . . . ," she paused. I could sense her
calculating what she wanted to tell me. "There was this one occasion, an anniversary . . . Martín and I used to celebrate every holiday, birthday, and family event at the cabaret. There was always a
head table. I did the seating arrangements, but his sisters would always insist on sitting to one side of him. That night a journalist
came up to me and said, 'You should consider seating the family
next to other guests, so other people get to sit beside Martín.' I
spoke to the sisters. I said, 'Would you mind changing your seats
so you could help me attend to our other guests?' I put it in those
terms. And I seated them with interesting, important people. Angela, who we called Lita, was at the table of a prominent psychia-
trist. Domitila, who we called Tila, sat with Roberto Ortíz, a
retired baseball player who'd been with the Washington Senators
and Philadelphia Athletics."

"So what happened then?"

"Nothing. But I felt Tila tense up. She became very quiet. She never said anything though. It never came up again."

HAD THERE been any ongoing ill will over the seating issue, Ofelia would probably have learned of it sooner or later. The two families were together almost all the time. After the four seaside buildings were completed in 1954, Martín sent for his sisters, who were then living in Matanzas and New York, and gave each of them one of the buildings. Martín's widowed sister Lita would often accompany them to Boston when Martín went for his annual checkup. Martín gave Ofelia the third building from their house for her family. Fara occupied an oceanfront three-bedroom on the third floor, and Ofelia's brother Osvaldo lived in a spacious ground floor four-bedroom with Cuca, their mother, as well as his wife and children. La Niña lived in Vedado, also in an apartment that Martín had purchased for her. On Sunday mornings all members of both families would gather for a roast pork lunch at Martín and Ofelia's house. "It was the only time we ever entertained outside of Tropicana," said Ofelia. "We'd eat and have drinks, sometimes play dominoes. By two we'd send everyone home so we could nap before it was time to go to Tropicana." Given that all of the men in the family worked at the cabaret, most of the lunchtime conversation revolved around Tropicana. Martín was especially eager to *descargar* with his brother Pedro of course; his nephew Alvaro, who was the titular head of the corporation that owned the nightclub; as well as Ofelia's brother Oswaldo, a baccarat dealer, and her brother-in-law Atilano, the casino's comptroller. ("Before he died, Ardura told me a story of how he and Martín tested Atilano," said Ofelia. "They used to do this to all the employees who dealt with money. Unfortunately, many of them were only too happy to slip a little into their pockets. In Atilano's case, they once put extra cash into one of the money bags he was counting. He immediately reported the difference, and ever since then Martín trusted him like almost no one else.") Ofelia, meanwhile, hosted the women of the family when they came to Tropicana, which was generally only on holidays, opening nights, or other special occasions. Of all the Tropicana wives, she was the only one who spent most nights at the cabaret.

The night of March 2, 1956, was a night when all of their relatives came to Tropicana. There had never been a night like this. It had never been this busy, not even during the unveiling of Arcos de Cristal or the opening of *Omelen-ko*. A month earlier, in February, there had been another gala for La liga contra el cancer, which overall had been more elegant, but tonight all of Havana, not just the bejeweled cream of its high society, was focused on the Tropicana cabaret. The number of people who had called for reservations was triple the club's capacity. So many extra tables had been set up in the aisles of Bajo las Estrellas that there was almost no room to maneuver in the space between the cabaret and the casino. Even Martín, who loved nothing so much as a packed house, was concerned that in an emergency people might not be able to get out. Not that he was anticipating a problem. Tonight was Tropicana's graduation party. It was the night the cabaret was going to catapult itself into a league all of its own.

Credit for the moment belonged to Alberto Ardura. As Ofelia's table began filling up with her family and members of the press, she took a moment to go over to Ardura's table and greet his wife, Carmelina. The presence of the other Tropicana wives, Carmelina Ardura, Ñica Fox, and Marta Echemendia, only added to the excitement of the evening. (Ofelia claims that she and Martín considered having children, but decided that it would have been impossible, given their lifestyle. And Tropicana, as she had seen repeatedly, was no place to leave a husband alone.)

The lights dimmed. Miguel Angel Blanco entered the spotlight and announced the first show of the evening. "Ladies and Gentlemen, *señoras y señores*, the Tropicana cabaret is proud to present . . . *Fantasía Mexicana!*" The next half-hour was a blur of Aztec sun masks, pounding drums, and dancers hurtling across the stage. The scene included a mariachi band, Ana Gloria and Rolando's mambos, Jenny León in chiffon with gold stripes and hoop earrings that grazed her shoulders, and Alicia Figueroa (by then Miguel Angel Blanco's steady girlfriend) in a bikini with satin scarf tied around her head. Sandra Taylor wore an organza skirt and a straw hat with dangling fruit. A bikini-clad Nora Osorio danced in a headdress consisting of a four-foot-high stack of sombreros.

Halfway through the show, the music drifted into something more romantic. The lights dimmed again and the cast slipped offstage. The catwalks lit up gradually, as if a cloud had just unveiled the moon. Eleven of Tropicana's modelos glided out onto the catwalks, holding huge black discs in front of them. Each disc carried the words "Capitol Records." Rolling the records like wheels, the women moved along the catwalks to the stage, forming a line before the audience. Then they spun the discs around. The backs were hot pink. On each was printed a bold black letter, spelling out N-A-T K-I-N-G C-O-L-E. The audience began to cheer and clap, as the voice of Miguel Angel Blanco boomed out once again: "Ladies and Gentlemen, *señoras y señores!* The Tropicana cabaret is proud to present the one and only . . . Nat 'King' Cole!"

The line of modelos parted to either side of the stage and the music started up again. Only this time it was not the Armando Romeu orchestra playing, but the celebrated Nat "King" Cole Trio, including John Collins on guitar, Charlie Harris on bass, and Lee Young, brother of the great Lester Young, on drums. The "King" himself, one of America's biggest recording stars, a man who had earned so much money for Capitol Records that its signature cylindrical building in Hollywood was known as "the house that Nat built," came out in his white tuxedo with black lapels, wrist cuffs, and a matching bow tie. Cole sat at the piano and began to pound out one of his hits. Which one, exactly, is lost to memory, but it was probably "Caravan," "Lover Come Back to Me," or "It's Only a Paper Moon." Though most of the audience was Cuban, many mouthed the words as he sang "Nature Boy," "Mona Lisa," and his signature song, "Unforgettable."

When the performance was over, the audience was on its feet, demanding more, but Cole had to perform again that night and the crowd had to content itself with the second half of *Fantasía Mexicana* while he went backstage. "No one loved the Tropicana shows more than me," Ofelia admitted, "but after hearing Nat 'King' Cole, I didn't want to hear anything else!" Neither, apparently, did the rest of the audience. While Nat Cole was singing, the silence had been so palpable it seemed to throb. "No one moved, not even a fork was lifted," said Ofelia, who had been worried earlier that Cole's romantic style would demand too much from a raucous Cuban audience that had been drinking heavily. But once Cole was offstage, people could barely wait for the next set, which was slated for one forty-five A.M.

One person who was more than happy to watch the rest of *Fantasía Mexicana* was Maria Cole, Cole's wife, who had accompanied her husband to Cuba along with Dick LaPalm, Cole's record promotion director. That first night at Tropicana, Maria Cole was as enthralled by Tropicana as Tropicana was by her husband. "My mouth just fell open. The Cubans just love show business, but this was something else. There was so much color, so much movement. Seeing women walk out of trees! And the orchestra! The house band had forty musicians. In Chicago you'd see eighteen tops, or sixteen men at the Copacabana in New York. I said to Nat, 'That's the house band? That many showgirls?' It was breathtaking."

LaPalm, meanwhile, was uneasily eyeing a group of thuggish bodyguards who sat with their guns on their laps. "They were protecting the general, that dictator who ran the country. Nat Cole wasn't too happy about it," LaPalm told me. But both Ofelia and Valentín insist that Batista was not there the night Nat "King" Cole played Tropicana. "And even if he had been," said Ofelia, "in my nine years at Tropicana I never saw someone openly brandishing a weapon inside the cabaret."

Backstage, as he waited for his second set, which would take place in the middle of a Cuban revue called *Noches del Tropico,* Cole was enjoying another part of Tropicana—the camaraderie of the cast members. "There was a patio outside the dressing rooms," recalled dresser Pastora Guerra, "and the cast was always *armando la rumba* [starting a rumba, meaning a party, in this case] between shows. The girls would come out and say, 'Pastorita, get me a bottle and a picnic basket, we're having a rumba.' And then Los Papines would start playing, and all of us would start dancing. Nat 'King' Cole was fascinated with us and with the Cuban rhythm. He was recording *"El bodeguero"* (The Shopkeeper) and he'd sing the chorus to me, *'Dale Pastorita, toma chocolate, paga lo que debe!'* He never got the rhythm right. I always had to correct him."

Nat "King" Cole's appearance at Tropicana was part of an attempt among the original big three cabarets to stave off competition from the new hotel-casinos by headlining big-name American stars. In March of 1956, Dorothy Dandridge completed a one-month run at Lefty Clark's Sans Souci. Later that year, *Show* announced Sans Souci's plans to bring in Frank Sinatra, Tony Bennett, Xavier Cugat, Abbe Lane, Silvana Pampanini, and Sarah Vaughan. Maurice Chevalier was scheduled to debut at Montmartre on April 15, and would be followed by Lena Horne and Edith Piaf.

"Tropicana invests $230,000 in three months for artistic talent!" announced *Show* in January 1956. It was an astonishing amount of money, but Cole was one of the most famous musicians in America, and immediately after his appearances ended, Tropicana opened a four-week run with singer Billy Daniels, the man known as "Mr. Black Magic" because of his close association with the Johnny Mercer and Harold Arlen song from the 1942 film *Star Spangled Rhythm.* On stage Daniels was the opposite of the elegant Cole—alternately raucous, romantic, tender, and exuberant.

The propulsive Daniels (along with Cole, he was one of the first African-Americans to host his own television show) was accompanied by his regular pianist, Benny Payne, and backed by Cuba's own Cuarteto D'Aida.

The use of big-name headliners was a formula adapted from Las Vegas, where the casino-hotels, like the Sands, Desert Inn, and Riviera, routinely spent millions on talent. To maintain its competitive edge, Tropicana also began offering a nightly bingo game with prizes that ranged from cash (the jackpot was 10,000 pesos), to plane tickets to Miami, to cars. The game was run by Johnny Williams, formerly a Boston-based gambler whom Martín had met there in 1953 while having his annual checkup. Williams earned approximately $80,000 in cash between 1956 and 1960, in addition to receiving housing and meals at Tropicana. But even signing Nat "King" Cole and giving away cars and money couldn't reduce the growing threat posed by the half-dozen new casinos being built. In addition to Lansky's Riviera, there were the Capri and Comodoro, both of which were going to feature casinos run by Santo Trafficante. Then there was the Hilton, which was going to be financed by the culinary workers union pension fund, and run by a consortium of shrewd and well-connected American gamblers with ties to the Mafia. (Investigators in New York linked the 1957 murder of Albert Anastasia to his attempts to muscle in on the Hilton casino concession.)

"I'm thinking of expanding the operation," Martín announced to Ofelia during one lunch at the Miami Restaurant. Their daily lunches at the Miami were the only time they had to be alone. Martín would relax visibly, leisurely sipping his highball glass of Ancestor whiskey, and greeting everyone who approached him. Cuba's most colorful street character, the long-haired Caballero de Paris, "Gentleman of Paris," waited outside the restaurant for Martín to emerge and give him a coin, at which time the Caballero would present a flower to Ofelia.

"China, what do you think about the idea of a Tropicana hotel?"

It was rare for Martín to ask Ofelia to comment on an aspect of his business. Their conversation mostly revolved around personal or family issues. But Martín had asked, so Ofelia ventured an opinion: "It seems like an immense proposition, Martín. It will take your energy away from the cabaret. But if you want to . . . You know I am 100 percent behind you."

Martín squeezed Ofelia's hand and nodded.

"And that," said Ofelia fifty years later, "was the first and last time that I heard anything about a Tropicana Hotel."

Martín was wise to abandon the hotel project, for in spite of his robust appearance and boundless energy, his health was precarious. There was some question about how much longer he could continue to handle the stress of running a cabaret. Most days Ofelia was able to keep his diabetes under control with shots of insulin. But sometimes, especially after they'd hosted important guests after Tropicana hours, or been out all night at other cabarets, or left Tropicana in the middle of the night for Varadero, where a rented yacht waited for them to host guests for the morning and afternoon, he would appear sluggish and pale to her the following evening. Ofelia watched him carefully. She would ask him to stay with her for longer periods at their table, pretending she needed him there. Had she asked him directly to slow down he would have simply laughed.

A number of Tropicana regulars, including Olga Guillot, remembered several tense weeks in 1956 when a rumor coursed through the dressing rooms that Martín's doctors told him that he had to slow down for his health, and that he was considering selling the cabaret to an American. "All of the employees worried he would do it," said Guillot. "Finally one day everyone gathered outside with placards that said 'Don't Sell, Martín! Tropicana is Cuba!' Everyone stood out there and repeated it. 'Cuba is Tropicana, Martín! Don't sell!' The Americans were offering him something like $20 million." When Martín got out of his car that afternoon, he saw the signs. "He was moved to tears," remembered Pastorita Guerra. "Finally he said, 'Don't worry, *gente*. I am not going to sell.' Then all of us began to clap and shout: '¡Viva Martín! ¡Viva Tropicana!'"

Rather than sell Tropicana, Martín and his brother Pedro came up with another plan to make the cabaret the premier tourist attraction in Cuba. "On January 15, Tropicana inaugurates its special service with *Cubana de Aviación*," reported *Show* in its January 1956 issue. The flight, known as the Tropicana Special, was a weekly charter aboard a forty-six-seat Lockheed Constellation. It was part of a package deal offering the flight, dinner, and drinks at Tropicana, a room at the Hotel Nacional, and breakfast, all for $68.80 (around $500 today). The best part was the flight itself. The plane was outfitted with a tiny six-foot stage beneath an Arcos de Cristal-style proscenium arch at the front, and the seat covers bore the Tropicana name and ballerina emblem. It was a miniature version of the cabaret, a cabaret-in-the-sky, with all the elements of Tropicana's entertainment except gambling. As soon as they were airborne, the passengers were served frozen pink daiquiris. A row of lights came up from underneath the arch and a gold lamé curtain opened to reveal a quintet of musicians in ruffled-sleeved shirts. The pilot throttled back to lower the noise of the engines as the conjunto launched into a blazing cha-cha-cha on trumpet, drums, guitar, maracas, and a sixty-six-key piano specially designed to fit in the confines of the cabin.

And if live music and grenadine-tinted daiquiris were not enough to put the passengers in the Tropicana spirit, when the plane crested over the darkening Florida Keys, Ana Gloria and Rolando came out to perform a truncated version of their gymnastic repertoire. There were cha-cha-chas, mambos, and dance lessons for some of the more adventuresome passengers. "Some of the lucky males find their hair mussed, their cheek patted as [Ana Gloria] passes . . . A few find her in their laps, smiling impishly and bounding out again before they regain their wits," wrote Henry Durling in the January 1957 issue of *Cabaret* magazine. The hour-long show ended with a conga line along the narrow center aisle, just as the twinkling lights of Havana appeared to starboard. The sky was the limit.

What days those were! Like Paris in the 1890s, Berlin in the 1930s, New York in the Studio 54 days, Cuba was an endless party, and Tropicana was its epicenter. Marlon Brando, Liberace, Tyrone Power, Ava Gardner, Ernest Hemingway, Debbie Reynolds, Dianne Carroll, Edith Piaf, Elizabeth Taylor, Eddie Fisher, Mamie van Doren, Cesar Romero—everyone who came to Cuba, every performer who worked at other cabarets, every movie star who lunched in the outdoor patio of the Hotel Nacional or dove off the platform diving board at Lansky's new Riviera Hotel, or swam in the saltwater swimming pool built into the rocky coastline of Trafficante's seaside Comodoro, eventually spent a night under the stars at Tropicana, drinking rum, dancing the mambo, or playing roulette. The cast basked in the glory of it all. "Ava Gardner was there the night we did *Luisa Fernanda en Chemise*," remembered Eddy Serra. "I did a modern dance interpretation of Peggy Lee's hit song, 'Fever.' Afterward, many of the cast went to the Cabaret Nacional, and there was Ava with her entourage. We used to go down there all the time. We'd eat *pan con bistec* [steak sandwiches], or *una rubia con ojos verdes* [a blond with green eyes, referring to a dish consisting of rice with avocado], and keep partying until morning."

Show chronicled all of it. There was Broadway dancer Taybee Afra, who was brought in to star in Tropicana's *Hello Broadway*, with *Pajama Game* producer Hal Prince and its director, George Abbott. Philippine actress Erlinda Cortes, star of the pan-Asian musical *En un Paraíso del Asia*, sat out a rehearsal next to Martín and Ofelia. In September 1956, *Show* featured a four-page spread on the filming of *Tropicana*, a Mexican romantic comedy shot at the cabaret that featured not only Tropicana's own Alicia Figueroa, Nora Osorio, Miguelito Checki, and Jenny León, but Mexico's most important composer, Augustín Lara, who sang his own composition, "Señora tentación," "Lady of Temptation," from the stage of Bajo las Estrellas. Mexican actress Evangelina Elizondo starred in the film, and that year's Miss Mexico, Ana Berta Lepe, played the starstruck fiancée of the "owner" of the Tropicana cabaret, in a zany plot with overtones of Lucille Ball. (Unbeknownst to her fiancé, the character played by Lepe participates in a competition to find the next great Tropicana modelo. Naturally, she wins.) Celia Cruz, Olga Guillot, Omara Portuondo, Elena Burke, Celeste Mendoza, Xiomara Alfaro, Mercedita Valdés, Miguelito Valdés—the Cuban greats played Tropicana regularly. Between the shows many would dance the rumba by the dressing rooms. Afterward they'd move the party to the Marianao beach cabarets or to those in Central Havana, or go to a nearby club called Tropicanita, or stay on the premises to eat at El Eruto— "The Burp"—Rodney's irreverent nickname for the little café that Martín had built for the artists. Rodney himself would hold fiestas on weekends at his *finca*—"country home"—located a half-hour from Havana. There was always suckling roast pork turned over an open fire, rice, black beans, fried plantains, beer, and lots of rum, and gossip: *Did you hear that Ardura keeps bugging Alicia to go out with Fernandez Miranda? Did you see the orchids in Nora's dressing room from Miguelito Valdés? Was that woman in the back of Bajo las Estrellas the mother of Oscar Echemendia's son? The kid looks so much like him, he's like a carbon copy! How does Taybee always manage to leave with the richest man in the casino? What did Pedro's wife say when she caught him getting on a bus with* otra mujer *in Central Havana? Is it true that after the last lipstick incident, Alberto Ardura started keeping a spare suit in his office?*

Some afternoons Rodney did not even feel like rehearsing. He would sit down on the stage and gather his cast around him, regaling them with tales of his early years as a chorus dancer and singer, of traveling to South America or working at the Shanghai. The stories were lusty, rowdy, and hilarious. "The rumba was never-ending," said Pastorita Guerra referring to the constant merriment. "We were *la gran familia*—'one big family.'"

In late 1956, after promising Ofelia that if she interceded on his behalf with Tropicana's management, he would deliver an excellent performance, with no alcohol-related incidents, Benny Moré got to join the Tropicana party. Ofelia took Moré's request to Ardura, and beginning on November 17 El bárbaro del ritmo and his orchestra played a two-week stint during the run of *Prohibido en España* (Banned in Spain) at ten thirty P.M., *Noche Cubana* (Cuban Night) at midnight, and *En Tragos* (Loaded on Drinks) at two A.M. Moré was a sensation. The crowds poured in to watch him crooning, mugging, tipping his guajiro's hat, cradling his cane and microphone. As he promised Ofelia, Moré arrived on time every night and completed his entire set without a single bout of onstage drunkenness. Afterward, he would stay late into the night, drinking and carousing at the Bajo las Estrellas bar—often with Ana Gloria, who was also featured in the shows—until the chairs were being stacked around him.

It was during this same spate of shows, which were preceded, at nine, by bingo in "Lefty Clark's Casino" and prizes of six 1957 model cars—Cadillac, Oldsmobile, Buick, Mercedes-Benz, Pontiac, and Chevrolet—that the Tropicana party came to a crashing halt. It happened on New Year's Eve, the busiest night of the year at Tropicana. About an hour and a half after the cast had released the traditional doves into the air, after the champagne toasts, kisses, and the eating of twelve grapes for good luck, when the patrons were back on the dance floor, a bomb ripped through the bar of Bajo las Estrellas.

There was instant pandemonium. People grabbed their partners and began running toward the carport and gardens. Fearing that another bomb might be hidden in the trees or fountains, some ran past the towering acacias of the entryway and down toward Truffin Avenue. The casino cleared out before the roulette wheel had stopped spinning. A young woman was rushed out, her arm severed near the shoulder.

No other bombs went off that night at Tropicana. But others went off at other cabarets around the city, the culmination of a month-long surge in violence that had until then been concentrated primarily in far-off Oriente Province. The escalation appeared to have been sparked by the December 2 landing of a fifty-eight-foot yacht named *Granma* on a tract of swampy coast near the town of Manzanillo. The vessel had been filled with guns and ammunition, and on board were Fidel Castro and eighty-two of his followers, including his brother Raúl and twenty other veterans of the attack on Moncada. Reports in *Diario de la Marina*, the Associated Press, and the *New York Times* conjectured that the landing was an even bigger failure than Moncada. The rebels had apparently been betrayed. Lost, confused, and, according to all eyewitnesses, leaderless—Castro had been reported killed in a fierce battle with Batista's army—they fled.

But the bombs across Havana signaled a different outcome. A war had begun.

CHAPTER 18

Esta es mi Cuba, Mister

On the 10th of this month—the opening
of the Hotel Havana Riviera . . .
In person—super-star, GINGER ROGERS,
and her grand revue
The hotel cost twelve million dollars and
has twenty floors.

from *Show*, on the opening of the
Hotel Havana Riviera, December, 1957

A new cast of characters waited in the wings and it was only a matter of time before they took center stage. First and foremost there was the leader of the would-be revolution, Fidel Castro. Like his sworn enemy, Batista, Castro was a native of northern Oriente Province. His father had come to Cuba from Galicia, in northwest Spain, and worked on the United Fruit railway until he accrued enough money to buy a small farm. A few miles south of the Bay of Nipe, near a village called Birán, Angel Castro grew mostly *caña*, which he sold to the Central Miranda, one of two large mills in the vicinity owned by the United Fruit Company. Despite his dependence on United Fruit (or possibly because of it) Angel Castro hated the United States. As in Banes, the town twenty-five miles to the north from which Batista hailed, the company was the dominant force. It owned much of the land, the railway, and the stores. It had its own small army, which was legally permitted to bear arms. Even the local post office was on company land.

Castro's mother, Lina Ruz González, had been Angel Castro's cook and mistress. She bore him five children—Ramón, Fidel, Juana, Emma, and Raúl. Angel married Lina so that his sons could be baptized and schooled in proper Catholic seminaries. Eventually Fidel went to Havana to study at the Colegio de Belén, the prestigious Jesuit school located on the other side of Villa Mina's gardens. In 1945 he entered the University of Havana. This was during the period when the anti-Machado political action groups had devolved into gun-wielding gangsters who settled scores from the windows of black sedans. Fidel joined Rolando Masferrer's Movimiento Socialista Revolucionario. Whether or not he ever pulled the trigger on an opponent remains a matter of speculation. He was a brilliant student and formidable orator, and exceedingly well read, especially in history. He was a talented baseball player as well—a decent pitcher; but rumors about his being recruited by the Washington Senators were untrue. Castro was politically ambitious from the outset. He studied law and joined the Ortodoxo party's youth movement. Yet his attacks on the Moncada and Bayamo barracks were carried out without consulting the Ortodoxo leadership. He was certain of his destiny as a great world leader. By the time he was in jail on the Isle of Pines, his letters were filled with references not only to José Martí, but to Napoleon and Julius Caesar.

While Castro was in jail, two events took place that shaped Cuba's future. The first was the 1954 presidential election. Though the general reaction to the bogus vote was resignation, the outcome made it clear that Batista had no plans to relinquish power. The second event took place in Guatemala. On June 18, 1954, that country's legally elected president, Jacobo Arbenz Guzmán, was removed from office in a swift, nearly bloodless *golpe de estado* that was planned and financed by the United States Central Intelligence Agency. Arbenz was a leftist politician who had begun a program of literacy for the peasant classes and legalized the Communist Party in his country. Moreover, his government had instituted a program of agrarian reform whose intention was to expropriate tens of thousands of uncultivated acres of land owned by United Fruit, the largest landowner in Guatemala. The program did not take the land outright (instead, the government made loans available to peasants to purchase the land at the value United Fruit declared for tax purposes); but Washington viewed the attempt to circumvent United Fruit's historical clout in favor of the peasants as a harbinger of communism. This was the height of the Cold War, when America was gripped by fear of Soviet expansion. In sessions similar to the Kefauver Committee hearings, the Senate's Permanent Subcommittee on Investigations, led by Senator Joseph McCarthy, interrogated anyone it suspected of harboring communist sentiments, including respected scientists, Hollywood actors, and even members of the United States Army. Arbenz's government was seen as an intolerable presence in the Western Hemisphere.

Though the American press colluded with the government to keep the CIA's involvement secret, outside the United States, and especially in Guatemala, the truth about what had happened to Arbenz was well known. Among the firsthand witnesses were several veterans of Moncada who had been exiled in Guatemala. Another was a twenty-six-year-old Argentinian doctor named Ernesto Guevara. For years, Guevara, or Che, as he was known by then (*che* is a term of affection used frequently in conversation in Argentina), had been traveling through South America on a motorcycle when he ended up in Guatemala. The son of a middle-class farmer whose family was active in left-wing politics, Guevara had been deeply affected by the condition of the poor throughout the continent. He arrived in Guatemala in early 1954 to see what a revolutionary government could do for its people. When Arbenz was toppled, Guevara sought refuge in the Argentine Embassy in Guatemala City. Eventually he made his way to Mexico City, where in November 1955 he met Fidel Castro. Though it remains unclear whether Guevara was already a communist, the events in Guatemala solidified his commitment to revolution and his anti-American sentiments. As he was later to say, "I was born in Argentina, I fought in Cuba, and I became a revolutionary in Guatemala."

Fidel Castro, his brother Raúl, and Che Guevara embarked for Cuba from Tuxpan, Mexico on November 24, 1956 with seventy-nine other men. The expedition, which was largely financed by deposed president Carlos Prío Socarrás, was to join up with other members of the 26th of July Movement upon landing in Oriente. Other organizations were also working to topple Batista. Earlier in December 1955, students from the University of Havana founded the Directorio Revolucionario in order to unite students and workers willing to join the fight. With the Ortodoxos, Communists, and Auténticos also calling for action against Batista, it was anyone's guess as to who was responsible for the bomb at Tropicana on New Year's Eve 1956.

The day after the blast, Martín and Ofelia rushed to the hospital to see the girl whose arm had been severed. Her name was Magaly Martínez, and she was a seventeen-year-old who had been spending her first New Year's Eve at Cuba's most glamorous cabaret. Ofelia could barely contain her anguish as she stood beside the young woman's hospital bed. There she was, maimed for life in the prime of her youth. At the moment that Ofelia and Martín arrived she was asleep on painkillers, surrounded by her weeping relatives. Martín was also deeply moved by what had happened to Magaly. He did what he usually did in these situations: paid for all the hospital bills, and told the family that he would give her a yearly stipend for her education and also find her the best prosthetic arm available in either the United States or Cuba.

After leaving the hospital, Martín and Ofelia drove directly to Tropicana. They had missed the bomb by minutes because that night they had been invited to see the show at the newly opened Hotel Capri. With its rooftop pool and a casino whose host and part owner was the American actor George Raft, the Capri had become one of the city's hottest tourist destinations. Martín had nonetheless been confident that his Paradise Under the Stars would not be overshadowed. "China, the show does not even compare to ours, does it?" he said to Ofelia while watching the show. Ofelia had agreed heartily. Now as she and Martín entered Tropicana for the first time since the New Year's Eve explosion, she was frantic with worry. How bad was the damage? More importantly, how would this affect the public's confidence in its safety? Several months before, in October of 1956, at Montmartre, two university students had shot into a group of off-duty policemen as they left the Vedado cabaret, killing Colonel José Blanco Rico, chief of the island's feared military intelligence service, and wounding Lieutenant Colonel Marcelo Tabernilla, the son of the army's chief of staff, and his wife. Several American newspapers, including the *New York Times,* described how women in evening gowns, some of them bleeding from cuts, stumbled into the mirrors of Montmartre's foyer as they tried to flee. The cabaret reopened, but attendance had thinned considerably, since almost no tourists were coming. There were rumors that it would close soon.

Bajo las Estrellas was a sea of policemen. Ofelia watched them comb through the splintered remains of the bar, carefully sorting shards of mirrored glass and skirting dangling electrical wires. By some minor miracle, all of the damage was confined to the immediate area. Even the injuries—apart from Magaly Martínez's— were limited to cuts and bruises. The bomb, said the police, had gone off before it had been securely placed. It was a small package-bomb of homemade composition, similar to others that had been set all over the city that New Year's Eve. The police had no clue who was responsible.

"WHO WAS *responsible? Ay, m'hija, por favor!* It was that girl who was injured!"

It was a rainy morning in the hilltown of Guanabacoa and I was sitting with La China Villamíl and Alicia Figueroa, poring through a stack of photo albums. The subject of the bomb had come up several minutes before, and La China was expressing a point of view I had heard once before—that Magaly Martínez was about to place the bomb when it went off by accident.

"It makes sense," continued Alicia. "No one saw anyone place the bomb. And no one else was injured."

"Do you mean her?" I asked, pulling out a photocopy of a picture from Ofelia's album. It had been taken several months after the blast, when Magaly had become a regular guest of Martín and Ofelia's.

"That's her!" exclaimed La China.

"*Sí.* She became Martín and Ofelia's favorite. They practically adopted her," Alicia added.

"Why would Martín and Ofelia take someone under their protection if that person had planted a bomb at Tropicana?" I wondered.

"That's the way Martín was," said La China, serving us cups of Cuban coffee.

"Martín and Ofelia had good hearts," added Alicia. "They weren't going to blame a girl who lost her arm, even if she did it." This sentiment was echoed by Martín's nephew Emilio Fox. "She had the bomb in her purse, under her arm. We all knew it."

In Glendale, Ofelia was pensive when presented with this theory about Magaly. "In some ways, it's logical. I have also heard that the son of Felipe Pazos [first president of the National Bank of Cuba and the country's top economist] planted the bomb. But I can tell you that it never crossed our minds. We felt so bad in the hospital that we couldn't think of anything else but this young girl who was so terribly injured. And nothing about Magaly suggested that she was involved in any revolutionary activities. She was a good girl from a fine family."

But it was precisely good girls and boys from fine families who were at the forefront of the burgeoning revolutionary movement. The youth of the island were joining the 26th of July Movement and Directorio Revolucionario in droves. In January 1957 bombs exploded all around the island. Constitutional guarantees were suspended on January 15. Though the government staunchly insisted that Fidel Castro had been killed after his landing near Manzanillo, news of his survival hit the world by force on February 24, when *New York Times* reporter Ruby Hart Phillips arranged for veteran senior editor Herbert Matthews to meet Castro in the Sierra Maestra mountains of Oriente (Felipe Pazos set up the interview and his son, Javier, accompanied Matthews). Matthews's article was published on the front page of the *New York Times*—albeit with exaggerated accounts of the size of Castro's forces. The Cuban government reacted swiftly. Minister of Defense Santiago Verdeja sent a cable to the *New York Herald Tribune* calling the article a "chapter in a fantastic novel." Minister of the Interior Santiago Rey stated publicly that it would have been impossible for Matthews to make his way around the army to reach the Sierra Maestra and rejected the claim that Castro was alive. The *Times* responded to the government by publishing a photograph of Matthews with Castro.

The *Times* report gave the revolutionary movement much-needed publicity. It also helped to galvanize the opposition, and in the following months the violence escalated, with the youth of the island leading most of the attacks. Wrote Ruby Hart Phillips: "Only boys and girls from twelve to twenty-five believed [the overthrow of Batista] could be done, and they went into action. Terrorism flared. Bombs exploded; trains were derailed; towns were blacked out by sabotage of power lines; incendiary fires were started by young revolutionists. Molotov cocktails, bottles of gasoline capped with a piece of waste and set afire, were hurled into trucks, government buildings and warehouses, the exploding gas scattering fire in every direction." The army and police responded with exceptional brutality aimed at young people. "The bodies of youths began to appear on the streets and roads of towns in the interior, especially in Oriente Province," wrote Phillips. "Once, I reported that the army had found twenty-one bodies in twenty-four hours around Holguin in the northern part of Oriente. The soldiers arrested the boys and killed them, then announced their bodies had been 'found.'" Havana's bus and train stations were targets for police roundups of young men and women who arrived from the countryside. "Pepe," the hustler who came to Havana from Cienfuegos in mid-1957, had heard about these random detentions. "I had no political affiliation, but when my bus approached Havana, I was scared to death," he told me. "The driver let me out before we got to the station and gave me an address where I could stay until I found a place to live."

Unbeknownst to Martín and Ofelia, among the "good boys and girls from fine families" who were actively sympathetic to the brewing revolution were members of their own families. Ofelia's first cousin once called her in the middle of the night at Tropicana. "She was hysterical," recalled Ofelia. "She said, 'They've got Angelito.' 'They' meant the police, of course. They were accusing him of handing out leaflets. My cousin didn't believe them. She said, 'He had nothing to do with any of this. But we don't want him transferred to a jail outside of Havana,' because sometimes when that happened people never came back alive. I had Martín call Santiago Rey and Santiaguito intervened. The boy was kept close to home until his case was decided." (Ofelia met her cousin's son again a few years ago when he came to visit Los Angeles. Now in his late sixties, and a high-ranking administrator with a natural history museum in Cuba, he and Ofelia had dinner. "I said to him, 'You know, my husband, Martín, saved you.' And he said, 'I know.'")

Another late-night phone call came from Ofelia's sister Fara. "She said to me, 'Ofelia I have these books in the house and I need to get rid of them. The books belong to Raúl. He was in a meeting, and the government is saying that it's communist. But even José Pardo Llada [a prominent radio personality, Pardo Llada had been part of the November 1955 anti-Batista meeting that took place at Havana's docks] was there,' my sister continued." The following night, after Ofelia returned with Martín from the cabaret, Fara brought her son's books to her sister's house. While a confused lion looked on from his cage inside the garage, the two sisters lit a fire in a metal trash drum and burned the offending books. As she was throwing them onto the flames, Ofelia chanced to look at two of the jackets. One was *Das Kapital* by Karl Marx. Another one was a title by Vladimir Ilych Lenin. At the time, Ofelia did not compute that her nephew's possession of these books signified anything political. "Even if I'd known, I probably still would have done everything I could to help my family," she said ruefully. There was no such thing as neutrality in those days. One night in 1958, Nat Cole's limousine was halted en route to Tropicana. "We didn't know who [the men] were or what they wanted," recalled Maria Cole recently. "They were all carrying guns. One of them was talking to our driver, and another stuck his head into the window of the limo. Suddenly they all started talking to each other. They were speaking so fast we couldn't understand a thing. I was getting worried [until] we heard them saying the words 'Nat "King" Cole! Nat "King" Cole!' Then they waved us off and let us go."

NAT AND Maria Cole had fallen in love with Cuba. They loved the people, the beauty of Havana, the balmy climate that coincided with the star's annual gig at Tropicana in February, and especially the music. In 1958 Cole had his third two-week run at Tropicana and the Coles felt themselves honorary habaneros. At Tropicana, Cole's yearly visit was as exciting as the annual *carnavales*, which sometimes coincided with his visit. The day of his arrival, the staff and performers would wait for him outside the dressing rooms, applauding and hugging him like a returning member of the family. The between-show party took on a special liveliness when Cole was present. Afterward, the cast watched from the wings as Cole took the stage to a hushed audience in Bajo las Estrellas. In 1957, Cole's performances had coincided with Rodney's Afro-Cuban *Tambó*, and a Brazilian revue, *Copacabana*. His ease with the Tropicana orchestra and his rapport with Armando Romeu had grown steadily. Now, in 1958, concurrent with the star's appearance in the middle of the Haitian show, *Vodú Ritual*, and a revue of Cuban folkloric song and dance that was entitled *Esta es mi Cuba, Mister*, "This is My Cuba, Mister," he had decided to record a Spanish-language album in Havana with the orchestra, using Romeu's arrangements for several key tunes.

For Martín and Ofelia, the Coles' annual visit had become a personal highlight of their social year. All year long they thought up new places to take the Coles after his show was over. As they had with Carmen Miranda and her husband, they would squire them around to other cabarets and nightspots, such as the Bambú Palace, where China Villamíl had worked for a brief period in 1956. By 1958, there were lots of new nightclubs to show them. During this third visit to the island, the Coles found themselves thinking about maintaining a more permanent address in Cuba. One day when they were having lunch with Martín and Ofelia at La Bodeguita del Medio, a hole-in-the-wall Old Havana bar and restaurant that was one of Ernest Hemingway's regular haunts (and where, according to Ofelia, Nat Cole loved to order the avocado salad with onions and olive oil), they asked their hosts what part of town would be best for them to buy their own apartment. Martín hesitated. He did not want to scare his guests, but neither did he want to mislead them. Despite the construction boom and rise in tourism, Cuba had become a shaky place to live. Revolution had spread across the island with the speed of a virus. From Oriente Province, where nearly anyone who was not in the military or police was a supporter of Fidel Castro and the 26th of July Movement, came daily reports of rebel bombings, sabotage, sugarcane field burnings, and kidnappings. Outside Tropicana, cars had been set on fire. The government, typically, responded with brutality. Soldiers prowled the streets, looking to pick up anyone who appeared the least bit suspicious. They were like "big cats, looking for someone to pounce on," as Ruby Hart Phillips put it. Reports of police torture and summary executions filtered daily into the *Times'* Havana office. The government did all that it could do to censor stories of both their abuses or rebel victories. They leaked out anyway. The information got broadcast over Radio Rebelde, the revolutionaries' clandestine radio station, or picked up in foreign papers that were smuggled in, filling the nation with a blend of elation and dread.

In March of 1957, just weeks after Cole had completed his second two-week gig at Tropicana, the Directorio Revolucionario mounted an assault on the presidential palace in broad daylight. The intent had been to kill Batista. Instead, forty people were gunned down, mostly by police. Among those killed were Directorio Revolucionario leader José Antonio Echevarría (who had helped seize the CMQ radio station control room to broadcast that the government had been overthrown) and an American tourist. The following year, three days after Cole's opening, ten separate bombs exploded in Havana. "You would hear the explosions sometimes," said Ofelia. Six months later, on March 3, 1958, *Life* magazine reported on the rebel kidnapping of the favored driver in the Gran Prix Cuba, Argentinian Juan-Manuel Fangio, the night before the race. (He was released unharmed after the race had ended in a fiery accident that had no relationship to revolutionary activity.) Alicia Figueroa narrowly missed being the victim of a volley of bullets when her car, parked on L Street in Vedado while she was at the beauty parlor, was caught in the crossfire of an assassination attempt on anti-Batista radio commentator José Pardo Llada. My father, Leonardo Lowinger, who had a wholesale business with his father selling eyeglasses and dry goods—costume jewelry, pocket knives, condoms—had to stop taking business trips to see clients because it had become too dangerous to drive around the country. "The army used to stop me constantly and search the car," he told me recently. "The worst time was at night. They'd come out of nowhere, groups of five or six soldiers. They'd shine a flashlight into the car. I never had guns, of course. But if they saw the merchandise, then they'd want you to give them things. This one wanted a pocketknife, this one some jewelry for his wife. Before you knew it, they took everything."

Despite the escalating violence, my father expected the political situation to stabilize as soon as Batista was out. "The consensus at that time was that one government comes in, steals enough to get rich, then leaves when another one takes over. Then that one gets rich and moves on. It's the Latin American way, and we'd seen it with Grau, with Prío. Ever since Cuba was liberated from Spain it had been like that. We figured Batista had made enough money with the gambling that he'd go soon and then Fidel or whoever took over would make a deal with the Americans and let the rest of us keep living our lives."

Martín was also sanguine about the future. "It's better to wait a few months to buy a place," he told Nat and Maria Cole. Translating for Martín, Ofelia explained to the Coles that neither of them expected Batista to hold on too much longer. "We've seen this kind of thing before," she told them. "When a new government takes over, things settle down rapidly." The important thing, of course, was for the conflict to end before tourism became seriously affected. The hotels had been crowded throughout the holidays (both the heavyweight champion Jack Dempsey and Senator John F. Kennedy had been to Cuba in December 1957); but in early

1958, Martín had seen a drop in attendance at the cabaret. Normally it was practically impossible to get a table during the winter season without a reservation. Now some nights there were empty tables. The Cubans were the ones staying home, but if the violence did not end soon, Martín knew, the Americans would stop coming.

Although he relied on government protection for his business, when it came to politics Martín maintained he had no ideology. Whether Fidel Castro or Fulgencio Batista was president mattered little to him. What mattered was that those in power protect gambling. The Batista status quo was obviously satisfactory, but Martín was also optimistic about his chances with the revolutionaries. Once, they sent a representative to Tropicana looking for donations. The young man came to the casino office late at night. The second show was over and Martín and Ofelia were waiting for their car, ready to leave, when Martín was called back to the office from the carport.

"They're looking for donations," Ofelia's brother-in-law, Atilano, told Martín. The man had gone directly to him—most likely because he was the casino's accountant. "Or because his son the revolutionary had sent them," speculated Emilio Fox.

"Give him five thousand pesos," said Martín. The young revolutionary shook Martín's hand and thanked him warmly. Then Martín took Atilano aside. "Make sure it's in small bills, in case someone stops him."

THE STORY of the donation came up one morning when Ofelia, Rosa, and I were heading back to Glendale after an aborted research mission to the Burbank Airport. A few years earlier, Ofelia and Rosa had been there to pick up a friend (Ofelia only flies if she has to), and when they had entered the terminal they encountered a photo exhibit having to do with aviation highlights. There, on the wall before them, was a blow-up photo-mural of Ana Gloria dancing with a passenger aboard the Tropicana Special. After their friend left, Ofelia and Rosa went back several times to see the photographs. Five years later, we were unable to get any information by phone. When we tried to make an inquiry in person, we were summarily turned away by airport security.

"I think of these times as similar to what was going on in Cuba in the '50s," said Rosa Sanchez as we drove back to their house. "The fear of terrorism had people by the throats. The police only became intolerably repressive after all the bombing started."

"And you know that those reports of repression were often exaggerated," added Ofelia.

I was not in any mood for a political argument, but couldn't let that one pass. "How so, Ofelia?"

"Years later, after Cuba was lost to us, the editor of *Bohemia* admitted that they—the press—had exaggerated the reports of torture and missing people. They had claimed that there had been twenty thousand dead by the hands of Batista, and it was not true. The editor wrote a long letter of apology then killed himself."

I had heard that story several times. I had read the text of the note left by Miguel Angel Quevedo, the editor of *Bohemia*, prior to his suicide in 1969. The letter is an anguished mea culpa in which the one-time journalist admonishes himself, his reporters, the United States government, and the Cuban public in general for allowing its hatred of Batista to create what he termed "the disgrace of Cuba." It is one of the many gut-wrenching tales of misgiving and self-doubt on the part of people trying to make sense of what happened to their lives and to the lives of their families. It is disheartening to hear people who once fought against tyranny retract their positions simply because a more ruthless and intransigent dictator followed Batista. But that is the sad history of Cuba. As one strongman replaces another, idealists harden into reactionaries. The posturing, obduracy, and historical distortions make change feel distant, almost impossible. I really did not want to get drawn into the battle with Ofelia. But I saw no way around it.

"Okay," I said, "let's say that *Bohemia* did exaggerate. And though I seriously doubt that the *New York Times* did the same, let's say that they were given misleading information, revolutionary propaganda designed to make the government look bad. How do you explain Martín's extreme worry that night that he made a donation? Why was he so concerned about making sure that the guy from the 26th of July left Tropicana only carrying small bills?"

"It's simple. If the police searched him and he had small bills on him, he could say he had won the money gambling. But if he had five hundred-peso or thousand-peso notes, it would look . . . suspicious."

"In other words, Martín, too, was afraid of the police."

Exasperation crept into Ofelia's voice. "Rosa, in those days you had to be careful."

"What I'm trying to get at here, Ofelia, is that there was a climate of fear in the country and that in large part it was caused by Batista's police and military."

"There was a war! Terrorists were setting off bombs in movie theaters. Of course the police was trigger-happy! How would it look now if someone caught the owner of, say, Caesar's Palace giving money to al-Qaeda?"

"There's actually no *owner*, per se, of Caesar's Palace," remarked Rosa Sanchez off-handedly.

"*Bueno,* you know what I mean," said Ofelia.

Though the analogy appeared relevant, it didn't quite fit. "It's not the same as what's going on now," I said. "And the main proof is that people like Martín *did* give them money. Do you think he would have done that if they were simply terrorists?"

"I don't think you understand. Most Cubans just wanted an end to the violence. The majority didn't care who came after Batista. If another group would have won, they would have supported them. All Martín was trying to do was protect his business. He was just speculating."

Like the good gamblers that they were, other Cubans also speculated. As the bombs exploded and the jails filled, people hedged their bets, made donations, and worked actively to support the insurgents. By late 1958, only those Cubans with ties to the government supported Batista. But as Basil Woon pointed out in 1928, in addition to being avid gamblers, Cubans seek diversion when there seems to be no ready solution to a problem. And there was diversion aplenty in Havana in 1958. Early in the year there was the long-awaited opening of the Ciudad Deportiva, a new sports complex in Vedado that was the brainchild of Sports Director Fernandez Miranda. Ofelia and Martín attended the opening night event—a boxing match between world lightweight champion Joey Brown and Cuban contender Orlando Echeverría. The sports complex next featured the rodeo show of Gene Autry, the first time that cowboys and cowgirls would be seen in a sports arena in the middle of Havana. The large casinos kept drawing in outside stars. Jimmy Durante played the Parisien. Vic Damone sold out for two weeks at the Havana Riviera. George Raft continued as the "social host and master of ceremonies" of the Casino de Capri in a show that starred Mitsuko, the dancer who had filled in at Tropicana when Leonela was on maternity leave, and a cadre of dancers dressed as Ginger Rogers, Mae West, and Marilyn Monroe, a few of Raft's Hollywood leading ladies. ("He was charming as can be," said Ofelia of the night Raft visited Tropicana.)

In February, *Show* celebrated its fourth anniversary as "the only genuinely international magazine in the world" with gala receptions in Caracas, Miami, Rio de Janeiro, and Madrid. The parties and accompanying performances were chronicled in an issue that featured Ana Gloria Varona on the cover and included a special two-page report on the Hollywood wedding of Robert Wagner and Natalie Wood. The issue also announced the gala Havana opening of 20th Century Fox's adaptation of Hemingway's *The Sun Also Rises,* starring Tyrone Power, Ava Gardner, and Errol Flynn, all of whom had visited Tropicana. September's *Show* had photographs of Jack Paar at La Bodeguita del Medio. The American talk show host had come to Havana to broadcast from Tropicana via Cuba's Channel Ten, following the earlier success of Steve Allen, who had brought his entire variety show, including the Skitch Henderson Orchestra, comic Lou Costello, singer Steve Lawrence, and bombshell Mamie Van Doren, to Meyer Lansky's Hotel Riviera in January. The Riviera, whose Copa Room had opened the previous year with Ginger Rogers, was by then the most elegant of all Havana's casino-hotels. Its rooms were booked throughout the winter of 1958 and into 1959.

Tropicana, however, remained unmatched in its entertainment offerings. To the shock of some, including Ofelia, Ardura arranged for the hiring of the first transsexual, singer Christine Jorgensen, for a two-week performance that sold out every night. The ribald comedy *Diosas de Carne* opened in May with Jenny León as Helen of Troy and a host of other Tropicana models playing the parts of Antigone, Medusa, Medea, Diana, and Minerva. Notably absent from the list of goddesses was Alicia Figueroa, who, after breaking up with Miguel Angel Blanco ("I left him in tears at the table, and I said, 'You, *güempa*, the perfect little postcard, are going to cry now?'") had left Tropicana for the Casino Parisien and eventually was offered an exclusive contract as the spokesperson-model for Trinidad y Hermanos. But Cuba had an endless supply of guitar-shaped women, so that by the time Rodney mounted his seventh anniversary show, *Su Majestad la Prensa*, "Your Majesty the Press," he had no problem filling the catwalks. The Performing Artists Union hosted a gala performance of *Esta es mi Cuba, Mister* to honor Martín Fox for his contribution to the field of cabaret entertainment. The show was performed at Havana's new five thousand-seat, air-conditioned theater, the Teatro Blanquita, on Miramar's First Avenue. There was a heavy police presence at the entrance to the theater, but no incidents of sabotage or violence.

After the New Year's Eve bombing a year before, there were also no further incidents at Tropicana. The cabaret was now heavily guarded by police and infiltrated by government informants (these ubiquitous snitches came to be called "thirty-three" because their salary was thirty-three pesos and thirty-three centavos a month). Few outsiders would have noticed their presence at Paradise Under the Stars. Certainly Steve Allen and his wife, Jayne Meadows, didn't when they visited Tropicana in January 1958. However, a month after Allen's show from the Copa Room was aired, the American Federation of Television and Radio Artists (AFTRA) began requiring that any of its members working in Cuba obtain additional accident insurance coverage to compensate for violence-related injury, and life insurance policies in the amount of $300,000.

Armed guards were in plain sight in the spring of 1958 at Tropicana, but they were there to protect several million dollars' worth of jewels owned by the House of Harry Winston. Neither Ofelia nor Valentín remembers how the emerald and diamond necklaces, ruby rings, and sapphire tiaras came to be exhibited for one night only in the baccarat lounge of the casino. Still, both remember the excitement of that night, of people filing past the jewelry as if it were the British crown jewels. In late November, Tropicana sent its own jewels—Rodney's full production, including the Armando Romeu Orchestra, Leonela González, the Tropicana dance corps, and a host of lighting and costume technicians—to New York to perform *Rumbo al Waldorf* for the American Society of Travel Agents (ASTA) convention. It was a big marketing coup arranged by Pedro Fox and Alberto Ardura in anticipation of the following year's ASTA meeting, which was supposed to take place in Havana. During the show, a man jumped onstage waving a pistol and shouted, "*¡Abajo Batista!*" (Down with Batista!). The Waldorf-Astoria security wrestled him offstage and the show went on. The cast returned to Cuba in December and went directly from the airport to Tropicana, where a rumba awaited them outside the dressing rooms and lasted well into the night.

As Christmas neared, Martín finally agreed to put his partners' percentages in writing. According to Valentín, up to that point he had been evasive about the matter, preferring to keep everything on handshake terms. For the partners it was a great relief and the best Christmas gift they could have been given. Martín also gave Ofelia an unusual gift that year. It was a white satin gown, a Pierre Balmain couture original with brightly embroidered flowers on the hem. The dress had been named "Havana" by the designer, and it was first displayed during a French fashion show at Tropicana that featured designs by Dior, Chanel, and Givenchy, as well as Balmain. Martín wanted Ofelia to wear it on New Year's Eve. But a few days after Christmas, she woke up with a sharp twinge in her back. It only got worse as the days progressed, and by New Year's Eve day she was barely able to stand without assistance or walk without a cane. She had caught a violent cold in the process and could barely hear because of congestion. Every time she sneezed, she felt she would crumple from the pain. Still, it would have taken a lot more than that to keep her home from Tropicana on a New Year's Eve. Martín, who helped her zip up her Pierre Balmain creation, clasp the white gold chain that held her four-inch diamond cross pendant, and put on the diamond earrings he had given her seven years before as an engagement present, understood the meaning of this effort. "China, you're the best thing that's ever happened to me," he said as he put on his tuxedo jacket.

"No, I'm the second best thing," said Ofelia with a pained smile.

As Martín and Ofelia headed to the door the phone rang. It was Carmelina Ardura. Her uncle had died suddenly that afternoon, and she was going to the wake that night instead of to the cabaret. She called to wish her friends *felicidades* for the coming year, and that they enjoy health, peace, and prosperity.

The next time the phone rang in Ofelia and Martín's house, the caller was Alberto Ardura. It was five thirty on the first morning of 1959, and he was getting ready to leave the country.

PART IV

CHAPTER 19

Shattered Slots

Carmelina Ardura: The afternoon of New Year's Eve, when I returned from the hairdresser, my mother-in-law was waiting for me. She said, "Carmelina, don't bother going upstairs. Your uncle died and you have to go directly to his house." I had my dress, shoes, and accessories laid out since morning. Alberto looked so sad. We always spent the New Year together. I said, "Don't get that way, Alberto, don't worry, you go and take care of business, and we'll see each other later." I got home from my uncle's around midnight. At two in the morning, a friend called and woke me. She said, "Carmelina, what's happening?" I had no idea. A few minutes later, another friend called. "Carmelina, what happened to Alberto? Fernandez Miranda came to pick him up at Tropicana." I knew nothing. I had been sleeping!

Valentín Jodra: Fernandez Miranda's chauffeur showed up all of a sudden. I said, "*¿Qué pasa, compadre?* What are you doing here?" He said, "I can't tell you, *mi hermano.*" People were afraid already because the revolutionaries were infiltrated everywhere.

But I already knew because another client of mine, Anibal Duarte, had been called earlier, and he and his wife left in a hurry. Ardura rushed in and out of his office, picking up papers. Then he went off without saying good-bye.

Eddy Serra: On New Year's Eve we performed only one show. Later, I left the cabaret to go to the Hotel St. John with some friends. The bar was pretty empty, which was strange for New Year's Eve. In the streets we heard *pah! pah! pah!*—gunshots. "Something's happening," people shouted, but we didn't know what. Later I took a bus home to Santiago de las Vegas. When we passed by La Cabaña [fortress] to pick up the Avenida de Rancho Boyeros, there was more gunfire. The bullets went across the bus. The passengers threw themselves on the floor. We didn't know where the bullets were coming from. The bus driver managed to speed away without any of us getting hurt.

Carmelina Ardura: At four in the morning I finally got through to Alberto's secretary. She said they'd come for Alberto and taken him but didn't say who. I was going crazy! At five he arrived at the house. He said: "Batista's gone. Pack a suitcase, we've got to leave, too." I was in shock. We didn't do anything. But he said they were going to come for him if we didn't leave. "What about the girls?" I asked. We had two small daughters—ages five and fourteen. He said, "The girls have to stay, because we don't know if we'll make it out of here safely." At that moment I had to decide between my husband and my children. I knew that the girls would be safe, so I left them with my mother-in-law. I gave the fourteen-year-old her father's pistol and said, "Defend yourself if you have to." I took them to their bed. I gave them kisses. Then we left for the airport.

Leonela González: People began saying, "Oye, Batista se fue—'Batista left,' " but I was caught up in the business of the show and wasn't paying attention. Things always happened around me without my noticing. All I used to care about was ballet. The [other cast members] used to call me *la despistada* [the spacey one].

Carmelina Ardura: When we arrived at the airport, the officials didn't want to let us go. These men were still dressed in the uniforms of Batista's people, but they were all infiltrated. I didn't understand the problem! Sure, we used to spend weekends at Kuquine [Batista's country house]. Every Sunday we were there, playing ball, dominoes, eating. But since childhood we'd been personal friends of Roberto's [Fernandez Miranda]. When I was nine years old he was a *medio-novio* [half-boyfriend] of mine. Alberto and he grew up together. This had nothing to do with politics. Our driver talked the soldiers into letting us go. We had a four-seat airplane. Normally Alberto flew himself, but that night our pilot wouldn't let him because he was so nervous. We flew to Daytona Beach. In the morning the officials came to the house looking for Alberto. They said to my oldest daughter, "Your father was a criminal. He killed people." She answered, "My father ran a cabaret. He didn't kill anyone. As a matter of fact, he used to be a good friend to all of you!" The pilot turned around and went back for the girls, but they did not arrive in Daytona until January fourteenth.

Alicia Figueroa: I was a pretty well-known personality because I was on television every day, on the CMQ news at one fifteen, and every Saturday I also appeared on the boxing show at nine P.M. I no longer did cabaret work because the ad agency that dealt with Trinidad y Hermanos had set that as a condition of my contract. I had broken up with Miguel Angel and I had no boyfriend. So I was home that night. At least that's what I remember. It's curious how my memory fails me about such an important night. I know I heard the news from my father, who was in the military. And I felt great uncertainty. Not happiness. The following month I was named "Model of the Year."

Valentín Jodra: I stayed [at Tropicana] all night with Atilano Taladrid and Efrain Hernandez, who used to service the slot machines. My brother was there too and also some custodians. At five, I said to Efrain, "We should go down to [Central] Havana and take the money out of the slots." He said, "*Figúrate* [go figure], that money belonged largely to Fernandez Miranda and Ardura. They're both gone, so why should we risk ourselves?" And I just blew up. I said, "What risk? This is our work." In reality, I knew there was going to be trouble. We'd heard people talking when we went to service the machines. In the bodegas and cafés . . . there was plenty of anger at Batista. The *maquinitas* were a symbol. I knew they were going to attack. And they did. Later that morning, they destroyed everything—the parking meters, the casinos . . . the ones belonging to the Americans. But no one came to Tropicana. Their anger wasn't directed at us. We were a 100 percent Cuban place. Anyone who thinks that Tropicana was Mafia-owned should stand before me and say it. I'll set them straight. Around six or seven I went home. Atilano stayed and so did some custodians. Other staff appeared, even people who were with the 26th of July came in to protect the workplace. Martín showed up after I was gone.

Rosa Sanchez: To me, Batista's departure meant that Cuba's problems were over. At the time I was living in Miami and someone called me and said that a bunch of Cubans were going to the airport because *los esbirros* [henchmen] *de Batista* were coming. I usually shy away from all demonstration, mostly because I don't want anyone to speak for me. But I, too, went to the airport to see what was going on. On the way there, the Cubans were honking their horns. It was very exciting. The people were getting off planes from Cuba carrying their suitcases and the Cubans on the ground were screaming "*Esbirros! Esbirros!*" The word was that their suitcases were full of money.

Jenny León: The next day we had rehearsal but no one went out.

Valentín Jodra: I went back a few days later. The place was closed. My brother and I did the accounting for the traganickels in the casino. This was in case things got back to normal rapidly and Fernandez Miranda came back wanting his money.

Ernesto Capote: Martín had me hide all the traganickels under the stage of Bajo las Estrellas. It was me, Martín, and two or three other employees. We thought it would be a matter of a few days. A *chivato* [snitch] finally told on us and they came and took them away.

Jenny León: It was a total shock that Batista left, as much as if Fidel Castro suddenly left Cuba now. And he did it only because things got out of control for him. But the people of Cuba were sick of Batista. We were sick of the government, the thieves, the violence, the *relajo* [joke] that Cuba had become in those years. *Caballero,* make no mistake about it—the people were with Fidel!

Ofelia Fox: I don't have any memory of those first days. *Figúrate,* I was in bed on painkillers. My doctor came by the first day . . . maybe it wasn't New Year's Day . . . *no sé* . . . He gave me a shot of something for my back. He diagnosed me with two herniated discs. I had a cold so they couldn't operate immediately. After the surgery, I woke up in a room filled with flowers. There were so many flowers that Martín paid for the room next door just to keep them. My favorite was this basket with twenty-one lavender orchids. It was sent by Santiago Rey and his wife. At the time I didn't know that they were hiding in an embassy. It was probably the Dominican Republic's, because that's where they eventually ended up. Later they went to Miami. Santo [Trafficante] was in jail at Trescornia [immigration and detention center], where later we went to the wedding of his daughter. *Claro,* no one said anything to me about what was happening during the first days. Martín made a pact with my mother and sisters that no one should tell me what was going on. I asked about Ardura. I was concerned for them, but Martín told me they were safe in Florida. I remember something on television: the people with placards that said "Gracias Fidel," the streets jammed. Probably it was the day that Che Guevara and Camilo Cienfuegos came in from Santa Clara. I had surgery a few days later. My sisters brought pictures of Sunan to the hospital because that always cheered me up. Olguita Guillot came by and sang to me. All the nurses and orderlies came running in when they heard her. She sang "Noche de ronda"—my favorite. And something she had made popular: "Palabras calladas." "*Siempre estoy en ti pensando y tu de mi no sabes nada* [I am always thinking of you, and you know nothing of me]." You can imagine the commotion when Olga was singing. She was already very famous.

I was in the hospital about ten days. In the middle of my stay, I watched Fidel Castro when he entered the city. It was on January 8, and they showed the whole thing on television. The streets were jammed. Cars couldn't move. He came in a jeep or a tank, I don't remember. There were dozens of *barbudos* [bearded ones, the popular term for the 26th of July fighters] with him, all in uniform. Many still had rifles. They stopped at the presidential palace and Fidel went up the steps to see [Provisional President Manuel] Urrutia. Everyone was cheering. They went from there to Campamento Columbia. We watched in the hospital—my sister, my mother, me. Martín was pacing in and out of the room. The cabaret was closed but he was trying not to make a big deal about it. "China, don't worry," he said. "Everything's settling down and getting back to normal." Now I realize he was pretending, but at the time it didn't occur to me to question it.

Leonardo Lowinger: I think every single person in Cuba was watching Fidel Castro that day. Our whole family was gathered together in the living room. We were all pretty excited. The only one not too excited was my aunt Fanny. She had survived the Holocaust by running from country to country until she got to France, and a Catholic priest hid her in a convent. After the war she returned to Hungary. Then in 1956, she fled when the Russians marched into Budapest with their tanks. She also told us that they came with rosaries and crucifixes hanging from their necks, and white doves flying. When we were watching Fidel on television that day, someone released some doves—there were two or six, I can't remember—and a pair of them landed on his shoulders as he talked. My aunt stood up and pointed to the television: "Those men are communists!" We all laughed at her. "Ah, come on, what do you know?" My father—her brother—called her a silly old maid. But she insisted. "You don't know. I saw this before. Communists act like they're holy people, but watch out," she said. She and my father argued in Hungarian for a long time.

Ofelia Fox: I don't think anyone was worrying about communism that day. There was nothing but joy in Cuba. It was like the day Hitler fell, when World War II was over and everyone came together. Probably never before had so many Cubans felt the same. And how could that not have been for the good of the nation?

CHAPTER 20

Rumba at the Presidential Palace

Nosotros los cubanos o no llegamos o nos pasamos.
(We Cubans either don't arrive or we overshoot
the mark.)

popular Cuban saying

New Year's Day 1959. The morning was bright and sunny. A light winter breeze made the Cuban flag above the presidential palace flutter. The streets were almost empty—no revelers straggled towards home, no crowds emerging from the favorite breakfast spots. Around nine, people began trickling into the streets. Cars coasted along the Malecón. Horns were honked. People shouted, *"¡Abajo Batista! ¡Viva Fidel!"* A crowd began to gather near the statue of José Martí in the Parque Central, in sight of the former Edén Concert. The cheers grew louder, bolder. Before long, the shouting turned raucous, the cheers hoarse and angry. Maybe someone threw a rock. Maybe someone saw a policeman. However the mob formed, by noon it was coursing down the shaded terrazzo pavement of the Paseo del Prado, stopping to smash windows, slash tires, hunt for members of the police, military, or anyone who could be accused of being a collaborator.

Just as Valentín had predicted, the slot machines became particular targets of the people's wrath. So did the parking meters, which everyone hated because they knew that the proceeds went straight into the pockets of Batista's family. The mob swarmed across Central Havana, yanking the meters from their bases. They burst into bars and bodegas, pulling the traganickels off the walls and smashing them. At the Sevilla Biltmore they rushed up the Moorish tiled steps and through the doors of the newly renovated casino, upending tables, tearing the felts, prying open the traganickels and pocketing the change. "I had seen this before, in 1933," wrote Ruby Hart Phillips in her book on Cuba. "It was for me like sitting through a bad movie a second time. Mobs speak with the same voice in every generation."

Because Batista had had such a cozy relationship with the gamblers and American organized crime, the mobs of January 1959 reserved most of their destructive vengefulness for anything and everyone associated with casinos. In Vedado, they stormed through the Capri and St. John hotels. Near the Malecón they hit the Hotel Deauville. Back at the Parque Central they tore through the Hotel Plaza and the Cabaret Nacional, though neither had casino gambling. Across the Almendares River, they raced past the topiary along Miramar's Fifth Avenue, attacking the homes of former Batista officials and suspected collaborators who had fled. They ravaged the beachfront Pennsylvania cabaret and Rumba Palace. They made their way to Sans Souci and scaled the gates.

At Tropicana the staff waited. By noon, waiters, cooks, busboys, and parking attendants, anyone who had heard about the destruction of the other cabarets, poured in to protect their workplace. Many now openly declared their alliance to Fidel Castro, and wore red and black armbands in support of the 26th of July. By mid-afternoon, however, nothing had happened. The city had been under the control of revolutionary militias for hours. From Truffin Avenue you could hear voices on loudspeakers ordering everyone to stay inside or risk being shot. The looting had been halted. Many were arrested at Sans Souci, caught in the act of destroying the casino. But Tropicana was spared. The mob never arrived.

OFELIA FOX gazed pensively at the twilit California landscape. It was an unseasonably hot night, and we were sitting out the Santa Ana winds on chaise lounges on the top tier of her and Rosa's terraced patio. Before us the hills of Glendale slowly darkened. The freeway lights blurred past. Next to us stood a greenhouse filled with bonsai trees—a miniature forest of juniper, cedar, oak, and redwood trees that Ofelia had coaxed into submission, stunting their roots, binding their trunks and branches. Ofelia sighed. "I suppose I should be comforted by the fact that no one tried to destroy Tropicana."

We all had heavy hearts that night. It had been five months since our visit to Chiquita's home in Malibu. She had since passed away awaiting a liver transplant. Ofelia's friend Santiago Rey had also died. And two dear Cuban friends of mine had also recently died within a week of each other. One was the mother of my artist friend. The other was a restoration architect. The suddenness of these deaths (one of which might have been prevented had the person been able to come to the United States for cancer treatment) underscored the terrible cost of the distance that after nearly fifty years still divides countries that are only ninety miles apart. Rhetoric continued to fly across the Straits of Florida, and it was becoming more and more apparent that relations between the countries would probably grow worse before they got better. Ofelia maintained that the United States should continue to pressure the Cuban government into accepting democratic reforms. But she felt my fury and my sadness.

"Now you know how I felt when we left, not knowing when we would see our families again," said Ofelia softly.

"I think you guys need another drink," said Rosa as she turned to me. "Nobody wanted to worry Ofelia, so she never got any details of what happened at Tropicana during the first days."

"Yes, tell me what I missed," added Ofelia.

WHILE OFELIA slept and got over her cold, Havana settled down to welcoming its new heroes. Militias formed by soldiers of the new regime began policing the streets the afternoon of January 1, and the destruction stopped. The following day, hundreds of thousands gathered near the Havana bay tunnel entrance to greet the first revolutionary commanders from Las Villas Province. Che Guevara, who had led some of the most decisive battles of the war in Las Villas Province, came through first. The crowd cheered wildly as Che's column of tanks and jeeps went up the ancient stone rampart of La Cabaña fortress. Another hero of Las Villas, Camilo Cienfuegos, followed Che's convoy through the streets of Havana en route to Campamento Columbia, where he was to assume command. Unlike the Castro brothers and Guevara, Cienfuegos was a jovial habanero with a great sense of humor who hailed from the working classes. Like many Cubans of his generation, he had spent several years in the United States, traveling from New York to Chicago, Kansas City, and San Francisco, and working in restaurants, hotels, and factories. Cienfuegos wrote humorous letters to his parents about life as an illegal immigrant. ("Today I filled out 60,000 forms and told 999,999 lies...," he wrote while looking for work in Chicago. About April in New York he wrote, "When it rains here, it gets so cold that you turn into a penguin.") In late 1955, Cienfuegos returned to Cuba for several months and was shocked by the escalation in police brutality. He wrote to friends of his house being ransacked repeatedly while the police looked for communist literature, of being shot in the leg, and later beaten after attending a student demonstration.

Cienfuegos returned to San Francisco in May of 1956, already determined to join Fidel Castro in Mexico. Embarking with Castro on the *Granma,* he later fought in the Sierra Maestra, and led decisive revolutionary battles in Las Villas Province.

At roughly the same time that Camilo Cienfuegos's motorcade arrived at Campamento Columbia, Martín, Valentín, and another member of Tropicana's staff were driving eastward into Central Havana in a paneled truck filled with a good portion of Tropicana's traganickels. The truck threaded through miles of cheering, honking, flag-waving minions and parked in front of the apartment building of Niquita, Martín's old paramour from Ciego de Avila. Valentín and the other staff member unloaded the machines and hid them. Those that did not fit in the truck were put under the stage of Bajo las Estrellas, where, according to Ernesto Capote, they were discovered several days later. If Capote's memory is correct, that would have been on January 5, when Ofelia was admitted to the hospital for surgery. Martín insisted on being in the operating room, holding her hand. That was also the day that Manuel Urrutia, Fidel Castro's handpicked choice for interim president, arrived in Havana by airplane from Santiago de Cuba and took up residence in the presidential palace. A somber judge who had presided in Santiago at the trial of the *Granma* survivors, Urrutia had been chosen because he had called for the acquittal of the captured men. He had little platform other than a vehement opposition to gambling and prostitution, which he linked and vowed to abolish.

On January 8, Fidel Castro entered Havana and made the speech from Campamento Columbia that Ofelia watched from her hospital bed, and which provoked a heated argument between my Hungarian grandfather and my great aunt. The following day, Castro gave permission for the cabarets to reopen. But not the casinos. Urrutia spoke out repeatedly against gambling; Fidel, Che, Raúl, and Camilo remained silent on the matter. Martín and his gambling cohorts understood that the president's invective meant little if Castro was not in agreement. Yet, unlike in the past, when he had a clear line of communication to government, Martín could not think of any way to exert influence. By January 9, when the cabarets opened, all his old friends in government had fled. Most of his police contacts had been arrested, and those who had not been arrested were of dubious reliability at this stage of the game. It was a different world; something fundamental had changed. Before, it had not much mattered who occupied the presidential palace—there was always a way to get around the rules. As the Cuban saying went, *"El que hizo la ley hizo la trampa,"* meaning, roughly, "Whoever makes the rules also makes the loophole." But now there were no more loopholes. The government was of one mind.

IN POGOLOTI, a ramshackle neighborhood on the outskirts of the (now-famous) Buena Vista section of Havana, Pedro Antonio Calvo, the Tropicana kitchen worker who went by the nickname Goyito, told me a story of the first day that the cabaret workers went back to work. "We were in the kitchen getting things ready," said Goyito, "when Pedro [Fox] came in and started handing out red and black 26th of July armbands. He said, 'Put these on, *gente*, so we show solidarity with the new government.' There was this one guy on staff who had been a member of the movement all along. And when he saw us all with armbands he said, 'Take them off. You aren't really supporters.' And we took them off."

In the past, no one would have dared contradict the order of their boss at Tropicana. Now it was apparent that a different power structure was in place in Cuba. The bosses were still the bosses, but there was a greater order, almost monolithic in nature. A mere ten days after the revolution, it was already eminently clear that no one dared to question even a lowly supporter of the new regime. At Tropicana there was concern that the whole airplane theme of

Rumbo al Waldorf—the landing projected onto the curtain, and then the song-and-dance number around the tail of a Cubana de Aviación plane that opened the show—might be construed as pro-Batista, since the former president had enjoyed excellent relations with Cuba's national airline. And to be seen as pro-Batista now meant certain arrest. Rodney immediately cut the opening number. The show now began (somewhat incongruously, given its title) with drums pounding in the darkness and the lights coming up on a lamé curtain sparkling with flecks of 24-carat gold. The music was Cuban composer Ernesto Lecuona's "Marta, capullito de rosa." Eight modelos, the tallest and most striking of the Tropicana lineup, stepped through slits in the curtain wearing low-cut dresses of the same material, platinum blond wigs adorned with egret feathers, and long gloves encrusted with beads and rhinestones. It was pure Tropicana glitz. The public that trickled in that night seemed to enjoy itself with the same gusto that it had before January 1, but to the careful observer it was clear something fundamental had changed. The freewheeling spirit was self-conscious. Tropicana was like a patient getting over a serious illness.

There were fewer people those first days, and hardly any foreigners. Most Americans had fled within the first week of the revolution, using United States embassy cars guarded by Marines to shuttle them to the docks and airport. There were also other changes. The absence of Alberto Ardura was deeply felt by Martín and his remaining partners. Who would now work out the contracts, offer salaries, decide which stars were worth their fees, and generally work with Rodney so that he had what he needed to work his magic? These worries were compounded when one day in late January Tropicana's bank accounts were frozen and its safety deposit box sealed by the government. "I read about it in the paper—in *El Mundo*," remembered Valentín. At the time the casinos were still closed, but Valentín would make a daily visit to Tropicana.

I found Martín sitting in a chair with his head in his hands, practically in tears. I'd never seen him like that. He said, "*Acabaron con mi vida, chiquitico* [They've ruined my life]." But I had a few ideas. In the safety deposit box there was a bounced check from this guy whose brother worked in the bank. The guy himself had a little factory that made machines for extracting *guarapo* [sugarcane juice]. When he'd come in to play craps, Lefty Clark had asked me to see about his credit, and we gave it to him, but then his three hundred-peso check bounced. I had the guy in the bank open the safety deposit box with the promise that we'd give him back his brother's bad check. I then went with my uncle—don't say his name this time, because he was a communist—to the *Ministerio de Recuperación y Bienes Malversados* [the Ministry to Recuperate Diverted Funds, a government agency that had been newly created to seek out ill-gotten gains]. We saw the man in charge and told him that hundreds of families depended on Martín's being able to pay them. And they agreed to temporarily unfreeze the account. Remember, it cost four thousand pesos just to open the door at Tropicana. And we didn't have any casino revenues. Three days later, the guy in the bank shot himself. It's not clear if it had anything to do with the matter, *pero tú sabes*, in those days anything could damage a reputation, get you arrested.

Though Martín now had Tropicana's bank account temporarily available to him, Urrutia's anti-gambling declarations grew increasingly more fervent and la bolita no longer enjoyed police protection. Martín desperately needed contacts in the new government. He needed to talk to someone with clout and make them see that Tropicana was different than the places that had been run by Americans. As he liked to put it, Tropicana was, and always had been, 100 percent Cuban, as Cuban as the royal palms. If he could just get someone in the top tier to come to a show, he could also demonstrate how vital gambling was to these productions. But for the first time since his days as a *tornero* in Ciego de Avila, Martín was not sure where, or to whom, to turn.

A solution presented itself a week after the cabaret reopened. It began with a misunderstanding. A 26th of July *miliciano,* dressed in uniform and sporting the ragged beard of a proper revolutionary, came to the cabaret asking to change a five hundred-peso bill. It was afternoon, well before the cabaret had opened. The man was sent to the kitchen. Pedro Fox turned him away, saying that they didn't have change for a bill that size. Later that evening, when the salads and coffee were being prepared and the dinner plates being set, a crowd of revolutionary soldiers suddenly appeared in Tropicana's kitchens. At the center was none other than Camilo Cienfuegos himself. Goyito was in the kitchen that night and heard the commotion when the bearded revolutionary leader came in with his escorts. "People embraced him," he recalled.

> He was in full uniform with his signature *campesino* hat and his .45 strapped to his side. Pedro was outside, but he came running in, saying, "*Compadre,* Camilo, how great to have you here, what would you like? For us you're like family." But we could all see he was pretty worried. Pedro put a good bottle of whiskey on the stainless steel table. He had the cooks prepare a plate of those giant shrimp. They put lemon, parsley, and pepper on them, marinating them well, then frying them up in an egg batter. We served them on a huge tray with mayonnaise. I was washing dishes and Camilo called me over. He said, "*Ven acá, chico,*" "Have a drink with us." And I didn't really drink, but I shared a whiskey with them. The photographer came and took our picture with Camilo.
>
> At around one A.M. Camilo said to his assistant, "Pay the bill." And Pedro said, "*¿Cómo?* After all you've done for us?"

But Camilo insisted that they were not allowed to accept money or food or services from anyone. Then he took Pedro aside and complained about the five hundred pesos. Pedro said, "I'm sorry, Camilo, we normally don't change bills that size, but we didn't know it was from you." Camilo just nodded while Pedro went to get the change.

According to Pedro Fox's daughter, Tillie, this was all a show. "My father and Camilo were great friends," she recalled recently. "He used to come to our house all the time. He had this huge beard, and I asked him once if he was related to Santa Claus." Tillie Fox credits Camilo Cienfuegos for saving her father's life when he was arrested. "Ofelia's nephew Raúl Taladrid accused him of stealing money. My father was stripped and searched and Camilo said he had been at the club and nothing happened, so they let him go." Camilo Cienfuegos continued coming back to Tropicana. He always entered through the kitchen and stayed there until the show was over, surrounded by his escorts. The *Comandante* was a *buena gente*, a "good guy," and a prankster who put salt in his escorts' coffee when they weren't looking. He also had a keen eye for the ladies. Soon it became apparent that his whole reason for coming to Tropicana was to be there after the show, when the modelos and dancers left their dressing rooms. He was dashing and charming and the women adored him. Many accompanied him and his staff to late-night parties at some of the mansions that had been appropriated by the revolutionary government after their owners had fled the country. Among his favorites was China Villamíl. "One night he invited me to a party in a private house," she recalled. "It was after the show, around three in the morning, and Camilo was so tired that he just fell asleep with his head on my lap. I sat there, not moving. He woke up about an hour later and insinuated, with enormous elegance, that I spend the night with him. And with equally enormous elegance,

I declined. He insisted on taking me home at that hour—by himself, not by sending a chauffeur. He was quite a man."

OFELIA SPENT the month of January recuperating from back surgery. It was her longest time away from Tropicana since she had met Martín. He tried to keep his troubles—about the closure of the casino, about his mounting sense of powerlessness—from her. "Martín kept information from Ofelia because he didn't trust [Raúl] Taladrid," insisted Tillie Fox. Still, he told her about his frustration with Camilo Cienfuegos. "He's there all the time," Ofelia recalled him saying one day, "but he never lets me approach him to talk seriously." That Martín was sharing any work problems alerted Ofelia to the fact that things were not going well. Other indications were the trials and executions. Hundreds of so-called collaborators were put to death by firing squad right in front of television cameras. Undoubtedly some of those convicted and sentenced were torturers and murderers, but many were not. There was something deeply unsettling about it all. Worst were the bloodthirsty cries of spectators shouting for the *paredón*, "the firing squad." "Never before, in all the history of Cuba, had I seen so many people aching for revenge," Ofelia said.

In early February, Ofelia's doctors gave her the okay to resume normal life, which in her case meant staying out until dawn with Martín. At roughly the same time a ray of hope regarding the casinos appeared. At the Teatro Blanquita, singer Ramón Veloz announced publicly that the artists relied on the casinos as much as the gamblers, sparking thunderous applause. A few days later, when President Urrutia openly called for an end to gambling, Fidel Castro, who was already beginning to distance himself from Urrutia on other matters of governance, responded testily on television: "From an air-conditioned office it is very easy to take bread from the mouths of casino employees." Still, nothing was decided one way or the other, and the Tropicana cabaret began, for the first time since Martín had taken over from Rafael Mascaró, to incur debt. Without readily available cash, Martín and Pedro ran around the city trying to establish credit with their vendors. Martín's secretary placed phone calls to their American suppliers, trying to do the same. The problem was that Tropicana had no credit history, because Martín and Pedro had always paid for everything in cash.

Then, on Friday, February 13, the food service, entertainment, and casino workers decided to take matters a step further. Said Valentín, "We were all worried, frustrated about our jobs. There was some talk of a strike, even. But that morning a big group of us—from Sans Souci, the Parisien, the Riviera, the Hilton, Capri, Tropicana—gathered at our workplaces and headed for the presidential palace." Everyone went in uniform: cooks in their whites, the botones boys in their double-breasted jackets and pillbox caps. There were models, dancers, makeup artists, choreographers. There were waiters, busboys, and parking attendants. Valentín went in his tuxedo. Armando Romeu and his orchestra led the group with all their instruments (except the piano). The parade swelled as it approached the gilded 1919 neo-baroque palace, so much so that by the time Tropicana's big band orchestra launched into a rousing rendition of Cuba's national anthem, it was as if a city-wide rumba was taking place in front of the presidential palace. President Urrutia, knowing that he had no real authority (and now, no inclination to intervene) in the matter of the casinos, never came out, but he sent word to the crowd that they were to go that afternoon to the *Palacio de los Deportes*, Cuba's premier sporting complex, and plead their case directly to Fidel Castro. "We went on foot," Pastorita Guerra told me in the one-room apartment where she lives in the Havana neighborhood known as El Cerro. Tropicana's wardrobe assistant and onetime rumba partner to Nat "King" Cole was eager to recall the festive spirit of the afternoon: "Some people carried *tambores* [drums]. Some had hidden bottles. That's the way we are in Cuba. All of us from Tropicana went. When we got there, Fidel was waiting for us. He listened to us. Then he talked and talked and said that he understood our problem, and assured us that no one would lose his job. Many people took pictures."

The casinos were allowed to reopen in March. The government imposed a gaming tax, however, payable to the newly created *Instituto Nacional de Ahorro y Vivienda,* the "National Institute of Savings and Housing." "Tropicana has removed several of its tables in order to reduce its tax base to the *Instituto Nacional de Ahorro y Vivienda,*" reported the monthly magazine *VEA* in April. "With all of its prior tables of roulette, craps, Big Six, and Twenty-one, the cabaret was due to pay eleven thousand pesos monthly. With its reduction in tables, it is now only responsible for eight thousand pesos."

And to insure that no back room wheeling and dealing took place, that no money was skimmed and taken abroad, that no illegal bolita lotteries were being held, the government placed four of its employees on Tropicana's staff—at the cabaret's expense. For Martín, this was a humiliating outrage. But he bit his tongue and tried to make the best of things. As Ofelia put it, "What choice did he have?"

CHAPTER 21

Bongo Congo

*Late-edition news flash! Tropicana's show will be
performed on July 4 in Miami and on the 26th in
New York. Henry Boyer mounts a production to take
to a hotel in Miami. . . .*

*The Cabaret Nacional has closed its doors . . . They
were heroes to maintain a show for such a long time,
given that only two or three tables were occupied each
night.*

from *Show*, July 1959

Despite the tumultuous political change, the show went on.
Throughout 1959, Carlos Palma's magazine continued its
coverage of the season's productions, giving full-page spreads to
the offerings at the Deauville, Hilton, Comodoro (where the
Llopis quartet was featured in July), and the Capri, where Alberto
Alonso mounted a show with the patriotic title *"Consumiendo Pro-
ductos Cubanos,"* "Consuming Cuban Products," that starred the
blond vedette Rosita Fornés. George Raft was long gone. So were
Norman Rothman, Lefty Clark, and Meyer Lansky. Santo Trafficante, Dino Cellini, and Jake Lansky were still in custody at the
Trescornia detention center on the Malecón. Trafficante's name
was on the executions list and he was trying frantically to use any

influence he had to get out of the country. After months of back-and-forth negotiations and visits from his lawyer, Frank Ragano, to Havana, Trafficante was released, and he left for Tampa. Meanwhile, for the first time in five years, *Show* did not report on "the magic of Rodney" or other goings-on at "Martín Fox's emporium—the Paradise Under the Stars." Tropicana was hardly mentioned at all in its pages. The reason was political, of course. By mid-1959, the American managers and owners of the remaining cabarets—the Comodoro, Parisien, Capri, Riviera, and Hilton—had fled the island, leaving their establishments in the hands of the Cuban government. Tropicana alone remained under the control of its owner. Palma was probably skittish about giving it too much press. The cabaret's prior associations with the top echelon of *batistianos* also did not help.

Heralded or not, Tropicana's winter season began on March 5, 1959 with *Bumki Bun,* a Brazil-themed show, and a vaudeville-style revue called *Tropicana Vodevil.* The shows starred the usual Tropicana cast; but by May 29, when they were replaced by two Cuban revues titled *Bongo Congo* and *Canto a Oriente,* there were significant changes in the lineup. Though both productions starred Celia Cruz, longtime Tropicana ballet stars Henry Boyer and Leonela González were notably absent from the roster. Right before the opening, Leonela and Henry left Cuba to perform at Miami's Biltmore Terrace Hotel, where the show was produced by none other than Alberto Ardura. On July 4, when *Bongo Congo* was performed at the Dade County Auditorium in Miami, the cast, including Celia Cruz, was heckled by Cuban exiles in the audience. It was a first for Tropicana. Once the most Cuban of establishments, Martín Fox's Paradise Under the Stars was now seen by some as anti-Cuban. "It was devastating. Like having your own family turn against you," said dancer Leowaldo Fornieles. The rift between Cubans on either side of the Straits of Florida was just beginning. Though Castro had not openly aligned himself with any political system, in Miami, anyone who supported the regime was labeled *comunista*. Conversely, in Cuba, those who had fled were considered *gusanos*, "worms," who had abandoned their country. The rhetoric notwithstanding, many in the cast of *Bongo Congo* headed directly to the Biltmore Terrace after the show. There was a joyous reunion and, of course, a party that lasted practically until morning. Even the normally reticent Ardura was overjoyed to be back among his Tropicana family.

Tropicana's *Diario de la Marina* advertisements in mid-1959 (which included a large photograph of a dancing Celia Cruz in a tiered Cuban dress) described *Canto de Oriente*, the season's second show, as "an homage to agrarian reform and ... the indomitable province of Oriente, birthplace of heroic *mambises* and rebels [the term used for Castro's revolutionaries]." Indeed, the Miami performance of *Bongo Congo* had an ulterior political motive: the money earned with the performance was to be used to support the Instituto Nacional de Reforma Agraria (INRA), an agency that oversaw a program of land redistribution that was one of the priorities of the new government. The initial idea of agrarian reform was to take large tracts of government-owned land that had been used by private parties or large companies, or land that had been left behind by fleeing batistianos, and parcel it out among poor guajiros. Even before the program extended to land owned privately by both Cubans and American firms, it smacked of communism to many in Cuba, and certainly to the communist-obsessed United States government. Indeed, agrarian reform's chief proponent and administrator, Che Guevara, had already made public his commitment to implementing Marxist principles in Cuba. So had Raúl Castro, the commander of the armed forces. Castro himself remained deliberately vague on the matter. During a whirlwind trip to the United States in April, he alternately denounced communism and refused to censure those in his government who were committed to it. Castro met with a myriad of journalists and government officials during his trip, and among them was a CIA agent named Gerry Droller (also known as Frank Bender), who was the agency's chief expert on communism in Latin America. Droller came away from the meeting with the impression that Castro was not only not a communist, but a strong anti-communist. Others were not convinced. Vice President Richard Nixon wrote, "Castro is either incredibly naïve about communism or under communist discipline," after he met with the bearded revolutionary. Admittedly, as a former member of the House Un-American Activities Committee, Nixon was quick to so label anyone with the slightest leftist leaning.

In this case, however, the handwriting was on the wall. In July, Urrutia resigned as president after repeated clashes with Castro, many of them over the president's insistence that the *Comandante* speak out irrevocably against communism. In October, Huber Matos, another of the top-tier revolutionary leaders, resigned from his position as military governor of Camagüey Province. The issue, again, was communist infiltration of the revolution. Matos was tried and sentenced to twenty years in prison for "anti-patriotic and anti-revolutionary conduct," and his Camagüey post was turned over to Camilo Cienfuegos. But Cienfuegos did not hold it for long, either: on October 28, 1959, his twin-engine Cessna 310C disappeared on a routine flight from Camagüey to Havana. Many suspected foul play. Among these was Pedro Fox. "My father went crazy," said Tillie Fox. "He shouted, 'Fidel killed him!'" The country went into mourning as officials searched for the wreckage off the Caribbean coast. "On one of those days of the search there was a false report that he'd been found," recalled Ofelia. "We were all so excited. I remember driving in my car along the Malecón when the radio announcer asked for everyone to honk their horns. Of course, I honked, too."

For Martín, matters of political ideology were irrelevant. What was becoming clearer every day was that the new government demanded absolute loyalty. The homage to agrarian reform was clearly a way to show allegiance to the regime. During the run of those shows, Martín did something else that was politically expedient. Ofelia believes it also came from his heart. "One night this large group of guajiros came to the cabaret. They'd been brought to Havana to attend a 26th of July rally where Fidel Castro spoke. There were several hundred of them, and they all came in their pressed guayaberas. Martín paid for everything—the food, drinks. All the men had their pictures taken between pairs of modelos and the photographs were also given to them." Whether or not this was a genuine gesture from a guajiro to his brethren, it was certainly a smart move. There was no one to bribe anymore. The currency of influence had changed from cash to gestures of revolutionary zeal. It was also a good idea to keep quiet when you didn't approve of what the government was doing. This was what Martín did in 1960 when the "inspectors"—who officially became "administrators" in late 1959—began firing his most loyal staff members. First to go was Ernesto Capote, the lighting designer who lived across the street from Tropicana. Capote quickly found work at the Teatro Móvil Moderno, a theater in the Víbora section of Havana, but it was not the same. He had been at Tropicana his entire professional life. The next victim of the purge was Valentín Jodra. "I could not believe that they were putting me out of my home," he told me. Forty years after the fact, the former roulette dealer's eyes still welled with tears as he remembered being told he was let go. Though things were spiraling out of his control, Martín found Valentín a job at the Casino de Capri. In August, *Bohemia* quoted Martín and Oscar Echemendia as saying that they had lost around $300,000 since January. Yet the loss of money was nothing compared to the inexorable whittling away of their control.

FOR OFELIA, there are two vivid memories of those early years after the revolution. The first is of a train ride through the parched Sonora landscape of northern Mexico in August of 1959. She and

Martín had gone to Mexico City to deposit money in a bank account they had opened with $400,000 in 1957. Afterward, they headed north by train to the United States. When they crossed the border at Laredo, Texas, a porter came into the bar car and took away their cocktails. "Within a half hour, the drinks were back, topped off and filled with fresh ice," recalled Ofelia. "And then a few miles further up, when we were back in a dry county, they took them away again. It was back and forth all through Texas. It made no sense."

But less and less was making sense. "Martín became even more secretive than usual. And not just Martín. My friends, my sisters, everyone was careful about what they said. You didn't know who was your friend or enemy anymore. It was unwise to question the revolution." Martín's reticence was due to the fact that he was moving money out in earnest and he did not want Ofelia's nephew Raúl to find out about it. Ofelia did not realize what was going on. Neither did the inspectors on Tropicana's staff—otherwise Martín would have surely been arrested. "Martín hadn't been the bolita king for thirty years without knowing something about skimming cash," remarked Ofelia proudly. On that first trip, Martín gave Ofelia $50,000 to put in her makeup case. From Texas they flew to New York, where they were to spend a few days at the Essex House before returning to Havana. The morning after they arrived, Martín awoke Ofelia early. "*Vamos,* china," he said without warning. "Let's go to Niagara Falls."

Martín managed to look genuinely surprised when they ran into Fred Bosque, a gambling associate from Havana, in Niagara Falls. Bosque's wife always sat at Ofelia's table while their husbands took care of their business transactions. Ofelia found herself once more entertaining Mrs. Bosque while the men went off to "have a drink." The women took the tour boat under the Falls. "It was so chilly and misty," remembered Ofelia. It was dark before Martín returned, and she had run out of what to say to her companion long before. Luckily, she and Martín left immediately for New York City.

"Of course now I realize that the meeting with Bosque was no accident," said Ofelia. Later that year and well into the next, Martín and Ofelia made a number of other trips to move money out of Cuba. They traveled to Miami once during June of 1960 and once in August, then flew to Mexico again, returning to Miami before flying back to Cuba. "There were about five trips in total, but sometimes I get confused. Sometimes Martín wouldn't tell me that we were going away until the day before our trip." By the middle of 1960 it became too difficult for Martín to move much of the money himself. He relied, instead, on his former American contacts—men like Lewis McWillie, who had been his last credit manager at Tropicana.

Ofelia's second vivid memory of those years took place at the bar inside the casino. "It was early 1960," she remembered. "Things were very shaky by then. Santa Claus and Christmas trees had been banned for the holidays because they were American symbols. There were already troubles with the United States. Many of our friends had left for Miami. It never occurred to me that we would also leave Cuba. Martín wanted me beside him all the time, instead of how we usually did things, with me waiting at the table. I sat at the bar of the casino. This man sitting there struck up a conversation with me. He was a member of the electrician's union and he said that for years he'd been a regular patron of Tropicana. 'Martín Fox is a hero to us union men,' he said to me. 'He took this place over with twenty employees and turned it into a business that gives jobs to over a thousand people.' The man's numbers were exaggerated, but his sentiment made me proud, and it gave me hope. If regular working people felt that way about Martín, it could only mean good things. For Martín and Tropicana."

But Tropicana was on a different course by then, along with the rest of Cuba. In February 1960, the government announced that all salaries would be automatically capped at five hundred pesos per month. Rodney, whose monthly salary had been two thousand pesos, immediately began making plans to mount a show in Mexico. Then he learned that Sandor, the choreographer of the Parisien, had thought the same thing, and that he had already left for Mexico with many of Tropicana's best modelos and dancers. Rodney collapsed from the stress. His ulcer began to bleed. Armando Suez took over while he was bedridden. In May, Rodney was back, but it was not to last. In September 1960, he, too, left for Mexico. Choreographer Gustavo Roig left for Miami, taking Eddy Serra with him to perform at the Biltmore Terrace. Frank and Jenny Llopis left with the Llopis Quartet for Mexico in April, fully intending to return. Soon, however, there was renewed talk of closing the casinos. Cuba began sending diplomats to the Soviet Union, China, Poland, and Czechoslovakia (in the latter case, to buy armaments). The nation's remaining sugar mills and agricultural lands were taken over by INRA after the end of the *zafra*, or "harvest." The Catholic Church openly criticized the regime. Radio and television stations and newspapers that did the same, like *CMQ*, *Diario de la Marina*, *Bohemia*, *Prensa Libre*, and *El Mundo*, were either taken over by the government or shut down. With much of his money safely out of the country, Martín was more than prepared for exile. Still, the idea of leaving Tropicana in the government's hands was unbearable. So he held on, even as nationalization of all businesses looked imminent. In July, the government demanded that larger businesses, including American firms such as Woolworth, Sears, International Harvester, Remington, and General Electric, provide sworn statements detailing their inventories and cash holdings. Martín began the humiliating task of compliance while being carefully watched by the government's administrators. "Those administrators would talk to him like he was *una mierda* [a shit]," said a former worker who asked not to be named. The man once walked past Martín after one of these scolding sessions. His boss hung his head and said, *"Caballero, ni en mi propia casa puedo hablar yo* (Folks, I can't even speak in my own house)."

Then one day in late August of 1960, upon returning from one of his and Ofelia's trips to Miami, Martín arrived at Tropicana and found himself face to face with a group of administrators who had never been to the cabaret before and did not recognize him. As with the previous group, the men were wearing olive green military uniforms. When Martín tried to enter, they got into a shouting match. "You can't come in here!" one of them barked. Something in Martín snapped. He shoved the man who'd yelled at him and knocked him to the ground. Then, knowing he had crossed a line, he jumped into his Cadillac and sped back home to Ofelia.

He was pale and his eyes were round as plates. I'd never seen him like that before. He was breathing heavily. I thought he'd have a heart attack. I rushed to get him some water and some pills to calm him down. He began telling me about the fight at Tropicana, and then there was pounding on the door. I looked out the window and saw a group of *milicianos* banging with the butts of their rifles. They shouted, "Open up, or we'll break down this door!" I called my sister, Fara. Her son Raúl already had some high-up position with the government. Raúl wasn't home, but Fara came down in a few minutes and she spoke with the *milicianos*. The men left a few minutes later.

Ofelia never found out what her sister said to the soldiers who'd come to arrest her husband. The next day, instead of going to Tropicana in the morning, Martín went to the Pan American airlines office. When he came home he sat her down and said: "China, I think we should go spend a few months in Miami."

PART V

CHAPTER 22

The House on
Beacom Boulevard

It was October and the weather was just starting to cool in Glendale. "Soon it will be possible to go back to Las Vegas," said Ofelia jauntily. "I told Valentín we'd try to get there next month. I want to see Carmelina too, *la pobre*. Maybe we can get Frank and Jenny and Eddy up for it also, and maybe Leonela will come out." As the years passed and their numbers dwindled, the Los Angeles and Las Vegas-based members of the Tropicana family grew closer. Ofelia felt this strongly. "It's what time does. When you know you might lose someone, they become more important."

In 1960, Ofelia found herself clinging to her mother while she prepared to leave Havana.

It was only supposed to be for a few months, but even that seemed like an eternity. My mother was seventy years old, and she'd never been sick a day in her life. But at that age you never know. I used to see her every day. Since that time that I had worked in Sumter [South Carolina], I'd never been away from home for a month. Martín and I traveled but it was always for very short periods of time. Our longest trip was the honeymoon cruise to South America and that lasted three weeks. Poor Martín was miserable the whole time. He'd say, "china, what do you think's happening at Tropicana now?" Another woman would have been insulted. Frankly, I was thinking the same thing. Now I realize that Martín's obsession with Tropicana was contagious. I found myself wondering if I shouldn't be at our table in the cabaret entertaining somebody. Like when we weren't there to greet Marlon Brando!

While Martín arranged for visas and exit permits for the trip to Florida, Cuca spent all day with Ofelia. She helped her pack and prepare instructions for the house staff. "She promised me that she'd come visit Sunan, Choni, Tito, and Negrita every day so they wouldn't miss me so much." On the day before she was scheduled to leave, Ofelia noticed her mother listing to one side. "We were in the hallway, going from the kitchen toward the dining room. Martín was out running an errand. Suddenly she slumped awkwardly. I thought she would fall." Ofelia cried out for help and Carmen, one of her housekeepers, came running. The two women eased Cuca onto Ofelia's bed. Her eyes were open but not focusing. Ofelia called Dr. Ramirez Corria, a top neurologist who frequently went to Tropicana. The doctor arrived in minutes, diagnosed the matter as a stroke, gave Cuca a shot directly into the carotid artery, then rushed her to the hospital.

The next morning, Cuca awoke disoriented. "She said to me, anxiously, 'I've got to go, I have to make breakfast.' When I tried to unwrap the bread that had come with her breakfast, she wouldn't let me. Boy did she struggle with that wrapper. She was determined to do it herself, even though it took her ten minutes." Ofelia's eyes watered at the memory of her mother's tenacity. "How could I leave her? But how could I ask Martín to stay? He wasn't safe in Cuba anymore. If he'd gone back to Tropicana and they hadn't let him go in? Can you imagine? He would have been capable of anything!"

Martín and Ofelia decided that he'd leave on his own, and that she would follow as soon as her mother was sent home from the hospital. This was not expected to take too long. The shot administered by Dr. Ramirez Corria (Ofelia does not know exactly what was injected into her mother's artery, but it seems to have been a precursor of current TPA therapy, wherein thrombolytic dissolving agents are injected into clotted arteries to avert strokes and heart attacks) had averted any serious damage. Cuca had sustained no severe paralysis or incapacitating residual effects. She had no memory of the event; however her mind seemed otherwise intact.

It was blazingly hot when Martín and Ofelia left for the airport. Martín took only one small suitcase. Thunderheads rolled in from the south, blackening the sky. Ofelia raised the top of the Eldorado.

My hands shook as I gripped the wheel. I didn't realize how hard it would be to say goodbye, even for a few days. Since the wedding we had never been apart. The airport was pure chaos—multitudes of people, families pressing towards the door, so much crying! I could not help crying too, though I knew I'd see him in a few days. At least I thought so. There were milicianos everywhere now, and everything was being inspected. I thought about his gun, which he'd insisted on packing. Luckily it was inside his checked luggage. I guess they didn't open his suitcase. The waiting lounge was behind a glass partition. They called it *la pecera*—"the fishbowl." It felt like more than a physical separation. There was now an ideological separation between those who stayed and those who left. We all were all Cubans, but now we were totally alien from each other. Two worlds separated by glass and water.

The days that followed Martín's departure proceeded with agonizing slowness. At night Ofelia slept in the hospital. This was no hardship, because she could not have imagined sleeping in their bedroom alone. Martín called several times a day, but that did not allay Ofelia's fears. Who would give him his daily shots of insulin? And how was he to get along without her when he didn't speak the language? Mostly, she worried that something would keep her from joining him.

It almost did. A week after Martín left, Cuca was home from the hospital. Again Ofelia began her round of good-byes to friends and family. In one home, that of a friend whose name she no longer remembers, there was a stranger present. The man looked at her oddly. "Do you have plans to leave the country?"

"*Sí,* tomorrow," Ofelia answered.

"You are not leaving tomorrow," he said.

I think my heart stopped. Things were changing so quickly in Cuba. I thought the man somehow knew of a reason why the government wasn't going to let me go. But he explained that he was a *santero*. As soon as he saw me he had a premonition. That made me even more worried. But he told me that it was only going to be a short delay. Sure enough, when I went to the airport I couldn't leave. The reason was the exit permit, which was required to prove that we'd done nothing against the government and were free to go. Martín had the one with both of our names. It took three days to get another permit. After two weeks apart, I was able to join Martín in Miami.

IN THOSE DAYS, Miami was a city in turmoil. Though its population had reached half a million in 1950, the city and its surrounding beach towns were relatively quiet, catering mostly to northeasterners who came down in the winter and the Cuban middle and upper classes who came regularly to shop. Suddenly, in 1959, thousands of the same Cubans who would come up for three or four days every summer, staying at hotels like the Deauville, Fountainbleu, and Delano on Collins Avenue, and eating at Wolfie's Delicatessen and Howard Johnson's restaurants, and clearing the dress racks at Burdine's, Three Sisters, and Saks Fifth Avenue on Lincoln Road, began arriving to stay, often with little more than the clothes on their backs. Rosa Sanchez was working at WMIE, a popular Miami radio station.

The arrival began as a trickle at first—a slow nightmare. The exiles were in shock. They came not knowing what had hit them, what the future held, or how to conduct themselves. The majority spoke no English. No one had any money. The Refugio [a government agency created to give aid to the arriving Cubans] helped people get settled. They gave out bags of food with jars of things people had never seen before, like peanut butter. People would ask me what it was, some with tears in their eyes because they'd never before received charity. Cuba's best actors and announcers came to the station desperate for any kind of work. There was this one woman—she was the spokesperson for Coca-Cola . . . all she could find was a part-time job at a dress shop in Miami Beach. A friend of mine who'd been the owner of a radio station in Sancti Spiritus came to see me, but we had nothing for him. He wound up working the swing shift at the *Miami Herald*, cleaning ink off the presses. There was a quiet desperation to these people. It was so sad. And most weren't batistianos. On the contrary—many had supported the revolution. At the station we saw it as an opportunity to tap into a market that was beginning to emerge and there was no other station with Spanish programming. So we began to offer programs in

Spanish. We gave away prizes—like radios, because many exiles didn't even have a radio. They'd gather in houses where there was a radio to listen to us.

With much of their money safely out of the country, Martín and Ofelia didn't face the same dire situation as other exiles. Yet, soon after arriving, Ofelia realized life was not going to be easy. After her joyful reunion with Martín at the airport, he took her in a car he'd borrowed from Alberto Ardura to the White House Hotel on Miami Beach. The place was a far cry from the hotels they were accustomed to. The bedspreads were musty and the bathroom tiles cracked. The broad porch that faced the ocean was filled with elderly retirees in rocking chairs. "It was obvious that Gladys, Martín's secretary, had not made the reservation," said Ofelia. Yet the choice of hotel was not half as surprising as what Martín told her. "China, I've seen a house and I want to make sure you like it before I rent it. There's no telling how long this situation will last in Cuba and I can't go back while this government is in power."

"The next day," Ofelia continued, "Martín took me to see a house at 225 Beacom Boulevard. It was a 1950s pink house with three bedrooms, two bathrooms, and a maid's room with a separate entrance. It was on a piece of land that was like an island in the middle of the street, so it had no houses next to it. I liked it, of course, which was a good thing because Martín had already bought it. I didn't know that. He'd bought it in June."

Martín and Ofelia's life in exile took on some semblance of their life in Havana. Ofelia would wake up late, then they would go to lunch at a Cuban restaurant downtown ("I can't remember its name, but we used to call it El Rancho") and take afternoon naps. There were social engagements almost nightly. By year's end, Oscar Echemendia, Pedro Fox, and Martín's sister, Lita, had also moved to Miami. Santiago Rey and his wife went back and forth between properties in Miami and the Dominican Republic. Alberto Ardura was busy with a nightclub called Café des Artistes, and often the old Tropicana crowd would gather there to eat, see the show, and have cocktails late into the night. Martín and Ofelia's house became the gathering locale for friends and family, especially on weekends. Martín bought Ofelia a little black mongrel, which she named Pachi. The only thing missing was gambling— or at least that's what Ofelia thought. Apparently, Martín, Ardura, Pedro, and Oscar had begun to run bolita numbers from various locales around Miami. "Years later, Marta, Oscar's wife, came to visit Rosa and I here in California, and she was the one who told me that on Saturdays she and Oscar always went to sleep in other houses where the bolita was thrown. This was to avoid the police, because here they couldn't buy people off the way they did in Cuba. I only learned this later, from Marta. Martín never told me about the bolita." Acting typically secretive, Martín also did not tell Ofelia that he bought a house for Niquita Valles, his old paramour from Ciego de Avila, and this was one of the places where he and Echemendia ran the bolita. Ofelia smiled when I asked if she'd been angry when she found out. "There was nothing romantic about it. Poor Niquita devoted her life to Martín. Marta Echemendia had been her friend since they were young girls in Ciego de Avila. It wasn't unusual for Martín not to tell me about these things. There were many inconsistencies in his business dealings, but I never gave it any thought back then."

There was no reason for Ofelia to think they were living off illegal gaming because Martín then had a legal source of income. In 1956, Tropicana had sued Dallas resident Kerby McDonald in a Texas court for losses he incurred while playing roulette. ("We'd nicknamed the guy Chupeta [lollipop] because he was always smoking these big cigars and he sucked on them like a lollipop," said Valentín, in his inimitable fashion.) The judgement against McDonald, which came through in 1961, delivered an initial

$92,000 lump sum payment to the Tropicana partners. Divided according to their usual percentages, this gave Martín $40,480—equivalent to $250,000 today. Martín also began sending money back to Cuba so that he would have cash on hand in Havana in case things changed suddenly and he could return to Tropicana. On one occasion he sent $60,000 to his sister Domitila. Another time he sent money back with Benny Moré. "After that time that he worked at Tropicana, Benny was always *muy atento* [very cordial] with us and he called us one day when he was in Miami," explained Ofelia.

> Martín asked if he would do him a big favor. They met at a Miami restaurant. I am sure it was at El Toledo. Martín handed Benny $40,000 in large bills and asked if he could deliver the money to my sister Fara. Benny said, "Of course." Martín asked him again if he was sure, because it could be dangerous, and again Benny said "yes." Martín gave him the money, but he was worried about Benny, so he asked him to call from Cuba. When Benny called, he told Martín that he'd pretended to be drunk, staggered out of the plane, the people cheered him: "Benny, Benny!" and nobody stopped or searched him. From the airport, Benny went directly to Fara's apartment and when the neighbors saw him, they cheered like at the airport: "Benny, Benny!" He went up the service entrance and gave the money to Fara.

Ofelia also traveled back to Cuba twice to see her mother. "She looked so frail, like she had aged ten years in just months." During Ofelia's last trip, which was over Christmas, the revolutionary government appropriated all American businesses in Cuba. Castro began talking of an impending United States invasion and ordered the embassy to reduce its numbers. Washington responded by breaking off diplomatic relations on January 3, 1961. For many middle-class Cubans, like my parents, that was the signal to leave.

On the morning of January 6, after my grandfather's store had finished the last toy sales of *El día de los reyes magos,* my parents left for the airport. In those days it was common for people to be harassed for leaving even when they held proper exit papers and American visas. My parents hid in the back of a taxi so the revolutionary *encargado,* or "superintendent," of the building would not notice us as we left. Ofelia scrambled to get another set of exit papers. On January 11, 1961, she left Cuba for the last time.

"SOMETIMES I think back on the things I could have brought with me. I left behind everything. All my personal items. The gifts that Martín gave me—my rings, my diamond cross, and earrings. The irony is that I could have brought everything because they never searched me." Ofelia rubbed her eyes. This was dangerous territory for her.

"But they didn't let you take your pinky ring," said Rosa Sanchez. As usual, she was trying to keep Ofelia from growing sad. "Why don't you tell Rosa that story?"

Ofelia shook her head. "It's unbelievable. See this?" Ofelia held out her left hand. On her pinky was a simple gold ring depicting two wishbones. "They were worrying about this! On my last trip they said I couldn't take it out of the country. So I gave it to La Niña who was with me in the airport. Years later, Rosa's mother brought it to me. But you want to hear something really funny? They wouldn't let me take this little ring, but they said nothing about the silver mink that Santo had given me. And that was far more valuable."

It was uncomfortable to listen to Ofelia's lament about her lost valuables. Unlike my parents, who had made their peace with their losses, it was a sore subject for her even after nearly fifty years of exile. I didn't understand this fixation, especially coming from someone who did not otherwise appear materialistic. "I imagine that the milicianos had no idea what was of value," I said. "They were probably just ordered to keep people from taking jewelry out of the country."

"How could they do that? By what right? The things Martín bought for me with money he had earned? My memories?"

"*Ya, Ofelia, ya,*" said Rosa, now standing and walking to the bar. On the way she gently squeezed Ofelia's shoulder and shot me a warning glance. "Rosa, don't you want to hear about Sunan? Ask Ofelia to tell you how he recognized her in the zoo when she went back to see him."

Ofelia did not want to change the subject. "It doesn't make sense. Forty years, and I still don't know how things got this out of hand."

For me it was evident. But it would have been cruel at that moment to bring up Batista's excesses and the complacency of those who had allowed him to remain in power.

"I think it's time to take a break," said Rosa. "Who wants a drink? Ofelia, make me a vodka and cranberry juice. I'll put on music."

ROSA SANCHEZ and Ofelia met one morning in 1961 at the radio station. By then the hope of any rapid resolution to *el problema de Cuba*—as exiles referred to the events that had transformed their country from a freewheeling dictatorship into a tightly controlled communist regime—had been shattered. The final blow had come that April, when fifteen hundred CIA-trained Cuban exiles invaded the island at Bahía de Cochinos, "Bay of Pigs," only to be overwhelmed by the Cuban army. The defeat was a huge triumph for Fidel Castro and demoralizing to the exiles. Almost the entire assault brigade was captured and held for ransom. The exile community grew even more heartbroken and bitter. They blamed President Kennedy for failing to authorize sufficient air power to back the invasion.

In response to her community's despair, Ofelia began to write. In the passionate, achingly patriotic style of José Martí, she wrote essays and poems to lift the spirits of her countrymen. Many evoked God. Others asked Cubans to reflect on the past and look to the future. *"¿Por qué no somos mejores?"*—"Why are we not better?" asked Ofelia of her brethren. "Why don't we forget all the different political systems and form a single one that contains all of the good of all eras of the past and present—without exception—and create a unique government that would be the pride of the world?" Some of the writings were diatribes against Castro and Communism. But most were messages of hope, entreating Cuban exiles to be reflective and to accept responsibility for what had happened to their nation. In September, Ofelia convinced Martín to fund the publication of her work in Mexico. The result was *Patria en Lágrimas: poemas de dolor, de lucha, y de esperanza*—"Fatherland in Tears: Poems of Pain, Struggle, and Hope" which was penned under the name Li-An-Su, an amalgam of syllables in Ofelia and Suarez, with the "an" thrown in to give it greater musicality. ("Just try saying Lia-su minus the *n* without your tongue getting tied," she pointed out.) *Patria en Lágrimas* quickly became a favorite among Martín and Ofelia's friends. Now Ofelia wanted to do something that would reach out to even more members of the exile community. She became involved in a discussion forum called Patronato por Cuba. Eventually she realized that radio was the best method of communicating with her bereaved countrymen. With Martín's approval, Ofelia funded a half-hour radio show on WMIE; it became one of the first Cuban talk shows in Miami.

"The first time Ofelia and I spoke she came over to me to explain why they were late paying for their airtime," recalled Rosa Sanchez.

In those days people paid weekly and practically everyone was late. So when she came over, I just said, "No problem.

Bring in the money when you can." I guess she was grateful, because after that she would stop by my office to make small talk. She'd ask about my life, how long I'd lived here. Whether I was married, had children. And I made a point of listening to her show. It was a half-hour segment done together with a man named Alfredo Otero and an announcer named Eduardito González Rubio. They would discuss issues, sometimes bring in guest speakers. It was unique because the tone was so measured. Other programs were full of these guys screaming and yelling and all that rhetoric, but they had this intelligent discussion going on, and this woman who had a voice made for radio. You should've heard Liansu on the air. She had a captivating, emotional voice. She seduced her audience, flirted with them—kind of Clintonlike.

Anyway, a few months after their show began, Martín decided it was too costly. Remember, all he cared about was saving his money to go back to Tropicana. But Liansu already had a following. So I decided to try to keep her on. It was a practical decision. We needed Cuban women on the air, especially in the afternoons when the housewives were listening. I arranged with a producer for her to do a short message—five minutes at most. It was called "El mensaje de Liansu," "Liansu's Message." I would hook the audience with her and then deliver other programming that would bring in the big sponsors, like Carnation. The women who came from Cuba didn't know many American food brands, and marketing surveys indicated that their loyalty was really important. I came up with the idea for a show called "De mujer a mujer," "From Woman to Woman," and created El club de oyentes de mujer a mujer, "The Club of Listeners of From Woman to Woman," with a large mailing list so we could do promotions at theaters. Whenever we announced that Liansu would be there among the personalities, we filled the house.

Ofelia flourished in her new role as a spiritual spokesperson for the community. Her world expanded. She became a sought-after speaker. Her friendship with Rosa Sanchez opened her to other people not connected to the cabaret world or to gambling. Indeed, Rosa was her first close friend who wasn't associated either with Tropicana, Martín, or their families. With both of their families back in Cuba, the two women became inseparable. On weekends, when the house on Beacom Boulevard would fill up with Martín's family and the Tropicana old guard, Rosa and her toddler son were always invited too. Martín doted on Ralph Sanchez. When Rosa, who was divorced from the boy's father, wanted to put him in a Catholic nursery school, Martín quickly made the arrangements for a second baptism because Ralph had originally been baptized Presbyterian.

But all was not as well as it appeared on the surface. Martín was growing restless and dejected. Unlike his wife, who had a public life, the onetime "King of Tropicana" had nowhere to go and little to do. His business dealings, which centered mainly on the weekly bolita run, were illegal and demanded secrecy. His lack of English made it hard to communicate. He also found himself hounded by federal agencies wanting information about American organized crime figures who'd done business in Cuba. In late October 1961, the IRS called Martín in to testify about Boston mobster Johnny Williams. Martín himself was not under investigation; however, he was subpoenaed and made to prepare an affidavit detailing his payments to Williams for running the bingo games at Tropicana in the late 1950s, a task that must have seemed degrading to someone used to fixing problems by picking up the phone and calling a general or police chief. Occasionally Martín would see Santo Traffi-cante; but this, too, was risky in a country where "el Solitario" was regarded as a criminal. In 1962, Martín was called in by the FBI and questioned about his relationship to Trafficante. Ofelia, who translated, recalled the meeting.

We went to an office in downtown Miami. It was a federal building. There were two men with a tape recorder. There were no lawyers. They asked simple questions first: How long have we been in the United States? How are we? What are we doing to earn a living? Martín said he had plans to buy a business. Then they showed Martín a photo of Santo and asked, "Do you know this man?" Martín looked at it and said, "No, I don't." Then the other agent said, "We know that on thus and such a day you had dinner with Mr. Trafficante and his wife at the Carrillon Hotel." I thought, "Oh, God, what's going to happen now?" So I said to him in Spanish, "Martín, look at the picture a little more closely." He took his time, then said "Oh yes, yes. I think that's Mr. Santo Trafficante. Sure, I've known him for a long time." The men asked, "Do you have any business dealings with him?" Martín said, "No, he's only an acquaintance." And that was it. They said thanks and let him go and nothing ever happened again.

As Martín grew more frustrated with his situation, he became, for the first time in his married life, openly jealous. Though gossip about Ofelia tended to center on her alleged predilection for women, she explained this in other terms. "He was always a little concerned when we had male visitors at our table in Tropicana," Ofelia told me, "but all that meant is that he'd come around more frequently than usual. He'd spend a half hour sitting with us instead of fifteen minutes. Remember, he was still an attractive man, but I was twenty-eight years younger. Now that he had nothing to do, and felt himself without power, he became irrational. One night he even took a knife and menacingly placed it in the drawer of his night table." The strain in Martín and Ofelia's marriage exploded one day when they were having a fight over one of his jealous fits. In the middle of the argument it came out that their house on Beacom Boulevard, which by then Ofelia knew had been purchased, was owned by the New Tropicana Corporation, an entity that Martín had founded in June 1960, together with his brother Pedro. Ofelia's name was not on the title.

That day I took two hundred dollars, bought a plane ticket, and left for New York. You can imagine how I felt when I tell you that I didn't even take my clothes. Nothing! I felt so betrayed. In New York I stayed with a friend from my childhood. Our fathers had been in the military together. Nobody knew where I was. But after I cooled off, I became really concerned about Martín. So I called Santiago Rey's wife, Berta, and asked if they had heard from him and told her where I was. She told me that Martín had gone to see them and that he was devastated. That he had cried and told them he was very sorry. She also said, "Come back, Ofelia. Now that you've got the frying pan by the handle he'll do anything you say." I called Martín and a few days later I returned. He'd already put the house in our name. I should've also gotten him to tell me other things, like where our money was. But I didn't. After that day we never fought again.

ON JULY 9, 1963, Liansu delivered the following noontime message:

Yesterday an old man committed suicide. He hanged himself. The obituary in the newspaper said, "due to health problems and nostalgia for his country." The obituary is insignificant, lost on the last page of the paper. A death in itself is not important, except to the family. The same is true of a suicide, although there's a bit of increased morbidity in that case. But that a Cuban should die in this fashion is a shame for all Cubans. A few days ago, a woman ill with cancer was on her way back to Cuba. At the last minute they removed her from the plane because they did not think she'd get there alive. She wanted to die there and could not. If only she could have been unconscious and died believing that she was back in her yearned-for Cuba.

When a Cuban commits suicide because of nostalgia for his country, as this son said of his father, our hearts are rent by terrible anguish. And we ask: until when, Lord? We ask God that these Cuban tragedies give us the strength to continue battling certain negligence that morally deadens many. Let those of us who have health, willpower, and dignity rise up and lift the spirits of the fallen. We need to confront those Cubans who would divide us, those pocket idealists who plant intrigue and infinitely lengthen our exile. All the circumstances that surround us can delay our future, but to get down on our knees? Never! And those old people who feel nostalgia for their country need not corner themselves. Let them use their remaining strength to ask us for an accounting. They deserve it. And so does Cuba.

Ofelia's call for moderation and introspection was one of the last messages she would ever deliver. Later that summer, she and Martín traveled to Boston for an unscheduled checkup at Peter Bent Brigham Hospital. Though he appeared strong and healthy, Martín had begun to complain of dizzy spells. One morning he almost collapsed in a post office. After running tests, Martín's longtime physician, Dr. Harold Levine, diagnosed the dizziness as the likely result of a narrowing he'd found in Martín's spine. Surgery was performed to correct the problem and Martín recuperated quickly. Shortly thereafter, however, the dizzy spells resumed. Dr. Levine felt that given Martín's age, which was sixty-eight, his diabetes, and arteriosclerosis he had also found during testing, nothing further should be attempted. According to Ofelia, Martín was not satisfied and insisted that she contact Dr. García Bengochea, the surgeon who had operated on her back in 1959. He was now at the university hospital in Gainesville, and he agreed to see Martín.

"On September 22, 1963, they left for Gainesville on a train, leaving their live-in maid that they'd brought over from Cuba, Carmen Carnero, to take care of the house and pets," wrote Rosa Sanchez in a lengthy e-mail to me detailing those events. I received the note one morning after I had mentioned to Rosa that I wanted to go over the chronology of Ofelia's last months in Miami. Rosa had written to me at four A.M., and begun with an entreaty: "Please do not ask Ofelia too much about those dark days. If you had any idea how hard they were . . . Today looking through all of my files it has all come back to me vividly. I hope this will give you the details you need." Rosa continued with her version of the visit to Gainesville:

That night they checked in at the University Inn, U.S. Route 441 South, in Gainesville. The next morning Martín was admitted to the J. Hillis Miller Health Center of the University Hospital at Gainesville. His patient number was 047190. After a number of tests, Dr. García Bengochea told him that the only way to get a conclusive diagnosis was by having a myelogram [an X-ray examination that involves injecting fluid to detect abnormalities of the nervous system]. He didn't recommend that Martín go through it because there was a danger of stroke. Ofelia tried to dissuade him also, but when Martín made up his mind that was it. The myelogram took place the next day—September 24. Ofelia was at Martín's side and she saw one of his eyelids droop and he began to speak nonsense. She knew immediately that something was wrong. The doctors acted quickly, but Martín had suffered a debilitating stroke.

Alone and terrified, Ofelia called no one but Rosa Sanchez. "She told me that she feared Martín had [had] a stroke and asked me not to tell anyone. I believe that perhaps she had the feeling that if the people who surrounded them knew that Martín was incapacitated, something bad was going to happen. She was not wrong." Later, Ofelia called Rosa again and asked her to call Lita, Martín's sister, and tell her only that Martín wasn't doing well. Rosa did so, and the next day, right after she'd finished work at the radio station, Rosa went to Ofelia's house, where she left Ralph with Carmen Carnero. She picked up Lita in Ofelia's Chevrolet and drove 330 miles to Gainesville. "It was a terrible drive. There was construction in parts of the highway, the signage was poor, and the visibility was even worse. Twice we took incorrect detours. Once I had to hit the brakes in front of a big piece of equipment that was sitting in the middle of the road. It was way past midnight when Lita and I arrived at the University Inn. Ofelia was frantic."

Martín's condition failed to improve over the next few days. He could not speak, walk, or recognize anyone. Dr. García Bengochea told Ofelia there was nothing that they were doing at the university hospital that couldn't be done in Miami. Arrangements were made for his transfer to Cedars of Lebanon Hospital in Miami. He was discharged on the morning of September 30. It took an entire agonizing day for the ambulance to arrive, and then, for insurance reasons, they would not let Ofelia travel in it. "She went to pieces," wrote Rosa. "Lita was also in no condition to drive. So, again, I drove Ofelia's car from Gainesville to Miami. The tension of that drive was indescribable. I was trying desperately to keep up with the ambulance's pace. Once, the police stopped me for speeding. The ambulance stopped when they noticed. I explained to the officer that I was trying to follow the ambulance and that the wife of the gentleman in the ambulance was in my car and he let me go without giving me even a warning. To this day I avoid driving at night as much as possible."

The horror of Martín's condition became compounded for Ofelia as soon as she returned to Miami. Aware that she now had to assume the financial responsibility for their lives, including what was sure to be a whopping series of hospital bills (Martín, of course, had no health insurance) she began to look for money. The first place she looked was the locked drawer of Martín's night table, where normally he kept between twenty-five and thirty thousand dollars. When she opened it, not only was there not a dollar to be found, Martín's 13-carat diamond ring was also gone. Ofelia went immediately to see Martín's brother, Pedro, who claimed to know nothing about Martín's money. The following day she went to the Pan American Bank, where they kept their main checking account. The balance was $2,051.51. The same scenario repeated itself at the Greater Miami Federal Bank, where the Fox-Suarez account held only $477.40. "Martín usually traveled with around $20,000 in his pocket, but by some stroke of bad luck, he had only taken $3,000 to Gainesville. Most of that had already gone to the hotel, doctor, and ambulance bills," wrote Rosa Sanchez. There was, however, a check for $5,000, which Martín had given Ofelia the night before he went in for the myelogram, along with a note written on a sheet of paper from the University Inn that read, "Depositar en Pan American Banco en la cuenta P37-35-112 Martín Fox y Ofelia Suarez." ("I am almost sure this is the last thing that Martín wrote," noted Rosa.) The check was from an acquaintance of Martín's named Evaristo García, and it had been written on September 18, only five days before they left for Gainesville. Ofelia went to the First National Bank of Miami to cash the check. She was told that the account had insufficient funds.

Now Ofelia was close to hysterical. Martín's condition had not improved at all. At Cedars of Lebanon he lay in a semi-conscious state, unable to feed himself or walk. Though a member of his family was always by his side, Ofelia also maintained round-the-clock private nurses and a personal physical therapist to tend to him. One day on the way back from lunch at the cafeteria, Ofelia was stopped by Lita in the hallway: "The old woman in the room with Martín is Niquita," she warned. Ofelia introduced herself and took Niquita's hand. It was cold and trembling. "You are welcome to see Martín any time you want," Ofelia said. "I'll wait out here. Talk to him. See if he recognizes you." When Niquita came out she told Ofelia that she'd tried and tried but Martín had not recognized her. "She was so grateful to me," Ofelia said. Niquita's gratitude multiplied a few months later when she called Ofelia concerned about a paper she had signed for Martín just weeks before his stroke. "She didn't know what it was," said Ofelia, "but she feared it was about her house, which was the only thing she owned."

Meanwhile, the medical bills kept piling up, outstripping the funds Ofelia had found so far. With Rosa accompanying her, Ofelia went to see Evaristo García about the bounced check. The man told her that the money had been a loan he was making to Martín, a fact that seemed unlikely, given that Martín was always the one lending money to others. ("Anyway, why would someone make a loan on an account with insufficient funds?" asked Rosa incredulously.) Ofelia went to see Miguel Angel Cano, the owner of Miami's Toledo Restaurant, and offered to discount a note he had signed to Martín from $10,000 to $7,000 if he would only pay it quickly. He refused, and she collected, per the terms of the note, three payments of $65 for a total of $195. Again, Ofelia asked Pedro Fox if he knew where Martín had other bank accounts or hidden cash. "Ofelia was desperate and Pedro calmly told her that he didn't know anything about Martín's business dealings," said Rosa, seething with forty years of pent-up rancor.

Everywhere she turned the answer was the same. But it simply wasn't possible for $900,000 [the amount Ofelia and Rosa calculated had been deposited during Martín and Ofelia's travels] to disappear in an instant. Clearly they weren't spending that much on their lives. What's more, no one came forth to tell her about the bolita income. And you know that note from Miguel Angel Cano? When Pedro became Martín's guardian, he got Cano to pay it, in full, in two payments! In my book the way Pedro treated her was criminal. She wanted the money to take care of Martín. He had helped everyone all his life, and now that his wife needed them—*vaya*, he was the one who needed them!—nobody came to their aid. The saddest part is that so many people thought she had the money! She just couldn't convince them of her incredible situation.

Emilio Fox, who lived with Martín and Ofelia in their house on Beacom Boulevard, tells a very different story of those days. "Our family was the one taking care of Martín. We used to take turns at the hospital. Ofelia was often with Rosita [Sanchez]. One time she showed up late for her shift and I made a comment to the maid about her running around with women instead of taking care of her husband. She told Ofelia and Ofelia threw me out of the house. As for the money, my uncle simply spent it. He paid for everything—mine and my brother's private school tuition, my cousin Lenny's flying lessons, and Ofelia's radio time. When he went to the store people would line up and Martín would pay for their groceries. I once heard him say he lost $60,000 in a poker game. One thing seems certain: If there was any money lying around after my uncle's death no one found it, because more than 40 years later there isn't anyone in my landscape living large."

Martín was released from Cedars of Lebanon on November 2. For a while Ofelia maintained the registry nurses. When she could no longer afford them, she hired a retired Cuban registered nurse, and sold everything she could to pay the house bills and Martín's doctors, and for his medicines, special diet, and nurse. Because the assets of greatest value—namely, the cars—were in both of their names, she could not sell them unless she declared Martín incapacitated. So Ofelia asked the court to be declared her husband's legal guardian. "That's when all hell broke loose," wrote Rosa Sanchez. "Martín's brother and sister went crazy. They marched into court to protest her request. To this date Ofelia can't figure out why they turned against her. It had to be the money. When you're someone's legal guardian, you're the custodian of *everything they own*. And in Martín's case, you know what that also means: Tropicana. Remember, at the time people were still saying, *'La próxima nochebuena la pasamos en Cuba'*—'We'll be celebrating the next Christmas Eve in Cuba.'"

After listening to Pedro and Lita's objections to Ofelia's guardianship (which, according to Ofelia, included such absurdities as "She doesn't know how to cook"), Dade County Judge George T. Clark granted Ofelia custody of Martín. Ofelia assured the judge she would keep searching for the money to care for Martín; if she did not, and found herself unable to properly care for him, she'd transfer custody to his brother. Judge Clark ended the proceedings by admonishing those present and suggesting that they help her find the resources to support her husband.

On November 5, 1963, one day before her fortieth birthday, Ofelia transfered the meager remaining balances from the Pan American and Greater Miami Federal bank accounts into a guardianship account established at International Bank of Miami. Three weeks later, the court granted her permission to sell Martín's Cadillac and mortgage the house. She amassed $6,000. Rosa and Ralph moved into Emilio Fox's old room and Rosa gave Ofelia her entire paycheck. Meanwhile Ofelia continued contacting people who might know what had happened to Martín's money. "You say that you cannot find Martín's money. As you know I brought thousands to the bank for him while I was in Cuba," wrote Lewis McWillie to Ofelia in January 1964 in response to a letter begging for help. By then, "Mack" was working as a floor man at the Thunderbird Hotel Casino in Las Vegas. "[Martín] also had money in a New York bank. If I remember right he had me check his account in the Miami bank and it alone was over half a million dollars, surely he did not do away with that kind of money in the past five years. Pedro probably knows more about his business than he is telling you."

McWillie's second letter to Ofelia, which Rosa still retains, was postmarked on February 12, 1964:

> Dear Ofelia,
> Received your most welcome letter yesterday. Sorry to hear that you are still having troubles.
> In regards to the questions you have asked in your letter No. 1, I put money in a bank on Flagler Street the whole time I was in Cuba. . . . I put a large sum of money three times after Castro arrived in Cuba in the Pan American Bank. The last time I put thirty thousand there. I remember it very well because there were six counterfit bills in the money and the teller found them. They called the treasury men & the teller told them that it was a natural mistake as I had brought large sums of money from Cuba on previous occasions, and they knew me very well. . . . The balance in this account was close to six hundred thousand. The balance in the other account was ninety thousand. I had quite a bit of trouble getting them to give me this information. In fact, I had to make another trip from Cuba with an order signed by Martín authorizing them to give me the information. When I got back Pedro asked me to let him see the statement of the bank balance. After I let him see them he asked me not to let Martín know he had seen them. Which I didn't mention to Martín.

Mack also told Ofelia that Martín had a substantial account—"around $400,000," he wrote—and suggested she might ask "Valento Jodra" for details. "Now I am positive that Martín also had quite a sum in a New York bank," he continued, "because a friend of mine & yours [a reference to Boston-based mobster Johnny Williams] borrowed quite a sum of money for a few days and it was drawn on a New York bank." Mack asked Ofelia not to mention this to anyone, but suggested that she might "contact our friend and he would probably remember the bank it was drawn on." He ended with the following: "I really don't see how Martín could have did away with all that money as you and I know he wasn't too free with his money. . . . All I ask you is not to let Pedro or any one else in Martín's family to know about me writing you this letter."

OFELIA CONTACTED all of the people Mack suggested. She spoke with Valentín in Las Vegas and Johnny Williams in Boston. None had any further information about what could have happened to Martín's money, though many helped her out. Santo Trafficante came to visit Martín and gave her $1,000. Others gave her $50 here, $200 there. Even Evaristo García of the bounced check came through with $300. "Ofelia later tried to pay him back, but he refused," said Rosa Sanchez. "Every nickel she received was properly recorded. She was scrupulous in her accounting of her guardianship." Meanwhile, as Martín languished in his pitiful state, unable to speak or recognize anyone, Ofelia tried to awaken his memory. She invited people to the house to see him, especially friends who would evoke the cabaret. On one occasion, it worked ever so briefly. Ofelia had picked up Olga Guillot and brought her to the house. Guillot was crushed to see the man who, in her opinion, had built Havana's most spectacular entertainment empire looking so diminished. "I took his hand and said, 'Martín, Martín . . .'" Guillot recalled. "And that man, who was in another world, had a second of clarity: '*Negrita, pronto, pronto vamos a volver a Tropicana,*' he said. 'Negrita, soon, soon we will return to Tropicana.'"

ON MARCH 27, 1964, Ofelia, broke and disconsolate, asked Judge Clark to transfer custody of Martín to his brother. The action was filed and recorded on April 5, 1964 by County Court Clerk Melba C. Dick. Prior to that, Lita told Ofelia that she could stay in the house on Beacom Boulevard if she wanted to, but it would be best if she moved into the maid's quarters, which had a separate entrance. "There was no way she could do that," said Rosa Sanchez. "If Martín had at least recognized her, it would have been different. But since he didn't—*Vaya*, she was even afraid that if he fell, if anything happened to him—they'd accuse her of negligence." But Martín's niece and nephews scoff at that notion: "What the hell could cause someone to dump her husband after he becomes incapacitated?" said Emilio Fox, expressing the opinion of his relatives.

Ofelia made a detailed schedule for administering Martín's medications and gave it to his family. Then she kissed him, told him she'd be back soon, and left for California with Rosa Sanchez.

CHAPTER 23

Noche de Ronda

Tell her that I love her
Tell her that I'm dying
from waiting so long
for her to return.

From Augustin Lara's *Noche de Ronda*

The Avenida de los Presidentes in Vedado never fails to impress visitors to Havana. The long, tree-lined boulevard, which slopes down from Twenty-Seventh Street to its northern endpoint on the Malecón, is divided by a park-like median lined with empty pedestals, which once bore sculptures of Cuba's presidents. After 1959, most of the bronzes were removed as a symbol of breaking with the past. (Because he was also a Mambí general, the colossal multi-figured monument to José Miguel Gómez, Cuba's second president, was left intact.) The most curious of the vacant pedestals once supported a statue of Don Tomás Estrada Palma, Cuba's first president. For some reason, probably because the life-sized bronze was too firmly secured to its limestone base, the shoes were left behind during the dismantling process, creating what appears to be a monument to feet. I thought about possible meanings for such a sculpture one day while walking down the avenue to catch a taxi to Tropicana. It could be paying homage to Cuban stalwartness—our feet are firmly planted here, that sort of thing. One could also interpret the sculpture as a monument to the diaspora, to the political upheavals that have made so many of us, including José Martí, flee throughout the centuries. The piece's location, in view of the north coast, supports either interpretation. That day, walking through Vedado, I was alert to architectural significance. This happens to me often in Cuba. It's the conservator in me. Havana wears its history on its sleeve and anyone whose professional life has been dedicated to preservation can't help but feel the resonance of all those centuries of stucco, stone, and glass. The interiors often strike me as particularly suggestive. The Bacardi building smells of rum to me; the Capitolio's senate chamber resounds with oratory and the rustle of papers. Half a block away from the Estrada Palma "monument" is the apartment house built by my grandfather. Since the early nineties I'd passed the building dozens of times, but I never thought to go in. That day I decided to do it. The task, however, was not as easy as simply knocking on the door. Since 1994, when dollars began to circulate again in Cuba, locked entry doors and ornate metal gates, many of them garish and incongruous, had become ubiquitous in Havana. I entered through the open garage. Hearing some noise, I walked past a few Soviet-era cars to what was once the small basement apartment of the building's superintendent. A woman who came to the door looked at me suspiciously. I explained my reason for being there: "My grandfather built this building and I was wondering if there was any way to see the apartment where my parents lived."

"Was your grandfather Alberto?" she asked. I nodded. "So are you Rosita?"

Oh, was there excitement in that musty, low-ceilinged apartment when I said yes. The woman was María, the wife of José, the *encargado*. "*Mira*, it's Rosita!" she exclaimed to her husband as she led me in. She called her daughter on the telephone. She sat me on their one good chair, brought out her niece and grandson, and apologized for not having coffee to serve me. The residents of my parents' old apartment weren't home, so instead María regaled me with stories about my grandmother's obsession with me: "She'd feed you on the terrace so you'd agree to eat; she wouldn't let any of the neighborhood children get near you so you wouldn't catch a cold."

"Those were the people we hid from when we were trying to leave," my mother said, when I told her about my visit with José, who could not speak to me himself because he has throat cancer. Then she reconsidered her tone. "Ah! That was so long ago. A world has come and gone."

That same afternoon in Havana I went to Tropicana for my second meeting with Tomás Morales, the cabaret's new artistic director. Tropicana at this hour is like a showgirl primping in her dressing room. While I waited for Morales to finish a rehearsal, I watched gardeners clipping shrubbery and electricians struggling with cables. In the distance, a clarinetist ran scales. Dancers rushed past in their workout wear, improvising a rumba to the loud percussion music that poured out of Bajo las Estrellas. "We're going crazy getting the new show ready," explained Morales's assistant, María Salazar, when she finally met me at the stage door. Salazar, or "Mery" as she is known, wore a red sleeveless leotard and gray workout pants. Her long hair was in a high ponytail—a reminder of the years (1974 to 1990) when she performed at Tropicana as part of a quartet that included her identical twin sister, Enriqueta, and a pair of male dancers, Armando and Alberto, who also happened to be twins. When Mery suffered a knee injury and her sister immigrated to the United States, she began teaching ballet in Tropicana's dance school, a prestigious academy established by the Cuban government in order to train cabaret dancers and modelos. It is a position Mery continues to hold in addition to her grueling job as the artistic director's right hand.

"My friend's daughter, Greta, was recently admitted to the dance school here," I told Mery as she led me through a dingy labyrinth of backstage corridors toward Bajo las Estrellas.

"Gretica *la rubia?* Oh, she's very talented. We'll probably move her into the show very soon. In fact, there she is."

We were on a balcony, facing a rooftop terrace where about twenty girls in leotards and shorts or tights stood in three loose rows, practicing a routine that involved several complicated turns. The girls were tall and curvaceous, but much leaner than the *diosas* of the past. Long, reedy arms, representing all the skin tones of Cuba's diverse racial population, waved through the air. I saw Greta, whom I'd known since she was eight, pivot slowly near the back of the class, her face turned towards the dappled sunlight that filtered through the branches.

"*Mira,* Greta! Your mother's friend is here," Mery called out to her. Greta broke into a huge smile and came running over.

"Rosa, can you believe I'm here? I can hardly believe it myself," exclaimed Greta excitedly. The angelic blond daughter of a conservation scientist mother (Raquel Carreras is one of Latin America's leading experts on preservation of tropical hardwoods) and a father who supervises a hog ranch was flushed and sweating, but more radiant than I'd ever seen her. "You know I never thought I'd get in," she confided, as Mery got called away by a male dancer. "It's very competitive around here. I'm exhausted all the time. I'm never home. I can't keep weight on. My muscles ache. You have to watch constantly for the *brujería* of the other dancers. But I'm going to give this everything I have and see where it takes me."

"With her attitude and talent, she should go very far," said Mery approvingly, returning with a lit cigarette.

Greta trotted back to class. Mery and I made our way down to Bajo las Estrellas. Tomás Morales was still in the middle of rehearsal. The drumming was infectious. Mery started stepping to the conga rhythm as she smoked. Morales waved at us, and he, too, began dancing as he started toward us.

Morales had just replaced Santiago Alfonso, an accomplished choreographer who had held the post for ten years, and, like all new leaders, he was thinking about making changes. "I'd like to return to some of Rodney's broader themes and concepts," he explained, when the music finally ended. Under Alfonso's direction in the 1990s, Tropicana had, again, become Cuba's must-see attraction. His signature show, *Tropicana: La Gloria Eres Tú* (Tropicana: You Are Heaven) ran for five years, toured Europe repeatedly, and even made it to the United States in 1998, at which time the performances took place while placard-waving exiles protested outside. Because the current Tropicana audience was composed almost entirely of tourists who paid between sixty-five and eighty-five dollars a seat, the repertoire leaned heavily towards generic Afro-Cuban themes that played to stereotypes. The dive that Chiquita had once made famous became a nightly feature. "In a sense, I've worked here on and off longer than anyone," said Morales pensively. "I've been here since the fifties, as a dancer and choreographer. I was at the [Hotel Riviera's] Copa Room for a while, but this is my home. If I can get the funding, I want to bring back variations of certain things that were done in the early years, like a great waterfall, or fire, and dangling cables so acrobats can fly over the public." Morales planned to call his first production *Tambores en Concierto* (Drums in Concert), and use a Rodney-inspired thematic device: a male dancer would rise out of the drum, symbolizing its spirit, and guide the audience through a history of Cuba's musical roots.

As I listened to Morales, I found myself imagining Ofelia's reaction to his plans. I thought that she'd probably bristle, and I wondered whether she would ever recognize that what Martín had wrought went beyond politics and ownership. Then I noticed where I was standing—on the stage of Bajo las Estrellas, right behind the geometric sculpture where Chiquita and La China had done the famous dive, on the boards that Leonela, Ana Gloria, Alicia, Eddy, and Jenny once trod regularly, and in clear view of Ofelia's table, one tier up from ringside. I took a mental picture to bring back to Glendale. Then I asked Morales if I could enter Arcos de Cristal.

I was guided to the spacious cabaret and left alone. There was no breeze that afternoon, and outside the leaves were still against the glass. Nonetheless, the building seemed alive with movement. The arches pulled my focus towards the stage. I could almost hear the trumpets and the clinking glasses, the voices of Celia Cruz and Olga Guillot, the piano of Bebo Valdés. Because it was daytime, the indoor-outdoor illusion wasn't so apparent. Still, it was not so very hard to picture the trees lit up, the pinpoint ceiling lights, the feathers and the rhinestones, and, of course, Martín walking down the tiers holding his highball glass, shaking hands and slapping backs. I indulged in the reverie for a few minutes. Then I noticed two acrobats in a corner, rehearsing a Chiquita and Johnson-style move. Oblivious to me, the muscular young man braced his feet and lifted up a small woman. She worked her way into a one-handed handstand against his upturned palm, her body soaring upward, a human arrow. It seemed, at that moment, like a perfect reflection of the building itself—weightless, illusory, magical.

A WEEK LATER, while having lunch with Ofelia and Rosa at the Los Angeles Farmers Market, located in my part of town, I was eager to describe to them those moments at Tropicana. That day, however, they had a different topic in mind.

"Go ahead. Ask me the question," Ofelia said. She looked at me, knowingly. Rosa busied herself unwrapping our fish sandwiches.

It took me a moment to figure out where she was headed. Then I got it. But I didn't want to let her off the hook so quickly. "Ofelia, I've got nothing to ask. Only you can decide what are the important points in the story of your life."

She nodded and folded her hands. "Okay. Rosa and I are a couple."

The three of us began to laugh, out of relief and nervousness. Then Ofelia asked, "Don't you want to know if I'm gay?"

"Does it really matter?" I asked.

"Come on," Rosa insisted. "Just ask her if she's gay."

I was used to their subtle manipulation around this matter, so I decided to play along.

"Okay. Ofelia, are you gay?"

Ofelia smiled at me coquettishly. "I suppose you could say I'm a late-bloomer bisexual. I married Martín without having ever been with anyone. While we were married, I lived with Martín and Martín alone. People always tried to say things about me—that I had been with this woman or that one. One rumor had it that I would give a diamond ring to any woman who I wanted to have sleep with me." I had been told that Olga Guillot was in love with Ofelia, that her hairdresser used to have a secret back room where Ofelia would meet lovers for trysts, and that both she and Martín were gay and their marriage was simply a convenience. Ofelia chuckled to hear these stories, then looked at me with dead seriousness. "Here's the point: no one could believe 'me and Martín,' because it didn't make sense. He, the owner of this glorious cabaret, is rich, powerful, surrounded by women beautiful beyond belief, and all he wants is me. I'm twenty-eight years younger, but always by his side, every night of the week. No one could see it for what it was—two souls who got together because they had so much in common and loved the same thing, which was Tropicana. Rosa, we were closer than any two people could ever be. I know people wondered why I was always surrounded by women. It was because Martín got restless if there were men at our table. He would keep coming around to check up on me. One night, he got jealous simply because I had gone to sit at Santiago Rey's table, even though Berta [Rey's wife] was the one who had invited me. Can you imagine that? But when he got ill and I was forced to leave—" Here Ofelia paused and breathed heavily. "When Martín got ill and I had to leave, when everyone abandoned me, Rosa Sanchez stayed. I had no money, no one to turn to. My family was in Cuba. I could not remain there in that house, in a maid's room as my sister-in-law suggested. I was helpless with Martín in that condition. He didn't even recognize me. Rosa was my closest friend. And we left Miami just as friends."

"Maybe we should eat," interjected Rosa Sanchez. "Just so you know, I never wanted to talk about this, but when you were half through with the book, I knew I couldn't do anything about it."

"We can eat and talk," said Ofelia as she divided their sandwich. I noticed, for the first time, that Ofelia and Rosa almost always shared their food.

"Here's the thing," Rosa continued. "People didn't understand, but I needed her, too. I was divorced. My family was in Cuba also. My son was little and lived with me. I had given up child support from his father in exchange for full custody. I used to spend so much time with Ofelia and Martín. Their house was always full of children and Ralph was made to feel like one of the family. Believe me, I liked my job and didn't plan to move away from Miami, but when I saw how desperate Ofelia was, I didn't give it a second thought. Looking back, I know it seems strange, but I was only in my twenties, and Ofelia was older and wiser. Quite frankly, since I've known her, she's been the voice of reason in my life. We figured that if she found the money to take care of Martín, we would go back. If she didn't, I had business contacts in Los Angeles and could get a job right away."

"It was fate," said Ofelia. "Two years later, we were living in Glendale—"

"Wait," said Rosa to Ofelia. "There's another part that has to be told first, and that was the moment you drove away leaving Martín in Miami. I was the only witness to that. It was like a woman that has to give up her baby, put him up for adoption because she can't take care of him anymore. It's easier said than done. Martín was like a baby at that point. He didn't know who she was. If he would have had his mind she wouldn't have had the heart to leave. No matter what. Did people talk? Did they say terrible things about her? You bet they did."

"Many thought I had taken his money," said Ofelia.

"Look, if she had left alone, they would have said she was leaving to meet a man somewhere. If she'd left with a man, *imaginate!* If she stayed, living in the little back room, they would have said that she was there only to wait for the old man to die and take his money. So she left with a woman, and they made up stories about that, too. It was a no-win situation for her."

"I left Miami to see if we could find the money," said Ofelia. "We went to Las Vegas to see McWillie."

"During the trip Ofelia was sick from the stress. We went to emergency rooms and hospitals all over the South. She had this blood condition that mimics leukemia. Can you imagine when she heard that on top of everything else? In Vegas she had some tests, and it turned out to be fine."

"Mack was great to us. His wife took care of Ralph so Rosa could take me to the hospital. He helped us make calls and write letters to banks. We wrote to Mexico and every place we could think of. Nothing turned up."

"What do you think happened?" I asked.

Ofelia and Rosa both looked at each other. "Who knows!" said Ofelia. "We didn't have money for private investigators and lawyers. We'd go to banks and, as incredible as it may sound today, they stonewalled me."

Ofelia paused. Rosa sighed deeply. "I tell her that there are only two possibilities. The Mafia or Pedro."

Ofelia shook her head. "I can't believe Pedro would do that. Martín and I baptized his only daughter. Besides, it was so much money. If he'd managed to get his hands on all of it there would have been a sign—some change in his lifestyle . . . *Pero mira*, it's over. Pedro made his peace with me long before he died. When I heard he was sick I called him at the hospital. He was very loving. He died a day or two later. We also saw Lita years later. I hadn't seen her since Martín's death. We were in Las Vegas. She was ninety-two. We hugged and I could tell she was really happy to see us. It was almost like old times, when we'd walk arm in arm through the cold in Boston, while Martín was having his checkup at the hospital."

"Ofelia wrote to Pedro asking about Martín all the time," said Rosa. "I kept copies of all the letters. And then one day she got a telegram from Pedro—"

"I know it practically by heart. It came on the eighth of April, 1966. I got home from work and found a special delivery letter and a telegram. The letter was postmarked the day before. Its first paragraph said: 'A few words to let you know that after suffering a terrible flu, Martín has developed kidney problems. He's been in bed for four days and today the doctor found him slightly better, without fever.' The telegram was dated April 8, and was sent at 6:32 A.M. It said simply: 'Martín died this morning. Pedro.'"

"Ofelia flew to Miami the next morning. She stayed with Marta Echemendia. I sent her money via Western Union to the Miami counter of National Airlines with instructions to hold the cash for her."

Ofelia wiped her eyes with her napkin. "Well, ladies, that's enough of that. I need a beer. Anyone else?"

As soon as Ofelia was gone Rosa visibly relaxed. "Do you see now why we didn't want to talk about the two of us? How could she make you understand her love for Martín and be open about the relationship with me? Ofelia will always be the wife of Martín Fox. I've known that from the beginning. She was never going to find another man like him. When we got to California there was so much struggle. I got a job immediately. For Ofelia, it wasn't as easy." Rosa's lengthy description of Ofelia's reintroduction to the work force sounded like a comedy of errors. Her first job, as a translator for radio station KWKW, lasted just weeks. The Mexican-American announcers could not make any sense of Ofelia's translations into Cuban Spanish, and they flatly told the station manager they'd quit en masse if she was not fired. In her second job, at a mailing house where she had to rapidly sort letters by zip code, Ofelia was painfully slow compared to the other workers. Nonetheless, she wept upon receiving her first paycheck—seventy-nine dollars for two weeks of work. After that, Ofelia sold perfume and cosmetics at Bullock's Department Store ("she wore high heels the first day, *la pobre*," Rosa told me, "and after eight hours on her feet she thought her back would break"). Eventually Ofelia found a steady job in a bank where she remained for ten years, until she retired because of a heart condition. "The worst thing of all was that people thought she'd found the money and was living well," said Rosa as Ofelia approached with two Coronas and three glasses. "I can show you old letters from people asking Ofelia to borrow money."

"Now we have to get back to the story about *Rosa y Yo*," said Ofelia as she poured beer.

"You tell her," said Rosa.

Ofelia took a sip of beer. "Ahh! That's good. Okay. Many years ago, when I was seventeen years old, this boy that I liked very much took my hand and said he wanted to ask me for something. I knew it was a kiss. So I waited. And I waited. And in the end he chickened out. That day I swore I'd never be in that weak position again. So now jump forward to 1967. It was three years since we'd left Florida. Martín was gone. Rosa and I had been through hell together. And one day we just realized that we were attracted to each other."

"*Bueno,* for me it wasn't that simple," said Rosa. "After we got on our feet financially, I went out on a few dates. There was this salesman who was interested in me. I'd go to lunch with him, but quite frankly, he bored me to death. And I couldn't just see any man raising my son, who was seven years old. Believe me, the last thing I ever expected would happen to me was that I'd fall in love with a woman. But one day, I opened my eyes and saw this magnificent, fascinating, incredibly beautiful person next to me. I hadn't realized how much she meant to me, how much I loved her. When I was with Ofelia, nothing else mattered. I still feel the same way."

"Yes, but how did it actually happen?" I asked, emboldened by their candor.

"Ahhh, so you want juicy details," said Ofelia.

"*Ay, por dios,*" groaned Rosa.

"Well, I'll tell you. One day we were at the post office in Glendale. Rosa was standing in line and behind her were two women speaking Cuban Spanish. You know how Cubans are. Within minutes they were talking to each other about where they were from, when they had come to California. Rosa told them that we'd come from Miami, that I was a widow, and that she was divorced and had a son. Addresses and telephone numbers were exchanged. Anyway, to this day we don't know how or why the women called us and invited us to a party. Rosa didn't want to go—"

"It was nothing personal. I'm just not the fiesta type," Rosa interjected.

"Yes, but you've learned to like it. Now that I think about it, I probably thought we were going to meet other Cubans. The party was in Topanga Canyon. When we got there it turned out that it was a private club and the doorman had our names. He rang a buzzer to let us in. It was gorgeous, with a pool and a bar. When we went in, it was obvious that it was a gay club, and the party was an anniversary for two women. The privacy was all about keeping this from the police, because they would raid those places."

"When I realized where we were I was a wreck!" said Rosa. "I'm not very liberal when it comes to those things. And it wasn't as if they were our good friends. We had only seen them once at the post office. They probably assumed we were gay, too, because we lived together. But Ofelia said we couldn't leave. We would look ridiculous, and we'd insult the people who invited us."

"We were seated at this table with twenty or so people. And when people got up to dance, it was men with men and women with women. I sat there briefly. Then I thought about my seventeen-year-old self, waiting for that kiss. I looked at this person sitting next to me, who had been with me through all my hard times, whose friendship had evolved into love, though neither of us had said anything. And I stood up, took her by the hand and said, 'Come on, Rosa. *Vamos a bailar.*' She was trembling. But she got up and danced with me. When I finally had her in my arms, dancing, we both realized the need to love again. And here we are, almost forty years later." It was a beautiful story, and I was not sure I believed much of it. But if I'd learned anything while writing about Cuba and Tropicana, it was that life abounds with illusion, and in the end it's the love and good memories that endure.

"It's an amazing coincidence that it should happen on a dance floor," I said.

Ofelia took Rosa's hand. "There are no coincidences," she said, now taking my hand as well. "The first part of my life was miraculously spent with a great man, who showed up in my life without warning and deserved my love, respect, and greatest admiration. The second part has been with someone equally wonderful and deserving. And then, when it was almost over, you arrived—another Rosa—to tell the tale. Whether you know it or not, I had been waiting for you for a long time. I tell you, it's always fate."

Now it was my turn to say something I had held back for two years. "If it's fate you believe in, don't you think I'm also in your life to take you back to Tropicana?"

Ofelia and Rosa glanced at each other. Neither said a word.

TROPICANA'S NEW show, *Tambores en Concierto,* opened in February 2005. Bajo las Estrellas continued to be packed with tourists from around the world, though now, because of even tighter travel restrictions, there were hardly any Americans in the audience. Tomás Morales expanded the cast, adding several new dancers, among them Greta González Carreras. The day after her onstage debut, Greta wrote me a lengthy e-mail from her mother's laboratory:

I got to Tropicana that day, like any other day, and Fernando, the school's director, told me I was going onstage that night. I finished my classes (from now on, you know, I have to take classes during the day, rehearse some afternoons, and perform every night), and at dusk I was taken to wardrobe and fitted with my costume. I was so nervous. The headdresses are huge and heavy, and it was hard to do the dance steps wearing them. The catwalks are narrow and so high up. I was worried about falling. But when the lights were upon me, I felt the greatness of the moment. Dancing on that stage was amazing. I'd waited so long for that moment! I don't mean to sound silly saying so, but I felt beautiful.

Wondering how Ofelia would react, I showed her Greta's e-mail. She wrote back to Tropicana's newest cast member. Unfortunately, Raquel's computer was having problems. So I called their house, and read it to Greta on the telephone.

Dear Greta,

I was deeply moved when I read how much dancing on the stage of Tropicana meant to you. That place is built on the sweat, money, and soul of a man who dedicated his life to a dream. From wherever he is, Martín is surely looking at you with a smile, knowing that Tropicana is still standing, in spite of the time and the circumstances. A thousand congratulations to you, and always remember a simple philosophy that will never fail to bring you happiness: At the end of the day, fate determines everything.

Ofelia

Ofelia Fox (1924–2006)

In November 2004, a month after we completed the manuscript of *Tropicana Nights*, Ofelia Fox was diagnosed with stage-four colon and liver cancer. The prognosis was poor—four months was the life expectancy; however, Ofelia lived another year, long enough to see the book's publication. She passed away on January 2, 2006, at the age of eighty-two.

ACKNOWLEDGEMENTS

This book is a testament to all who ever worked at Tropicana, whether or not their names appear in these pages. We are deeply grateful to those who shared their stories, especially Jenny León, Frank Llopis, Eddy Serra, Leonela González, Alicia Figueroa, Bebo Valdés, Carmelina Ardura, Hector Leal, Emilia Villamíl, Leowaldo Fornieles, Erna "Chiquita" Grabler, Valentín Jodra, Olga Guillot, Tomás Morales, Maña Salazar, and the great Max Borges Recio.

Several individuals provided valuable information on the artistic and political atmosphere of mid-twentieth century Cuba. Especially helpful were Helio Orovio and Armando Romeu III on music; Eduardo Luis Rodriguez, Isabel Rigol, and Lee Cott on architecture; Celida Villalón, on ballet and Pro-Arte Musical; Saul Srebnick, on memories of Victor de Correa; Maria Cole and Dick La Palma, on Nat "King" Cole in Cuba; José Rodriguez for Tropicana show chronology; and Marvette Perez on Celia Cruz. Carolina Miranda and Anne Louise Bardach helped in ways too numerous to mention, and Reinaldo Taladrid set fate in motion with a phone number. We thank Zoe Blanco-Roca and the Cuban Heritage Collection at the University of Miami for access to Diario de la Marina and old Show magazines, and our friends at Cuba Tours and Travel and the Copperbridge Foundation for coordinating trips to Cuba.

I am deeply grateful to the generous and gifted Alexandre Arrechea, whose original drawing graces the cover of this edition. We thank Ellen Levine of Trident Media, original agent for this book, and Tim Bent, its editor at Harcourt, as well as the Wolfsonian at FIU, the Los Angeles Conservancy, and the National Trust for Historic Preservation for providing me ongoing reasons to research Cuban architecture.

Our friends and family who encouraged us during the period of writing are chronicled in earlier versions of the book. Most significant in every way is Rosa Sanchez, whose diligent recordkeeping made it possible to recreate Martin and Ofelia's life and whose devotion was the heart and soul of the original writing. For this edition, I want to thank the hardworking staff at RLA Conservation, Inc., Danny and Wendy of Little Gables Group, Joanne Bolton, the staff of In Situ Press, Jorge Hernandez, Hilario Candela, Ruth Behar, Gloria Estefan, Frank Luca, and my favorite honorary Jewban Vicki Gold Levi. Our greatest debt, of course, is to our families—the Lowingers, Kesslers, Shipps, Sanchezes, Peresechenskys, and Brandfons. I give a special shout out to Ben Brandfon for his big heart and relentless humor.

Lastly, there is Todd Kessler. You listened to the clamor for another edition of this book, and decided it was necessary. You are a constant inspiration to me.

Rosa Lowinger Los Angeles 2016

APPENDIX

A List of Rodney's Tropicana Shows

THE FOLLOWING chronology has been assembled from articles in *Show* magazine (after April 1954) and Tropicana advertisements in *Diario de la Marina* (from 1952–1960). There were two to three shows nightly. We have used the most common spelling of names for the groups, as they varied in the advertisements. All performers mentioned are in addition to the Tropicana corps of dancers and modelos.

1952

June, 1952: Rodney begins at Tropicana. His name first appears in the cabaret's *Diario de la Marina* advertisements on August 2. Beginning August 9 the ads had the following billing: "Two different shows nightly with choreography by Rodney: *Goyescas* [Goya's Women], *Prende la Vela* [Light the Candle], and second shows *Paris-Havana* and *Chinos en la Habana.*" Throughout the summer and fall of 1952, these shows, featuring soprano Zoraida Marrero and mambo dancers Ana Gloria and Rolando, run in rotation. Beginning August 9, the billing changes to "Production and choreography by Rodney."

September 13: *Las Viudas Alegres* (The Merry Widows), an adaptation of the Franz Lehár operetta about the amorous adventures of a rich widow in the imaginary land of Marsovia, is first advertised. Featuring Zoraida Marrero and tenor Miguel Angel Ortíz.

October 10: Chiquita and Johnson join the cast.

October 18: *Orquídeas Para Usted* (Orchids For You) added to repertoire. Featuring Chiquita and Johnson, and Ana Gloria and Rolando. *Las Viudas Alegres* is done as a second show after this date. *Goyescas* and *Prende la Vela* continue to run in rotation with these shows through mid-December.

November 8: *Malagueñas* (Women of Malaga), featuring Spanish singer Amparo Garrido, is rotated in with prior shows.

December 22: *El Omelen-ko* and *Caribbean Island* open, featuring Chiquita and Johnson.

December 27: A third show, *Batanga* (no translation), is added.

1953

Through mid April: *El Omelen-ko, Caribbean Island,* and *Batanga* run together.

April 18: *El Guajeo* (a *cubanismo* meaning, roughly, "a party without limits"), featuring traditional Cuban dance set to music composed by Bebo Valdés, runs together with *Core di Napoli* (Chorus of Naples) and a third show, *El Yoyo* (The Yo-yo). Featuring Celeste Mendoza, Chiquita and Johnson, and Italian singer Emma Puvo.

June 10: *Sereneta Gaucha* (Gaucho Serenade), a show of Argentinian music and tango. Second show is *El Marara* (a title without translation, in *Diario de la Marina* ads it is said to have "*sabor criollo*" or "Cuban flavor"). Featuring Celeste Mendoza, dance pair Doris and Robert, singers Gaston Vila, America Crespo, and tenor José Le Matt.

August 22: *Europa, Año Cero* (Europe, Year Zero), a three-part show depicting the most famous historical personalities of Europe. Parts one and two were performed together and focus on Italy and France. The second show (part three) focuses on Germany. Featuring dancers Leonela González, Luis Trapaga, and modelo Sandra Taylor.

October 30: *Majas y Toro* (a *maja* is a term for a Spanish brunette beauty as depicted in Francisco de Goya's *The Nude Maja* [1800]). Ads in *Show* say the production is based on Colombian music and dance. The second show is a Spanish-themed production, *Patio Andaluz* (Andalusian Patio). Featuring Paulina Alvarez, the Spanish musical group Los Xey, and the Senén Suarez conjunto.

November 7: *Prende la Vela* is added as the third show.

December 19: *Mayombe* (no translation) and *Carnaval Carioca* (roughly, Carnival in Rio). Featuring Celia Cruz, Maño Lopez, Paulina Alvarez, Kiko González, Emilia Villamíl, and Marta Castillo.

1954

Through April: *Mayombe* and *Carnaval Carioca.*

April 10: *Rodneyscope,* a revue of Rodney's prior output, and *Pregones de mi Cuba* (a show that features *son pregón* music, like "El manisero"). Featuring Italian tenor Pino Barratti, *vedette* Niola Montes, Leonela González, and the Orlando de la Rosa quartet.

June 15: *El Circo* (The Circus) and *Luna de Tropicana* (Tropicana Moon). Featuring acrobats and animal tamers from Cuba's national circus, dancers Leonela González, Henry Boyer, Miguelito Checki, and Maricusa Cabrera.

August 13: *Ritmo en Fantasía* (Rhythm in Fantasy), *Polynesia,* and *Canciones de Ayer* (Songs of Yesterday). Featuring Miguelito Valdés, Olga Guillot and Los Rufinos.

November 5: *Prohibido en Televisión* (Prohibited on Television) and *Mambo Versus Cha-cha-cha.* Featuring Leonela González, Henry Boyer, Los Rufinos, and the Tex Mex Trio.

December 1: *White Christmas* substitutes *Mambo Versus Cha-cha-cha* and plays through January, 1955.

1955

February 7: *Karabalí,* a show of Afro-Cuban liturgy, originally entitled *Abakua,* and *Embrujo en la Noche* (Nighttime Spell) a carnival-themed show. Featuring dancers Darvas y Julia, Leonela González, Raúl Díaz; and the Cuarteto D' Aida (a female quartet led by director Aida Diestro, and consisting of singers Moraima Secada, Omara Portuondo, Haydée Portuondo, and Elena Burke); the Cuarteto D'Ruff (formerly Los Rufinos); Mercedita Valdés; and Orlando de la Rosa.

April 27: *Las Viudas Alegres* (The Merry Widows), and *Las Pasiones* (The Passions), which is described in a *Diario de la Marina* ad: "Rodney subtly expresses the passions that reside in the soul of a woman, using symbols that represent her irrefutable need to possess: gold, jewels, furs . . . eternal founts of feminine vanity." Featuring Rosita Fornés, Italian singer Armando Bianchi, Leonela González, Henry Boyer, Raúl Díaz, the Cuarteto D'Ruff, and acrobats Antonio Fleitas and Roberto Berenguer (the latter was a Mr. Cuba).

July 8: *Bahiondo,* a Brazilian-themed show, and *Flamingo Rhapsody,* a Cuban-music show. Featuring Carmen Miranda and Bando Da Lua (for two weeks in August), Olga Guillot, Afro-Cuban singer Gina Martin, Colombian singer Nelson Pineido, pianist Felo Bergaza, and pianist and singer Juan Bruno Tarraza.

September 11: *Casa de Té* (Tea House) and *Feria de Mujeres* (Women's Fair), both Asian-themed shows. Featuring dancers Ana Gloria and Rolando, Leonela González, Henry Boyer, Gladys Robau, Raúl Díaz, Chinese martial arts group Moc-Kan-Sent, and *vedette* Nancy Morén.

November 20: *Hello Broadway* and *Madonnas de Capri*. Both shows described in *Diario de la Marina* ad as "two frivolous revues that gather various international artists on Tropicana's stage, headlined by Italian composer Alberto Barberis, author of *Gira Gira*." Also featuring Ana Gloria and Rolando, Leonela González, Henry Boyer, Miguel Angel Ortíz, soprano Ana Julia, the Cuarteto D'Aida, Puerto Rican singing star Lucy Fabery, and Broadway dancers Julio Solano and Taybee Afra.

1956

January 12: *Fantasía Mexicana* and *Noches del Trópico* (Nights in the Tropics). Featuring Ana Gloria and Rolando, Leonela González, Henry Boyer, Johnny Puleo and his Harmonica Gang, singers Xiomara Alfaro, Dandy Crawford, Lolita Chanquet, Miguel Angel Ortíz, the Cuarteto D'Aida, and Mexican dancers Columba Dominguez and Alicia Lira. Performance attended by Joan Crawford and Alfred Steele, and Marlon Brando.

March 2–15: Nat "King" Cole.

March 16–April 15: Billy Daniels and pianist Benny Payne.

April 21: *Evocación* (Evocation) and *Seis Lindas Cubanas* (Six Pretty Cubans—a reference to a song that extols the beauty of the six original provinces of Cuba). The shows were both described as nineteenth century reflections on Cuban dance and music. Featuring Ana Gloria and Rolando, the Cuarteto D'Aida, the Cuarteto de Carlos Faxas, Xiomara Alfaro, tenor Manolo Alvarez Mera, soprano Estelita Santaló, the Hermanas Lago Trio, *guajiro* singers Celina and Reutilio, singer Ramón Veloz, Leonela González, and Henry Boyer.

June 22: *Lola y el Rey* (Lola and the King) and *Prohibido en Televisión* (the second, 1956 version of "Prohibited on Television"). Both shows were farces, the first based on *The King and I*, the second based on television commercials and the English language. Featuring comedian-impersonators Tito Hernández (known for his "Ramón Grau San Martín" bit), Armando Roblán (known for his Liberace impersonation), Milos Velarde, and Pepe Biondi; Puerto Rican singer Raffi Muñoz, the Hermanas Lago Trio, the Cuarteto de Carlos Faxas, and Ana Gloria and Rolando.

August 30: *En Serio* (Seriously) and *En Broma* (Joking), a pair of musical revues based on the Alhambra Theater in Havana's Chinatown. Featuring *vedette* Blanca

Varela, singer Wilfredo Fernández, the Hermanas Lago Trio, the Cuarteto Los Faxas, and Ana Gloria and Rolando. Performance attended by Liberace.

September 14: Blind Mexican organist Ernesto Hill Olvera begins a two-week run.

November 15: *Prohibido en España, Noche Cubana,* and *En Tragos* (Loaded on Drinks). Featuring Paulina Alvarez, Ana Gloria and Rolando, the Cuarteto D'Ruff, Argentinian *vedette* Elsa Marval, Spanish dancers Carmela Vásquez and Carmen Reyes, Spanish singer Miguel Herrero, Leonela González, baritone Ramon Calzadilla, actor/dancer Adriano Vitale ("Italy's Gene Kelly"), and (for two weeks in December) Benny Moré and his orchestra.

1957

January 15: *Tambó,* an Afro-Cuban show, and *Copacabana,* a Brazilian revue (and the show where a zeppelin "flew" in on wires carrying *vedette* Kary Russie). Featuring Celia Cruz, Paulina Alvarez, Merceditas Valdés, Richard Robertson, Adriano Rodríguez, the Vocal Chorus of Paquito Godino, Johnny Puleo and his Harmonica Gang, Ana Gloria and Rolando, Leonela González, Afro-Cuban drumming group Los Tambores Batá, and Adriano Vitale.

February 1–14: Nat "King" Cole.

April 14: *Primavera en Roma* (Springtime in Rome), a showcase of Italian music, and *Música del Alma* (Music in the Soul), advertised as "Rock and Roll at Tropicana." Featuring Italian singer Jula de Palma, Argentinian singer Alberto Rochi, Mexican singer Pedro Vargas, Cuban singer Carmen Lastra, the Vocal Chorus of Paquito Godino, the Llopis Quartet, and Leonela González.

June 14: *Rodney Circus,* the second circus production, and *Las Viudas del Calypso* (The Calypso Widows), a calypso revue. Featuring Alberto Rochi, singer Luis García, and Cuarteto Los Riveros, dance pair Gladys y Freddy, Mitsuko, and animal tamers Los Gauthier.

September 6: *Tambores Sobre la Habana* (Drums Over Havana), a tropical showcase of the work of Cuban composers, and *Tropicana Souvenier,* a revue of Rodney's prior output, including the song "Sun Sun Babae," and emphasizing the music of *Las Viudas Alegres.* Celebrating Rodney's sixth anniversary. Featuring Alberto Rochi, Blanca Varela, the Cuarteto Los Riveros, Gladys y Freddy, *vedette* Monica Castell, Mexican actress Gina Romano, and the traditional Cuban singing group Los Guaracheros de Oriente.

November 8: *En un Paraíso del Asia* (In an Asian Paradise) and *Chinatown.* (Note: almost all former Tropicana staff regard this as the most sumptuous and costly pair of shows ever produced at the cabaret. It was notable for Gladys and Freddy's performance of the Javanese dance called *tinikling* and for the all-Asian menu served during the run of the show.) Both productions were based on Asian dance and culture, blended with Cuban music. Featuring Philippine actress and dancer Erlinda Cortes, American specialist in Hindu and Siamese dance Ana Correja, Hong Kong folkloric ballerina Vie Voon Hum, hula dancer Loma Duke, Chinese dancer Denise Quam, Monica Castell, and the Cuarteto Los Riveros.

1958

January 12: *Vodú Ritual* (Voodoo Ritual), a Haitian-themed show, and *Esta es mi Cuba, mister* (This is my Cuba, Mister), a Cuban comedy revue featuring traditional song and dance. Featuring Haitian singers Marta Jean Claudet and Rosita Jean Ophilias, Cuban singer Berta Dupuy, the Cuarteto Los Riveros, Gladys and Freddy, baritone Richard Robertson, Monica Castell, and Los Guaracheros de Oriente.

February 7–21: Nat "King" Cole

April 18: *Diosas de Carne* (Goddesses of the Flesh), based on the women of Greek mythology, and *Canciones para Besar* (Songs for Kissing), a revue built around famous love songs. Featuring Gladys Robau, Leonela González, Henry Boyer, the Hermanas Lago Trio, and the Cuarteto de Carlos Faxas. The goddesses were portrayed by *modelos* Teresita Rodríguez (Medusa), María Magdalena Hernandez (Friné), Esperanza Muñoz (Xerxes), Wilda Walter (Antigone), Jenny León (Helen of Troy), Dulce María Valdés (Medea), Miriam del Valle (Minerva), Ivette Ramos (Diana), Zita Coalla (Venus), Emy de Mendoza (Selene), and Rosalía Fernandez (Anfitrite).

June 20: *Luisa Fernanda en Chemise* (Luisa Fernanda in a Chemise), a comic production based on Spanish light opera, and *Una Hora Contigo* (An Hour With You), a revue of romantic songs. Featuring Blanca Varela, Argentinian singer Daniel Riolovos, Leonela González, Henry Boyer, Marta Castillo, and Miguelito Checki.

September 29: *Su Majestad la Prensa* (Your Majesty, the Press), an homage to Cuban newspapers and magazines, and *Show de Papel* (The Papers Show), billed as a humorous and audacious criticism of French fashion. Featuring Xiomara Alfaro, Berta Dupuy, Los Guaracheros de Oriente, comedienne Eloisa Alvarez Guedes, singer Gladys Lorenzo, and dancers Leonela González, Henry Boyer, Miguelito Checki, Eduardo Perovani, and Marta Castillo.

October (date unconfirmed): Christine Jorgensen performs for one week.

November 26: *Rumbo al Waldorf* (To the Waldorf), featuring the music of Cuban composer Ernesto Lecuona, and *Ritmo en Color* (Rhythm in Color), advertised as "a kaleidoscope of atomic rhythm." Featuring Berta Dupuy, Maria Teresa Tolón, Leonela González, Henry Boyer, Gladys Lorenzo, Miguelito Checki, Marta Castillo, the Conjunto Vocal de Tropicana, and Los Guaracheros de Oriente. Los Armonicos de Felipe Dulzaides play in the casino bar.

1959

March 7: *Bumki Bun,* a Brazilian production, and *Tropicana Vodevil,* a revue of contemporary Latin American music. Featuring Berta Dupuy, María Teresa Tolón, Los Riveros, Miguelito Checki, and Marta Castillo.

June 6: *Bongo Congo* and *Canto a Oriente* (A Song for Oriente). The second show is an homage to agrarian reform and the province of Oriente, "birthplace of heroic *mambises* and rebels." Featuring Celia Cruz, Los Riveros, Miguelito Checki, and María Teresa Tolón.

October 17: *Cubanacan* (later spelled *Kubanacan*), described as "a sumptuously colored show of Cuban song and rhythms"; and *Rodneyrama,* "a kaleidoscope of the most famous Cuban music and dance." Opening coincided with ASTA world congress in Havana. Featuring Los Riveros, Miguelito Checki, Marta Castillo, Berta Dupuy, and Emilia Villamíl.

1960

February 6: *Tropicana Alrededor del Mundo* (Tropicana Around the World) replaces *Rodneyrama. Kubanacan* is second show. Featuring singer Esther Borja, Los Riveros, María Teresa Tolón, Marta Castillo, and Miguelito Checki. When Rodney becomes ill in mid-1960, his position is filled by Armando Suez, who eventually assumes his post as choreographer with *Pachanga en Tropicana,* a show which substitutes for *Kubanacan.*

Author's Note on Sources

THE BACKBONE of this story comes from the recollections of Ofelia Fox. Most of the information about the workings of the Tropicana casino and the *bolita* industry come from roulette dealer Valentín Jodra. Their stories were recounted to me in a series of conversations that took place between 2000 and 2004. Rosa Sanchez was present for almost all of the conversations with Ofelia Fox, and she contributed additional material, as seen in the text. Additional interviews were conducted with individuals who appear as sources in the text and several others who do not appear as subjects. Except where noted, I conducted the interviews on the dates indicated below. Ofelia was a source for all of the chapters. The dates of my conversations with her and Rosa are not always included, as they occurred over a four-year period. The chronology of events and shows at Tropicana derives from articles in *Show* magazine and weekly advertisements in the Saturday edition of *Diario de la Marina* from 1951–1959.

Quoted sources are noted below. Additional reference materials used to create the atmosphere surrounding the Tropicana cabaret are also listed. In addition to *Show*, and *Diario de la Marina*, the following three books were especially helpful in recreating the social, political, and musical climate of Cuba during the time period described:

Phillips, R. H. *Cuba, Island of Paradox*, New York: McDowell, Obolensky, 1959.
Sublette, Ned. *Cuba and its Music: From the First Drums to the Mambo*, Chicago: Chicago Review Press, 2004.
Thomas, Hugh. *Cuba: The Pursuit of Freedom*, New York: Harper & Row, 1971.

Prologue   The Flight

Interviews/Conversations with Rosa Lowinger

Valentín Jodra
Leonardo and Hilda Lowinger
Eddy Serra

Additional Sources

Kihss, Peter. "Batista and Regime Flee Cuba." *The New York Times,* January 2, 1959.

Phillips, R.H. *Cuba, Island of Paradox.* New York: McDowell, Obolensky, 1959.

Thomas, Hugh. *Cuba: The Pursuit of Freedom.* New York: Harper & Row, 1971.

"Counting Batista's Days," *Newsweek,* December 22, 1958.

Chapter 1   Introductions

Interviews/Conversations with Rosa Lowinger

Lee Cott
Eduardo Luis Rodríguez

Additional Sources

Cirules, Enrique. *El imperio de la Habana.* Havana: Casa de Las Americas, 1993.

Kefauver, Estes. *Crime in America.* New York: Doubleday, 1951.

Messick, Hank. *Lansky.* New York: Berkeley Medallion, 1971.

Pyron, Darden Asbury. *Liberace: An American Boy.* Chicago: University of Chicago Press, 2000.

Ragano, Frank, Nancy Ragano, and Selwyn Raab. *Mob Lawyer.* New York: Charles Scribner and Sons, 1994.

Rodríguez, Eduardo Luis. *The Havana Guide, Modern Architecture 1925–1965.* New York: Princeton Architectural Press, 2000.

Diario de la Marina, September 15, 1956.

Show magazine, September 1956, pp. 62–63.

Chapter 2   A Nickel on the Butterfly

Interviews/Conversations with Rosa Lowinger

Cesar Quesada
Rosa Sanchez

Additional Sources

Barbour, Thomas. *A Naturalist in Cuba.* Boston: Little, Brown & Company, 1945.

Foner, Philip S. *The Spanish-Cuban-American War and the Birth of American Imperialism 1895–1902.* New York: Monthly Review Press, 1972.

Greene, Graham. *Our Man in Havana.* New York: Viking Press, 1972.

Moreno Fraginals, Manuel. *El ingenio.* La Habana: Editorial de Ciencias Sociales, 1978.

Rodríguez, Eduardo Luis. *La Habana: Arquitectura del siglo XX.* La Habana: Art Blume, 1998.

Sublette, Ned. *Cuba and its Music: From the First Drums to the Mambo.* Chicago: Chicago Review Press, 2004.

Terry, T. Philip. *Terry's Guide to Cuba.* Boston: Houghton Mifflin, 1926.

Thomas, Hugh. *Cuba: The Pursuit of Freedom.* New York: Harper & Row, 1971.

Chapter 3   The Boulevard of the New World

Interviews/Conversations with Rosa Lowinger

Valentín Jodra
Rosa Sanchez
Saul Srebnick

Quotes

"Havana . . . Prohibitionists." Woon, Basil, *When It's Cocktail Time in Cuba.* New York: Horace Liveright, 1928, p. 33.

"everyone is drinking . . . drunk." Ibid., p. 38.

"healthful drink." Ibid., p. 38.

"He always believes . . . lottery." Ibid., p. 103.

"The boulevard . . . world." Thomas, Hugh. *Cuba: The Pursuit of Freedom.* New York: Harper & Row, 1971, p. 12.

"Here . . . nervs." Caruso, Dorothy. *Enrico Caruso: His Life and Death.* New York: Simon & Schuster, 1945, p. 185.

"The Casino . . . continent." Woon, p. 129.

"Gambling . . . wheel." Lacey, Robert. *Little Man, Meyer Lansky and the Gangster Life.* New York: Little, Brown & Company, 1991, p. 85.

Additional Sources

Clark, Sydney A. *Cuban Tapestry.* New York: McBride, 1936.

González Echevarría, Roberto. *The Pride of Havana: A History of Cuban Baseball.* New York: Oxford University Press, 1999.

The Journal of Decorative and Propaganda Arts: Cuba Theme Issue. Miami: Wolfsonian Foundation, 1996.

Phillips, R.H. *Cuba, Island of Paradox.* Ibid.

Schwartz, Rosalie. *Pleasure Island, Tourism and Temptation in Cuba.* Lincoln, Nebraska: University of Nebraska Press, 1997.

Chapter 4   The Peanut Vendor

Interviews/Conversations with Rosa Lowinger

Olga Guillot
Valentín Jodra
Rosa Sanchez
Saul Srebnick

Interview by Marisel Caraballo

Armando Romeu, June 2000.

Quotes

"can refer. . . . Atmosphere." Sublette, Ned. *Cuba and its Music: From the First Drums to the Mambo.* Chicago Review Press, 2004, p. 257.

"I have not doubt . . ." Cugat, Xavier. *Rumba is My Life: American Autobiography.* (Library Binding) Reprint Services Corp., 1949, p. 101.

"There is no . . . do it." Ibid., p. 161.

"Young, mild-mannered . . . vocalist." Ibid., p. 118.

"It was. . . . streets." Marisel Caraballo interview with Armando Romeu Jr., June 2000.

"*Entre palmeras y flores . . . para ti.*" Lam, Rafael. *Tropicana, un paraiso bajo las estrellas.* La Habana: Editorial José Martí, 1999, pp. 21–22.

Additional Sources

Acosta, Leonardo. *Cubano Be Cubano Bop: One Hundred Years of Jazz in Cuba.* Washington: Smithsonian Books, 2003.

Carpentier, Alejo. *La música en Cuba.* Editorial Letras Cubanas, Havana, 1998.

Calloway, Cab. *Of Minnie the Moocher and Me.* New York: Ty Crowell Co., 1976.

Fajardo, Ramon. *Rita Montaner.* Editorial Letras Cubanas, Havana, 1993.

Gil-Montero, Martha. *Brazilian Bombshell: The Biography of Carmen Miranda.* New York: Dutton, 1989.

Orovio, Helio. *Diccionario de la música cubana.* Editorial Letras Cubanas, Havana, 1992.

Orovio, Helio. *El son, la guaracha y la salsa.* Santiago De Cuba: Editorial Oriente, 1994.

Sweeney, Philip. *The Rough Guide to Cuban Music.* London: Penguin Group, 2001.

Chapter 5   Valentín

Interviews/Conversations with Rosa Lowinger

Valentín Jodra

Rosa Sanchez

Quotes

"He was a brutish . . . house." Lam, p. 23.

Additional Sources

Schroeder, Susan. *Cuba: A Handbook of Historical Statistics.* Boston: G.K. Hall, 1982.

Chapter 6   Waiting Things Out

Interviews/Conversations with Rosa Lowinger

Valentín Jodra

Rosa Sanchez

Quotes

"Havana was . . . was boss." Gosch, Martin A., and Hammer, Richard. *The Last Testament of Lucky Luciano.* Boston: Little Brown & Company 1974, p. 318.

"There was a strange . . . things." Phillips, p. 225.

"His mind works . . . gaping." Ibid., p. 157.

"Boss Batista . . . 4,000." "Cuba: Evolution of a Dictator." *Time,* June 12, 1944, p. 22.

"[Havana] was a place. . . . supposed to." Gosch, Ibid.

"[Grau] did a great. . . . left behind." Thomas, pp. 757–758.

Additional Sources

"Cuba's Boss Batista." *Time,* April 26, 1937.

"Foreign Trade: High Jinks in Cuba." *Time,* June 15, 1942.
"Cuba: Evolution of a Dictator." *Time,* June 12, 1944.
"Cuba Elects Grau." *Life Magazine,* June 12, 1944.
"Cuban Housecleaning: Grau Urges Batista Henchmen From Country's Army and Police." *Newsweek,* November 20, 1944.
"Cuba's Mr. A." *Newsweek,* May 1, 1944.
"Cuban Upset." *Newsweek,* June 12, 1944.
"Cuba: The Diamond Mystery." *Newsweek,* April 8, 1946.
"Cuba: Lost Milestone." *Time,* April 8, 1946.

Chapter 7   Covering Your Bets

Interviews/Conversations with Rosa Lowinger

Valentín Jodra
Rosa Sanchez

Additional Sources

Cugat, Xavier. *Rumba is My Life: An American Autobiography.* (Library Binding) Reprint Services Corp., 1949.
Dubivsky, Barbara. "A Working Girl's Debut in Shipboard Society." *The New York Times,* December 16, 1951.
Orovio, Helio. *Diccionario de la música cubana.*
Pujol, Jordi. *Chano Pozo: el tambor de Cuba.* Barcelona: Alemendra Music, 2001.
Schwartz, Rosalie. *Pleasure Island: Tourism and Temptation in Cuba.*
Sublette, Ned. *Cuba and its Music: From the First Drums to the Mambo.*
Suchlicki, Jaime, *Cuba from Colombus to Castro and Beyond.* Washington, D.C.: Brassey's, Inc., 1997.

Chapter 8   Arcos de Cristal

Interviews/Conversations with Rosa Lowinger

Max Borges Jr.
Lee Cott
Valentín Jodra
Eduardo Luis Rodríguez
Rosa Sanchez

Quotes

"social dictator," Woon, p. 135.

Additional Sources

Hitchcock, Henry-Russell. *Latin American Architecture Since 1945.* New York: Museum of Modern Art, 1955.

Lam, Rafael. *Tropicana: un paraiso bajo las estrellas.* La Habana: Editorial José Martí, 1999.

Le Corbusier. *Towards a New Architecture.* New York: Dover Publications, 1986.

Rodríguez, Eduardo Luis. *The Havana Guide: Modern Architecture 1925–1965.*

Scarpaci, Joseph L. *Havana: Two Faces of the Antillean Metropolis.* Chapel Hill: University of North Carolina Press, 1997.

Suchlicki, Jaime. *Historical Dictionary of Cuba.* Lanham, Maryland and London: The Scarecrow Press, Inc., 2001.

Chapter 9   The Santos and the Song-and-Dance Man

Interviews/Conversations with Rosa Lowinger

Luis Carbonell
Hector Leal
Tomás Morales
Helio Orovio
Eddy Serra

Quotes

"wealthy victims . . . health of the family." Stanhope, Dorothy, "Havana's Leper Colony." *The New York Times,* May 20, 1900, p. 6.

"our closer . . . present time." "Dr. Ashmead Calls Lepers a Menace." *The New York Times,* February 4, 1900, p. 14.

Additional Sources

Bolívar Aróstegui, Natalia, and Carmen González Díaz de Villegas. *Ituto: la muerte en los mitos y rituales afrocubanos.* Miami: Editorial Arenas, 1992.

Bolívar Aróstegui, Natalia. *Los Orishas en Cuba.* La Habana: Ediciones Unión, 1990.

Lam, Rafael. *Tropicana: un paraíso bajo las estrellas.*

Roberts, Adolphe. *Havana: Portrait of a City.* New York: Coward-McCann, Inc. 1953.

Rosell, Rosendo. *Vida y milagros de la farándula de Cuba.* Miami: Ediciones Universal, 1992.

Sublette, Ned. *Cuba and its Music: From the First Drums to the Mambo.*

"Leprosy." Britannica.com, http://www.britannica.com/eb/
    article?eu=48992&tocid=0&query=leprosy%20in%20carribbean&ct=eb.
"Dr. Matias Duque: Former Secretary on Health in Cuba, Expert on Leprosy."
    The New York Times, February 16, 1941.
"Leper Found in Bronx." *The New York Times,* January 11, 1931.
"To Attend Leprosy Congress." *The New York Times,* April 1, 1948.

Chapter 10   The Two Loves of Martín Fox

Interviews/Conversations with Rosa Lowinger

Max Borges, Jr.
Eddy Serra

Additional Sources

Lam, Rafael. *Tropicana: un paraíso bajo las estrellas.*
Suckling, James. "On the Road to Tobacco Country: A journey into the Vuelta
    Abajo, land of the world's best cigar leaves." *Cigar Aficionado,* May/June,
    2001.
Westfall, Glenn L. "Florida's Cultural Legacy: Tobacco, Steam and Stone." *South
    Florida History Magazine,* vol. 23, no. 4 (Fall 1995/Winter 1996), pp. 13–23.

Chapter 11   The Coup

Interviews/Conversations with Rosa Lowinger

Max Borges, Jr.
Ernesto Capote
Valentín Jodra
Rosa Sanchez

Quotes

"pirate king. . . . bodyguards." Thomas, p. 761.
"chaotic conditions. . . . lives and property." Phillips, p. 259.
"In Havana . . . old scores." "Cuba: Killers Beware." *Newsweek,* September 23,
    1946, p. 54.
"On July 4 . . . ever found." Phillips, pp. 253–254.

Additional Sources

Acosta, Leonardo, Olivier Cossard, René Espí, and Helio Orovio. *Fiesta Havana.*
    Paris: Editions Vade Retro, 1999.

"Cuba: Batista at Work." *Newsweek*, March 24, 1952.

"Cuba's Batista: Dictator with the People." *Time*, April 14, 1952.

"Cuba: Crime Wave." *Time*, September 23, 1946.

Phillips, R. Hart. "Cuba Preens Itself for the Tourist." *The New York Times*, December 14, 1952.

Schwartz, Rosalie. *Pleasure Island: Tourism and Temptation in Cuba.*

Chapter 12   Mambo a la Tropicana

Interviews/Conversations with Rosa Lowinger

Roberto Cabrera

Julieta Jimenez

Helio Orovio

Armando Romeu III

Gilberto Torres

Bebo Valdés

Emilia Villamíl

Quotes

"If you . . . jazz." Sublette, p. 326.

"It's hard . . . recycled as nostalgia." Ibid., p. 508.

Additional Sources

Acosta, Leonardo. *Cubano Be Cubano Bop: One Hundred Years of Jazz in Cuba.*

Acosta, Leonardo, Olivier Cossard, René Espí, and Helio Orovio. *Fiesta Havana.*

Adler, Barbara Squier. "The Mambo and the Mood." *The New York Times Magazine*, September 16, 1951.

Erlewine, Michael, with Vladimir Bogdanov, Chris Woodstra, and Scott Yanow. *The All Music Guide to Jazz*. San Francisco: Miller Publishing, 1996.

Figueroa, Frank M. *Israel Lopez "Cachao": Highlights and Review of his Smithsonian Jazz Oral History Interview.* www.picadillo.com/figueroa/cachao.html.

Figueroa, Frank M. *Mario Bauza: Highlights from his Smithsonian Jazz Oral History Interview.* www.cubanmusic.com.

Gillespie, Dizzy, with Al Fraser. *To Be or Not to Bop*. New York: Doubleday and Company, 1979.

Gleason, Ralph J. "Prado's West Coast Tour Proving a Huge Success." *Downbeat*, October 5, 1951.

"Mambomania." *Newsweek*, August 16, 1954.

Orovio, Helio. *Diccionario de la música cubana.*

Orovio, Helio. *El danzón, el mambo, y el chachacha*. Santiago De Cuba: Editorial Oriente, 1994.

Pujol, Jordi. *Chano Pozo: el tambor de Cuba*.

Salazar, Max. "Who Invented the Mambo?" *Latin Beat*, 1992.

Watrous, Peter. "Mario Bauza, Band Leader Dies; Champion of Latin Music Was 82." *The New York Times*, July 12, 1993.

Wilson, John S. "Ga-ga Over Cha Cha." *The New York Times*, March 15, 1959.

Chapter 13　　The Leap

Interviews/Conversations with Rosa Lowinger

Erna Grabler

Hector Leal

Eddy Serra

Additional Sources

Deitche, Scott M. *Cigar City Mafia*. Fort Lee, New Jersey: Barricade Books, 2004.

Eisenberg, Dennis, Uri Dan, and Ali Landau. *Meyer Lansky: Mogul of the Mob*. New York: Paddington Press, 1979.

Gosch, Martin A. and Richard Hammer. *The Last Testament of Lucky Luciano*. Boston: Little, Brown & Company, 1974.

Kefauver, Estes, *Crime in America*.

Lacey, Robert. *Little Man, Meyer Lansky and the Gangster Life*. New York: Little, Brown & Company, 1991.

Messick, Hank. *Lansky*. New York: Berkeley Medallion, 1971.

Letter from U.S. Treasury Department to the Commissioner of Customs, March 27, 1958, viewed at: Cuban Information Archives, http://cuban-exile.com/doc276300/doc0288.htm.

"Testimony of Lewis McWillie, Las Vegas, Nevada." *The House Select Committee on Assassinations:* Volume V, viewed at: http://jfkassassination.net/russ/jfkinfo2/jfk5/mcwill.htm.

Chapter 14　　The Circus

Interviews/Conversations with Rosa Lowinger

Alicia Figueroa

Olga Guillot

Leonela González
Jenny León
Frank Llopis
Bebo Valdés
Célida Villalón
Emilia Villamíl

Quotes

"Leonela González . . . Miss Universe." *Show* magazine, April 1955, p. 7.

"I warn. . . . carefully." Fidel Castro. "La historia me absolverá," La Habana: Editorial de Ciencias Sociales, 1981. Quote taken from online version: Castro Internet Archive, http://www.marxists.org/history/cuba/archive/castro/1953/10/16.htm.

"In the first show . . . business." *Show* magazine, July 1954, p. 15.

Additional Sources

Bardach, Ann Louise. *Cuba Confidential: Love and Vengeance in Miami and Havana.* New York: Random House, 2002.

Orovio, Helio. *El bolero cubano.* Santiago De Cuba: Editorial Oriente, 1994.

Thomas, Hugh. *Cuba: The Pursuit of Freedom.*

Chapter 15 On Diamonds, Razzle, and Goddesses of the Flesh

Interviews/Conversations with Rosa Lowinger

Roberto Cabrera
Pedro Antonio Calvo
Alicia Figueroa
Leowaldo Fornieles
Carlos Gomery
Helio Orovio
Eddy Serra
Pepe Tuero
Bebo Valdés

Quotes

"If a proving ground . . . just that." Rob Ruck. "Baseball in the Caribbean," in Thorn, John, Phil Birnbaum, Bill Deane, Rob Neyer, Alan Schwartz, Donald Dewey, Nicholas Acosella, and Peter Wayner. *Total Baseball.* New York: Total Sports, 2001.

"the architects . . . glass." Rodríguez, Eduardo Luis. *The Havana Guide: Modern Architecture 1925–1965.*

"Among the victims . . . salary." Velie, Lester. "Suckers in Paradise: How Americans Lose their Shirts in Caribbean Gambling Joints." *Saturday Evening Post,* March 28, 1953, p. 181.

"helmeted . . . banished." Ibid.

"In spite of the fact . . . those divisions." Langston Hughes. "Cuban Color Lines." Reprinted in: John Jenkins, ed. *Traveler's Tales of Old Cuba.* New York: Ocean Press, 2002, pp. 128–129.

"Monica Castell . . . battle." *Show* magazine, November, 1957, p. 63.

"The sculptural Mitsuko . . . life." *Show* magazine, April, 1958, p. 4.

"The sweet . . . public." *Show* magazine, April, 1955, p. 8.

"Speaking of Leonela's . . . legs." Ibid., p. 7.

Additional Sources

Darling, Juanita. "Legendary Cuban Hot Spot is Newly Hot." *Los Angeles Times,* December 16, 1996.

González Echevarría, Roberto. *The Pride of Havana: A History of Cuban Baseball.*

Hughes, Langston. *I Wonder as I Wander: An Autobiographical Journey.* New York: Hill and Wang, 1995.

Lacey, Robert. *Little Man, Meyer Lansky and the Gangster Life.*

Miller, Tom. "Cuba's All Stars." *Natural History,* April, 1999.

Perez, Louis A., Jr. *On Becoming Cuban: Identity, Nationality, and Culture.* New York: The Echo Press, 1999.

Schwartz, Rosalie. *Pleasure Island: Tourism and Temptation in Cuba.*

Thorn, Birnbaum, Deane, Neyer, Schwartz, Dewey, Acosella, and Wayner. *Total Baseball.*

"Cuba Ousts 13 U.S. Gamblers." *The New York Times,* March 31, 1953.

Peninsular and Occidental Steamship Company. *The Seahorse.* Miami: Transportation Advertising Service, Inc., 1949.

Reference to *Wide, Wide World* broadcast at Tropicana comes from advertisements in *The New York Times,* December 18, 1955, and Tropicana ad in *Diario de la Marina,* December 17, 1955.

Chapter 16   "The Guajiro has gone crazy"

Interviews/Conversations with Rosa Lowinger

Max Borges Jr.

Ernesto Capote

Valentín Jodra
Jenny León
Eddy Serra

Quotes

"The luxury . . . musical revues." *Show* magazine, January, 1955, p. 52.
"Here is one . . . say no more." Roberts, Adolphe. *Havana: Portrait of a City,*
pp. 227–228.
"man who in all . . . generations of Cubans." Thomas, p. 849, and n. 14.

Additional Sources

Halberstam, David. *The Fifties.* New York: Random House, 1993.
Havemann, Ernest. "Mobsters Move in on Troubled Havana." *Life,* March 10,
1958.
Perez, Louis A., Jr. *On Becoming Cuban: Identity, Nationality, and Culture.*
Schwartz, Rosalie. *Pleasure Island: Tourism and Temptation in Cuba.*
Sublette, Ned. *Cuba and its Music: From the First Drums to the Mambo.*
Thomas, Hugh. *Cuba: The Pursuit of Freedom.*

Chapter 17   Cabaret in the Sky

Interviews/Conversations with Rosa Lowinger

Maria Cole
Alicia Figueroa
Carlos Gomery
Pastora Guerra
Olga Guillot
Rosa Sanchez
Eddy Serra

Quotes

"Tropicana invests . . . talent!" *Show* magazine, January, 1956, p. 56.
"On January . . . *Aviación.*" Ibid., p. 15.
"Some of the lucky . . . wits." Durling, Henry. "Night Club in the Sky." *Cabaret,*
January, 1957, p. 35. Seen at: http://cuban-exile.com/doc_201-225/
doc0201.htm.

Additional Sources

Cole, Maria, and Louie Robinson. *Nat King Cole: An Intimate Biography.* New
York: W. Morrow, 1971.

Phillips, R. Hart. "Cuba Betting on Bustling Off-Season Season." *The New York Times*, April 8, 1956.

Ragano, Frank, Nancy Ragano, and Selwyn Raab. *Mob Lawyer*.

Rothman, Hal. *Neon Metropolis*. New York: Routledge, 2002.

"Cuba: Tonight at 8:30." *Time*, January 28, 1957.

"Cuba: Prosperity and Rebellion." *Time*, August 19, 1957.

Sworn statement to IRS signed by Martín Fox, October 27, 1961, regarding Johnny Williams's earnings in Cuba.

Chapter 18   *Esta es mi Cuba, Mister*

Interviews/Conversations with Rosa Lowinger

Maria Cole
Alicia Figueroa
Leowaldo Fornieles
Pastora Guerra
Valentín Jodra
Dick La Palma
Leonardo Lowinger
Rosa Sanchez
Emilia Villamíl

Quotes

"On the 10th . . . Marciano." *Show* magazine, December 1957, p. 38.
"chapter in . . . novel." Phillips, p. 300.
"Only boys . . . direction." Ibid., p. 291.
"The bodies. . . . found." Ibid., p. 292.

Additional Sources

Anderson, Jon Lee. *Che Guevara: A Revolutionary Life*. New York: Grove Press, 1997.
Halberstam, David. *The Fifties*.
Phillips, R.H. *Cuba, Island of Paradox*.
Schwartz, Rosalie. *Pleasure Island: Tourism and Temptation in Cuba*.
Szulc, Tad. *Fidel: A Critical Portrait*. New York: Morrow, 1986.
Thomas, Hugh. *Cuba: The Pursuit of Freedom*.
"Counting Batista's Days." *Newsweek*, December 22, 1958.
"Cuba in Dire Straits." *New York Times*, December 31, 1958.

"Cuba: The Church Says Stop." *Newsweek,* March 10, 1958.
"Cuba Faces Crisis as Rebels Cut Off Key Sugar Ports." *The New York Times,*
    December 4, 1958.
"Cuba: Into the Third Year." *Time,* December 1, 1958.

Chapter 19   Shattered Slots

Interviews/Conversations with Rosa Lowinger

Carmelina Ardura
Ernesto Capote
Alicia Figueroa
Leonela González
Valentín Jodra
Jenny León
Leonardo Lowinger
Eddy Serra

Chapter 20   Rumba at the Presidential Palace

Interviews/Conversations with Rosa Lowinger

Pedro Antonio Calvo
Ernesto Capote
Pastora Guerra
Olga Guillot
Valentín Jodra
Eddy Serra
Pepe Tuero
Emilia Villamíl

Quotes

"I had seen . . . generation." Phillips, p. 397.
"Today I filled out . . . penguin." William Gálvez. *Camilo: señor de la vanguardia.*
    La Habana: Editorial de ciencias sociales, 1979, p. 116.
"From an air-conditioned . . . employees." Thomas, p. 1197.
"Tropicana has removed several. . . . eight thousand pesos." *VEA Magazine,*
    April 1959, p. 25.

Additional Sources

Phillips, R.H. "Cuban Rebels Plan Provisional Rule." *The New York Times,* December 29, 1958.

―――. "Gamblers in Cuba Face Dim Future." *The New York Times,* January 4, 1959.

―――. "Liberty Carnival in Cuba." *The New York Times,* April 19, 1959.

Chapter 21 Bongo Congo

Interviews/Conversations with Rosa Lowinger

Pedro Antonio Calvo
Leowaldo Fornieles
Leonela González
Valentín Jodra

Additional Sources

Thomas, Hugh. *Cuba: The Pursuit of Freedom.*

Chapter 22 The House on Beacom Boulevard

Interviews/Conversations with Rosa Lowinger

Rosa Sanchez

Additional Sources

Li-An-Su. *Patria en Lágrimas: poemas de dolor, de lucha, y de esperanza.* Mexico, D. F.: Ediciones del Caribe, 1961.

Affidavit stating receipt of funds in Kerby McDonald case. Signed by Martín Fox, Alberto Ardura, Pedro Fox, and Oscar Echemendia, September 25, 1961.

Note on University Inn stationery and signed check from Evaristo García with stamp indicating insufficient funds.

List of Martín Fox's medications as prepared by Ofelia Suarez Fox, March 10, 1964.

Sworn statement to IRS signed by Martín Fox, October 27, 1961, regarding Johnny Williams's earnings in Cuba.

Letters of Lewis McWillie to Ofelia Fox and Ofelia Fox to Lewis McWillie, dated January 11 and February 12, 1964.

Letter of Ofelia Fox to Armando Cano, detailing checks returned to people. April 10, 1964.

Letter of Armando Cano to Ofelia Fox, detailing Martin's condition, May 29, 1965.

Letters of Pedro Fox to Ofelia Fox and telegram, dated April 8, 1966.

Chapter 23   *Noche de Ronda*

Interviews/Conversations with Rosa Lowinger

Santiago Alfonso
Greta González
Tomás Morales
María Salazar
Rosa Sanchez

Dates of Interviews

Denotes that repeated brief phone conversations also took place with subject.

Santiago Alfonso	November 5, 2003
Carmelina Ardura	November 17, 2002, April 10, 2003
Max Borges*	September 24, 2002, November 22, 2003
Roberto Cabrera	November 2, 2003
Pedro Antonio Calvo (Goyito)	November 1, 2003
Ernesto Capote	October 26, 2003
Luis Carbonell	November 3, 2003
Maria Cole	August 18, 2003
Lee Cott	January 11, 2003
Alicia Figueroa*	August 25, 2003, November 4–10, 2003, September 21, 2004
Leowaldo Fornieles	November 3, 2003, December 21, 2003, May 22, 2004
Carlos Gomery	October 22, 2003
Greta González*	January 27, 2005, March 3, 2005
Gladys González	January 18, 2004
Leonela González*	December 2, 2002, March 5, 2003, October 11, 2004
Erna Grabler	January 16, 2003

Pastora Guerra	February 18, 2004
Olga Guillot	November 26, 2002
Julieta Jimenez	May 9, 2003
Valentín Jodra*	September 17, 2002, November 16, 2002, December 4, 2002, January 6, 2003, January 14, 2003, January 22, 2003, June 29, 2003, July 21, 2003, August 23, 2003, September 11, 2003, September 18, 2003 (in Las Vegas), October 6, 2003, February 9, 2004, March 15, 2004
Dick La Palma	August 18, 2003
Héctor Leal*	October 21, 2003
Jenny León and Frank Llopis*	November 24, 2002; December 12, 2003
Leonardo and Hilda Lowinger*	August 28, 2002, May 10, 2003, July 6, 2003
Tomás Morales	May 21, 2004, January 27, 2005
Rolando Moreno	October 29, 2003
Helio Orovio	June 26, 2003, October 30, 2003
César Quesada	June 4, 2003
Eduardo Luis Rodríguez*	November 4, 2004
Armando Romeu III	October 20, 2003
Eddy Serra*	September 18, 2002, September 22, 2003, February 24, 2004
Saul Srebnick	November 15, 2002
María Teresa Tolón	December 20, 2003
Gilberto Torres	November 2, 2003
Pepe Tuero	November 7, 2003, December 29, 2003, February 23, 2004
Bebo Valdés	September 4, 2004
Célida Villalón	August 12, 2004
Emilia Villamíl	November 7, 2003, December 22, 2003

Interviews conducted by Ofelia Fox and Rosa Sanchez

Aristides Rodríguez Sastre	August 20–22, 2003
Valentín Jodra*	December 7 and 12, 2002
Olga Guillot*	November 24, 2002

Bibliography

Books

Acosta, Leonardo. *Cubano Be Cubano Bop: One Hundred Years of Jazz in Cuba.* Washington: Smithsonian Books, 2003.

Acosta, Leonardo, Olivier Cossard, René Espí, and Helio Orovio. *Fiesta Havana.* Paris Editions Vade Retro, 1999.

Alonso, Alejandro G. *La obra escultórica de Rita Longa.* La Habana: Editorial Letras Cubana, 1998.

Amado, Jorge. *Shepherds of the Night.* New York: Avon, 1988.

Ameringer, Charles D. *The Cuban Democratic Experience: The Auténtico Years, 1944–1952.* Gainesville: University Press of Florida, 2000.

Anderson, Jon Lee. *Che Guevara: A Revolutionary Life.* New York: Grove Press, 1997.

Arnaz, Desi. *A Book.* New York: William Morrow, 1976.

Barbour, Thomas. *A Naturalist in Cuba.* Boston: Little, Brown & Company, 1945.

Bardach, Ann Louise. *Cuba Confidential: Love and Vengeance in Miami and Havana.* New York: Random House, 2002.

Batista, Fulgencio. *Cuba Betrayed.* New York: Vantage Press, 1962.

Bettelheim, Judith, ed. *Cuban Festivals: An Illustrated Anthology.* New York: Garland Publishing Company, 1993.

Bolívar Aróstegui, Natalia and Carmen González Díaz de Villegas. *Ituto: la muerte en los mitos y rituales afrocubanos.* Miami: Editorial Arenas, 1992

Bolívar Aróstegui, Natalia. *Los Orishas en Cuba.* La Habana: Ediciones Unión, 1990.

Cabrera Infante, G. *Three Trapped Tigers.* New York: Avalon, 1995.

Calloway, Cab and Bryant Rollins. *Of Minnie the Moocher and Me.* New York: Ty Crowell Co., 1976.

Cañizares, Dulcila. *La trova tradicional.* La Habana: Editorial Letras Cubanas, 1995.

Carpentier, Alejo. *La música en Cuba.* La Habana: Editorial Letras Cubanas, 1998.

Caruso, Dorothy. *Enrico Caruso: His Life and Death.* New York: Simon & Schuster, 1945.

Castro, Fidel. *La historia me absolverá.* La Habana: Editorial de Ciencias Sociales, 1981.

Cirules, Enrique. *El Imperio de la Habana.* La Habana: Casa de Las Americas, 1993.

Clark, Sydney A. *Cuban Tapestry.* New York: McBride, 1936.

Clark, Sydney A. *All the Best in Cuba.* New York: Dodd, Mead, 1956.

Cole, Maria, and Louie Robinson. *Nat King Cole: An Intimate Biography.* New York: W. Morrow, 1971.

Collazo, Bobby. *La última noche que pasé contigo: 40 años de farándula cubana.* San Juan: Editorial Cubanacan, 1987.

Cugat, Xavier. *Rumba is My Life: An American Autobiography.* (Library Binding) Reprint Services Corp., 1949.

Deitche, Scott M. *Cigar City Mafia.* Fort Lee, New Jersey: Barricade Books, 2004.

Depestre, Leonardo. *Joseito Fernandez y su Guantanamera.* Santiago De Cuba: Editorial Oriente, 1994.

Eisenberg, Dennis, Uri Dan, and Ali Landau. *Meyer Lansky: Mogul of the Mob.* New York: Paddington Press, 1979.

Erlewine, Michael, with Vladimir Bogdanov, Chris Woodstra, and Scott Yanow. *The All Music Guide to Jazz.* San Francisco: Miller Publishing, 1996.

Fajardo, Ramon. *Rita Montaner.* La Habana: Editorial Letras Cubanas, 1993.

Fergusson, Erna. *Cuba.* New York: Alfred A. Knopf, 1946.

Foner, Philip S. *The Spanish-Cuban-American War and the Birth of American Imperialism 1895–1902.* New York: Monthly Review Press, 1972.

Gálvez, William. *Camilo: señor de la vanguardia.* La Habana: Editorial de ciencias sociales, 1979.

Gellman, Irwin F. *Roosevelt and Batista: Good Neighbor Diplomacy in Cuba 1933–1945.* Albuquerque: University of New Mexico Press, 1973.

Gil-Montero, Martha. *Brazilian Bombshell: The Biography of Carmen Miranda.* New York: Dutton, 1989.

Gillespie, Dizzy, with Al Fraser. *To Be or Not to Bop.* New York: Doubleday and Company, 1979.

González Echevarría, Roberto. *The Pride of Havana: a History of Cuban Baseball.* New York: Oxford University Press, 1999.

Gosch, Martin A., and Richard Hammer. *The Last Testament of Lucky Luciano.* Boston: Little, Brown & Company, 1974.

Greene, Graham. *Our Man in Havana*. New York: Viking Press, 1972.

Halberstam, David. *The Best and the Brightest*. New York: Random House, 1972.

————. *The Fifties*. New York: Random House, 1993.

Hitchcock, Henry-Russell. *Latin American Architecture Since 1945*. New York: Museum of Modern Art, 1955.

Hotchner, A.E. *Papa Hemingway*. New York: Random House, 1955.

Hughes, Langston. *I Wonder as I Wander: An Autobiographical Journey*. New York: Hill and Wang, 1995.

Humboldt, Alexander von. *Ensayo político sobre la isla de Cuba*. Miguel Angel Puig Samper, Consuelo Naranjo Orovio, Armando García González, editores. Madrid, Spain: Ediciones Doce Calles, 1998.

Jenkins, John. *Traveler's Tales of Old Cuba*. New York: Ocean Press, 2002.

Kefauver, Estes. *Crime in America*. New York: Doubleday, 1951.

Lacey, Robert. *Little Man, Meyer Lansky and the Gangster Life*. New York: Little, Brown & Company, 1991.

Lam, Rafael. *Tropicana: un paraíso bajo las estrellas*. La Habana: Editorial José Martí, 1999.

Lawrenson, Helen. *Latins are Still Lousy Lovers*. New York: Hawthorn Books, 1968.

Le Corbusier. *Towards a New Architecture*. New York: Dover Publications, 1986.

Li-An-Su. *Patria en Lagrimas: poemas de dolor, de lucha, y de esperanza*. Mexico D.F.: Ediciones del Caribe, 1961.

Savio Linares, Maria Teresa. *El Punto Cubano*. Santiago De Cuba: Editorial Oriente, 1995.

Martinez Rodríguez, Raúl. *Benny Moré*. La Habana: Editorial Letras Cubanas, 1993.

Martre, Gonzalo. *Rumberos de Ayer: Músicos Cubanos en México (1930–1950)*. Veracruz: Instituto Veracruzano de la Cultura, 1997.

McAuslan, Fiona, and Matthew Norman. *The Rough Guide to Cuba*. London: Rough Guides, 2000.

Messick, Hank. *Lansky*. New York: Berkeley Medallion, 1971.

Miller, Warren. *Ninety Miles From Home*. New York: Avon, 1961.

Miller, John, and Susannah Clark, ed. *Chronicles Abroad: Havana*. San Francisco: Chronicle Books, 1996.

Moreno Fraginals, Manuel. *El Ingenio*. La Habana: Editorial de Ciencias Sociales, 1978.

Nuñez, Luis M. *Santería, A Practical Guide to Afro-Caribbean Magic*. New Orleans: Spring Publications, 1992.

Orovio Helio. *Diccionario de la música cubana*. La Habana: Editorial Letras Cubanas, 1992.

————. *El bolero cubano.* Santiago De Cuba: Editorial Oriente, 1994.

————. *El danzón, el mambo, y el chachacha.* Santiago De Cuba: Editorial Oriente, 1994.

————. *El son, la guaracha, y la salsa.* Santiago De Cuba: Editorial Oriente, 1994.

————. *La conga, la rumba: columbia, yambú y guaguancó.* Santiago De Cuba: Editorial Oriente, 1994.

Ortíz, Fernando. *Contrapunto cubano del tabaco y el azucar.* La Habana: Consejo Nacional de Cultura de La Habana, 1963.

Perez Jr., Louis A. *On Becoming Cuban: Identity, Nationality, and Culture.* New York: The Echo Press, 1999.

Phillips, R.H. *Cuba, Island of Paradox.* New York: McDowell, Obolensky, 1959.

Pujol, Jordi. *Chano Pozo: el tambor de Cuba.* Barcelona: Alemendra Music, 2001.

Pyron, Darden Asbury. *Liberace: An American Boy.* Chicago: University of Chicago Press, 2000.

Quiroga, Orlando. *Muñecas de cristal.* La Habana: Letras Cubanas, 1998.

Ragano, Frank, Nancy Ragano, and Selwyn Raab. *Mob Lawyer.* New York: Charles Scribner and Sons, 1994.

Reid, Ed, and Ovid Demaris. *The Green Felt Jungle.* London: Cox and Wyman, 1965.

Roberts, Adolphe. *Havana: Portrait of a City.* New York: Coward-McCann, Inc. 1953.

Rodríguez, Eduardo Luis. *The Havana Guide: Modern Architecture 1925–1965.* New York: Princeton Architectural Press, 2000.

Rodríguez, Eduardo Luis. *Havana arquitectura del siglo XX.* La Habana: Art Blume, 1998.

Rosell, Rosendo. *Vida y milagros de la farándula de Cuba.* Miami: Ediciones Universal, 1992.

Rothman, Hal. *Neon Metropolis.* New York: Routledge, 2002.

Ryan, Alan, ed. *The Reader's Companion to Cuba.* San Diego: Harcourt, Brace and Company, 1997.

Santi, Enrico Mario. *Bienes del siglo, sobre cultura cubana.* Mexico: Fondo De Cultura Economica, 2002.

Sasuly, Richard. *Bookies and Bettors: Two Hundred Years of Gambling.* New York: Holt, Rinehart and Winston, 1982.

Scarpaci, Joseph L. *Havana: Two Faces of the Antillean Metropolis.* Chapel Hill: University of North Carolina Press, 1997.

Schroeder, Susan. *Cuba: A Handbook of Historical Statistics.* Boston: G.K. Hall, 1982.

Schwartz, Rosalie. *Pleasure Island: Tourism and Temptation in Cuba*. Lincoln, Nebraska: University of Nebraska Press, 1997.

Sublette, Ned. *Cuba and its Music: From the First Drums to the Mambo*. Chicago: Chicago Review Press, 2004.

Suchlicki, Jaime. *Cuba from Colombus to Castro and Beyond*. Washington, D.C.: Brassey's, Inc., 1997.

———. *Historical Dictionary of Cuba*. Lanham, Maryland and London: The Scarecrow Press, Inc., 2001.

Sweeney, Philip. *The Rough Guide to Cuban Music*. London: Penguin Group, 2001.

Szulc, Tad. *Fidel: A Critical Portrait*. New York: Morrow, 1986.

Terry, T. Philip. *Terry's Guide to Cuba*. Boston: Houghton Mifflin, 1926.

Thomas, Hugh. *Cuba: The Pursuit of Freedom*. New York: Harper & Row, 1971.

Thorn, John, Phil Birnbaum, Bill Deane, Rob Neyer, Alan Schwartz, Donald Dewey, Nicholas Acosella, and Peter Wayner. *Total Baseball*. New York: Total Sports, 2001.

Turkus, Burton B., and Sid Feder. *Murder, Inc*. New York: Farrar, Strauss and Young, 1951.

Turner, Wallace. *Gambler's Money*. Boston: Houghton Mifflin, 1965.

Woon, Basil. *When It's Cocktail Time in Cuba*. New York: Horace Liveright, 1928.

Articles and Documents

Adler, Barbara Squier. "The Mambo and the Mood." *The New York Times Magazine*, September 16, 1952.

"Batista's Bid." *Newsweek*, March 17, 1952.

"Bootlegging," Britannica.com, http://www.britannica.com/eb/article?eu=82848&tocid=0&query=bootlegging&ct=eb.

"Counting Batista's Days." *Newsweek*, December 22, 1958.

"Cuba: Batista at Work." *Newsweek*, March 24, 1952.

"Cuba: Caught in a War." *Time*, July 14, 1958.

"Cuba: Comeback." *Time*, August 25, 1958.

"Cuba: Crime Wave." *Time*, September 23, 1946.

"Cuba: Dictator with the People." *Time*, April 14, 1952.

"Cuba Elects Grau." *Life*, June, 1944.

"Cuba: Evolution of a Dictator." *Time*, June 1, 1944.

"Cuba Faces Crisis as Rebels Cut Off Key Sugar Ports." *The New York Times*, December 4, 1958.

"Cuba: Hit-Run Revolt." *Time*, December 1956.

"Cuba in Dire Straits." *The New York Times*, December 31, 1958.

"Cuba: Into the Third Year." *Time*, December 1, 1958.

"Cuba: Killers Beware." *Newsweek*, September 23, 1946.

"Cuba: Lost Milestone." *Time*, April 8, 1946.

"Cuba: Love & Bullets." *Time*, March 7, 1955.

"Cuba Ousts 13 U.S. Gamblers." *The New York Times*, March 31, 1953.

"Cuba: Prosperity and Rebellion." *Time*, August 19, 1957.

"Cuba: The Church Says Stop." *Newsweek*, March 10, 1958.

"Cuba: The Diamond Mystery." *Newsweek*, April 8, 1946.

"Cuba: Tonight at 8:30." *Time*, January 28, 1957.

"Cuban Housecleaning: Grau Urges Batista Henchmen From Country's Army and Police." *Newsweek*, November 20, 1944.

"Cuban Upset." *Newsweek*, June 12, 1944.

"Cuba's Batista: Dictator with the People." *Time*, April 14, 1952.

"Cuba's Mr. A." *Newsweek*, May 1, 1944.

Darling, Juanita. "Legendary Cuban Hot Spot is Newly Hot." *Los Angeles Times*, December 16, 1996.

"Dr. Ashmead Calls Lepers a Menace." *The New York Times*, February 4, 1900.

"Dr. Matias Duque: Former Secretary on Health in Cuba, Expert on Leprosy." *The New York Times*, February 16, 1941.

Dubivsky, Barbara. "A Working Girl's Debut in Shipboard Society." *The New York Times*, December 16, 1951.

Durling, Henry. "Night Club in the Sky." *Cabaret*, January 1957, p. 35. Seen at: http://cuban-exile.com/doc_201-225/doco201.htm.

Figueroa, Frank M. *Israel Lopez "Cachao": Highlights and Review of his Smithsonian Jazz Oral History Interview.* www.picadillo.com/figueroa/cachao.html.

Figueroa, Frank M. *Mario Bauza: Highlights from his Smithsonian Jazz Oral History Interview.* www.cubanmusic.com.

"Foreign Trade: High Jinks in Cuba." *Time*, June 15, 1942.

"For the Record." *Los Angeles Times*, March 12, 1997.

Fuentes, Norberto. "Mafia in Cuba." *Cuba International*, August 1979.

Gleason, Ralph J. "Prado's West Coast Tour Proving a Huge Success." *Downbeat*, October 5, 1951.

Havemann, Ernest. "Mobsters Move in on Troubled Havana." *Life*, March 10, 1958.

Kihss, Peter. "Batista and Regime Flee Cuba." *The New York Times*, January 2, 1959.

"Latin American Affairs." *Newsweek*, August 27, 1951.

"Leper Found in Bronx." *The New York Times*, January 11, 1931.

"Leprosy," Britannica.com, http://www.britannica.com/eb/
    article?eu=48992&tocid=0&query=leprosy%20in%20carribbean&ct=eb.
Miller, Tom. "Cuba's All Stars." *Natural History,* April, 1999.
"Pearl of the Antilles." *Time,* January, 1959.
Phillips, R. Hart. "Castro Moving to Take Power." *The New York Times,*
    January 2, 1959.
————. "Cuba Betting on Bustling Off-Season Season." Ibid., April 8, 1956.
————. "Cuba Preens Itself for the Tourist." Ibid., December 14, 1952.
————. "Cuban Rebels Plan Provisional Rule." Ibid., December 29, 1958.
————. "Cuba's Off Season." Ibid., April 14, 1948.
————. "Liberty Carnival in Cuba." Ibid., April 19, 1959.
————. "Gamblers in Cuba Face Dim Future." Ibid., January 4, 1959.
"Prohibition," Britannica.com, http://www.britannica.com/eb/
    article?eu=63069&tocid=0&query=prohibition&ct=eb.
Robinson, Eugene. "Cuba Begins to Answer Its Race Question." *The
    Washington Post,* November 12, 2000.
Salazar, Max. "The Miguelito Valdes Story." *Latin Beat,* 1992.
————. "Who Invented the Mambo?" Ibid., 1992.
————. "Chano Pozo." Ibid., 1993.
Secades, Eladio. "Con su admirable demostración de arte y ciencia, Kid Gavilán
    patentizó que es, en todos sentidos, un verdadero campeón." *Diario de la
    Marina,* October 7, 1952.
Show Magazine. Havana, Cuba. January 1955, April 1955, August 1955, October
    1955, October 1956, December 1956, June 1957, September 1957, November
    1957, December 1957, February 1958, March 1958, April 1958, June 1958,
    September 1958, June 1959, July 1959, September 1959, January 1960,
    November 1960, January 1961.
Stanhope, Dorothy. "Havana's Leper Colony." *The New York Times,* May 20,
    1900.
Stewart, Jack. "Cuban Influences on New Orleans Music." *Jazz Archivist,*
    1998–99.
"Testimony of Lewis McWillie, Las Vegas, Nevada." *The House Select Committee
    on Assassinations:* Volume V, viewed at: http://jfkassassination.net/russ/
    jfkinfo2/jfk5/mcwill.htm.
Velie, Lester. "Suckers in Paradise: How Americans Lose their Shirts in
    Caribbean Gambling Joints." *Saturday Evening Post,* March 28, 1953.
Wilson, John S. "Basie and His Boys." *The New York Times,* October 2, 1955.
Wilson, John S. "Ga-ga Over Cha Cha." *The New York Times,* March 15, 1959.
Watrous, Peter. "Mario Bauza, Band Leader Dies; Champion of Latin Music Was
    82." *The New York Times,* July 12, 1993.

Index